More praise for *All Deliberate Speed*

"Ogletree . . . movingly recounts his schooling in a poor and largely minority community in Merced, Calif., in the years immediately after *Brown*, his years at Stanford University as an early affirmative-action recruit, and his attendance at Harvard Law School during the years of the South Boston riots against busing." —Eric Arnesen, *Boston Globe*

"*All Deliberate Speed*, a provocative and intimate reflection on *Brown v. Board of Education*, is not only Charles Ogletree's story, it is the story of an entire generation, male and female of all races. *All Deliberate Speed* reminds us that the 'baby boomer' generation will also pass on a racial legacy. As the beneficiaries of *Brown*'s legacy, this work informs us that the struggle against racism is not completed until its promise of racial equality is realized for everyone." —Anita Hill

"*All Deliberate Speed* is a remarkable and very readable account of one young man's coming of age during the civil rights movement. It is downright exciting to read how the movement shaped the career of the author, Charles Ogletree, into a leading scholar-activist. Ogletree fully appreciates the work and sacrifices of Thurgood Marshall's generation." —John Hope Franklin

"Charles Ogletree's analytic memoir of the *Brown* case brings history alive. One of America's most distinguished professor-lawyers personalizes this historic case in a compelling and dramatic way. This is a must-read as well as a great read." —Alan Dershowitz

"The best part of [Ogletree's] book is an invigorating memoir of his rise from poverty. He found opportunity and hope in desegregation, which balance his disappointment with Brown's unfinished business." —David L. Chappell, *New York Times*

"An effective blend of memoir, history, and legal analysis." —Christopher Benson, *Washington Post Book World*

"Ogletree takes the reader on a more personal journey, tracing the arc of his life from growing up in a segregated rural town (Merced) in the Central Valley to his education at Stanford to his current position of professor at Harvard Law School."
—Paul McLeary, *San Francisco Chronicle Book Review*

"The memoir part of his story works well; you can't help identifying with a young black man who arrives as a first-year law student at Harvard just as South Boston is getting violently ugly over busing for desegregation."
—Harry Levins, *STL Today*

"Mr. Ogletree presents a broad and thoughtful survey of a half-century of progress and lack of progress in racial justice. His personal involvement with many aspects of post-*Brown* civil rights law makes *All Deliberate Speed* a wonderfully valuable combination of memoir and analysis."
—Philip Seib, *Dallas Morning News* (also in *Milwaukee Journal*)

"Readable, thoughtful, accessible—Ogletree's *All Deliberate Speed* is both a historical survey and a call to action. Ogletree has lived a remarkable—and quintessentially American—life."
—Susan Larson, *New Orleans Times-Picayune*

"[*All Deliberate Speed*] offers readers an honest . . . account of one man's firsthand experiences with one of the most significant court decisions of the twentieth century and brings new insights into America's continuing struggle with race and integration."   —*Publishers Weekly*

"Ogletree, born into an African-American family two years before the *Brown* ruling, covers so much more than the court case. . . . Ogletree achieves [his] goals through his considerable intellect, his passionate desire for a color-blind society and his clear and often compelling writing style. In fact, this is a rare book in that it delivers far more than promised in the introduction."
—Steve Weinberg, *Denver Post Book Review*

"*All Deliberate Speed* is a thoughtful memoir wrought with careful analysis and a look at the history of race in American society and an examination of the lasting effects, those intended and not, of the *Brown v. Board of Education* ruling."

—Zakia Munirah Carter, "What to Read Next"

"An absorbing and sobering look at the history of race and integration in the United States, Ogletree's *All Deliberate Speed: Reflections on the First Half Century of Brown v. Board of Education* exposes why *Brown*, the single most important decision on race in the twentieth century, should be carefully analyzed rather than celebrated on its fiftieth anniversary."

—*Seattle Scanner*

ALSO BY CHARLES J. OGLETREE, JR.

Beyond the Rodney King Story: An Investigation of
Police Conduct in Minority Communities
(coauthored with Mary Prosser, Abbe Smith, and William Talley) (1995)

Brown at 50: The Unfinished Legacy
(coauthored with Deborah L. Rhode) (2004)

ALL DELIBERATE SPEED

REFLECTIONS ON THE FIRST HALF CENTURY OF

Brown v. Board of Education

Charles J. Ogletree, Jr.

HARVARD LAW SCHOOL

W. W. NORTON & COMPANY

NEW YORK AND LONDON

Frontispiece: Thurgood Marshall and other lawyers for the plaintiffs celebrating May 17, 1954, *Brown v. Board of Education* victory. From left to right: John Scott, James M. Nabrit, Jr., Spottswood W. Robinson, III, Frank D. Reeves, Jack Greenberg, Thurgood Marshall, Louis L. Redding, U. Simpson Tate, George E. C. Hayes.

Photo credits: Frontispiece, courtesy of the NAACP Legal Defense and Educational Fund. Page 95, courtesy of the Panopticon Gallery, Waltham, Massachusetts. © Ernest Withers. Page 181, Reuters/Rick Wilking. Page 237, Angela "Amani" Davis, professor of law, American University School of Law. Page 257, James Kavin Ross/*The Oklahoma Eagle*.

Manufacturing by Quebecor World, Fairfield
Book design by BTDnyc
Production manager: Julia Druskin

Library of Congress Cataloging-in-Publication Data

Ogletree, Charles J.
   All deliberate speed : reflections on the first half century of Brown v. Board of
Education / Charles J. Ogletree, Jr.—1st ed.
      p. cm.
Includes bibliographical references and index.
   ISBN 0-393-05897-2 (hardcover)
   1. Race discrimination—Law and legislation—United States—History. 2. Civil
rights movements—United States—History. 3. Ogletree, Charles J. 4. African
American lawyers—Biography. I. Title.
   KF4757 .O35 2004
   342.7308'73—dc22

                                                              2003023131

ISBN 0-393-32686-1 pbk.

W. W. Norton & Company, Inc., 500 Fifth Avenue, New York, N.Y. 10110
www.wwnorton.com

W. W. Norton & Company Ltd., Castle House, 75/76 Wells Street, London W1T 3QT

1 2 3 4 5 6 7 8 9 0

This book is dedicated to the *Brown* clients and lawyers, Charles J. Ogletree, Sr., Willie Mae Ogletree, Pamela Ogletree, Charles J. Ogletree III, and Rashida Ogletree.

CONTENTS

ACKNOWLEDGMENTS

This book is the culmination of fifty years of blessings and good fortune as the result of the benefits I have received by being born near the time of the *Brown v. Board of Education* decision in 1954. The list of people who have been helpful is endless, but I would like to thank a few in particular for their assistance over the past few months.

First, I am very pleased that so many of my students worked hard to find obscure but important details about *Brown*. This deeply committed group of researchers includes Russell Capone, Clifford Ginn, Kristy Tillman, Cytheria Jernigan, Mandana Dashtaki, William Morehead, David Harkin, Walter Mosley, and Jia Cobb.

I am also pleased that many of my colleagues and former students, including Matthew Colangelo, Lydia Lin, Professor Eric Miller, Professor Gary Orfield, Erika Frankenberg, Professor Randy Hertz, Professor Goodwin Liu, Professor Mark Tushnet, Howard Manly, Warren Hayman, Henry Organ, and Derek Toliver, have been willing to offer their insightful and critical perspectives on this project.

I am privileged to have a group of staff members at Harvard Law School (particularly Melissa Hoffman, Patricia Tarabelsi, Ben Lambert, and Lauren McDowell) who have patiently worked with me to ensure that the book would be completed before the fiftieth anniversary of *Brown*.

This book would not have been possible without having been so enthusiastically embraced by my agent, John Taylor "Ike" Williams. The dedicated people at W. W. Norton & Company, in particular my primary editor, Robert Weil, his assistant, Brendan Curry, and my copy editor, Otto Sonntag, have been incredibly supportive and reassuring under real time pressures throughout the process of writing this book.

I would also like to thank my family, Willie Mae Ogletree Robinson, Charles Ogletree, Sr., Elna Dunn, Nadine Washington, Charlie Reed, Richard Ogletree, Robert Ogletree, Talia Hassan, Rose Atkins, Charles Ogletree III, Rashida Ogletree, and Rachelle Clarke, who have served as historians and archivists in finding important details about our family's history.

I want to particularly thank my wife, Pamela Ogletree, who has the patience of Job and has relentlessly pushed me to focus on this project in a way that I did not think imaginable.

Finally, I want to thank the *Brown* lawyers for their courageous work in the 1950s and particularly my mentors, A. Leon Higginbotham, Jr., Thurgood Marshall, Charles Hamilton Houston, and Judges Constance Baker-Motley and Robert Carter, and my mentor and professor, Derrick Bell, for offering unusual insights about the significance of *Brown* and making sure that those of us who have benefited so much from the decision do not forget from whence we came or our mission to continue to be of service to our communities. I stand on very broad shoulders today and it would not be possible without the incredible work of those responsible for *Brown v. Board of Education* in 1954.

INTRODUCTION

All Deliberate Speed offers my personal reflections on the historic civil rights decision *Brown v. Board of Education*, issued by the U.S. Supreme Court on May 17, 1954. I have three goals in mind. First, I want to explain why the *Brown* decision, coming at a time of great racial inequality in America, marked a critical effort by the Supreme Court to send to the country a strong message: that legalized racial inequality in America would no longer be tolerated. The Court's decision, stemming from a careful examination of our history of slavery and Jim Crow segregation, held that disparities in public education opportunities that were based on the race of America's children had to end. The Court sent this message to all the stakeholders in America, including Congress, the president, and the general public. At the same time, its decision, though unanimous, contained a critical compromise, which I argue undermined the broad purposes of the campaign to end racial segregation immediately and comprehensively. While ordering the end of segregation, given its corrosive effects on black children, the Court removed much of the force of its decision by allowing proponents of segregation to end it not immediately but with "all deliberate speed." Those three words form the title of this book and reflect, in my view, the slow and ultimately unsuccessful effort to eliminate segregated education.

This compromise left the decision flawed from the beginning. Over the past fifty years, the attempt to integrate the public education system and to achieve full racial equality in other areas has been resisted and openly defied, by policy makers and the public, to the detriment of the laudable aim of achieving racial equality in America.

My second goal is to discuss the important work of lawyers who started the legal fight for racial integration decades before the *Brown* decision, the obstacles they faced and overcame, and the disappointment they eventually experienced, as they saw a critical decision weakened not only by the legislative and executive branches of our government but also by the same Court, as its membership changed and as conservatives narrowed and, in the end, turned their back on the mandate articulated in *Brown*. The book chronicles the efforts of those who conceived the strategy and initiated the attack on Jim Crow segregation, like Charles Hamilton Houston, and those who led the effort to achieve true racial equality, like Thurgood Marshall. It also follows the course of *Brown*'s tortured history, from Marshall's successful argument in 1954 to his appointment to the U.S. Supreme Court and his retirement, and his replacement by Clarence Thomas, a conservative who has voted consistently with the majority of justices restricting and, in some instances, eliminating the *Brown* mandate.

Finally, I want to bring into this story my personal reflections on *Brown* over the past fifty years, contained mostly in the first four chapters of the book. I was born in 1952, and my life has been influenced, in numerous ways, by the 1954 *Brown* decision. This book tells how I, like millions of other African-Americans born during or after *Brown*, have experienced its celebration, condemnation, and evisceration. I take the reader through my childhood encounters with race, my experiences in college and law school, as a beneficiary of *Brown* and affirmative action programs, and my perspective on the persistence of racial conflict in America. I believe that I'm only one of millions of Americans whose life was impacted profoundly by the end of legal segregation. I hope others will share their own rich stories about *Brown*'s transformative qualities.

By the time of the *Brown* decision, the lives of my grandparents and parents had been shaped by the pervasive influence of Jim Crow segregation in America. I describe their lives, their lack of meaningful educational opportunities, their response to segregation, and their survival even though they lived in circumstances of abject poverty. I detail the many benefits that I received throughout the past fifty years as a result of the *Brown* decision, and my good fortune in being able to take advantage of the opportunities that integration, busing, and affirmative action provided, while at the same time being acutely aware that the majority of African-Americans did not enjoy these important benefits. I also reflect on the resistance to full racial equality in America, from the experiences of segregation in my hometown of Merced, California; to the rantings of Professor William Shockley, who, while I was a student at Stanford, argued that blacks were genetically inferior to whites; to the violent resistance by white families to the court-ordered busing in

Boston to achieve racial equality in education; to the efforts to narrow or eliminate the goals of *Brown* through lawsuits challenging programs designed to open the doors to black students where those doors were previously closed.

In the end, I reach the sad conclusion that the important goal of full equality in education following slavery and Jim Crow segregation was compromised from the beginning and that fifty years after *Brown* there is little left to celebrate. W. E. B. Du Bois's prescient words in 1903 informed us that "the problem of the twentieth century is the problem of the color line," but I maintain that, by refusing to acknowledge this country's history and to repair the harm done, we have allowed the problem of the color line to carry over into the twenty-first century. We need to examine our own individual resistance to full racial inequality, if we are to achieve true justice and equality in America. It is not enough for me to celebrate my good fortune in America in the half century since *Brown*, when a significant number of African-Americans were left behind during this period. I conclude with some alternatives to *Brown* that may not achieve the integrated society envisioned by *Brown* but that will directly benefit the communities of color that *Brown* and its progeny failed to help. We must address the problems of inequality and, in many respects, resegregation in America that the "all deliberate speed" approach to racial inequality has left unsolved and replace that approach with an unequivocal commitment—at the highest levels of government, in private industry, and in our personal lives—to full racial equality, and we must do it now. We cannot afford to wait another fifty years to find meaningful remedies to address the problems described in *Brown*.

We deal here with the right of all of our children, whatever their race, to an equal start in life and to an equal opportunity to reach their full potential as citizens. Those children who have been denied that right in the past deserve better than to see fences thrown up to deny them that right in the future. . . . [U]nless our children begin to learn together, there is little hope that our people will ever learn to live together.
—*Milliken v. Bradley*, 418 U.S. 717, 783 (1974)
(Marshall, J., dissenting)

PART I

Charles Ogletree with his mother, Willie Mae
Ogletree, and his father, Charles Ogletree, Sr.,
in Merced, in 1982.

CHAPTER 1

THE SIGNIFICANCE
OF *BROWN*

On May 17, 1954, an otherwise uneventful Monday afternoon, fifteen months into Dwight D. Eisenhower's presidency, Chief Justice Earl Warren, speaking on behalf of a unanimous Supreme Court, issued a historic ruling that he and his colleagues hoped would irrevocably change the social fabric of the United States. "We conclude that in the field of public education the doctrine of 'separate-but-equal' has no place. Separate educational facilities are inherently unequal."[1] Thurgood Marshall, who had passionately argued the case before the Court, joined a jubilant throng of other civil rights leaders in hailing this decision as the Court's most significant opinion of the twentieth century. The *New York Times* extolled the *Brown* decision as having "reaffirmed its faith and the underlying American faith in the equality of all men and all children before the law."[2]

President Eisenhower, who later described the appointment of Earl Warren as chief justice as the worst decision he had ever made, was not as jubilant. At a White House dinner, he told Warren, "[Southern whites] are not bad people. All they are concerned about is to see that their sweet little girls are not required to sit in school alongside some big overgrown Negroes."[3] Eisenhower added, "It is difficult through law and through force to change a man's heart."[4] His heart, however, seemed to be with the opponents of integration.

At the time, no one doubted the far-reaching implications of the Court's ruling. The *Brown* lawyers had apparently accomplished what politicians, scholars, and others could not—an unparalleled victory that would create a nation of equal justice under the law. The Court's decision seemed to call for a new era in which black children and white children would have equal opportunities to achieve the proverbial American Dream. It did not come too soon for the families whose children were victims of segregation.

The *Brown* case actually consisted of five different cases.[5]

In *Briggs v. Elliott*, thirty black parents from Clarendon County, South Carolina, sued the school district to improve the educational conditions for their children. They began organizing in 1947 with the help of local black ministers and the South Carolina chapter of the NAACP. The parents complained about the poor quality of the buildings, the lack of adequate transportation, and inadequate teacher salaries, among other things. The defendant in the case, Roderick W. Elliott, a sawmill owner and chairman of the board of trustees of School District no. 22, made no effort to supply black students with adequate educational facilities.[6] After the lawsuit was filed, Harry Briggs and his wife, the named plaintiffs, were both fired from their jobs and other blacks who participated in the lawsuit suffered threats and damage to their property from angry South Carolina citizens. Annie Gibson, another plaintiff, lost her job as a maid at a local motel, and her husband was forced from inherited land his family had sharecropped for decades.[7] One of the *Brown* lawyers, Jack Greenberg, has described the problem in South Carolina in blunt terms: "Soon many of Clarendon County's black leadership, their families, and other [black citizens generally] were fired from jobs, denied credit, forced to pay longstanding debts, refused renewal of leases on farmland, had trouble getting their cotton ginned, were sued for slander, threatened by the Klan, and one black person was even beaten to death."[8]

Lawyers representing the families in the *Briggs* case employed Professor Kenneth B. Clark and his wife, Mamie Clark, whose now famous study placed identical dolls differing only in skin color in front of black children. The children preferred the white doll to the black doll, picking the black doll as looking "bad"; more than half identified themselves with the "bad" doll.[9] Clark, a psychology professor at City College of New York, was brought into the desegregation cases as an expert witness to explain the psychological harm experienced by black children as a result of the racial caste system in the South. The doll test suggested to the Clarks that black children expressed positive identification with the white dolls and negative identification with the black dolls. Marshall's goal was to demonstrate forcefully, by means of such empirical data, the harm that continued segregation had on black children.

In *Brown v. Board of Education,* after years of fruitless negotiations with the Topeka school board, black parents sued to desegregate the Topeka school system.[10] Oliver Brown, the father of Linda Brown, wanted to eliminate the segregation that required his daughter to attend an inferior school a considerable distance from their home. Linda had to walk one mile through a railroad switchyard to get to her black elementary school, even though a white elementary school was only a few blocks away.[11] Brown tried to enroll his daughter in the white school near his home, but the principal denied his request.[12] The Brown family approached the NAACP, and other black families decided to join the effort to sue the Topeka school board.

Dorothy Davis, a ninth-grade black student and the daughter of a local farmer, had no choice but to pursue her education in the harsh conditions of the all-black Robert Moton High School.[13] In *Davis v. County School Board*, plaintiffs charged that Virginia's segregated school system violated the federal Constitution, or, in the alternative, that the white community in Prince Edward County, Virginia, refused to spend sufficient money to upgrade the substandard black schools.[14] The students conducted a two-week protest and called on the NAACP attorneys Spottswood Robinson and Oliver Hill. Hill and Robinson filed a lawsuit on their behalf.

In *Gebhart v. Belton*, plaintiffs charged that Ethel Louise Belton and the other black students living in a suburb of Wilmington, Delaware, had to commute eighteen miles to attend Howard High School in Wilmington. This segregated school, like many cited in the other *Brown* cases, was a poorly maintained facility, with very high pupil-to-teacher ratios and a curriculum that did not adequately prepare the children for higher education. The related Delaware case, *Bulah v. Gebhart*, involved Sarah Bulah, a working mother, and her husband, Fred, a foreman at a paper mill, determined to get equal bus transportation for their daughter Shirley Barbara.[15] Mrs. Bulah sought the help of Louis Redding, a local NAACP attorney, who agreed to represent all of the plaintiffs.

Bolling v. Sharpe, the fifth case, involved a Washington, D.C., parents group whose black children attempted to register for the all-white

Philip Sousa Junior High School. When the black parents arrived on registration day with the white parents, they were ordered to leave the school and their children were subsequently denied admission because of their race. In particular, twelve-year-old Spottswood T. Bolling, Jr., attempted to enroll at Philip Sousa Junior High. Turned away, he had no choice except to return to Shaw Junior High, the substandard school he was attending.[16] Charles Hamilton Houston represented the families until he became ill. The case was later handled by two Howard Law School professors, James Nabrit, Jr., and George E. C. Hayes, who sued C. Melvin Sharpe, president of the board of education of the District of Columbia, on behalf of Bolling and the other black children. The *Bolling* case posed an even greater challenge because the Fourteenth Amendment at the time applied only to states, and the District of Columbia was not a state. The lawyers in this case based their claim on the Fifth Amendment, relying on the argument that the plaintiffs suffered deprivation of life, liberty, or property without due process.[17]

The argument presented by the *Brown* lawyers, as well as Dr. Kenneth Clark's doll experiment, persuaded the Supreme Court of the magnitude of the problem and led Chief Justice Earl Warren, writing for the unanimous Court, to conclude,

Today, education is perhaps the most important function of state and local governments. Compulsory school attendance laws and the great expenditures for education both demonstrate our recognition of the importance of education to our democratic society. It is required in the performance of our most basic public responsibilities, even service in the armed forces. It is the very foundation of good citizenship. Today it is a principal instrument in awakening the child to cultural values, in preparing him for later professional training, and in helping him to adjust normally to his environment. In these days, it is doubtful that any child may reasonably be expected to succeed in life if he is denied the opportunity of an education. Such an opportunity, where the state has undertaken to provide it, is a right, which must be made available to all on equal terms. We come then to the question presented: Does segregation of children in public schools solely on the basis of race, even though the physical facilities and other "tangible" factors may be equal, deprive the children of the minority group of equal educational opportunities? We believe that it does.[18]

The Court's decision recognized the negative impact of segregation on black children in America and saw quality education as the appropriate means for beginning to eliminate the crippling effects of segregation. The Court applied these principles to the schools in question, but made it clear that the mandate applied to any school system with similar practices.

During oral arguments, the justices asked the lawyers probing questions, giving little indication of where they were leaning. Justice Felix Frankfurter seemed particularly interested in how a decree would be implemented if the Court were to rule that segregation was unconstitutional. Thurgood Marshall responded by emphasizing the importance of establishing the legal principle in these cases; in the event of a favorable ruling, the specific details would have to be hammered out by the district courts and implemented by the individual school boards. The *Brown* lawyers, however, recognized the Court's concern with, and indeed "fear" over, the implementation of a Court decree abolishing segregation, specifically noting that this "fear" was the most "persuasive factor" working for the other side.[19] To the lawyers arguing in favor of segregation on the basis of precedent, some justices raised several questions about whether changed circumstances could compel a result different from the one the Court had reached in the past. In response to this line of questioning, the representative of South Carolina, John Davis, replied that "changed conditions cannot broaden the terminology of the Constitution."[20]

After each day of oral arguments, the *Brown* lawyers considered the justices' line of questioning and attempted to discern which way the decision might come out. On the last day of argument, however, the lawyers were not quite sure how the justices would decide the thorny issue of ending racial segregation in education.

Segregation had been the law of the land since the country's inception; what the *Brown* lawyers were fighting in particular, however, was the infamous 1896 Supreme Court decision in *Plessy v. Ferguson*.[21] In that case, the Court gave a constitutional rubber stamp to segregated public facilities, finding that they did not violate the equal protection clause of the Fourteenth Amendment so long as they were equal. For the next fifty-eight years, with a few modest exceptions, the Court continued to interpret that clause so as to render it essentially without any bite. The *Brown* lawyers were thus faced with a challenge, particularly because NAACP lawyers had in prior cases pursued a strategy of "equalization" that implicitly did not challenge *Plessy*'s logic but instead focused on showing that separate facilities typically were not equal. In other words, despite *Plessy*'s moral reprehensibility, Fourteenth Amendment litigation leading up to *Brown* worked *within* the "separate but equal" framework. The Court had supported the "equalization" strategy, but *Brown* asked it to switch horses in midcourse and revisit *Plessy* as a whole. The behind-the-scenes discussion during the Court's post-hearing conference indicated that there was indeed resistance to the demand for integration. Some of the justices' personal records reflect a strongly divided Court. After a vote was taken in 1953, when the case was originally heard, the outcome was (according to some sources) 5 to 4 against the plaintiffs, with Chief Justice Fred Vinson holding the deciding vote.

On June 8, 1953, instead of issuing its opinion in *Brown*, the Court ordered that the cases be reargued. Even more surprising, it asked each side to answer five specifically targeted questions. The first asked the lawyers to discern whether the Congress and state legislatures that ratified the Fourteenth Amendment had the understanding that the amendment would compel integrated education. If the answer to this question was no, the next question was whether the Congress and state legislatures that ratified the Fourteenth Amendment understood that either future Congresses or the courts could construe the amendment as mandating integrated education in light of changed conditions. The Court also asked the lawyers whether they believed it was within the Court's power to reason that the Fourteenth Amendment required the abolition of segregation. The final two questions dealt with the Court's concern about the implementation of a decree mandating integration. Specifically, the Court wanted to know, if it overruled *Plessy,* should black students "forthwith be admitted to schools of their choice" or should the Court allow for a "gradual adjustment." Along these same lines, the Court asked who would implement and oversee this transition.[22]

In hindsight, it is pretty clear that these questions were meant to stall a decision on this important constitutional question. Some members of the Court felt that the newly elected and appointed Eisenhower administration would need some time to deal with the decision in *Brown*, regardless of its outcome.[23] It is also reported that Frankfurter, who viewed unanimity as necessary in a case of such grave import, wanted to hold off the decision for a year because the Court was divided. In fact, he drafted the five questions and persuaded his colleagues that the case should be reargued. The *Brown* lawyers viewed the issuance of the questions as favorable, especially since some of them indicated that the Court was seriously contemplating remedial action. In preparing to answer these questions, Marshall employed a team of historians and constitutional scholars, including Howard Graham, law librarian of the Los Angeles County Bar Association Library, John Hope Franklin, Constance Baker Motley, and C. Vann Woodward. Teams of scholars were given a discrete issue to research, and the lawyers would then incorporate it into the brief.[24]

On September 8, 1953, before the second round of oral arguments, Chief Justice Fred Vinson died, and President Eisenhower appointed Earl Warren the new chief justice. On hearing of his colleague's death, Frankfurter, no friend of Vinson's, is reported to have said, "This is the first indication I have had that there is a God."[25]

President Eisenhower's appointment of Warren, who had been attorney general and then governor of California, did not suggest a change of course for the Court. Warren, after all, was the attorney general who had defended the result in *Korematsu v. United States*, the 1944 case that ratified the internment of Japanese Americans for the first years of World War II and that was authored by another still-sitting justice, the Alabaman Hugo Black.[26] What most observers, Eisenhower included, did not fully realize was that *Korematsu* had troubled Warren and that, as a Californian, he was considered to be a moderate Republican. Warren immediately recognized the importance of the *Brown* case and began an effort to persuade all of his colleagues to reach a unanimous decision. By May 17, 1954, the day the *Brown* ruling was handed down, he had his unanimity, but at a cost that would prove to be exceedingly high.

In a break with tradition, the Court did not order the states to enforce the rights just announced, but instructed the *Brown* lawyers to return a few months later to address specific questions concerning the scope of their ruling. The *Brown* lawyers wasted no time in giving the Court their view of the urgency of ending segregation immediately. In their briefs, they argued it should end "forthwith" and certainly no later than September 1955.[27] Those representing the states forced to integrate after *Brown* argued that the Court's ruling could do irreparable harm; there would be sustained hostility by whites, withdrawal of white children from integrated schools, racial tensions, violence, and loss of jobs for black teachers. Some opponents of integration went to extremes, arguing that integration could bring blacks with lower IQs into the schools, that many black children were retarded, and that tuberculosis and venereal disease would spread, as would the enrollment of illegitimate children. Their point was that integration would destroy their way of life.

Having broadly proclaimed its support of desegregating public schools, the Supreme Court shortly thereafter issued its opinion—the opinion that legitimized much of the social upheaval that forms the central theme of this book. Fearful that southern segregationists, as well as the executive and legislative branches of state and federal governments, would both resist and impede this courageous decision, the Court offered a palliative to those opposed to *Brown*'s directive. Speaking again with one voice, the Court concluded that, to achieve the goal of desegregation, the lower federal courts were to "enter such orders and decrees consistent with this opinion as are necessary and proper to admit to public schools on a racially nondiscriminatory basis *with all deliberate speed* the parties to these cases."[28]

As Thurgood Marshall and other civil rights lawyers pondered the second decision, they tried to ascertain what the Court meant in adding the crucial phrase "all deliberate speed" to its opinion. It is reported that, after the lawyers read the decision, a staff member consulted a dictionary to confirm their worst fears—that the "all deliberate speed" language meant "slow" and that the apparent victory was compromised because resisters were allowed to end segregation on their own timetable. These three critical words would indeed turn out to be of great consequence, in that they ignore the urgency on which the *Brown* lawyers insisted. When asked to explain his view of "all deliberate speed," Thurgood Marshall frequently told anyone who would listen that the term meant S-L-O-W.[29]

The Supreme Court, in *Brown v. Board of Education*, did not craft the phrase "with all deliberate speed" out of thin air.[30] Justice Oliver Wendell Holmes first used it in his 1912 decision of *Virginia v. West Vir-*

ginia: "[A] State cannot be expected to move with the celerity of a private business man; it is enough if it proceeds, in the language of the English Chancery, *with all deliberate speed.*"[31] Justice Felix Frankfurter, Holmes's contemporary, used the phrase five times[32] prior to Chief Justice Warren's immortalizing it in *Brown.*

The phrase "deliberate speed" appears to be a derivative of "speed thee slowly" found in Sir Thomas Elyot's 1545 introduction of the word "maturity" into the English language. "Speed thee slowly" was taken from a Greek proverb and translated from the Latin *festina lente.*[33] One famous American use of the expression *festina lente,* particularly relevant to our subject matter, is by President Abraham Lincoln. When Lincoln was asked whether he favored the immediate emancipation of the slaves, he responded, "It will do no good to go ahead any faster than the country will follow. . . . You know the old Latin motto *festina lente.*"[34] Lincoln in this case was referring to Augustus Caesar's interpretation: "make haste slowly."[35]

Although Justice Holmes attributed the phrase to the English Chancery, no one has yet found a single quotable instance of that court's use of the phrase. The more familiar Chancery phrase was "all convenient speed."[36] However, "all deliberate speed" appears in the writings of many classic poets and novelists. Sir Walter Scott, in his 1817 novel *Rob Roy,* used the exact phrase "with all deliberate speed" in describing the progress of a lawsuit. The poet George Gordon, Lord Byron, the author of *Don Juan,* used it in an 1819 letter to his publisher; and the poet Francis Thompson wrote in his often quoted poem "The Hound of Heaven" (1893), "But with unhurrying chase/And unperturbed pace/Deliberate speed, majestic instancy. . . ."[37]

Even though the Court's ruling was unanimous, its reluctance to take a more forceful position on ending segregation immediately played into the hands of the integration opponents. The victory in *Brown* would be tested often and by a variety of methods. The efforts to give meaning to these decisions led to many organized civil rights marches. These protests, however, were frequently met with increasing hostility and violent resistance. In 1957, for example, nine black students, whose admission had been ordered by a federal district court, attempted to enroll at Central High in Little Rock, Arkansas. They were prevented from entering the school by the Arkansas National Guard, under orders of Governor Orval Faubus, who had declared a state of emergency. This incident gained worldwide attention and entered the Cold War dialogue, as Communists harshly criticized the United States for its policies. President Eisenhower also ordered federal troops to be available to enforce the desegregation laws in Little Rock, Arkansas, in 1957.

After a series of legal battles centering on court orders of desegregation, the issue made its way to the Supreme Court, which convened an extraordinary summer session in order to hear the case. Marshall served as the NAACP's counsel. The cause faced significant opposition from white segregationists. Governor Faubus called a special session of the state legislature two days before the Supreme Court hearing was scheduled and persuaded the legislature to pass bills that gave him broad power to oppose desegregation. Some of these bills were intended to establish legal pretenses for closing desegregated schools and transferring the money to private, segregated schools. Pursuant to one of these bills, Faubus called a local referendum, which produced a vote of 19,470 to 7,561 in favor of closing the public schools in order to avoid desegregation. Nevertheless, Marshall and the NAACP prevailed in the famous unanimous decision of *Cooper v. Aaron*, in which the Court rejected the Little Rock school board's reasons for delaying desegregation and stated that "law and order are not here to be preserved by depriving the Negro children of their constitutional rights."[38]

Not wanting to slow down the pace of litigation designed to bring the Jim Crow system to its knees, Marshall in 1961 assigned Constance Baker Motley, the first woman on his civil rights legal team, to assist James Meredith, a black student who had been denied admission by the University of Mississippi. After a series of court rulings that rejected his contention that the denial was based on race, and a series of appeals all the way to the Supreme Court, during which Meredith was arrested and rioting took place, he was finally allowed to enroll in the university in 1962. Motley, who later became a judge, stated that the *Meredith* case "effectively put an end to massive resistance in the Deep South" to the *Brown* decision.[39] History seems to suggest that Motley's optimism was premature, since both the South and the North resisted the mandate of integration for generations to come.

The success of Marshall's post-*Brown* litigation strategies was not limited to education cases. After the *Brown* victory, NAACP attorneys broadened their efforts to end segregation. Their strategy was to attack segregation in areas such as housing, travel, employment, voting, and public accommodations. The NAACP challenged segregation wherever it existed, including public beaches, parks, and swimming pools. Specifically, in 1955 the Supreme Court found segregation unconstitutional in requiring racial separation whenever blacks desired to enjoy the public beaches and bathhouses of Baltimore with whites.[40] At the same time, it handed down an opinion ruling that it was likewise unlawful to mandate segregation on municipal golf courses.[41]

In the following year, the Supreme Court declared Alabama's bus segregation laws invalid and thus assured blacks that they could end their bus boycott and resume riding the city buses without fear of arrest.[42] In 1958, attorneys for the NAACP achieved another victory for blacks: segregation in the use and enjoyment of city parks was held unconstitutional.[43] Again, in 1963 the NAACP fought and won the battle against segregation in the courtroom itself.[44] Finally, segregation was eventually declared unconstitutional in prisons and jails.[45]

By the 1970s, opponents of *Brown* had begun creatively to avoid the impact of integration. *Palmer v. Thompson,* decided in 1971, marked the start of a trend reflecting the Court's unwillingness to order measures that would require blacks and whites to integrate.[46] The NAACP had fought for the right of blacks in Jackson, Mississippi, to have equal and equivalent access to the public facilities, including its parks, auditoriums, golf courses, and city zoo. At that time, there were five publicly available swimming pools in Jackson—four for white residents and one for black residents. When faced with the prospect of having to desegregate public swimming pools, white residents refused to come to the swimming pools, and the city of Jackson preferred to close all the swimming pools rather than require integration.[47] Reasoning that it would not be economically feasible to continue maintaining the swimming pools, the Supreme Court embraced the defendants' creativity and did not fault them for violating the holdings of prior segregation cases.[48] It thus permitted the city of Jackson to avoid the integration problem altogether.

Brown's success in ending legal segregation in education is undeniable. It is appropriately viewed as perhaps the most significant case on race in America's history. Not only did the *Brown* opinion lead to more than a dozen unanimous decisions by the Supreme Court finding segregation of public schools unconstitutional or upholding desegregation remedies,[49] it also went a long way toward healing the black community's wound in the wake of *Dred Scott v. Sandford*, which held that blacks had "no rights which the white man was bound to respect,"[50] and *Plessy v. Ferguson*'s conclusion that the Fourteenth Amendment was not intended "to abolish distinctions based upon color, or to enforce social . . . equality . . . of the two races."[51]

While the *Brown* lawyers were right to celebrate this remarkable achievement, the evil that *Brown* sought to eliminate—segregation—is still with us, and the good that it sought to put in its place—integration—continues to elude us. The violent resistance to integration proved to be more than anyone had imagined. Yet, the more subtle forms of resistance, such as white flight, denial of funding for equalization, and rejection of *Brown* principles by a conservative Supreme Court, have been the most effective in limiting the promise of *Brown*.

As we reflect on fifty years of *Brown* in the context of where we are today as a country of diverse people, we have a clearer sense of its successes and failures and the challenge for the future. In the pages to follow, my goal is to share my assessment of *Brown* and its progeny, in the hope that others will seek solutions to these problems and meet the laudable goals of *Brown*, which have, regrettably, thus far not been achieved.

CHAPTER 2

THE LEGACY OF SEGREGATION: WHAT *BROWN* MEANT IN MERCED

What the Supreme Court described as a "separate and unequal" school system in Kansas, South Carolina, Virginia, and Delaware existed in my hometown of Merced, California, as well as in most communities across America in 1954. The parents of the children seeking relief in the *Brown* case were no different from my grandparents or my parents. Previous generations had grown all too comfortable with segregation and come to accept it as the norm in America. My parents and grandparents, typical of their generation, accepted segregation on buses, in housing, at water fountains, in restaurants, and even in schools. The Supreme Court ruling in *Brown* made little difference in Merced. Although it was welcome news for black families with children everywhere in America, it hardly changed the routine of life in Merced.

Most of the blacks in Merced had originally come from the South. My grandfather Willie Reed was born in Ozan, Arkansas, in 1898. Similarly, his wife, my grandmother Essie D. Nelson, was an Arkansas native, born in 1905. My grandfather told the family that the Reed name was given to my great-great-grandfather John Reed by a white plantation owner in Arkansas in the years before the Civil War. He also told us that the original family name from West Africa was Fuque, but I have had no success in confirming this precious bit of Reed family history.

When my grandparents moved to California in 1944, they first settled in northern California, near Oakland. They believed that the abolition of slavery, a horror experienced by their parents, was God's answer to their prayers; they never contemplated asking for something as unfathomable as equality. They were free to work and earn wages, move about the country, and take advantage of a modest form of citizenship. Their lives were infinitely better than those of their parents. It did not seem to matter that they could not vote, live in certain neighborhoods, or attend the better schools of their white counterparts. They could move from their segregated and impoverished conditions in the South and find more opportunities to work throughout the year out west. California provided relief from the painful memories of the past, and the potential for a new beginning.

Despite the West's promise, life in California was anything but comfortable. The Reed family initially lived on the outskirts of Merced, on the Marvin C. Baker Ranch on Jefferson Road. My grandparents and other African-American families, as well as poor whites, worked for Mr. Baker, as day laborers. The Baker Ranch contained a farm and a dairy. My family did not have much, but was happy to be working. The ranch was, in many respects, a way station from the hell that they recalled from Arkansas. But if they were looking for paradise, the Baker Ranch was far from it. They did not own a home, but were allowed to live on the ranch in one- or two-room cabins with no toilets or running water, and only kerosene lamps for light at night. The money they made by working for Mr. Baker was largely consumed in the rent they had to pay or for the credit they were given to purchase basic necessities between pay periods.

My grandparents both worked all day during the week and half a day on Saturday. My grandmother was a very religious woman, often reading the Bible, praying for her family's salvation. To lift her spirits and others', she would sing one of her favorite Negro spirituals, "By and By," with the words "by and by when the morning comes, all the saints of God come gathering home, and we will tell the story of how we overcome, and will understand it better, by and by." It was her song of hope to keep moving forward. Her son Charlie recalls her often praying for him, particularly when he was mischievous, saying, "Lord, have mercy on my child." She would read the Bible to deepen her faith in God's willingness to help them survive, and believing that God was answering her prayers, she garnered enough strength to return to work the next day. My grandparents toiled in a system comparable to sharecropping for the white farmers in rural Merced. They worked for the Bakers, the Schuhs, and the Hooper brothers, doing everything from my grandmother's shucking corn and picking cotton to my grandfather's driving tractors to irrigate the cotton, corn, and hayfields.

Though they engaged in extraordinarily hard labor, my grandparents did not move up the social ladder until an unfortunate, though ultimately profitable, accident that involved my grandfather. Big Daddy, as he was called by his children and grandchildren, was an imposing figure, over six feet tall, thin, and almost always attired in overalls. His face was dark chocolate, partly attributable to his African ancestry and partly influenced by the relentless days of working the fields under the hot sun. His facial features were rugged, and he sported a short salt-and-pepper beard that he rarely cut, but occasionally trimmed. His narrow eyes were penetrating; anyone who crossed his path did so at his own peril. He did not attend school as a child, at the height of the Jim Crow era. He started working at odd jobs from the time he was ten years old. He learned to read by talking with other blacks in the fields, and when he found time, read discarded newspapers, listened to the radio, and tried to keep abreast of the slow progress of achieving racial equality. Over time, he became the Reed family historian, and although he never wrote anything down, he told the stories of our family's background and expected his children and grandchildren to keep these stories alive for the next generations.

Big Daddy's hard exterior concealed an unmistakable tenderness when it came to his wife and children. He loved his family dearly. He tried to be stern with us, but we always found him giving in to our requests for more stories, or to stay awake a little later at night to listen to the radio, or to go through his pockets, rummaging for change with which to go to the store to buy candy.

My grandfather's life was altered by an accident that occurred in the 1940s. He owned a 1936 Chevy, and as he drove to the store with his daughter and son, on Highway 152, a group of sailors hit him head-on. The sailors were at fault, and two died as a result of the crash. My grandfather's ribs were broken, his daughter's nose was broken, and his son sustained an injury to his hip. The car was totaled, and he received a settlement of $1,240 as a result of this accident. It was without question the biggest payday in Big Daddy's life. With the money, he bought a 1941 De Soto, purchased two lots on Farmdale, and then bought two large wooden crates, used to haul Caterpillar tractors aboard trains;

with these he created his first wholly owned home. There was no concrete foundation for the wooden boxes. They sat on concrete blocks, and there were cardboard covers for the interior of the "home." The new home had a wood stove for heat and a butane stove for cooking.

Since there was no indoor plumbing, Big Daddy built an outhouse in the backyard; he dug a well to pump water for drinking, cooking, cleaning, and, occasionally, bathing. The family used a washtub for doing laundry, carrying drinking water, and heating water for the Saturday night bath.

The house on Farmdale was in a neighborhood populated largely by blacks and some poor whites. Families in this neighborhood in the 1950s were on friendly terms with one another, and some attended the Reverend D. H. Hall's church, Mt. Zion Baptist, on Rita Mae Street. Although all here had escaped the poverty of the South, they rarely complained about being poor. They really didn't know of any alternatives. My grandparents, one generation removed from slavery, had learned to survive on the things they found on the land. My grandfather was particularly proud of his ability to feed his family through hard work as a seasonal worker, and through his success as a hunter and farmer. He loved to hunt and to raise hogs. The hogs were almost sacred in the Reed house, and what some people considered a filthy, unhealthy animal, my grandfather considered to be poor people's answer to poverty.

Hogs were worshiped because, unlike most other animals, they served at least two distinct purposes. First, they were garbage collectors. Anything we could or would not eat, the pigs would eat. There were thus no bones or trash to be thrown away. Second, the hogs would produce a litter of pigs, which would provide food for the family in the future. My grandmother was an excellent and creative cook, who would not waste anything. She found remarkable ways to enjoy the many products coming from the hog and did not believe in wasting any food. Big Mama made sure that the family would eat ham, bacon, and pork sausage. She prepared chitterlings (or, as they were identified in the Reed house, "chitlins"), hog maws, salt pork, pork chops, hog head cheese, jowl bacon, pigs' feet, pig tails, pig ears, scrapple, pickled pigs' feet, and, of course, fried pork rinds. The Reed family ate the pig from head to tail. It is truly amazing how a little barbecue sauce, hot sauce, or other seasoning can create delicious delicacies.

My family and the other African-Americans found ways to create a real sense of community despite the economic and political barriers to progress. While Thurgood Marshall was convincing a once skeptical Supreme Court of the evils of segregation, we lived in our community, largely separated from whites and lacking equal resources, but content with our existence. Despite de facto segregation and prejudice, the residents south of the tracks developed a nurturing community and survived through perseverance and resourcefulness. The most prominent black families in the town were those who owned businesses, like Mr. and Mrs. Henry, proprietors of a small convenience store. Every time we had a few pennies, my siblings and I would run to the Henrys' to buy candy, ice cream, potato chips, and RC Cola. Mr. Henry was a stern man who would not suffer fools, even if they were children. He did not want us loitering around his store. He became impatient when we could not decide whether we wanted to buy jelly beans, fire balls (two for a penny), or Mary Janes. Mrs. Ella Henry, on the other hand, would not only let us take our time but even occasionally give us something free, like a piece of bubble gum or a jawbreaker.

Down the street from the Henrys' convenience store was the Knotty Pine Café, the leading social establishment in the black community. The café was a small greasy spoon, but extremely popular among those who lived on the south side of Merced. When you walked into the café, you saw a number of small tables and chairs and heard a jukebox blasting the big blues hits of the fifties. The dance floor in the center was invariably packed on weekends. Farther back were the bar stools and the kitchen, where you could be served lunch and dinner. The menu always included ribs and collard greens. On special occasions, you could get ham hocks and navy beans and Aunt Liz's famous sweet potato pie. You could also order soft or alcoholic drinks.

The real action in the Knotty Pine, however, was not visible to the public. Behind the kitchen and out of view was a gambling hall where men like my father and some women would spend nights and weekends. There were two tables in the back. The first was for the more casual gamblers; the second, for the addicts. My father was a charter member of the latter group. Gambling was his primary vice. The gambling table at the Knotty Pine was his primary residence, and our home was the place where he slept a few hours, bathed, and ate some meals. After working ten to twelve hours a day driving trucks up and down Highway 99, he would take his modest earnings to the gambling table. On occasion, he won and won big. More typically, he lost money and spent money he did not have.

One of the most impressive entrepreneurs on Cone Avenue was Mr. Lee. Moneyback Lee, as he was affectionately known, owned a business that was a combination pawnshop, antiques shop, scrapyard, used-furniture outlet, and, most important, dry cleaner's. He traveled to parts of the north side of Merced and picked up items the white families had discarded, bringing them to his shop to be resold. He was always well dressed, ready to make a deal, and willing to offer credit. His credit rates were usurious and clearly illegal, but the poor blacks in rural Merced were grateful to have someone who would give them credit. Moneyback Lee sold watches and other jewelry, furniture, car parts, and antiques that could sensibly be used only in the homes of the wealthy. He sold black folks items that he claimed were antiques, but weren't, and jewelry that he claimed was gold, when it wasn't. All that mattered to those who shopped with him was that the items looked good.

Down the street from Moneyback Lee lived the Reverend Roberson. He was the neighborhood Pentecostal preacher, who also had an entrepreneurial spirit. The Reverend Roberson was particularly effective in getting young people to come to Sunday school each week. His approach was creative and direct. He understood that the quickest way to reach a youngster's mind and heart was through his or her stomach. Every Saturday morning he would rise early and drive to the bakeries and supermarkets in Merced. He had an arrangement that allowed him to collect doughnuts, other pastries, and breads that were being thrown out on Saturday morning. He would collect the items, drive back to Cone Avenue, and, on reaching an area six blocks from his home, slow down and blow his horn to announce that these goodies had arrived and were available for us. We followed him, like the Pied Piper, to his home and the church and excitedly partook of his stale goods. The Reverend Roberson knew how to reach our families, too, giving us a loaf of stale bread to take home. His approach was always the same: "God is good. This food is free for you all. I want to see you and your families in church tomorrow. Do we have a deal?" He had a deal with us and would assuredly see us in church on Sunday. He was our Santa Claus every Saturday afternoon.

I recall that Charley Huddleston was also a popular figure and important role model in Merced. The consummate unofficial politician, Charley could communicate on a first-name basis with every major farmer in the San Joaquin Valley. He also was able to choose his own private fishing holes, hunting grounds, and camping grounds on the farmers' property, and had twenty-four-hour access to those areas. He invited motorcycle clubs from Oakland and San Francisco to come to Merced to entertain us. Charley himself was great on a motorcycle, doing wheelies, figure-eight spins, and other daredevil moves. Charley was also the unofficial traffic cop at funerals, wearing his black shirt, riding his motorcycle, and directing traffic for funeral processions. No one else in the black community wielded as much power, and no one else organized as many activities for the black youth of Merced. Charley raised money to build a skating rink on the south side of Merced and encouraged black children to learn to skate to keep us busy during the summer. He treated all the children as if they were his own. Most important, he kept my father employed as a truck driver when other work opportunities were nonexistent.

I remember other prominent Merced citizens. Bert Alexander, for example, had a very successful newspaper, magazine, and novelty shop, could surely have afforded to live elsewhere, but chose to live on the south side of town. Joe James had a successful vending and pinball machine business, and David Norfles owned a dry cleaning business. Sam Pipes, a mail carrier, was the first black to be elected to the Merced City Council. Vernon Roberts owned Vernon's barbershop, the natural gathering place for black people, particularly on weekends. Billie Alexander, Bert's wife, owned Billie's beauty salon, where black women gathered weekdays and weekends to gossip, and to keep an eye on their occasionally errant husbands. Some could afford to go elsewhere, but they all lived in south Merced. There were other locals who did not own businesses but were nevertheless significant figures in the community and important role models for me. Julia Beale, a substitute teacher and president of the Merced NAACP, was particularly memorable.

Mrs. Beale was a hearty woman with lots of children and a strong, clear voice. She always made sure the concerns of those who lived on the south side of Merced were frequently on the agenda of the city. She lashed out at racism, degradation, and prejudice, but she was equally critical of indifference in the black community. In the early 1960s, she urged black families to be vigilant in keeping their children away from drugs, violence, and negative peer pressure.

Many of the young people in Merced saw Mrs. Beale as being just a few ranks lower than God. When I think of her, I'm reminded of how well it was understood in the 1950s and 1960s that, in the black community, parenting was a community concern. We were told that people like Mrs. Beale were our surrogate parents. Our parents gave her license to observe our conduct when we were away from home and to discipline us whenever she deemed it appropriate. Mrs. Beale took this responsibility very seriously. She was everywhere and in everybody's business, but in a way that our parents appreciated. I firmly believed that Mrs. Beale had extraordinary powers permitting her to see through buildings and over distances miles away. She knew when, where, and how we were doing wrong and, in her God-fearing way, was committed to straightening us out. She took to heart the adage "Spare the rod, spoil the child." We were not spared her wrath. The worst part of my encounters with Mrs. Beale was not when she punished me. I accepted responsibility for my transgressions and would take my licks. However, for some reason that is beyond me, Mrs. Beale would not find her punishment of me sufficient. She would take me home, enumerate all of my transgressions to my mother, and set me up for a second round of punishment. That seemed utterly unfair to me and still strikes me as a case of double jeopardy.

RACISM HUNG LIKE A PERSISTENT CLOUD over the world of Merced, and while it seemed to be an undercurrent in my parents' conversations during my childhood, they were rarely explicit about discussing it in our house. They would sometimes talk about "Mr. Charlie"[1]—slang generally used contemptuously in referring to the white community as oppressors of blacks—but they did not belabor the point or try to raise us with a racist attitude toward white people. They appeared to accept their fate in the sincere belief that things would be better for their children.

The railroad tracks in Merced established critical boundaries in the 1950s and beyond. It was the dividing line between blacks and whites, between opportunity and despair. While there was no sign at the track saying "whites only" or "coloreds only," there were other signs of a divided community. As my father used to say about his childhood in Alabama, "There were certain places we just could not go. There were no signs stopping us, but we knew that we didn't belong in certain places. You didn't have to tell us twice."

There was a buffer zone just a few blocks north of the tracks that encompassed downtown Merced, where whites and blacks shopped, indifferent to one another. If you wanted to go to the theater to see a movie, you went downtown, north of the railroad tracks. If you wanted to go to a department store, you went across the tracks. If you wanted to go to Yosemite Lake, you crossed the tracks. If you needed to stay in a hotel, find a bakery, or go to a fast-food restaurant, you went across the tracks. These were rules children learned at an early age.

The wealthiest, largely white Merced families lived in an upper-middle-class community in north Merced, with street names like Bear Creek Drive and Cedar Crest Lane. The less affluent families lived on the south side of Bear Creek, but still north of the railroad tracks that ran through the center of town. Most of the businesses, both of the high schools, and Merced Junior College lay north of the railroad tracks as well. The vast majority of black citizens, like the poverty-stricken segment of the rest of the population, lived on the south side of the railroad tracks. The only significant "institution" south of the tracks was the Merced County Fairgrounds, the site of an annual weeklong county fair, at which interracial fights were as predictable a feature as softball games. Apart from the fair, high school football games, and summer modified-stock-car races, white students had little occasion to visit the south side of Merced, where my family lived. Except in one instance, our homes were either in the rural part of the city or on the south side.

On Saturdays, we were given one dollar to go to the movie theater, some three blocks north of the railroad tracks. We made the trip to the theater a full day experience, arriving when it opened at noon and staying until the early evening. We watched the double feature at least twice. We always sat in the balcony, but it is not clear to me whether we did so out of an innate sense of our place or a desire to be mischievous, using our vantage point to throw a piece of candy or ice at the whites sitting below. It never occurred to us that the balcony had until recently been reserved for blacks and that our parents could not have sat down-stairs. We were happy in the balcony and, long after the end of segregated seating in the theater, voluntarily sat where our parents had been forced to sit. The irony was lost on us.

Even with the railroad delineating physical and social boundaries, we persevered. In south Merced, as in many other African-American communities contending with segregation at the time, one found ways to create one's own centers of excellence, in a community short on resources. We had our barbershops and beauty shops. We had our dry cleaner's and convenience stores. We had our pool halls, cafés, and, most important, places of worship. We carried on the great tradition of the slaves, by placing our burdens in God's hands. When I was still in high school, we attended Antioch Baptist Church, where the Reverend T. C. Wynn would remind us every Sunday, "God will make a way, where there is no way." We would sing the songs like "Swing low, sweet chariot, coming for to carry me home" and hoped that God would not forget those of us, stuck in the throes of segregation, when he returned to take the saints to heaven. We didn't know whether Merced was on his route, but we sang the spirituals with conviction, if not always with precision, and wanted to make sure that he heard us, loud and clear.

Most important, my grandparents' and parents' generations made sure that their children went to school every day. In their own childhood, school had been a less desirable option than work, and so they worked. By the 1950s, when it appeared that education provided the vehicle for crossing the railroad tracks into the land of opportunity, we were encouraged to learn.

NEITHER THE *BROWN I* DECISION, on May 17, 1954, nor the *Brown II* decision, on May 31, 1955, generated much interest in Merced. Although my mother and my father had lived through the same forms of rank segregation that Thurgood Marshall experienced in his hometown of Baltimore, they did not share his optimism that the courts could eliminate segregation. When the Supreme Court ruled that segregation would be ended with "all deliberate speed," they understood all too well that little if anything had changed in American society generally or in their lives more specifically.

Despite my parents' less than modest circumstances, they were typical of our community in placing a high value on education. Although neither of them had finished high school, both encouraged their children in school. Born in Anniston, Alabama, my father left in the 1940s for Georgia, where he served in the military and then migrated to California. When he left Birmingham, the school system was still segregated. My father never had the opportunity to attend a desegregated school, much less to vote in the Jim Crow–dominated world of the 1940s. Born in Little Rock, my mother moved with her parents to California in 1944. Her formal education did not extend beyond the tenth grade. In 1949, at age sixteen, she gave birth to my stepbrother, Curtis Reed. My father also had a daughter, Taalia Hasan (born as Shirley Ogletree), in 1943 before he married my mother in 1950.

Their life together had an inauspicious beginning. You could say that my father's very existence depended on marrying my mother, for he was almost killed in 1950. There were myriad reasons why a black man was forced to deal with the almost constant threat of death at the time. El Nido, as my father's friends commonly called him, could have succumbed to the destructive forces of racism in Alabama, where segregation and racial hatred were especially pervasive. Given the bleak life of poverty in the South, many of my father's generation fell victim to inadequate nutrition and health care, and suicide was far more common than is generally known. My father's courtship with death, however, was far more personal—he was threatened with murder by my grandfather. In 1950, my father, already forty-one years old, was passionately involved with my mother, only seventeen at the time. My grandfather informed my father that if he did not marry my mother, he would kill him.

Neither my father nor my mother had the slightest idea that a team of lawyers was at the time working to end racial segregation in education. They were trying to make a life in a world that offered few possibilities, and they never imagined that they might one day live in a world without legalized segregation. Their most urgent concern was my grandfather's threat. My father was a strong and confident man, yet he could clearly understand the message of a shotgun pointed at him. He agreed to the ceremony.

The oppressive migrant work described by John Steinbeck in *The Grapes of Wrath* remained very much a reality. In their early years together, my parents experienced indignities that were routine for poor and minority workers, who had no ability to alter the way those with power viewed or treated them. They were seasonal farm laborers living in a work camp in a rural community called Chowchilla, a few miles south of Merced. They moved frequently, following the flow of work.

After my birth on December 31, 1952, four other children were born. My brother Robert Anthony came along in February 1954, my sister Barbara Jean in December 1955, my brother Richard Jerome in January 1957, and my second sister, Rose Marie, in September 1958.

From the time that I was born, until I left home to go to college eighteen years later, we moved constantly, always facing poverty. We lived with our grandparents in the country for a while, moved into a two-bedroom house a little closer to the city on Cone Avenue, and then moved even closer, living in south Merced in three different places. We never owned a house, and the apartments were always small and cluttered. From the time I started school at Weaver Elementary, in rural Merced, to the move to south Merced and Galen Clark Elementary, to another move to rural Merced and Franklin Elementary School, we lived in at least half a dozen places. It never quite felt settled, but we always had a roof over our heads. By the time I attended junior high, we moved to Home Avenue, also in south Merced, and we stayed there until I left for college. Every one of the houses we lived in, except the last, was ultimately condemned and replaced by parking lots, strip malls, or any other establishment able to offer more for the property than we could as tenants.

Although my parents valued education, they had little understanding of how to foster academic excellence. We did not discuss current events over dinner and we did not hear stories from our parents before we went to bed. We had few, if any, books at home and could only imagine what the world was like, convinced that everything we read about in books about white families was indeed a fairy tale.

When I read books about "seeing Spot run," my frame of reference was the greyhound dogs my grandfather trained to take out in the open fields in the country, to hunt the rabbits and birds that he shot and we ate for dinner. When the fairy-tale families ate breakfast, lunch, and dinner, we saw no comparable reality at home. We did not have a dining room or dining room table. We did not have a refrigerator, but an old icebox, with blocks of ice designed to keep our food from spoiling. Unlike "Dick," I never had my own room or my own bed. I grew up sharing a bed or, better, a place to sleep with my brothers. My family was on welfare, and we looked forward to the monthly checks. When the welfare check came, it was spent almost overnight, and we would celebrate by having "good food," like chili dogs, Spam sandwiches, and, occasionally, fried chicken.

There was one thing I had in common with little Dick, though. In the books we read, he was always dressed the same, every page and every day. That seemed fine to me. We wore the same clothes, hand-me-downs, as they were called, and had no shame in doing so. One day at Weaver Elementary School, however, that changed. I guess my first-grade teacher grew exasperated at my less than splendid wardrobe, which was a cotton shirt, pants that were dirty and old, or something close to it, and shoes that had seen better days, with a hole in the bottom covered by a piece of cardboard. She sent me to the principal's office with a note. Although I knew that I had done nothing wrong, I was upset, and she made it worse by not telling me why I was going.

When I got there, I was told to wait a few minutes, because I was to be taken to the gym, which also served as the cafeteria and assembly hall. At the gym, the physical education teacher told me to take off the old clothes I was wearing, adding he had a new set for me to wear. That puzzled me even more, but at the time I had no idea whether to reject this unexpected generosity. I did feel fortunate to receive some clean clothes. The teacher did not explain where they came from or why he was giving them to me. I only knew that I felt like a new kid.

My first-grade teacher, who I thought was going to ask if I had been punished, simply smiled when I returned to the classroom. She never said a word to me about it. The other kids made fun of my new clothes at recess, since they remembered my old ones. When they asked me whether I had to go home to get those clothes, I lied and said yes. I certainly was not going to tell them that someone gave me clothes and threw my old set away. Somehow, I think they knew that I was lying about the clothes, but, for whatever reason, they just let it go. When I came home and my mother saw the clothes, she could only shake her head. It took me years to realize that she viewed this small gesture by the school as a negative reflection on her parenting skills. The school had stepped up to do what it thought my mother should have done. It was a day that I would not forget.

While the material poverty we lived in was palpable, there was no poverty of values in our home. My grandmother could barely read, but she knew enough to read the Bible to us, and make sure we listened. I don't know why she read that Bible to us, but it started my curiosity in reading. I was so drawn into these biblical stories that I spent hours in the library and read lots of books. The more I read, the more I dreamed of being in another world, and the fascination with learning opened up avenues that I never imagined.

I was encouraged to keep up this interest in reading, as the school librarian was my enabler. She offered me new books to read, and seemed vicariously to enjoy my excitement. We established a nice partnership. She provided the books for me to read, and I told her stories about the wonderful things I learned. I treasured every moment, and whether I was riding home on the bus or sitting outside near the creek behind our house, reading a book became part of my daily routine.

Not everyone embraced the full scope of my endless interest in reading. My grandmother and mother, who were pleased to see me interested in reading, did not like the lack of self-imposed boundaries. Both would occasionally admonish me for spending all my time reading, and forgetting to do some of my chores around the house. At night, I would read until it was dark, and my mother would say, "Junior, you are going to go blind reading in the dark! Put that book down, and go to bed!" I always wanted to respond and tell her that reading in the dark doesn't cause blindness, that this was a silly thing to say. But I knew better. I followed her admonition, and when she fell asleep, I would use the moonlight to read as long as I could, and then fall off to sleep myself.

Books were my addiction, and I could not feed it fast enough. The books I read took me places that I suspected I would never visit in life. They took me to castles and caves, over the seas and atop the highest mountains. They allowed me to be by turns inventive, curious, melancholy, or frustrated. I would imagine riding on a riverboat with Tom Sawyer and telling him I did not appreciate his use of the word "Nigger." I would find myself enthralled by Daniel Defoe's classic work *The Adventures of Robinson Crusoe,* and travel the high seas serving as a mate for any captain looking for a gifted sailor. My most inspiring moments of reading and learning came on those summer nights, when it was just too hot to sleep. I would read about places all over the world and imagine getting there. These trips were made a lot easier when I heard the Southern Pacific trains travel through Merced, heading to destinations unknown. I imagined getting on those trains and journeying to places with no limits and no barriers.

It was becoming apparent to others around me, but not to me, that reading would be my ticket out of poverty and despair. I had witnessed a better place and a better life. I was patient but certain that, as I grew older, it would be time to move to another place and be someone else. It would be time to see the things my grandparents and parents had never imagined, and to do the things they had never dared even try.

Much has been written about segregation in the South during the years preceding and following *Brown,* but far less about life in places like Merced. During the 1950s and 1960s in the Central Valley of California—the heartland of the California farm belt—segregation was decidedly race based, but class based as well. Black and brown people, with rare exception, came in one shade—poor. Whites, on the other hand, came in three—dirt poor, better off, and affluent. Whites who had the misfortune of being poor went to school with black and brown children.

I recall that my first experiences in elementary school were fond ones. My classmates, all poor and working class, were predominantly black and brown, with a few whites. The topic of race never came up in those early days, and we all felt we were equal. However, when we left public school and returned to our respective homes, race mattered very much. The black, brown, and white families all lived in largely segregated communities. There was no interaction between our families. We did not play together outside of school. We did not dine or socialize in the same areas. There seemed to be an unspoken agreement that people would be cordial to one another, interact when necessary, but never raise the uncomfortable issue of race voluntarily.

The significance of race was evident in the economic disparities between the two sides of town, but I was too young even to know that we were economically inferior to our white counterparts. It was not the economic disparities that brought race to the forefront. No, it was the interaction with white students that made me realize that being black meant being different and that, in the minds of some of my white peers, it meant being inferior.

One of the numerous moves my family made landed us for a short time in a rural section of Merced, where schools were almost exclusively white and the families were generally poor. My mother had gained the support, or possibly sympathy, of a public assistance employee who placed us in a crowded home. My siblings and I were enrolled in the Franklin Elementary School, a school with few black or brown students. I embraced the label "good student" and earned recognition for being so, even in my all-white sixth-grade class. There were occasions, however, when on reflection I might have misinterpreted a special honor as a reflection of my academic achievements rather than of my racial identification. Although *Brown* was by 1964 settled law in the United States, there was little evidence that it had changed the hearts or minds of those to whom it was addressed.

There was no more enjoyable period of the school day than morning and afternoon recess. In California, the sun would shine generously and the clouds strike dramatic poses in the skies, making the weather conditions perfect. We could not wait to get outside and run around. Although new to the school, I was fortunate to make friends easily. I recall that the guys stuck together, throwing rocks on the pond, shooting marbles, or playing a little touch football. The girls played jump rope, hopscotch, or on the playground swings. At that age, our recess activities usually divided along gender lines or, as we preferred to call it in those days, boy-girl.

One nice day, the boys decided to play a game of touch football. Since I had some speed and decent moves, I was pleased that one of the teams quickly chose me to be on its side. Since recesses lasted only twenty to thirty minutes, these games had to be quick. We were doing well in the game and scored first. We then kicked off to our opponents, one of whom made a pretty good runback, but did not score. On an ensuing play, one of our opponents caught a pass, but I tagged him before he could score. Although it was unintentional, our bodies collided, and he fell down. He seemed more embarrassed than hurt. But it was his spontaneous response that changed everything that day. "You nigger!" he shouted and stormed off the field, startling me and everyone else who heard it. I was only eleven years old and had never been called a "nigger" before. I was shocked and deeply hurt by the experience and to this day cannot understand why I responded the way I did. I laughed and pretended that maybe I hadn't heard it, or that he hadn't really said it, or maybe that it didn't matter. My teammates wanted to follow my lead, before responding. No one said a word. Although I'm sure it was only a matter of minutes, it felt like an eternity before the recess ended. I was no longer reading a story, trying to anticipate what was next. I was living a very uncomfortable moment and had no clue how to proceed. We were spared further awkwardness when the bell rang.

I wanted to put the incident out of my mind and to forget that it had ever happened. Unfortunately, I did not have that luxury. For some reason that I cannot recall, I was the last student to return to the classroom after our recess. The class was unusually quiet after a recess, with the students in their seats, and all eyes on me when I walked in. Our teacher appeared particularly somber, for someone had obviously shared the recess incident with him. He began a discussion about the need for us to respect each other. He, too, was struggling with how to talk about race, without obviously talking about race. As he rambled on, it was clear that he had to confront the issue: a white student had called me, the only black in the class, a "nigger," intending to hurt me. He expressed how upset he was with all that had happened. He then went on personally to apologize to me on behalf of the class and asked whether I wanted to talk about it further. Being the only black student in the class, I could not imagine any benefit from discussing the incident any more, so I declined his invitation. I wanted to ignore the incident, and he wanted to hold a class discussion on the use of the "N" word. Although very well intentioned, my teacher's effort to discuss race did not make me feel any better. It was at that moment when I sat in that classroom as the only black student that I grasped the significance of my blackness and concluded that being black was not a good thing. What did the boy mean when he called me a "nigger"? I know, at a minimum, the word was intended to hurt me, and it did. I also know that it changed the way I saw myself going forward.

Later that year, one of my teachers organized a play depicting California's early history. Our teacher announced the different roles that each student would portray in the school play, and let me know that I was selected for a special role, that of master of ceremonies for the event. It was my job to introduce my fellow fifth-graders, describe the characters they were playing, and offer a narrative describing the California gold rush of the 1840s. My classmates were playing the roles of proud American pioneers who battled the terrain, disease, weather conditions, and other barriers as they sought to make California the state where their dreams would come true. As I watched the play unfold, I realized that there was no role or character for me in this story. Those in the gold rush were white women and men. If there was to be a mention of African-Americans, it would require the discussion of the difficult topic of slavery. Race was not mentioned at all that day. While I was told that my selection as master of ceremonies was a reward for being a good student, a subtle, more disturbing factor also was evident. The teacher created a role for me to play that I, as a black student, could play credibly in the discussion of this topic. It is true that I was a good student, but apparently not good enough to have a character role in a play about the gold rush.

By the time I reached middle school, in the mid-1960s, the issue of race had become more pronounced. Black and Hispanic students, with a small number of poor white students, largely populated the schools in the town. In the outlying areas, the schools and neighborhoods were virtually all-white, and these neighborhoods reflected that lack of diversity. At the beginning of the 1960s, our community had begun to experience the early effects of the *Brown* decision. Although segregation as we knew it had started to change with the requirement that black and brown students be bused from the city to the suburban high schools, segregation nonetheless persisted in some ways.

As I grew older, I realized the significance of race in some of my classes. I began to notice that I was usually one of no more than two or three black and brown students in math and science classes. I assumed that other black and brown students were simply choosing other options. As this trend continued into high school, I learned of another practice, well intentioned, but nonetheless pernicious in its impact. The public school teachers I encountered had developed rather firm views concerning the inability of black and brown children to compete successfully in the rigorous math and science courses. The teachers routinely tracked black and brown students, relegating them to lower-level and less challenging courses. Moreover, once students were placed in a lower academic track, it was nearly impossible for them to be placed in a more rewarding and challenging academic track. It became clear that students who were placed in the math and science classes were the chosen few.

I'm not sure what elevated me. I suspect it had more to do with behavior than with intellect. I responded to my family's extreme poverty and frequent moves from one bad living condition to a worse one by being withdrawn, quiet, and passive in elementary school—in other words, the perfect student. I did my work, followed the rules, and never complained. My shyness, combined with a great affection for sucking my thumb, made me perhaps a child seemingly deserving of sympathy, thus endearing me to my teachers despite the color of my skin. I was designated a "good student." I soon embraced that label, recognizing the benefits and favored status it conferred, and worked hard to hold on to it, not just through good behavior but through academic performance as well. Fortunately for me, the designation "good student" followed me to junior high school and made the difference between being placed on a track for future success and being placed on one for failure.

The teachers' power to decide our fate was exacerbated by our parents' failure to recognize that this tracking system would permanently banish their children to less rigorous academic courses and preclude them from opportunities in higher education. While the mechanism of busing as a means to promote *Brown*'s integration mandate was well intentioned, it was easy to recognize, even at that early stage, that little was being done to provide the overwhelming majority of black and brown children with a high-quality education. Achieving actual academic excellence for black and brown children was proceeding with "all deliberate speed" even in Merced. There were, of course, some wonderful teachers, like Mrs. Elsie Myers and Mrs. Edna McMaster, who pushed the children of south Merced to excel. Although they were both white and we were all black and brown, they were deeply committed to our success. Additionally, mentors like our Native American principal, Mr. Gather B. Haynes, pursued the same academic excellence for all children.

Both of the Merced High School's campuses and the private Catholic high school were across the tracks in north Merced. East Campus, used primarily for freshmen and sophomores, was just a few blocks across the tracks. North Campus, where most juniors and seniors attended, was the larger and more beautiful campus, where most of our athletic events and many of our top academic and cultural programs took place.

When I started high school, in 1967, it was the first setting in which blacks, Latinos, and whites, rich and poor, interacted as members of the same community. We were in the same classrooms, members of the same band, teammates on the athletic fields, and in every sense, together as one community for a few hours each day. After school, my friends and I boarded buses for the ride back to the community south of the tracks.

In my freshman year, I took Spanish and was the only black in the class. It was an honors class; as a reward for our academic success, we took a field trip to Baja California and crossed the border into Mexico, to have an opportunity to test our Spanish-speaking skills. I felt uncomfortable being the only black on a bus of forty students, teachers, and chaperones on the trip, but it was the kind of experience that I would come to expect while in high school.

My most consciousness-raising experience came later in the year when I met John Heflin, an African-American teacher and the basketball coach for the freshman team. I broke my ankle just before the start of high school and missed freshman football. I did get a chance to play basketball and spend some time with Coach Heflin. He was tall, articulate, and self-assured. He exposed me to a new set of readings that changed my life. Thanks to the gentle prodding of Heflin, I read such books as Harriet Beecher Stowe's *Uncle Tom's Cabin*, Claude Brown's *Manchild in the Promised Land*, and Richard Wright's *Native Son*. They gave me an entirely new sense of who I was and informed me about the misery that generations of black people had experienced.

In *Manchild*, essentially a memoir of Claude Brown's life, the brutal reality of urban disaffection that is fictionalized in *Native Son* is revealed as still in effect a generation later. Both Wright and Brown explored the numbing frustrations of midwestern (in *Native Son*) and northern (in *Manchild*) forms of racism, which were as brutal and stifling as their southern counterparts. Many African-Americans imagined that the trip up north or out west would spell freedom: as described by Brown, going to New York meant good-bye to the cotton fields, good-bye to "Massa Charlie," good-bye to the chain gang, and, most of all, good-bye to those sunup-to-sundown working hours. One no longer had to wait to get to heaven to lay one's burden down; burdens could be laid down in New York. But the reality of life in New York proved very different, and *Manchild* recounts Brown's experience as a preteen gang member who was confined to a reform school by the age of fourteen. In *Native Son,* Bigger Thomas, the novel's protagonist, disaffected and with few outlets for protest and fewer opportunities to assert his humanity, is propelled by events, as much as by his own acts, to his tragic death. *Native Son* is a savage indictment of the treatment of African-Americans in forties America. Both of these novels had a profound impact upon me, as well as on millions of other Americans whose parents had fled the South in search of a better life.

I began to understand more clearly why my grandfather mentioned that our ancestors were from Africa, but did not tell us more. I came to appreciate why my father would not look white people (and particularly not white women) in the eye—because of his sense of his role in society as a black man. I understood, better than ever, why we were in south Merced, when my white peers were in north Merced. These books awakened a consciousness that I didn't realize was within me. I never took, nor was there offered, any course on black history, the entire four years of high school. There was no discussion of slavery, or Jim Crow laws, or the Emancipation Proclamation. Was someone afraid that this information would arouse the black students and create a rebellion? Was it too divisive a subject for high school students? Were the teachers themselves ill equipped to teach it? Whatever the case, I was glad to have been directed by Mr. Heflin to learn a little bit about the history of black struggle in America, and I used this knowledge to take on new challenges in school. My generation, having been sheltered from much of the discrimination that our parents had experienced, took a different approach on issues of race. We did not fear white people. We did not feel unequal. We had no reluctance to speak and be heard.

The spark that set off my newfound black consciousness came during the spring of my freshman year of high school. On April 4, 1968, my father drove from the Blue Moon Café and Pool Hall, where he had been gambling, to our house and simply announced, "They killed King. I heard it on the radio. Turn on the TV." He had a forlorn look, but said little. If he was angry—and I'm sure he was—he did not show it. I couldn't understand why anyone would kill a black man who preached nonviolence and wanted only justice and equality in America. My friends and I walked around town, wandering aimlessly, but angry that our black leader was dead. We didn't know what to do to vent our anger.

In school, teachers praised King, whereas there had been no mention of him before. All the discussions focused on his message of nonviolence. Students were shown clips of his "I Have a Dream" speech. Within our community the message was the same. The local NAACP leaders told black students to remain calm and stay home. Our black ministers implored us to put this in God's hands. But we felt that God had let us down in allowing somebody to kill King. Out of frustration, we started an organization of black students called Operation Get Together; it was the precursor to the Merced High Black Student Union and a group where minorities could discuss civil rights issues.

We searched for other ways to vent our frustration and challenge our community. During my junior year, two of my classmates—Duke Fergerson and Avery Poncho Shelton—and I had a conversation about our interaction with the white guys on the football team. We got along well as players, but I wondered why we never saw them, ever, in south Merced, or why we were never in their homes. I suggested that we pay our friends a visit on the weekend. We decided to visit them at their place of worship, the Mormon Church in Merced. When we entered the church that day, appropriately dressed, church members reacted initially with a sense of alarm. A few then scurried over to greet us and help us feel welcome. We were the only blacks in the church that day. Ironically, the sermon focused on serving the needs of the community. I wondered whether the minister understood that serving the community extended beyond north Merced. At the end of the service, our friends greeted us as though happy to see us and said they would see us at practice on Monday. Having made our point, we returned across the tracks to south Merced.

We wanted not only to challenge what was white but also to claim something for ourselves. Our aim was to make sure that we, too, had pride in some of the institutions in our community. The largest facility in Merced, open to blacks and whites, was the Merced County Fairgrounds. The fairgrounds were located, as I mentioned, in south Merced and were used for our annual county fair, the Saturday night model car races, and the high school's fall Friday night football game. We felt the fairgrounds belonged to us, because they were in our neighborhood. This created repeated outbreaks of racial conflict and occasional violence. When the Merced County Fair came to town each summer, along with the white farmers, who were affectionately known as Aggies, there were repeated fistfights between blacks and whites. Fights typically started with someone's looking at us in a way that suggested he owned the fairgrounds or certainly had the right to move around with impunity. They were in our neighborhood, and we wanted respect. Almost nightly, the police broke up the fights and arrested a few of the principals, and life would go on. The expectation was that fights between blacks and whites were part of the annual entertainment at the fairgrounds.

Although no black drivers or crewmembers were involved in the stock car races at the fairgrounds, we would nonetheless go there to establish our right to be there. We also rationalized that since they were in our part of town, we need not pay to enter the races and routinely jumped over the fence and enjoyed our time in the stands watching the races.

Our willingness to question the status quo opened our eyes to the disparity among the city's parks and recreational facilities. The city operated two public swimming pools—one at the North Campus high school and the other in south Merced at McNamara Park. The high school pool was Olympic size, with more lanes than the pool at McNamara. City workers meticulously maintained it and supplied it with ample pool equipment. The McNamara pool, by contrast, was much smaller, poorly maintained, and often lacking basic supplies.

The two pools had one thing in common: all of the lifeguards were white, even though McNamara served the black and brown residents of south Merced. For years, my friends and I swam at McNamara, never questioning its condition or staffing, content to have an oasis from the summer heat. We decided in the summer of 1970 that it was time to change this, too.

My friends Glenn Williamson and Poncho Shelton, another classmate, Robert Runnels, and I questioned why the lifeguards at our pool were all white. We saw no reason why we shouldn't have black lifeguards in south Merced. We raised the question with Craig Smith and Sandy Harmon, who worked in the city's parks and recreation department. Craig responded in a positive manner, offering to discuss the matter with the director of parks and recreation. He came back to us with an answer and a challenge: the city would hire some black lifeguards if it could find some who were qualified. Since we were all good swimmers, he urged us to apply. We were prepared to rise to the occasion. For three weeks, we met at McNamara Park every morning at eight, for four hours, learned first aid, water safety, and pool care. We also learned how to rescue swimmers in distress and to resuscitate drowning victims. It was a grueling experience, but four weeks later we were certified to be lifeguards. I became the pool manager at McNamara Park.

We wanted the pool to be a center of activity, one that children, our peers, and even our parents would enjoy. We gave swimming lessons to youngsters and held swimming and diving meets where everyone won a prize. We extended the hours of operation, opening the pool some evenings so that those who worked all day could have a place to relax at night. Charley Huddleston opened up a game room in the hut located in the park, for shuffleboard, pool, horseshoes, and picnics. For the first time that I could remember, McNamara Park was full of life and excitement.

The broader question about the McNamara pool example is more complex. It took us until seventeen years after *Brown* to have black lifeguards at the pool for black people, in our part of town. By the same token, were we, as late as 1971, perpetuating the segregation that *Brown* tried to end? Why were we content to be lifeguards at McNamara Park, never even considering being lifeguards at the high school pool in north Merced? If we were going to the Mormon Church to make a statement, why not, in the spirit of Thurgood Marshall and Dr. King, push for full equality by working in an environment dominated by whites?

In 1970, my interest in politics and race became even more pronounced. I decided to run for vice president of the student body. No black student had ever been elected to a student body–wide office such as this. The sitting student body president, Jack Kanealy, and John Lenker, a teacher who was the adviser to the student government, insisted that my goals were not ambitious enough and urged me to run for student body president. I thought that I was not prepared for that role and that others were probably better suited, but decided to run nevertheless. My campaign focused on inclusion and unity among blacks, whites, Chicanos, and Asians. Perhaps my message of unity struck a positive chord in the aftermath of King's assassination, for I was elected student body president. One of the great pleasures in 1970–71 was meeting and working with Gil Grover and Alice Spendlove, two full-time employees of Merced High School who encouraged me in all of my efforts to increase student interest in civic affairs and other forms of community service. They arranged for high school students to volunteer to assist the elderly in the community and to host forums that allowed students and families from north and south Merced to work collaboratively.

Toward the end of my junior year, my counselor, Mrs. Jackson, talked to me about college options. I told her I was thinking of attending Merced Junior College or, as a stretch, might apply to Occidental College, a California college that had some brochures at the high school. Mrs. Jackson, a graduate of Stanford University, urged me to aim higher and recommended that I apply to Stanford. I responded, "Mrs. Jackson, I want to stay closer to home. I really don't want to go to Connecticut. It's just too cold." Mrs. Jackson laughed. I thought she found my concern about cold weather to be funny. When she finally controlled her amusement, she handed me a brochure about Stanford, saying, "Charles, Stanford isn't in Connecticut. It's in California. It's two hours north of Merced." I applied to Stanford more out of embarrassment than anything else.

As I left Merced in the fall of 1971, much had changed in my life. The *Brown* decision was instrumental in persuading colleges and universities to open their doors to students like me, and I was more than willing to enter. The opportunities that did not exist for my grandparents or parents were available to me. Still, I headed to Stanford with mixed emotions. I was leaving so many friends and classmates behind. I was one of five Merced high school graduates, but the only minority student, headed to Stanford. In our graduating class of several hundred students, only a few of the dozens of black students were attending a four-year college. While *Brown* gave all of us access to equal educational opportunity, it did little to transform an educational system that expected less from black and brown students than from whites and that disproportionately tracked black and brown students in courses that failed to prepare them for college.

CHAPTER 3

BROWN'S PROMISE:
BLACK STUDENTS AT STANFORD

Virtually all of the black freshmen who arrived at Stanford in the fall of 1971 were born near the time that the *Brown* decision was issued in 1954. We were, in every sense of the word, *Brown* babies, and we came to Stanford from every conceivable community in the country. Some came from Mississippi, Alabama, Georgia, and North Carolina. Others came from Texas, New York, Michigan, and Illinois. The largest contingent was from California, primarily from the urban areas of Southern California. A fair number of the black students, mainly black males, came from preparatory schools on the East Coast. All told a similar story of excelling academically in their all-black high schools and being selected by a counselor to attend an elite school such as Phillips Andover Academy, Milton Academy, or Phillips Exeter. The counselors felt that they would benefit from a year or two in highly competitive, academically challenging schools.

In our class of 1,500 freshmen, there were 68 African-American students, fairly evenly divided between men and women. We typified students of the 1970s. We wore our hair in Afros the size of small planets and donned bell-bottom pants for every occasion. We danced to the music of Earth, Wind and Fire and enjoyed the mellow sounds of Barry White, Isaac Hayes, and Aretha Franklin. We were also in constant search of reasons to protest.

My hometown was only 120 miles from Stanford, and yet it seemed very far away. My classmates were familiar with LA and Houston, or San Francisco and Detroit, but no one had ever heard of Merced. The first question, given my uninspiring wardrobe, southern accent gained from my parents, and "country look," was invariably, "Is

Merced in the South?" It was not, but being from the San Joaquin Valley was like being in exile, and no one knew or cared that it was where César Chávez organized farmworkers, or that John F. Kennedy rode a train through the valley in the early 1960s, or that Summer Bartholomew, the sister of one of my high school classmates, was once Miss U.S.A. I was from a place with a remarkable past, but no one at Stanford seemed even slightly impressed. I might as well have been the "Brother from Another Planet." Nonetheless, I was determined to be accepted at Stanford.

Many of those arriving that fall had never left the inner cities where they were raised and, like their parents before them, attended largely segregated public schools. When I arrived on campus, I met a contingent of black students, including my future wife, Pamela Barnes, who had all attended schools in Southern California. Pam and two of her black classmates, Billy Walker and Michelle Miller, graduated from Compton Senior High School. They ranked among the top students in a graduating class of 700 that consisted entirely of African-American, Mexican-American, and Pacific Islander students. From across town at Compton High's archrival, Centennial High School, a school with similar demographics, Paris Brooks and Sandra Henderson also became members of Stanford's 1971 entering class. A third public high school, Dominguez Hills High, on the outskirts of Compton, and more integrated than the other two, sent Margaret Owens. Reggie Turner, who would prove to be an ally on many of the projects we pursued at Stanford, traveled the shortest distance to Stanford. He lived in East Palo Alto, a predominantly African-American community in the shadow of Stanford.

Most of the black students who entered Stanford that fall were the first members of their families to attend college. Remarkably, the parents and family members who were college educated had, with few exceptions, attended historically black colleges and universities (HBCUs). Thus, in attending an elite, predominantly white university, we were, with rare exception, all beneficiaries of *Brown*.

Even though we came to Stanford from different places and with different experiences, our goals were similar. Many of us almost immediately chose academic paths to pursue careers in law, medicine, or business. We were determined to learn all that we could so that our communities would be proud of our accomplishments. At the same time, we chose to find ways to volunteer our modest talents to others, particularly children, who would also be thinking about their educational options in the coming years.

By the time we arrived at Stanford, much of the turmoil of the civil rights movement and the antiwar demonstrations had subsided. The 1960s had generated unparalleled student activism at Stanford and on college campuses around the nation. The push for civil rights, the protest against the Vietnam War, and the violent demonstrations at the 1968 Democratic National Convention in Chicago had galvanized young people nationwide. Student protests at Columbia University, for example, led to school closings, arrests, and constant clashes between students and police. The same fervor was rocking the West Coast as well, as students at Berkeley organized a free-speech movement and shut down classes on campus. Students at San Francisco State protested the war in Vietnam and found themselves under attack by the police, with the approval of the school's president, S. I. Hayakawa. The student protests there caused the campus to be shut down for four months in 1968.

In 1967, twenty black students at Stanford created an organization called Interact, designed to interact with black youth in neighboring East Palo Alto. Like many of us coming later, the early black Stanford students had arrived from predominantly black high schools and found the transition to Stanford a culture shock. Their goal was to find ways to be an integral part of the Stanford community. That same year, Dr. Martin Luther King, Jr., visited Stanford and made a speech that left an indelible mark on the black students. He urged them to be active wherever they were, pleading, "We may have to repent in this generation not for the violent actions of the bad people, but for the inaction of the good people."[1]

Dr. King's assassination on April 4, 1968, provoked a national reaction. The *Stanford Daily* newspaper reported that some white students cheered King's assassination, fueling the flames of black protest. Within days of the assassination, while demonstrations and riots were taking place around the country, black students at Stanford were organizing their own protests. On April 8, 1968, in light of the student anger and frustration, Stanford canceled all classes to host a universitywide convocation to address the students' concerns. As Richard Lyman, Stanford's provost and soon to be appointed its president, began to address the death of King, seventy black students walked onstage, seized the microphone, and issued a set of ten demands to the president. These included radically increasing black student enrollment, oddly adding that the administration do so "with all deliberate speed"; admitting five "marginal black students and five marginal students from other minority groups"; increasing financial aid; and hiring black faculty. The students were joined by Gertrude Wilkes, a black activist from East Palo Alto, who organized black youth and parents from the community to support the Stanford students. The students also succeeded in demanding the creation of an African and Afro-American studies program, which recruited the Chicago sociologist and anthropologist St. Clair Drake to run it.

The student protests at Stanford were raised a notch in 1970 when black students held a demonstration at the Stanford hospital in response to the alleged wrongful firing of a black worker there. To the surprise of many, Stanford called police in to break up the demonstration. Protesters were brutally assaulted, and others were arrested, including the Black Student Union (BSU) chairman, Willie Newberry. When we arrived that fall, the anger from the spring arrests permeated the campus. Stories about the protest were as much a part of our orientation as the campus tour. Knowing that the BSU chairman had been beaten and arrested, and was still in jail, inspired us to develop strategies for change that eschewed violence. It was now our time to advance the movement, but also to prove, contrary to what many suspected, that we were going to excel in the classroom as well.

During our years at Stanford, while focusing on the same national issues, we turned to local and international issues as well. On the local level, Stanford students organized demonstrations to support the farm movement inspired by César Chávez. On the international level, they held massive demonstrations to protest Stanford's investments in companies operating in South Africa. We were also active in Stanford campus politics, holding elected student government positions and contributing our time to the local black community by serving as tutors in East Palo Alto elementary schools. We revived the black student newspaper, previously known as *The Real News Motherfucker*, and later shortened it to *The Real News*, pushed for black faculty and students, fought for an increased number of black studies classes, attended Black Panther and African Liberation Day events in the Bay Area, and actively supported Angela Davis, the black Communist scholar who was fired from her post at UCLA as a result of her radical political views.

I was thrilled to be on the Stanford campus. The red-roofed buildings, country club–like setting, and countless bicycles were things to marvel at. For the first time in my life, I had my own bed, three meals a day, a hot shower, and complete independence. Also for the first time, I sensed that I was no longer an anomaly, but rather was surrounded by a critical mass of gifted and bright black students who excelled in disciplines as diverse as chemistry, biology, economics, math, and music. I couldn't imagine life being any better. Toward the end of my freshman year, I was elected chairman of the Stanford BSU. As the fall semester came to an end, and we began to study for final exams, a shooting a few miles away from the Stanford campus changed my life forever.

Jonathan Jackson, the brother of George Jackson, a Black Panther and political activist who was in jail, entered a courtroom in Marin County, north of the Stanford campus, and with weapons drawn, tried to free several black radicals who were in the middle of their criminal trial. Jonathan Jackson, the judge presiding over the trial, and two others were killed, and no one escaped. Within days, the police traced the weapons to Angela Davis, issued a warrant for her arrest, and indicated that, when they captured her, they would seek the death penalty. Having no faith in the American criminal justice system, Davis went underground and avoided police for months. She was finally captured in New York in 1972 and transported back to California for her trial. The trial of Angela Davis became the focal point of black student interest at Stanford in 1972.

Her brother, Benjamin Davis, and sister, Fania Davis, came to Stanford and urged us to get involved in defending people like Angela, who were not criminals, but political prisoners. I served as coordinator of Stanford Students for the Defense of Angela Davis. As if by divine providence, Professor Davis was held at the women's detention center in Palo Alto, right across the street from the Stanford campus.

Allowed to visit her in jail, I let her know how we were organizing the campus to support her. She was a tall, warm, and imposing presence that day and, contrary to my own sense of anxiety, seemed oblivious that she was in a prison cell. Her point was, I think, that the physical confinement would not imprison her sense of mental liberation. She sat there, with her signature Afro hairstyle, smoking a pipe and taking notes, and told me that our defense of her, though commendable, was misplaced. She urged me to change our focus to other political prisoners who lacked the notoriety and international support she received, but who needed the public to know about their plight in our criminal justice system. I was troubled by her comments in only one respect: we had already made the silkscreen T-shirts reading, "Stanford students for the Defense of Angela Davis." We had to change them that week to read, "The Stanford Students for the Defense of Angela Davis and All Political Prisoners." In the course of one meeting in prison, Davis had taught me how to broaden our message and to present our cause in such a way that the public would find it more acceptable.

The conflict between our sense of responsibility as *Brown* babies and our role as Stanford students was never more sharply drawn than when Stanford went to the Rose Bowl in January 1972. We cheered the team with a level of enthusiasm rivaling that of the most avid Stanford fan. Yet, when the national anthem was played, we raised a large banner, inscribed with the words "Free Angela Davis and All Political Prisoners," and released black balloons representing the dark cloud created by America's unjust prosecution of Professor Davis. Not surprisingly, a sea of white Stanford alumni, who strongly objected to our protest, surrounded us. We endured the boos and jeers of the crowd with an indifference developed through years of practice. When the Rose Bowl game ended with a surprising victory by Stanford, the underdog, we celebrated the win.

I was so convinced of Davis's innocence that I decided, during my trip home for the winter break, to enlighten the larger Merced community about her trial. I wrote a letter to my hometown newspaper, the *Merced Sun Star*, describing her poor health and the deplorable conditions of her incarceration in the Santa Clara Women's Detention Center. My letter drew a spirited response from several of my white Stanford classmates who were also from Merced. They challenged my claims of Davis's poor treatment and believed that she would receive a fair trial. Their response however, did not stop there. They went on to suggest that it was inappropriate for me, as a beneficiary of scholarships to attend a school like Stanford, to be so critical of the system that was largely responsible for paying all my educational costs. Not to be outdone, I replied to my classmates by indicating that, even if my scholarships were taken away, I would still exercise my right to speak out against injustices.

Many of us regularly attended Davis's trial in San Jose, thirty miles from the Stanford campus. The trial was a key factor in my decision to attend law school when I finished my undergraduate studies. I had never attended a murder trial, nor had I seen anyone other than white lawyers, all male, in a courtroom. The Angela Davis trial changed that. This was not Atticus Finch trying to save an innocent black man from unfair punishment. This was a multiracial and multigender defense team representing Davis, and unlike the poor and defenseless black defendant in *To Kill a Mockingbird,* she herself was intelligent, well educated, and well known and chose to be an active participant in her own trial. Her lead attorney was Leo Branton, a distinguished African-American litigator from Los Angeles, the younger brother of Wiley Branton, an Arkansas lawyer who had worked with Thurgood Marshall to file civil rights cases in Arkansas in the 1950s. He was joined by Howard Moore, a prominent African-American lawyer from Oakland.

Two women were also on the team. Margaret Burnham had grown up in Alabama with Davis and later worked at Thurgood Marshall's former office, the NAACP Legal Defense and Education Fund in New York. When the director and the board refused to enter the Davis case, Burnham resigned and moved to California to assist in the defense of her lifelong friend. The fourth member of the team was Margaret Brin Walker, one of the first women admitted to practice in California, a member of the Communist Party, and a public-interest lawyer. These lawyers worked well as a team and allowed their client to participate, by presenting her own opening statement and questioning witnesses. It was an amazing sight to watch. Since my only exposure to the legal system had been seeing police in encounters with black men in Merced, it was an empowering experience to watch skilled lawyers peel away the falsehoods and half-truths in the state's case against Davis. They convinced me that she was innocent, but the twelve people on the jury gave no clues as to how they were evaluating the case.

Aware that a verdict was going to be delivered on June 5, 1972, I and other Davis supporters organized a major demonstration. It was feared that the jury would convict this innocent woman, and we decided not to sit by and let this happen. I was so drawn into this case that I was prepared, after only one year of college, to drop out of school to fight for individuals like Angela Davis who found themselves involved in a corrupt criminal justice system. As we waited, I thought about what I had said in my hometown newspaper, and how my life would change when this verdict was issued. The jury came back, and to my utter surprise, found Angela Davis innocent of all charges. The massive demonstration that was planned had to be changed to a celebration. We were not ready for an acquittal. At that moment, I understood what a difference good lawyers could make in the lives of clients who are facing the loss of life or liberty in the legal system. I felt fortunate to be at Stanford during this historic case, and to have it influence my career path.

Most black students were proud to be at Stanford and to have been afforded the chance to compete with the best and brightest students. However, some members of the black community thought that "special efforts" to recruit and admit black students created a stigma, and that we should not support any effort, no matter how well intentioned, that created such risks. Those of us who were there as first-generation admitted students were not nearly as troubled. Our goal was to get in the door, excel academically, and prove our worth. We could not do that outside of institutions like Stanford, and we had enough self-confidence not to be deterred by what others said or thought.

We did not anticipate, however, that our access to such institutions did not engender real acceptance. Nearly twenty years after *Brown* and six years after the assassination of Martin Luther King, Jr., we found ourselves confronting the same demons that we thought Marshall's success in *Brown* and King's death had eliminated. We were prepared to be involved in many things at Stanford but were surprised when the next battleground was responding to a tenured professor who questioned the intelligence of blacks and our competence to be there.

William Shockley, whose name is no longer familiar to my children's generation, was born in 1910 in London, where his American parents were working at the time. Raised near the Stanford campus, Shockley then was educated at Caltech and MIT, where he received a Ph.D. in physics. While subsequently working for Bell Labs in New Jersey, he and his colleagues applied quantum theory to the development of semiconductors. This work led to the development of the transistor, for which Shockley won the 1956 Nobel Prize in physics. In 1963, he was appointed a professor of engineering at Stanford.

At Stanford, Shockley became interested in the field of genetics, though he had no genetics training, and began to take positions on race, genetics, and intelligence. Since I knew that Shockley was not a geneticist and that his statements linking racial intelligence to genetics were not credible, my thought was to ignore him. Interestingly, Shockley's ideas were rather summarily dismissed by Stanford scientists with some knowledge of genetics, but, undaunted, he presented his views at forums around the country. His views were so racist and shocking that we could not ignore them. He argued that the future of the American population was threatened because African-Americans had lower IQs and were producing low-IQ children faster than Americans with higher IQs.

His arguments were not new, for the same eugenics arguments about a master white race had already been aired by Adolf Hitler in the 1930s. Shockley gave an interview to *U.S. News and World Report* in 1963, claiming that blacks as a group scored 15 points lower on the IQ test and that this "deficiency" was hereditary. He went even further, though, by making a public spectacle of donating his sperm to a sperm bank for high-IQ whites, to preserve their presence and numbers in a future society. In the fall of 1972, after discussing Shockley's antics with some black faculty on campus, two black psychology professors challenged Shockley to a public debate of these theories.

On November 9, 1972, as the chairman of the Stanford BSU, I issued a public challenge to Shockley, to debate his genetics theories with the psychology professor Cedric Clark and the genetics professor L.L. Cavali-Sforza, both of Stanford. The debate was scheduled for January 23, 1973. At the same time that Professor Clark was preparing for the debate with Shockley, he also joined the Nation of Islam. As the debate approached, student, faculty, and public interest reached a fevered pitch. The debate was planned for Memorial Auditorium, which held nearly two thousand people.

Professor Clark, now known as Professor Cedric X, had a surprise for us. The panel was not balanced, he said, and he would not debate unless his colleague Professor Philip McGee, another African-American faculty member, was added to the debate. Philip Zimbardo, the moderator and the Psychology Department chair, objected to this arrangement, but Professor X and I told him that either McGee was allowed to participate or the debate would be canceled. With the electricity in the room, and the audience becoming more impatient in anticipating the debate, Zimbardo allowed McGee to participate. To no one's surprise, Memorial Auditorium was filled beyond capacity, with people in the aisles, the balcony, and jamming all the doors. If there had been an emergency that night, it would have been disastrous. The Stanford Fire Department knew that, but chose not to create any animosity among the Fruit of Islam, the young men who provided security for the Nation of Islam, or the black students.

That night, rather than make a serious case for his views, Shockley instead attacked those African-American students who were at Stanford. Not satisfied simply to restate his views, he went on to declare that the IQ of the average African-American increases one percent for every one percent of Caucasian ancestry. He suggested that Americans could learn from Nazi experiments with eugenics.[2] This was actually not surprising, since he had already proposed to sterilize persons who did not meet a minimum intelligence standard. Although he was booed after making these points, Shockley had, perhaps unwittingly, accomplished his goal. His debate points were weak, but they probably reinforced the views of those who believed blacks to be inferior to whites. Shockley lost the public debate, but we, the *Brown* babies, had to contend with the powerful impression even racist ideas can have on vulnerable minds.

Ultimately, our public strategy was successful. Although Shockley maintained his views until his death many years later, in 1989, he officially retired from teaching the year we graduated and never generated any serious following in the academic community in general or in the genetics field in particular.

Although the Shockley experience was a blatant challenge to our existence as eighteen-year-olds at Stanford, there were other challenges to our acceptance as full and equal members of the Stanford community that took more subtle, but no less disappointing, forms. During our senior year, we obtained a copy of a memo written by James Gibbs, an anthropologist and, as the Dean of Undergraduate Studies, the highest ranking African-American at Stanford. Gibbs's memo created a storm of controversy in that, among other things, he suggested that Stanford should alter the financial aid program for minority students, and seek to admit a different, and "better," mix of minority students, noting that those of us there spent too much time "trying to turn the institution around."

At the end of our four years at Stanford, we prepared for the moment we had all been waiting for. For many of us who were first-generation African-American graduates, this graduation meant everything to us and our extended families, who would be coming from all over the country to celebrate our moment. My three African-American roommates—James Rice, Calvin Dorsey, and Eric Phillips—all graduated in 1975, and each of us went on to graduate or professional school. Since we had no experience with college commencements, we sat around arguing whether we should tape special messages on our caps and gowns. We could not have been more excited about our graduation. We imagined that nothing could dampen our spirits on this special day. We had made it through, some of us graduating with honors, many going on to law, business, or medical school, while still others received coveted fellowships or found jobs in areas of their particular interest. The *Brown* babies were now young adults, about to take on the world.

A few weeks before the ceremony, the president of the university announced the commencement speaker. The graduates usually pay little attention to news of who the speaker will be, since the focus is on hearing your name called and seeing your family share in your accomplishment. I was also nearing the end of my year as one of the four student body copresidents.

The President's Office announced that our commencement speaker would be the former Harvard University political scientist, and pending nominee of President Nixon to be the U.S. ambassador to the United Nations, Professor Daniel Patrick Moynihan. We *Brown* babies were not at all pleased that Moynihan would be our commencement speaker, and we thought our concern was well founded. What I knew of Moynihan's work, I did not like. I was familiar with his highly acclaimed and controversial 1963 book, *Beyond the Melting Pot: The Negroes, Puerto Ricans, Jews, Italians, and Irish of New York City*, and with the 1965 Moynihan Report, entitled *The Negro Family: The Case for National Action.*[3]

Beyond the Melting Pot was explicit and, to many of us, deeply troubling. Early in the discussion of "the Negroes," Moynihan and his coauthor, Nathan Glazer, asserted, "The Negro immigrant [from the South] has not had the good fortune of arriving with useful skills and strong institutions, nor has he found a prosperous, well-organized Negro community to help him."[4] They also argued that African-Americans "did not develop the same kind of clannishness, they did not have the same kind of close family ties, that in other groups created little pools for ethnic businessmen and professionals to tap." The exception to this pattern was "the Negro church," and the authors found it unsurprising that "churchlike groupings" such as those of Father Divine, Daddy Grace, and the Nation of Islam established successful business enterprises.

In their discussion of education, the authors noted that the African-American community placed a strong emphasis on education and achievement, yet the school systems produced few top students. Moynihan was also skeptical that segregation had influenced the quality of education in the North, "where it is simply the expression of the existence of the Negro ghetto," as compared with the South, "where segregation is the formal and legal embodiment of society's effort to keep the Negro in a less than human position."[5]

The conclusions of Moynihan and Glazer did not sit well with many black students at Stanford because we were the products of the very family structure that they described as a formula for failure. These things, the authors wrote,

> do not necessarily mean poor upbringing and emotional problems. But they mean it more often when the mother is forced to work (as the Negro mother so often is), when the father is incapable of contributing to support (as the Negro father so often is), when fathers and mothers refuse to

accept responsibility for and resent their children, as Negro parents, over-whelmed by difficulties, so often do, and when the family situation, instead of being clear-cut and with defined roles and responsibilities, is left vague and ambiguous (as it often is in Negro families).[6]

In an analysis that relies heavily on the work of the sociologist E. Franklin Frazier,[7] the authors also attributed the weakness of the Negro family to the history of racism. Slaves who had no power over their chil-dren were less apt to take responsibility for them, and educating them was virtually impossible much of the time. "What slavery began, preju-dice and discrimination, affecting jobs, housing, self-respect, have con-tinued to keep alive among many, many colored Americans."[8]

In our view, Moynihan's work on the black family reinforced stereotypes about African-American mothers, welfare recipients, gender roles, and other matters. We felt that these stereotypes contributed to the negative view of blacks already held by too many Americans.

Moynihan's selection struck many of the black graduates as a slap in the face. Many of us were products of single-parent families. Our mothers, in our view, had done a great job in helping us through the challenges of life, and we were the examples of success that comes through perseverance. We immediately condemned the selection of Moynihan as our commencement speaker and demanded that the pres-ident rescind the invitation; he refused. We issued press releases with excerpts from Moynihan's writings and started organizing protests. We then faced a difficult decision. Do we attend our graduation since it means so much to our families and us? Or do we boycott out of respect for our families and as a tribute to them? We met for hours and engaged in heated debates over our options. There were strong views supporting a boycott and equally strong views supporting our attendance. What-ever action we took, we would represent the largest class of black grad-uates in Stanford history. It was not an easy decision.

After many hours of meeting, crying, and praying, we agreed on a course of action. First, we would call our parents before they arrived for commencement, tell them that Moynihan was our commencement speaker, and explain why we objected to him. Then we would ask our parents and families to come to Stanford a day early because we were organizing our own black graduation before the Stanford event and wanted them to attend. We told them that it was a tribute to them and that our keynote speaker would be Dr. St. Clair Drake, the esteemed director of Stanford's Afro-American Studies Department, a professor with a joint appointment in sociology and anthropology, and a fervent Pan-Africanist and author of *Black Metropolis*, a groundbreaking work when first published in 1945 and still a landmark study of race and urban life. Finally, we would tell our parents that the day following our black graduation, we would attend the Stanford commencement, peacefully distributing leaflets explaining our protest to the parents, students, and alumni attending, march into the ceremony with our classmates, and, as Moynihan got up to speak, quietly stand up and walk out. After Moynihan finished his speech, we would return, take our seats, and get our degrees.

That first black graduation was very emotional. Our meeting room was filled with parents and grandparents, aunts and uncles, cousins and siblings, and friends who had supported us throughout our lives. My mother and uncle, my younger brother Richard, my baby sister, Rose, and Evelyn Inman, a family friend from Merced, all came to my graduation. I was disappointed that my father, who had promised to attend, did not join them. Our families shared in our joy, aware that their lifelong sacrifices had paid off with their children's graduation from Stanford. We were surprised, too, as they stood up, one by one, and told us how proud they were of our standing up for them.

Dr. Drake made the special evening even more memorable by giving us credit for being courageous and defiant at a time when it would have been easier, and understandable, simply to accept the choice of Moynihan, get our degrees, and get on with life. I was given the task of reading the protest letter we would be distributing the next day. When I finished reading it, the parents all stood up and applauded us again.

Significantly, the "Black Graduation" we started in 1975 is now a tradition at Stanford. Every year, black students have a special ceremony with their parents and families, and each graduate has a kente cloth placed around his or her shoulders by a parent, grandparent, or, in some cases, the graduate's child. Hundreds attend the ceremony. In fact, the Latino, Native American, and Asian-American students hold similar celebratory ceremonies with their families. Few of these current graduates are aware that our protest ceremony marked the genesis of these annual ethnic celebrations.

On commencement day we arrived early to distribute fliers of our protest to all of the graduates, alumni, family, and friends. We marched in with our classmates and took our seats as expected. As Moynihan was introduced and approached the podium, we stood up and began to walk out quietly. We expected our classmates and their friends to boo or, at least, hiss as we walked out. They did not. To his credit, Moynihan delayed giving his remarks until we had left the amphitheater. In light of our strongly worded protest, we were a bit surprised that he did not turn the crowd against us. And most surprisingly, we were joined by dozens of Chicano graduates and their families and quite a few white students who sympathized with our protest. In particular, I remember seeing Rick Kelly, a Stanford basketball star and later a successful professional basketball player, join us in the walkout. At seven feet one inch, he was hard to miss.

The most poignant moment came when an elderly black woman, clearly in her seventies, called me and said, "Son, come help me up, I'm going with you." The woman was Mrs. Ruby Edwards, the grandmother of Belinda Edwards, one of our black classmates from Atlanta, and a devout follower of Atlanta's native Martin Luther King, Jr. She told me that she had marched with Dr. King for good causes and that there was no reason to stop marching now. As I helped her up the steps of the amphitheater that morning, I began to understand what Thurgood Marshall, Martin Luther King, Jr., and so many others had accomplished. Mrs. Edwards was the embodiment of those who sacrificed so much of their own lives, hopes, and dreams for us to attend schools like Stanford. As I walked out, feeling a rush of adrenaline, she was calm and dignified. I revealed my youthful nervousness by wanting this moment to end right away, and to get back to the commencement ceremony. Her mood was different. She had marched before and knew that she was not to let anybody turn her around. She was fully aware that the slower your pace, the less evidence of fear. She wanted those watching us leave to understand that she was someone who had done this before, without fear. Mrs. Edwards was also letting the world know that she didn't march to end segregation in the South only to see her granddaughter, and her peers, disrespected on what should be the happiest day of their young lives.

As I reflect back on the Stanford experience, I think the Shockley and Moynihan events were our calls to service as the next generation of leaders. Furthermore, I think both Martin Luther King, Jr., and Thurgood Marshall would have been proud of us that day and believed that their sacrifices were not in vain.

CHAPTER 4

BROWN'S FAILURE: RESISTANCE IN BOSTON

When I arrived in Boston in August 1975, eager to obtain the legal training that Harvard Law School promised, the resistance to integration had reached a fever pitch. Just fourteen months earlier, Judge Wendell Arthur Garrity, Jr., had issued his controversial busing order.[1] My wife and I drove into the Boston area for the first time at dusk and prayed that we would find 17 Hunting Street in east Cambridge before nightfall.

The 3,000-mile drive across the country from Compton, California, where we had been married one week earlier, had been filled with a series of mishaps and misadventures. Not the least of these were a regrettable stop in Las Vegas, where I lost money I could ill afford to lose playing poker, and a stop in Oklahoma City, where I foolishly argued with an auto mechanic, demanding that he remove the new shocks he had installed on our car at a price twice what I had agreed to pay. My wife and I drove the next 300 miles expecting that the engine might at any moment drop from the car or that a truckload of angry, vengeful friends of the mechanic might pursue us.

On the sixth evening of our drive, we reached Memphis, Tennessee, exhausted and barely speaking to each other because my wife had urged me to stop much earlier, but being the stubborn man that I am, I insisted on driving until after midnight. It seemed everyone else on the highway had the good sense to check into a motel earlier in the evening or make reservations in advance, for we searched in vain for a vacancy at an affordable chain motel. After being disappointed at five or six places, we were ready to give up and sleep in the car when we saw a beckoning "Vacancy" sign. The motel looked neglected and in utter disrepair, what would commonly be called a flea bag. Our small room was shabbier than the exterior. The full-size bed was covered with dingy, worn linen. The pattern and color of the carpet was unrecognizable, matted with years of soil and stain. We considered whether it might be better to sleep in the car, but fatigue made us stay. We slept fully clothed and with the lights on to protect ourselves from fleas, bedbugs, and other non-paying guests. We learned later that we had spent a night in the infamous rooming house from which James Earl Ray fired the fatal shot in the assassination of Martin Luther King, Jr.

No part of the drive across country caused more apprehension than our final few miles. I had enlisted the help of a Stanford classmate, Larry Terry, who was attending Harvard Medical School, to find us a suitable apartment in Cambridge. He acted as our intermediary in arranging the rental of an apartment in east Cambridge and also gave us frequent updates about the racial climate in Boston, sending us news clippings and telling us about the latest racial incident. When we entered the Boston area, I held the steering wheel tightly with both hands and leaned forward, intently reading street signs. My wife sat next to me, rigid with tension, her hand gripping the door handle. Our worst fear was that we would accidentally end up in South Boston instead of Cambridge. Fear has a way of driving you to do exactly that which you fear doing. So it was with us.

We found ourselves in an area of debris-strewn streets and police barricades. We stopped to call our landlord, and, on hearing his voice, breathed a little easier, thinking we were just a few blocks away from our new home. When I described where we were, he quietly told me to get in the car, turn around, and look for the freeway marked I-93 North. He also insisted that we not get out of the car, unless we saw a police officer who could help us with directions. I did not understand why he had turned from cheerful and friendly to stern.

We soon saw a police officer and told him we needed directions to Cambridge. Without saying so, he seemed to know that we were not from Boston. Maybe it was the West Coast accent. Or maybe the California license tags and the U-Haul trailer gave us away. Maybe it was two black people driving through that neighborhood after midnight. We were out of place. He gave us directions to I-93 and mentioned the

Monsignor O'Brien Highway in Cambridge. We followed his directions and, on reaching O'Brien Highway, stopped and called the landlord a second time. He was pleasant again and told us we were five minutes away. I began to wonder whether Larry Terry had found us a landlord with a Jekyll and Hyde personality.

When we arrived, our landlord came out to greet us and seemed relieved to see us. I did not ask about his behavior earlier, but he volunteered to explain. "Do you know where you were when you called me? That was South Boston, where they are having all those problems with busing." This unceremonious arrival, as it would turn out, was the beginning of a relationship with South Boston that I could not have imagined.

BOSTON'S DESEGREGATION BATTLE IN THE 1970S occurred in the framework set by a series of Supreme Court decisions, handed down more than fifteen years after *Brown*, that established some constitutional parameters for desegregation. In *Green v. County School Board*, the Court imposed an affirmative duty on southern school boards that had previously operated racially segregated school systems to "take whatever steps might be necessary to convert to a unitary system in which racial discrimination would be eliminated root and branch."[2] To assist trial court judges in crafting desegregation plans, the Court listed six factors or benchmarks to be measured and balanced: facilities, staff, faculty, extracurricular activities, transportation, and student assignments.[3] A few years later, in *Swann v. Charlotte-Mecklenburg Board of Education*, a unanimous Court authorized trial courts to use a variety of remedial tools to oversee and implement desegregation plans, chief among which was crosstown busing.[4] These decisions clarified the scope of the school board's duty in desegregation conflicts, established the boundaries of federal judicial authority, and more clearly articulated the constitutional imperative behind the desegregation agenda.

To some extent, the mandates worked. Focused judicial and executive enforcement of desegregation orders in the South in the late 1960s and 1970s "resulted in the South becoming the most integrated region of the country by 1988, with 43.5% of black students in majority white schools by that year."[5] Desegregation was particularly successful and long-lasting in metropolitan districts or areas in which the affected geographic region covered most of the local housing market.[6]

But the desegregation in many places was neither easy nor clearly successful. Boston, a city of racial contrasts from the beginning, was one such place. It had seen a remarkable number of black firsts. Crispus Attucks, a black man, was the first American killed in the struggle for freedom that eventually became the Revolutionary War. The city was a hotbed of abolitionism before, during, and after the Civil War. Massachusetts and Ohio proved the most indefatigable abolitionist states, and few cities matched the resolve of Boston on this score. Harvard graduated its first black Ph.D., W. E. B. Du Bois, in 1895, and Charles Hamilton Houston, the first African-American on the *Harvard Law Review*, in 1923. More recently, the Boston Celtics, the town's second secular religion (after the Red Sox), had in Bill Russell the first African-American coach in the NBA and then the first all-black starting five. Yet Russell found the racial tensions in Boston so severe that when he left, he vowed never to return.

The long struggle to gain equality in Boston public school education reflected racial contrasts as well. Boston was home to one of America's first segregated schools. Contributions from black and white people alike, combined with a pittance from the thrifty school committee, made possible the establishment of a separate primary school for black children in the early nineteenth century. Not long thereafter, white abolitionists and Boston's small black community tried to eliminate the segregated schools in the late 1840s; they argued that the "African" grammar schools were "unhealthy and inadequate."[7]

In 1849, reformers brought a suit to the Massachusetts Supreme Court on behalf of a black youth named Sarah Roberts, who was forced to walk a mile every day in order to attend a segregated school. That court decided against integration, but five years later the state legislature ordered Boston schools to desegregate.[8] This state law, like the desegregation laws that followed it, led the country in equality of laws for blacks, but was disregarded by the majority white immigrant community in Boston and subsequently abandoned. Shortly after the Civil War, black children were again placed in separate schools, and for the next century Boston's black population remained comparatively small, residentially segregated, and politically disadvantaged.

Between 1940 and 1970, Boston experienced an increase in the black population of 342 percent. Simultaneously, it experienced white flight as middle-class whites left for the suburbs, allowing the percentage of blacks in the city to rise from 3 percent to 16 percent by 1970.[9] The majority of blacks who entered Boston were those fleeing from the overtly racist South and finding homes in Boston's North Dorchester, South End, and Roxbury. The migration of the poorer newcomers to the growing black middle class in Boston created more disparity in the separate black schools.

Boston's school desegregation movement in the early 1960s sprang from the admixture of national events, internal strains in the black community between middle-class blacks and those migrating from the South, improved economic conditions for native black Bostonians, and the condition of black schools.[10] The Boston NAACP, led by Thomas Atkins and supported by the emerging black middle class, took action, following the mandate of Charles Hamilton Houston and Thurgood Marshall.

Even with *Brown* as the law, desegregating the school system in Boston was arduous and often involved violence. The NAACP was fighting an uphill battle just to get the city to recognize its de facto segregation. In its 1961 report, the Massachusetts Commission against Discrimination (MCAD) stated that race was not a "determining factor" in the quality of the schools or in the assigning of students. Two years later, the NAACP brought its case directly to the Boston School Committee, which refused to admit that the schools were segregated.[11] The committee asserted, "We have no inferior education in our schools. [The problem is] we have been getting . . . an inferior type of student,"[12] suggesting that the problem was migrating blacks trying to escape from the South. The NAACP, with the help of a team of Harvard University consultants, however, had the data to prove otherwise.

The data showed that of the thirty-five schools enrolling 60 percent or more black students, twenty-seven were built before 1914. Several predominantly black schools were "simply hazardous to the health of their occupants." The Bates School in Boston's South End, for example, had wooden stairs, a very small playground, and an exterior "charitably described as deteriorating." Inside the school, the "window sashes and frames [were] rotting; the classrooms [were] drab and in need of paint and the toilet facilities require[d] a great deal of renovation."[13]

The Harvard Divinity School chimed in with a report of its own, showing that the school department expenditures were 10 percent lower for textbooks in black schools, 19 percent lower for library books, and 27 percent lower for health care per pupil. Boston's in-class expenditures averaged $275 per student, but in black schools they averaged only $213 per student.[14]

Employing the strategies used in the Deep South, such as school boycotts and demonstrations, the NAACP had initial, but short-lived, success in the Massachusetts legislature. The Democratic Party leaders teamed up with liberal suburbanites to pass the Racial Imbalance Act of 1965, which concluded that "racial imbalance was educationally harmful and should be eliminated."[15] The Massachusetts act barred the Commonwealth from supporting school systems whose nonwhite enrollment exceeded 50 percent and mandated that the school districts of Boston, Springfield, and Cambridge create a racial balance.[16] By so doing, they would receive a variety of incentives, including up to 90 percent reimbursement of school construction costs.

The Boston School Committee's response to the act was to refuse to acknowledge that racial imbalance was a problem that should be eliminated, as well as to challenge the constitutionality of the act in court. Only one legislator in Boston, the city with the most representatives, voted for the act, which had no significant impact on the composition of Boston's public schools.[17] The school committee was able to delay the implementation of the Racial Imbalance Act for nine years.[18]

The NAACP did not give up the fight. The parents and children continued to boycott and petition the school committee and the state government for equality in public schools. One black mother in Roxbury noted about Boston, "I used to feel that things like boycotts and demonstrations belonged in Birmingham and Mississippi. Now I know that . . . this is the Boston problem as well, here in the deep North."[19]

On March 15, 1972, after years of fighting, a class action suit was filed on behalf of fifteen black parents and forty-three black children. The lead plaintiff was Tallulah Morgan, a twenty-four-year-old mother of three; the named defendants included the Boston School Committee, chaired by James Kerrigan. Morgan brought suit claiming that Boston had intentionally developed and maintained a racially segregated public school system, citing racial discrimination with respect to the allocation of instructional materials and resources, and maintained a pattern of lower instructional expenditures in schools attended by black children. Morgan also accused the city of manipulating district lines to reflect segregated neighborhoods and failing to implement policies reasonably available to eliminate racial segregation.[20]

Judge Garrity found that 80 percent of Boston's schools were segregated; 84 percent of Boston's white students attended schools that were more than 80 percent white, and 62 percent of black students attended schools that were more than 70 percent black. The teachers in the Boston school system were segregated as well. Some 75 percent of black teachers were in schools that were more than 50 percent black, while eighty-one schools had never seen a black teacher in their entire history.[21] Uncertified schoolteachers abounded in black schools, while white schools had less than one uncertified teacher per school.

Because of the overwhelming data in favor of the plaintiffs and the judicial precedents of *Brown* and *Keyes* on June 21, 1974, Judge Garrity handed down a 152-page opinion in favor of the black children and parents. He held that the Boston school system had knowingly carried out a systematic program of segregation affecting students, teachers, and school facilities, and had intentionally brought about and maintained an unconstitutional dual school system.[22]

This lawsuit, *Morgan v. Kerrigan*, was to result in a citywide busing program that lasted twenty-five years. While many have argued that the busing plan has fostered racial understanding, the immediate impact was to split poor, urban Bostonians along racial lines and to foster divisions even within the African-American community, reviving the debate over the merits of equalization of services compared with integration, of adequate school facilities compared with a massive program of busing.

The central figure in any education desegregation litigation strategy was the district court judge to whom the case was assigned. The NAACP depended to an extraordinary extent upon the judiciary's continued identification with its aims. It needed the Supreme Court to continue to ratify the "integrate at all costs" policy, the intermediate court of appeals to keep the pressure on sometimes recalcitrant district courts, and the district courts—which are located within the community and serve, in many ways, as the community's conscience—to approve the desegregation proposals by making extensive findings of fact favorable to the plaintiffs. A district court judge, whose major power is to settle the record and to frame the issues for purposes of appeal (as well as entering the orders enforcing desegregation), is thus the primary point of contact between plaintiffs, defendants, lawyers, the community, and the law itself. In Judge Wendell Arthur Garrity, Jr., the NAACP found a powerful, courageous, and fiercely independent jurist.

W. Arthur Garrity, Jr., as Judge Garrity was officially known, was born in 1920 in the western Massachusetts city of Worcester. In the mid-nineteenth century, his great-grandfather emigrated from Ireland to Charlestown; later, the Garritys moved to Worcester. His father, Wendell Sr., named after the well-known nineteenth-century Boston-bred abolitionist and reformer Wendell Phillips, became a prominent local lawyer and was a member of the NAACP in the 1940s and 1950s. Garrity Jr.'s upbringing was comfortably upper class and quite remote from the tougher, "more abrasive" existence of his Boston relatives.[23]

Like his father, brothers, uncles, cousins, and one of his sons, Garrity attended Holy Cross College, where he graduated cum laude in 1941. He enrolled in Harvard Law School, but left during his second year to become a sergeant for the Signal Corps. He served on a command ship in the Normandy invasion and won five battle stars during his service in France and Germany. At the end of the war, he returned to Harvard and received his law degree in 1946. In 1952, he married his local sweetheart, Barbara Ann Mullins, and bought a home in Wellesley.[24]

For the first fifteen years of his legal career, Garrity engaged in private law practice, held a few minor public office positions, and was active in various political efforts for the Democratic Party. The latter endeavor resulted in his meeting John F. Kennedy at a fund-raiser. Garrity was sufficiently impressed by the young, wealthy local son to commit his efforts and hitch his fortunes to Kennedy's political ambitions. In 1958, Garrity, along with the future Kennedy cronies Kenneth P. O'Donnell and Lawrence F. O'Brien, organized scheduling for Kennedy's U.S. Senate race. Two years later, during JFK's presidential campaign, Garrity ran the Milwaukee campaign headquarters in the critical Wisconsin primary and teamed up with Robert F. Kennedy to organize a

Democratic voter registration drive. In return for his service, Kennedy named Garrity the U.S. attorney for Boston in April 1961.[25] Consistent with local patronage practices at the time, Garrity in return named the president's cousin Joseph F. Gargan as his first assistant.

Subsequently, Senator Ted Kennedy recommended Garrity as a federal judge, and he was accordingly nominated by President Johnson to preside over the district court in Boston in 1966. Garrity developed a reputation for being a painstaking and thorough judge, obsessed—almost to a fault—with fairness and orderly procedure in his courtroom. As both a prosecutor and a judge, he was reputed to rarely allow emotion to disproportionately shift the balance in his precise and legalistic method of issue analysis. He was active in the socially conscious Boston Bar Association and reflected in his rulings the common judicial approach of the 1960s and 1970s of judicial activism and liberal social philosophy. In his highly disciplined personal habits he was described by colleagues as "puritanical," particularly in his sticking to rigid schedules and moderation in living. He became known for meting out stiff penalties in criminal cases.[26] Finally, Garrity was known for his gentleness and sensitivity, described by the *Boston Herald American* as "the most gentlemanly of men, quiet and informally courtly, exceedingly polite."[27]

In the 1960s and 1970s, the district court appeared to be the best forum in which to undertake social change. Judges, many of them Democratic appointees, were receptive to the civil rights program. More important, district court judges were experimenting with new types of relief that required them to take a more active part in the conduct of the litigation. The use of injunctions and "injunctive relief" permitted the court to create or approve remedial plans directing a variety of institutions—prisons, legislatures, and school districts, among them—to alter the manner in which they were run, and allowed the judge to undertake a more active scrutiny of the resulting programs. Whereas state legislatures, municipalities, and school boards had declined to enforce the provisions of the Constitution, or even state statutes such as the Massachusetts Racial Imbalance Act, judges were willing to override even staunch and well-organized local opposition to enforce integration.

The NAACP-sponsored plan for the Boston public school system attempted to achieve a racial balance in each school that roughly corresponded to the population of whites, blacks, and others in the community.[28] To achieve this goal, the Boston litigation mandated the busing of about twenty thousand children. In fact, the court ordered the city, in Garrity's 152-page opinion, to transform the school system from a racially discriminatory, "dual" system into a unitary one and, in the process, to consider a variety of methods for so doing, including "busing, the pairing of schools, redistricting with both contiguous and non-contiguous boundary lines, involuntary student and faculty assignments, and all other means, some of which may be distasteful to both school officials and teachers and parents . . . . [I]f necessary to achieve a unitary school system, they must be implemented."[29] The court-ordered solution involved transporting not only large numbers of African-American students to white schools but also large numbers of white students to black schools. The latter were sometimes in a serious state of disrepair.

Garrity faced staunch opposition on the part of the people of South Boston. Enraged by his rulings, they appealed them all the way up to the Supreme Court, but to no avail. Taking matters into their own hands and blatantly disregarding Garrity's judicial orders, the people of South Boston, led by Louise Day Hicks, began a fight reminiscent of that put up by white southerners in Little Rock, Arkansas, some seventeen years earlier.[30]

Hicks, described as a "pudgy South Boston mother of two," rose to prominence entirely by opposing busing.[31] Her political career included stints on the Boston school committee, city council, and Congress. As the head of an antibusing group called Restore Our Alienated Rights (ROAR), she led twenty thousand white protesters on a march on Beacon Hill, to pressure Governor Francis Sargent to sign a bill limiting busing to students whose parents voluntarily chose it.[32] Although Judge Garrity quickly ruled the bill unconstitutional, Hicks's leadership in the antibusing movement was undeniable.

Hicks was particularly critical of Garrity, describing him as an affluent suburbanite who was severely out of touch with public sentiment. Her views were shared by other Bostonians, from public officials to affected parents, especially people living in South Boston, who routinely attacked Garrity as a privileged, suburban tyrant removed from the urban realities that shaped Boston's neighborhoods and public schools. Notwithstanding Garrity's Irish roots and faithful membership in the Clover Club, a social organization for Irish Bostonians, Jimmy Flaherty, the head of the South Boston Civic Association, was particularly virulent in his personal attacks on the judge, calling him "[t]hat black Irishman, no, he's no Irishman. That . . . that . . . protestant."[33]

Across the city, slogans appeared on walls, bridges, and roadways, such as "Bus Garrity," "Fuck Garrity," or "Kill Garrity."[34] Garrity was bombarded with menacing telephone calls and letters at his home and office. He was called "nigger lover," "Nazi," "child murderer," and "hoper"—Boston slang for a man who goes to bed Irish and hopes to wake up Yankee.[35] The larger question that arose out of this criticism of Garrity's ethnicity is, of course, whether he was expected to view judicial decisions in light of his "ethnicity." Indeed, one wonders whether Garrity saw himself as an "Irish judge"—such a categorical definition of him would undermine the notion of judicial independence. This level of attacks on judges' biases stemming from their ethnicity has a long history, and similar, though less personally antagonistic, claims were made against other judges in other contexts.

Many decried the fact that busing did not affect Boston's more affluent suburbs, where Garrity and many of the liberal supporters of his ruling lived. Some insinuated that Garrity would not have entered the busing order if he had been affected by his own order:[36] Clay Smothers, a Dallas talk show host and strong busing opponent, dared Garrity to "move to Roxbury," while meanwhile the chant "Bus Garrity" became popular among antibusing demonstrators.[37] Others expressed dissatisfaction with what they saw as meddling in city affairs by outsiders, removed from urban realities. Kathleen Sullivan, considered by many the most liberal member of the school committee, said,

> I don't want to have suburbanites and outsiders, the State Department of Education, Tom Atkins [a black leader], Charley Glenn [a white liberal minister who drew up a busing plan for state officials] and the League of Women Voters deciding our fate. In terms of the reality, I would rather have us in charge than some crowd who do not understand and love the city of Boston as we do.[38]

A motorcade of several hundred antibusing demonstrators—about 75 percent of whom were from South Boston—attempted to bring the controversy to Garrity's insulated suburban gates. To the disgust of his urban detractors, Garrity responded to this incident and multiple death threats by placing outside of his home two U.S. marshals on permanent guard.[39] Garrity, however, ignored the constant needling about his suburban address. Staying on point, he repeatedly insisted that he saw no other way to enforce the constitutional guarantee of desegregated education without busing.[40]

The criticisms of Judge Garrity as either a softhearted liberal or a hardheaded one were similar to the staunch resistance that other judges, usually white and male, experienced in the 1950s and the 1960s, in their push to make the principles of *Brown* applicable in the South. Although much has been written about the heroics of federal judges such as Judge William Wayne Justice in Tyler, Texas, Judge J. Skelly Wright in New Orleans, and Judge Frank Johnson in Alabama (including his role as the judge presiding over the Montgomery bus boycott of 1955) and about the reports of death threats each encountered, Garrity never received the national acclaim as a champion of equality that the others did. This may, upon reflection, be due in part to the general perception, and perhaps overstated assumption, that racism is a regional or southern problem, and to an unwillingness to believe that in the home of Harvard University, MIT, and Dr. King's alma mater, Boston University, the virulent racism of the 1970s could be anything more than an anomaly. Much as the generalization of southern racism may have been overstated, an equally plausible case can be made that the tolerance of racial bigotry among whites opposed to integration in the North was grossly understated. Garrity inherited a hornet's nest with the Boston busing cases, but he did not allow the resistance to impede his judgment that he had to enforce the Constitution, no matter how much opposition he generated.

Given his judicial activist philosophy and the extensive scope of his busing rulings, many referred to Garrity as a "dictator." A young white man who had called the judge a "dictator" was caught with a homemade bomb while on his way to Garrity's home.[41] Lorraine Faith, whose seventeen-year-old son, Michael, was stabbed by a black student in South Boston High School on December 11, 1974,[42] told a crowd of six thousand antibusing protesters assembled in the Boston Common that Garrity "seems to have more power than any dictator that ever crawled on the face of this earth." She continued, "My son was stabbed, and Judge Garrity's reaction was to heap more indignities on South Boston."[43] After the third week of the busing program, thousands of protesters marched through South Boston, reciting in unison a new antibusing version of the pledge of allegiance: "I will not pledge allegiance to the court order [of] the United States District Court, or to the dictatorship for which it stands, one law, incontestable, with liberty and justice for none."[44]

The busing of black students into South Boston and of white junior and senior high school students into Roxbury was perceived by many whites in South Boston as a distinct threat not only to their fragile place in the social order but also to their children's future.[45] The resulting racial tension manifested itself in many forms of protest, both violent and nonviolent.[46] This is not to say that the nonviolent protests were the more benign forms of dissension. In Charlestown, for example, hundreds of residents staged a "funeral procession" to mourn what they said would be the "city's death" if court-ordered busing continued.[47] These protests reflect the ease with which these residents were able to justify their racism by a desire to maintain their sense of home. Some attempted to justify these actions by pointing to traditionalist arguments, focusing on the Constitution and the purpose of education. Perhaps in an attempt to regain ownership of their concepts of what education ought to look like, many white parents took their children out of public schools and placed them in private institutions. In particular, most of the white junior class from a South Boston neighborhood boycotted the move to Roxbury. Some transferred to Roman Catholic or other private schools, while others decided to use their relatives' addresses to go to high schools in other neighborhoods. This white flight was an exercise in protest that impeded the success of integration and stripped away resources from schools that desperately needed them.[48]

Unfortunately, there was a pervasive belief that in order to get back to the "business of education," one must use violent and destructive means. After Judge Garrity's desegregation plan was revealed, the office of the local chapter of the NAACP was firebombed. The violent dissension on the part of whites, however, neither began nor ended with the firebombing. The violence occurred both inside and outside of the schools. White and black students routinely engaged in physical altercations, name-calling, and spray-painting of racist graffiti on many public buildings, and the persistent violence reached such a pressure point that the Boston police commissioner petitioned Judge Garrity to have one school remain closed until a plan of action could be formulated to handle the intraschool violence.[49] Garrity declined to grant this request. Meanwhile, the violence continued to escalate.

At South Boston High, for example, a black student stabbed a white student, leading what was described as a "mob" of at least fifteen hundred protesters to trap the black students inside the school building and prevent them from going home. The crowd ominously chanted, "Give us the niggers, give us the niggers, and send 'em back to Africa." It eventually attacked the police and their vehicles. Three white men were arrested for assaulting police officers outside of South Boston High.[50] Attacks on the police, black motorists, and black employees were prevalent after the schools opened. One mob awaiting buses carrying black students from Roxbury carried a dummy dressed in blue overalls bearing the sign "Nigger Beware."[51] Black students were bombarded with rocks, bottles, and other missiles on their way to and from South Boston. When the head of the Klu Klux Klan, David Duke, visited South Boston, he further ignited sentiments of white supremacy and black hate by saying, "[T]he federal government is taking money out of your pockets to finance the production of thousands of little black bastards." The next day, gunshots were fired through the front doors of a local black high school.[52]

A black resident of Boston, who was dragged out of his car and beaten by four white men, expressed his fear poignantly when he stated, "For twenty-one years I walked the streets of the city of Boston without fear. Now I'm afraid of this city. I'm almost afraid to go out of the house. I wake up in the middle of the night and I think about it. I have to sit on the edge of my bed, shaking, until I can fall back asleep."[53]

As fights continued throughout the city, the Pentagon alerted the Eighty-second Airborne Division, based at Fort Bragg, North Carolina, for possible deployment in Boston.[54] The national alert underscored the explosiveness of the tension and animosity between the citizens of Boston following Garrity's ruling.

BOSTON'S EXPERIENCE, while certainly not an aberration in terms of cities' experiences nationwide, was perhaps among the most extreme. Over the past thirty years, moreover, data do show that support for integrated action has grown.[55] The evidence about parents and students whose kids are in desegregated schools is consistently positive, even when busing is involved.[56] A number of school systems around the country are now in that odd position of being forced by courts to abandon desegregation plans that they want to continue.[57]

This was not so in 1970s Boston, where I happened to be attending law school right as the desegregation of public schools was facing its greatest resistance. Hard as I might try, it was impossible for me, as an African-American law student, pursuing my legal training within the shadow of the busing crisis, only a few miles away from Harvard, to ignore it. The explosive racial conflict in Boston and the intimidating aura of Harvard Law School combined to focus my attention on the complexity of applying rules of law to the everyday problems ordinary people experience in their lives. While I understood why the South Boston residents did not want a judge to force them to do something they found to be unconscionable, I also understood Judge Garrity's goal of trying to find measures, any measures, that would promote the goal of ending segregated education, something that *Brown* had mandated more than twenty years earlier. Garrity, in my view, was not initiating a legal order, as an activist judge, to further his personal views about busing. On the contrary, he was trying, as required by the Constitution, to respond to a serious legal challenge by black parents, who felt that their children were denied a basic right: quality education in public schools.

Boston's busing crisis would become part of the fabric of my experiences as a law student. When I arrived at Harvard in September 1975, the focus of most law students was not on busing in Boston but on finding ways to reduce the competitive pressures of being a law student. It seemed that the more we claimed to be trying to reduce competitive pressures, the more we exacerbated the situation. Just before I attended law school, the movie *The Paper Chase* (1973) had been released. Portraying Harvard Law School as inhospitable to all incoming students, it created terror in the minds of those thinking about law school, regardless of race, sex, or ethnicity. That the movie had little evidence of race only heightened the anxiety of the law school's black students. Like every law student, black or white, I resisted the idea of seeing a movie about the intimidating atmosphere at Harvard Law School; at the same time, though, my eagerness to learn more about Harvard led me to watch it at the first opportunity. I was struck by the relative absence of blacks in the movie, and in the Cambridge community, and even with a critical mass of blacks in my law school class, I still wondered whether my decision to attend Harvard was a mistake.

Unlike our white counterparts, most of the black students were first-generation college graduates and certainly the first to go to law school. A few of the black students had parents who had attended HBCUs, but none, to my knowledge, had parents who were Harvard Law School graduates. In the class the year before I arrived was Chris Edley, Jr., whose father, Chris Edley, Sr., president of the United Negro College Fund, was a Harvard Law School graduate. In the class two years behind mine was David Wilkins, whose father, Julian Wilkins, a prominent Chicago lawyer, had also attended Harvard Law School. The number of second-generation black graduates could be counted on one hand.

A number of our white peers came from prominent or wealthy families; generally, we did not. A number of them had lawyers in their extended families; we did not. Many of our white peers felt entitled to be at Harvard, and easily fit in; we felt neither entitled nor welcome. Moreover, our peers' assumption that we were "special admits" made the environment even less hospitable.

I wanted to live up to the high expectations of the *Brown* lawyers and Dr. King, who had forced the doors of places like Harvard open to us. I wanted to prove that I had the ability and the discipline to obtain the necessary legal skills to graduate and serve the interests of the community that sent me to Harvard. I wanted so badly to work hard and excel, to stay focused on my objectives. I tried diligently to do that the first few weeks, attending every class, reading every case, discussing and debating legal concepts with my peers. I strived to be a typical Harvard Law School student, whatever that meant.

It did not take me long to find levels of discomfort at Harvard. Some students arrived with study groups already in place. Others boasted, within four weeks of arriving, of having sent letters to firms for jobs in New York, the prize city for law students. Most obnoxious were those students who seemed to find something to say, every day in class, without being called upon. They annoyed me, since I did not warm to the idea of responding to theoretical questions. As it turned out, some of these obnoxious and arrogant individuals who dominated class discussions became my closest friends in law school, and afterward.

I wanted facts and clear answers to my straightforward questions. When I would express my concern about the fuzziness of the discussions in class, and wondered whether the professors could clear it up, their responses were remarkably the same: there are no clear answers, just more questions. Well, since this experience in asking questions with no answers was going to leave me with a 1970s debt approaching $20,000, this response, from reputedly smart people, was unacceptable. I wanted a refund. If you don't get your money's worth in buying a house, shopping for a car, or groceries, you are, as a matter of law, entitled to a refund. Here I was at Harvard Law School, and the legal geniuses were telling me that I did not have an actionable case. Not a good way to start a legal career.

While I tried to keep my focus on understanding such critically important legal concepts as the rule against perpetuities, fictitious interlopers, the importance of stare decisis, *quasi in rem* jurisdiction, and *qui tam* actions, I was drawn, with increasing forcefulness, to legal matters outside of Harvard Law School. When I took a break from reading the endless cases we were required to review each night, I would become distracted by the scenes of violence on the evening news, or, as I listened to morning radio for a weather update, I was puzzled to hear the angry, condemning voices on talk radio. When I wanted to see the sports scores to check up on my favorite teams, I confronted regular coverage in screaming headlines of local newspapers. Just across the river, a race war was in progress, and I could not sit in the relatively quiet obscurity of my law school classroom and ignore it.

It was, I would learn, a variation of the challenges to racial integration in the South that I had heard or read about and that I had experienced at Stanford, but it was also a unique experience in another way. This was the North, it was Boston, and the targets were children. This was twenty-one years after *Brown*, twelve years after Dr. King's historic March on Washington, and seven years after his assassination. I could not believe that what seemed imaginary when I heard of the resistance to integration in the South was a real daily occurrence just a few miles from where I was being trained to be a lawyer.

There was a great disparity between the examination of esoteric questions of law, in the sedate halls of Harvard Law School, and the seemingly routine exercise of racial violence in response to black children's being sent to public schools with white children. In 1975 in Boston, a bus carrying black children to school would be attacked by white mobs with rocks, paint, and other objects. Black children were chased out of a school building. Whites in South Boston marched to proclaim white pride. Public officials challenged the right of black children to attend schools in South Boston. A black lawyer whom I knew, Theodore Landsmark, who was dressed in a suit on his way to work in the mayor's office, was beaten with the sharp end of a flagpole, which waved an American flag, by angry whites in front of the state capitol. Landsmark suffered a broken nose and was left severely beaten and bloodied. Another talented African-American student, a potential college and professional athlete, was shot in the back, and paralyzed for life, by another group of white students from the same area that was generating resistance to busing.

During the same period, students would jog along the Charles River, which separated Cambridge from Boston, or enjoy a slice of pizza in the afternoon at Three Aces, a Greek pizzeria a block from Harvard Law School, and find themselves in intense debates about whether persons who choked on a fish bone at a seafood restaurant had a right to sue the owner or whether their own negligence in not spotting the bone prevented them from succeeding in a lawsuit. Similar arguments could be heard as law students stood in line in Harvard Square to watch a movie on Saturday night, or took the subway, locally known as the T, to Boston to do a little shopping, or attended the seemingly life-and-death football game between Harvard and Yale on a fall Saturday afternoon. For those Harvard law students who had attended either Harvard or Yale as undergraduates, and went to the annual final game of the season at Harvard's Soldier's Field, the only thing more important than who won was the endless debate in the bleachers about whether a harm you committed in Illinois could subject you to a court proceeding in

Massachusetts, or whether contracts of adhesion were nonetheless enforceable.

These were the all-important questions at Harvard Law School, not whether the *Brown* decision was under vigorous assault decades after it had been decided. I knew full well that, despite the growing anxiety I experienced by sitting on the sidelines in Cambridge, it would be necessary to concede that my classmates were focused on the right issues— learning to be not just lawyers but excellent lawyers. Yet, the reality of what was happening to children, through no fault of their own, just a few miles from Harvard, challenged me to rethink my priorities. I chose—rightly, I feel—to set aside for the moment the pressing legal questions of the day, and to join some of my African-American classmates in aiding black families in their struggle for equality. My interest became more personal on February 14, 1976, when our son, Charles J. Ogletree III, was born. We were blessed with a Valentine's Day baby during a time when the future of black children was hotly contested. My son's birth invigorated my resolve to fight for equal educational opportunities for blacks.

The first effort by black law students to lend help took the form of daily visits to the Boston NAACP office, on Massachusetts and Columbus Avenues. The black families were represented by Tom Atkins, a gifted lawyer with incredible vision and commitment. The cramped offices did not offer great working conditions. We also lacked a few basic supplies, like a working mimeograph machine, forms on which to fill out client information, and typewriters for taking down clients' complaints. The paint peeling from the walls and the occasional leaks during the rains were minor distractions, and part of the environment within which we worked at the NAACP office. The urban atmosphere also created an ambiance characteristic of Boston. All day long, you would hear the sounds of frustrated truck drivers, trying to get their products to market and finding tourists driving too slowly, or attempting to sightsee from their cars, afraid to walk through the streets, and keeping traffic at a snarl. Double-parking on the main thoroughfares was the rule, not an exception. You could smell the pretzels being hawked by peddlers along the streets, and feel the occasional rumble of the T as it passed through parts of Boston near Symphony Hall.

Across the river at Harvard, it was a different world. Our classrooms were soundproof, to ensure that all we heard each day was the arrogant bellowing of our professors, trying to make us understand the inherent complexity of studying law and reminding us that many are called, but few are chosen. There was an undeniable order to our existence at the law school. First, we learned to call it "The Law School," as if there were no others worth mentioning. Like the prisoners we represented in the law school clinics, we too had to follow rules with precision. We were assigned a number that was used for everything from class assignments to small-group gatherings and the designation of which section we were in. We were given assigned seats in classes always beginning and ending on time. Even as a heated debate erupted in class, on a Friday afternoon, with the diametrically conflicting choices before us, the professor would leave the question dangling in the air, where it would remain, even though we would not meet again until the following Wednesday.

Unlike grade school, where a bell would ring and send us from one class to another, Harvard Law School had no bells. You would look up, and like robots, when the professor closed his book, you would leave and head to the next class. We were assigned lockers on campus, so that as we strolled from a class on torts to one on contracts, we could drop off one set of books and materials and pick up another set.

As law students, we received other benefits not accorded to the public-interest lawyers trying to defend the children who were being attacked during the busing crisis. Harvard allowed us complete discretion in how we used our spare time (though, in reality, there was very little spare time). A number of students used it to get involved in clinical programs assisting clients in Boston who desperately needed free legal services. The assistance of an idealistic Harvard law student was readily accepted by the law offices, and clients welcomed us, even when their most generous comment was that our services were better than no services at all—perhaps a backhanded compliment. Through the clinical office, we not only volunteered our time but also occasionally took advantage of Harvard's generous supply of office materials to help the public-interest agencies, like the NAACP. Some of the items we could bring—pens, scissors, thumbtacks, paper, and notepads—were critically needed. If we wanted to copy something, we had an account. We also had multiple phone lines, forms for clients to fill out when interviewed, and a supervisor to look over our shoulders when we did our work. It seemed to me that the NAACP clients' needs were of great urgency, and we had the resources to provide some representation to those clients.

Despite the tight quarters and limited supplies, we worked in the second-story office helping students and their parents fill out forms raising claims of racial harassment. The targets were not only white families from South Boston but also police officers whom parents identified as being less than vigilant in protecting their children from verbal and physical assaults. We also researched legal remedies families could pursue against anyone who harmed them. Although we had only a few weeks of legal training when we started volunteering, the parents treated us like real lawyers and accorded us a level of respect and deference that we certainly did not deserve. Interestingly, while we were there to assist the victims of attacks associated with the busing crisis, we would also receive requests to help a son who was incarcerated on unrelated charges, or to give advice in dealing with a hostile landlord or even a rude conductor on the T. We always gave the parents thoughtful, legalistic, and probably wholly inaccurate advice.

When the community held marches or rallies, we were asked to serve as legal observers. Even though we really did not know what that meant at the time, we went along anyway because it sounded like an impressive title. We rarely asked questions about the value or utility of our efforts, since we saw ourselves as the beneficiaries of *Brown* and felt that we had a mandate to keep the educational-opportunity doors open for the next generation, in the same spirit that Charles Hamilton Houston and Thurgood Marshall had opened them for us. We would never have made it to Harvard, I believe, if communities like Roxbury, Dorchester, and Mattapan had not forced the Harvards, MITs, and Boston Universities to open their doors to us. We were simply paying our debt to the communities that had made our entry into the prestigious halls of academia possible.

As I reflect on these early efforts to promote the *Brown* mandate of integrated education, I'm struck by our failure ever to ask the hard and obvious questions about what we were doing. Why were black children being forced to go to white schools, without anyone's raising the question of more resources for black schools? Why did I fail to see the parallel with the 1960s policy by which black and brown children were bused across town to attend the predominantly white schools, but scarcely any white children came across the tracks to our schools? Did anyone ask whether the black parents were getting the best for their children by sending them into white schools and neighborhoods where the chance to study and learn, given the intense racial hostility, was marginal at best? What message were we sending to our children, having them leave their neighborhood schools and sending them to white, presumably better, schools? We didn't ask these questions then, to our regret, and perhaps to the harm of our children.

CHAPTER 5

BROWN'S CHALLENGE: CARRYING THE TORCH

When I left Harvard Law School in 1978 and moved to Washington, D.C., the judicial system was undergoing an enormous transformation, which would have a profound impact on *Brown*'s legacy and the legacy of Justice Marshall and Dr. Martin Luther King, Jr. The civil rights lawyers on the outstanding team assembled by Marshall in the 1950s had by 1978 moved on to new challenges, having been appointed to positions in the government or to the bench.

By 1968, Thurgood Marshall had become not only the first African-American solicitor general but also the first African-American justice of the Supreme Court. Two years earlier President Johnson had appointed Constance Baker Motley to the federal court in the Southern District of New York, the largest federal trial court in the United States. President Nixon appointed Robert Carter, who had argued one of the *Brown* cases, to the federal bench in the Southern District of New York in 1972. A presidential term later, President Jimmy Carter was in the White House and kept his promise to diversify the federal judiciary.

Professor Louis Pollak, a former dean and law professor, and a consultant on the *Brown* case and a member of the NAACP board of directors, was appointed to the federal court in Philadelphia, while the Columbia Law School professor Jack Weinstein was appointed to the federal court in New York. Spottswood Robinson, a Richmond Virginia civil rights lawyer who worked on the *Brown* cases, was appointed to the District of Columbia Court of Appeals in Washington, where he later served as chief judge. President Carter was still in office when Judge Motley assumed the position of chief judge of the Southern District Court. Other prominent *Brown* lawyers, such as William Coleman and Oliver Hill, continued to practice in their respective jurisdictions, rather than accepting possible judicial appointments. Jack Greenberg, who had worked with the NAACP since 1949, replaced Thurgood Marshall as director counsel until he left in 1979 to teach at his alma mater, Columbia Law School.

Ultimately, America's first true "dream team" left a huge void when its members were appointed judges. It was a refreshing change in the diversity of the federal court, but a devastating blow to the civil rights movement.

Carter's success in appointing the *Brown* lawyers and other African-Americans to the bench was short-lived, however, for he served only one term and was replaced in 1981 by Ronald Reagan, a fervent opponent of affirmative action. President Reagan's record on minority judicial appointments was inexcusably poor. In two terms, Reagan appointed fewer black federal judges than George Bush did in one term. More appallingly, President Carter appointed more black federal judges in his one term than Presidents Nixon, Ford, Reagan, and Bush in all their terms combined.[1]

While Reagan was successful in appointing conservatives to the Court, he could not stop the growing effort to immortalize Dr. Martin Luther King, Jr., who had emerged as the icon of the civil rights movement. When King was assassinated on April 4, 1968, many thought that progress in race relations was doomed. The immediate reaction, riots in many American cities, certainly created a sense of failure of the movement. At the same time, the wide respect that King had generated, among blacks and whites alike, created a grassroots campaign to memorialize his contributions to improved race relations in America. The biggest push was for the unthinkable—a national holiday in the name of an African-American, a distinction not available to other well-known and revered individuals. For example, George Washington now has to share Presidents' Day with other presidents. Many African-Americans did not want a civil rights holiday or a black history month holiday. The goal was to establish a King holiday, and nothing less was acceptable. A key figure in the effort to create a national holiday was the popular recording artist Stevie Wonder. He wrote a song entitled "Happy Birthday" dedicated to Dr. King, and it became the theme song for the movement. Every January in the early 1980s, many marched on the Capitol, often trudging through the snow, demonstrating for a national holiday in King's name. King was responsible for making Americans more conscious of issues of racial equality and tolerance. Moreover, the challenge was to persuade the entire nation to accept some responsibility for his death and, as a nation, make a commitment to a national holiday to preserve King's legacy.[2]

It did not occur to me at the time that the architect of the *Brown* decision, Justice Marshall, was perhaps not enamored of our efforts, and probably thought that they were unwise and inappropriate. Here we were again, giving King credit for everything good that happened to African-Americans in the twentieth century, but paying little tribute to the *Brown* lawyers, who successfully argued the case that created so many of the opportunities that we enjoyed. The irony was even more apparent in the early 1980s. While King's reputation only increased after his death, the beneficiaries of Marshall's brilliant strategy largely took him for granted. At the same time, some of Marshall's toughest days as a jurist came during the 1980s. Marshall slowly but unmistakably saw the Warren Court's "rights revolution" disappear, and the hard-fought gains that followed the *Brown* decision were being systematically dismantled before his eyes. He went from writing opinions in the majority to writing dissents from the new positions asserted by the conservative majority on the Rehnquist Court.

AFTER I GRADUATED FROM HARVARD LAW SCHOOL IN 1978, my focus shifted from the battle to preserve affirmative action to the battle to represent people, particularly black people, caught up in the criminal justice system. Although I was deeply concerned about the need to maintain the modest gains in affirmative action that flowed from the *Bakke* decision, my focus was on trying to aid those who rarely benefited from affirmative action.

From the time I was a teenager, I viewed disparities in the criminal justice system as the most pressing priority for an oppressed community. I was certain that the doors of opportunity would eventually open up to minorities after *Brown*, but concerned that contact between police and African-American citizens, usually on the street and away from judicial review or oversight, would remain unchanged without diligent intervention by someone. I had witnessed the way police treated African-Americans when I was a child, and it alarmed me. I observed the growing disparity, along racial lines, between those caught in the criminal justice system and those who meted out justice. My calling, as I saw it, was to get the proper training through the study of law and to serve as a buffer between the community and law enforcement. Being a public defender seemed the most direct and appropriate way to do it at the time. I wanted to return to the area of law that inspired me—criminal justice.

In the 1970s there was no better place to do that, in my view and that of many others, than the District of Columbia Public Defender Service (PDS). Formed in 1960, PDS maintained an excellent reputation in the District of Columbia criminal justice system, and was nationally recognized for its excellence in the delivery of enthusiastic legal representation to D.C.'s indigent population. Driven by a strong desire to ensure that the rights of poor people were not compromised because of their inability to afford legal services, PDS attorneys often worked evenings, weekends, and holidays in order to prepare for upcoming cases.[3] In addition to litigating cases in the local and federal courts, PDS devoted itself to ensuring the soundness of criminal justice policy decisions.[4] This office and its work seemed to match my interests and talents.

While in law school, I had spent time on criminal justice issues, working at the Harvard Prison Legal Assistance Project and handling criminal cases through the clinical program. It also helped that my faculty supervisor at Harvard, Gary Bellow, had worked at PDS for three years shortly after graduation from Harvard Law School and encouraged me to take the job. Gary, a terrific public defender, was credited with using his considerable talents to spark criminal justice reform. Before *Miranda v. Arizona* became law (in 1966), Gary had raised serious questions about police tactics to extract confessions from clients. He was consistently successful in persuading judges that when police exceed the limits of their legal power to arrest or search suspects, they should pay the heavy price of losing their seized evidence. After leaving PDS in the early 1960s, Gary continued his legendary advocacy in the civil justice arena, working in California with César Chávez and the farm laborers and later representing members of the Black Panthers in disputes with the police. His path to becoming a scholar and activist led him to the University of Southern California School of Law, where he helped establish a law clinic, training students to represent indigent clients in a range of legal matters. In 1971, he returned to his alma mater, Harvard Law School, where he developed its first full-fledged legal clinic tied to academic courses, while producing clinical scholarship that has influenced clinical legal education for decades.

I was fortunate to have Gary as a teacher while I was at Harvard, and he became a mentor in many ways. His stories about PDS intrigued me and helped me decide where I wanted to work after graduating from law school. I wanted to follow in his footsteps. Even though PDS was highly selective and in the 1980s probably hired more former Supreme Court clerks than most of the firms who coveted these highly skilled new lawyers, I was hired.

As a public defender, I found my true calling. All new hires were put through a rigorous six-week training program before we ever went to court, a luxury (some would argue a necessity) not afforded to most public defender offices, given financial constraints and an urgent need to get to court immediately to handle very heavy caseloads. Our training covered both theory and practice. We learned all aspects of criminal law and procedure, drafted motions and briefs, heard lectures on forensic evidence, criminal investigation, sentencing alternatives, and offender rehabilitation options, and participated in mock trials. We worked ten to twelve hours a day in training, in addition to doing our nightly homework assignments. At the end of six weeks, we began our first year in either juvenile court or writing appellate briefs, to ensure a proper period of maturation as public defenders before handling adult misdemeanors and felonies. We also had extensive supervision by other public defenders in the office. It was an amazingly taxing, yet exhilarating, learning experience.

My first year at PDS was tumultuous as a result of a superior court judge's action on the topic of affirmative action. Judge John Fauntleroy, an African-American in the D.C. Superior Court, was a quiet and plain-spoken jurist. He was one of a generation of African-Americans who worked during the day and attended Terrell Law School at night.

Fauntleroy was sensitive to the double standard of race, and he would not tolerate discriminatory efforts to deny blacks opportunities for advancement. A very conscientious and highly regarded jurist, he was widely admired by both the public defenders and the prosecutors who appeared before him. On a September day in 1978, Fauntleroy, who was responsible for assigning new cases to public defenders and court-appointed lawyers, called the public defender picking up cases that day, Barbara Corprew, an African-American woman, to the bench. He told Ms. Corprew he would henceforth refuse to appoint new cases to PDS because of what he perceived as a lack of commitment to affirmative action. He lamented that PDS, a District of Columbia agency financed by city funds and serving a largely minority population, employed an embarrassingly small number of black lawyers. He also expressed similar concern about the U.S. attorney's office, but conceded that he had no power there.

Judge Fauntleroy's appointment power would enable him to effect change at PDS. Never had I imagined that affirmative action, an issue of paramount importance to me while a student at Stanford and Harvard, would find some relevance outside of higher education and reappear at PDS. It certainly was a logical step in the *Brown* analysis, but I naïvely assumed that the battle would involve efforts to hire minorities in law firms or in government institutions. I was wrong.

Fauntleroy ordered the director of PDS, J. Patrick Hickey, to appear before him and explain why PDS hired so few African-Americans. Hickey visited with the judge, along with the recently hired deputy director, Frank Carter, an African-American. Fauntleroy's concerns were well placed. PDS did have an affirmative action program, like most governmental agencies in the United States in the 1970s. In 1978, however, I was only one of two African-Americans in a class of fifteen new lawyers. I was hired along with two of my white Harvard Law School classmates and friends, James McComas and James Klein. The other African-American hired was Laura Christine "Chris" Strudwick, who had grown up in D.C., where her parents were doctors, and she had clerked for H. Carl Moultrie, the first African-American chief judge of the D.C. Superior Court.

Moultrie had grown up in D.C. during the height of segregation and was limited to attending Terrell, a D.C. law school created during the Jim Crow era to provide legal education for African-Americans. By the 1970s, Terrell had been closed, and precious opportunities for a larger group of African-Americans to attend law school had been eliminated. But Terrell had proven its point in training the talented man after whom the H. Carl Moultrie I Superior Courthouse was eventually named. The irony for Moultrie was that right across the street from this courthouse was a public agency, serving indigent African-American clients, which failed to achieve the changes *Brown* mandated. I'm sure he had to wonder whether progress was really being made.

An even greater irony was the fact that Deputy Director Frank Carter had applied to PDS in the early 1970s after clerking for Chief Judge Moultrie, but was not offered a position. Very much committed to public service and criminal defense work, Frank worked for a while with his father-in-law and gained a reputation as an exceptional lawyer. Whereas PDS had earlier found him unacceptable as a staff attorney, in 1977, when the agency got into trouble because of its poor affirmative action record, it enthusiastically hired him as the agency's deputy director; just two years later, it made him director.

In a city that was more than 70 percent African-American in the early 1980s, and with a clientele that was nearly 90 percent African-American, PDS showed a lack of diversity that was shameful and inexcusable. Again, I found race mattering in my life, but in a way I had not contemplated. Much as PDS was fair game for criticism for its lack of diversity, I worried about something else: Who would be hired and for what reason?

As I served on PDS's hiring committees during my tenure at the agency from 1978 to 1985, I continually faced a deeply troubling question: Was I a gatekeeper, in some ways influencing the number of African-Americans to be hired by PDS? It was a difficult dilemma, triggered by two factors. First, the number of minority lawyers increased over the years, but only slowly. Second, many who were hired had attended elite law schools.

In my first few years at PDS, we hired some remarkable African-American lawyers, who were highly successful as public defenders. Many of them became great trial lawyers, like Michele Roberts and

Dennis Sweet, or highly regarded judges, such as Rhonda Reid Winston. Some became acclaimed law teachers, such as Randolph Stone at Chicago Law School, Kim Taylor-Thompson at NYU Law School, and Amani Davis at American University, Professor Isabelle Gunning of Southwestern University Law School in Los Angeles, and Professor M. Shanara Gilbert, who taught at CUNY Law School and died in a tragic car accident in Johannesburg, South Africa. Still others went on to have distinguished careers as public defenders, including Penny Marshall, Henderson Hill, and Avis Buchanan.

Virtually every year one or two African-American students from Harvard and other leading institutions were hired by PDS. I recruited heavily at my alma mater and used my former contacts as the national president of the Black Law Students Association to recruit at other law schools. The more African-Americans I recruited, the more applied. Yet, even with the increased applicant pool, our hiring numbers for African-American attorneys did not grow as quickly as I had hoped. It dawned on me that, in our effort to develop the best public defender service in the country, providing for our clients a level of representation rivaling, if not exceeding, that of the most prestigious law firm, we were in some respects impeding affirmative action goals.

The interview process at PDS was rigorous, with ten applicants for every position. Few made it through the various rounds and into the finals. It was impossible to bluff your way into a job at PDS. The committee of at least six public defenders asked applicants about the extent of their clinical or public-interest work in law school, their summer jobs while there, their capacity to empathize with the poor, their commitment to work seven days a week, their loyalty to defense work, and their ability to handle the pressures of hard cases and difficult clients.

An applicant was scrutinized for his or her fitness not to join a firm but to join a struggle. The admissions criteria were much more rigorous and nuanced than anything these applicants had gone through before. We posed more than the standard "How can you defend guilty people?" questions. We were looking for people willing to talk to a mother whose son had allegedly been murdered by a PDS client, and see what disparaging things she might offer about her deceased son. We were looking for people willing to seek witnesses, in the middle of the night if necessary, and find them in drug dens, pool halls, homeless shelters, jails and prisons, or wherever else they might hide. We wanted individuals committed enough to go to the medical examiner's office, view an autopsy, if possible, and review the findings, looking for errors, omissions, or exaggerations in the evidence. We wanted bold, courageous people, willing to stand up to judges and face the real risk of being held in contempt. In short, zealous defense of our clients knew no bounds, except lawlessness.

If you passed the interview process, you were considered a prospect for bargaining with the devil, since so many other parts of the criminal justice system regarded many of our clients as evil. I was among the strongest advocates of PDS's arrogance and toughness, and believed unequivocally that we should hire only people who exhibited, by everything they said and did, an unwavering commitment to the work. An applicant's race was important to me, but what was more important was a commitment to zealous defense work and a deep respect for the black and poor clients PDS served. I applied the same standards to all applicants, and those who demonstrated a special commitment had the best chance of being hired.

Another disturbing pattern was that we were hiring African-Americans from Stanford, Berkeley, Harvard, and other Ivy League schools, but few from Howard, Thurgood Marshall (Texas Southern) Law School, or Southern Law School, all historically black institutions. Were we doing precisely what Thurgood Marshall had fought to eliminate? I came to realize that even well-intentioned hiring practices could easily limit diversity in hiring. For example, an applicant from Harvard or Howard who expressed an interest in public-interest law, but not a deep interest in defense work, or who saw both defense and prosecution as similar public-interest opportunities, was not someone I easily embraced, whether or not the candidate was African-American. It meant that interested and interesting candidates from all schools who would add to our diversity faced an uphill battle if they failed my litmus test of genuine interest in the specific work we were doing. One has to wonder, in hindsight, whether these "high standards" were, in effect, another form of exclusion that *Brown* had fought to remedy. Were we, the black elite at the public defender's office, preventing the promise of *Brown* from being realized, by our desire to have the best, most dedicated lawyers for our clients? Had I moved from being someone grateful for the opportunities given to me in the post-*Brown* period by the Stanfords and Harvards to someone who, when placed in a position to aid the next generation of aspiring African-Americans, held them to an unachievably high standard? Rather than being part of the solution, had I become part of the problem? I realized that achieving the goals of *Brown* was more difficult than I had contemplated. I realized that achieving the goals of *Brown* would impact not only future generations but my own son and daughter as well.

Our second child, Rashida Jamila Ogletree, was born in January 1979 during my first year at PDS. A perky and precocious child, Rashida, like her brother, was full of promise. I wondered whether or not the doors unlocked by *Brown* would be open to them. I wondered whether or not the opportunities available to me would be available to them. The fact that we were still grappling with affirmative action issues at PDS, and just a few years earlier black families in Boston were fighting the battle to desegregate schools, gave me cause for concern.

MY EXPERIENCES AT PDS challenged my commitment in another significant way. Three years after joining PDS, my colleagues and I decided to seek admission to practice before the U.S. Supreme Court. The swearing-in ceremony and the events leading up to it offered an occasion to reassess my life in the context of the lives of two men I greatly admired: Justice Thurgood Marshall and my father, Charles J. Ogletree, Sr.

My father never thought he would see the day when a black man would have a holiday named after him. But he did live to see it. He also never thought he would have a chance to meet that "colored lawyer" who won all of those civil rights cases in the 1950s and 1960s. But he was able to do that, too. My father never wanted to be a lawyer. More often than not, he needed the services of a lawyer as a result of his temper and unwillingness to turn the other cheek.

My father's Alabama was a hotbed for hate groups that aggressively opposed civil rights for blacks in America. In the 1930s and 1940s, the state not surprisingly witnessed an exodus of many of its African-American residents who were seeking a better life and hoping to escape the racist-fueled violence that characterized their lives in Alabama. The court system there was also flagrantly biased against

African-Americans. Alabama juries, which in those times were exclusively white and male, typically depended less on reason and more on their passionate hatred for black skin in delivering verdicts in cases that involved people of color. These juries were often known to disregard evidence exonerating accused blacks, relying on perjuring witnesses and dispensing unduly harsh and cruel penalties to allegedly guilty African-Americans. State-deputized lynching was also popular in Alabama.[5] Naturally, my father's roots in Alabama left him with bitter memories of civil rights and criminal justice.

My father was aware of Marshall's work as the "colored people's lawyer," as he was known. Marshall, of course, was unaware of my father, for there was no reason that he should know him. In 1983, though, they did come together in the same place on the same day: the U.S. Supreme Court in the District of Columbia. Each had taken a quite different path to get there that day, and, not surprisingly, each entered the Court with many scars that were a direct result of America's racist past. My father arrived nearly five years after a fractured majority had decided the *Bakke* case. Getting him to Washington was a difficult feat—one that I achieved by grossly exaggerating the significance of the Supreme Court swearing-in ceremony.

In a conversation with my mother, I mentioned that we would be sworn in later that spring, and she expressed interest in coming from Merced, California, to Washington to attend the ceremony. She had never seen me in court, even though she told everybody she met that her son was a "Washington, D.C., lawyer," whatever that meant. I asked her whether my father would want to come to the Court ceremony as well, so that they could see the first African-American on the Supreme Court. She suggested that I call and persuade him.

By 1982, my parents had been divorced for close to twenty years, but both still lived in our hometown and actually got along quite well. My father often invited himself over to the house to eat, or my mother took him food at his house. He saw all of the kids regularly at the house and occasionally showed up at one of our football or baseball games. He also gave us birthday gifts and allowances when he had the money and drove us places when we needed a ride.

When I graduated from Stanford in 1975, it was a great moment in my family's history. The Ogletrees would have their first high school *and* college graduate. My mother, uncles, brother, and others attended the Stanford graduation, but my father was conspicuously absent. I went from being puzzled to being concerned. I knew how difficult it was for my father to survive the many racial indignities that were a part of his formative years in Alabama. I thought he would finally feel a sense of fulfillment or vindication to see his oldest son graduate from college. It was not to be.

Three years later, I achieved an even greater milestone in our family. It was not so much my completing professional school, though that was important. It was that I would become a lawyer, an unthinkable option for my parents, but a member of a profession that affected their lives, usually adversely, with a regularity that was uncanny. By now, I not only did not expect my father to attend but had concluded that if he didn't care, I wouldn't care either. It was his loss, I told myself. Much as I tried to convince myself that it didn't matter, I knew in my heart that these absences were a continuing disappointment.

If I could not get my father to my high school, college, or law school graduation, how in the world could I persuade him to come to an event before the Supreme Court that was, at best, only ceremonial? I would have to make an argument that left him no room to decline, and to get him to make a promise that he would keep. I devised a strategy to reunite him with his brother Robert Ogletree, Sr., whom he had not seen for nearly forty years, since they were both young men growing up in Alabama.

Reuniting my father and his brother became all-important to me and increased the significance of having them both in Washington that spring. My father's brother Robert lived at the time in Buffalo, New York. When my father left Alabama in the 1940s, he never went back, and apparently his brother had never returned either. My father rarely talked about Alabama at home, and even though his older brother, Clifford, who passed away in the 1970s, and other relatives remained there, most of what we learned we gleaned from letters to and from his family.

My cousin Zemora Ogletree, the daughter of Robert Ogletree, also lived in the D.C. area. We conspired to reunite our fathers. I could not have been more pleased when Zemora told me she had succeeded in persuading her father to travel to Washington. The night before the scheduled trip to D.C., I received a call from my father, who said he would not be able to make the trip. I think I stopped breathing for a few seconds.

The conversation with my father was a bit surreal. I recall it today with unmistaking clarity.

"Junior, I can't make it to D.C.," he said.

I asked simply but sternly, "Why?"

I should not have been so stern with my father, since on this occasion he was at least calling me to tell me he was not coming. I should have been grateful for the call, but instead was close to being indignant.

He calmly responded, "I can't travel, because I don't have a hat."

I wanted to laugh at this preposterous excuse, but instead I chose to listen. I was not, however, willing to allow my father to cancel this trip so easily, having worked hard to arrange the trip and prepare for his visit. I had bought a new suit (he didn't own one that was less than a decade old, nor did he think he needed a new one) and shoes and even sent him some spending money.

I thought that I had taken care of all of my father's needs. It was inconceivable to me that he would cancel because of a hat. There had to be another reason behind the latest cancellation. Was it an indirect reference to his fear of flying? Was he nervous about being in the Supreme Court—or any court? Did he think that he would be out of place in a big city like Washington, far away from the comfort zone of the pool hall, his gambling buddies, and the barbershop trash-talking crew? I was dumbfounded.

"Why do you need a hat?" I asked.

He responded with honesty and clarity: "If I'm traveling that far, I need to look good. I have these nice clothes, but I don't have a good hat."

What is wrong with him? I wondered. Forgoing a trip to D.C., a Supreme Court ceremony, and a chance to reunite with his brother after forty years of separation, all because of a hat, seemed ridiculous to me. Nevertheless, I told him I would call Stefani's men's store in Merced (where we bought other clothes for the trip) and give them my credit card number over the phone, so that he could buy a hat. I was fuming by then, but did not express any frustration to my father. He agreed to go to Stefani's to purchase a hat, and then with my mother drive to San Francisco to catch the flight to Washington.

When I talked to my mother, she thought the whole thing was ridiculous. "Just like your father. Waiting until the last minute to think of a hat. He has lots of hats at home. Why does he need a new one? I'm not getting a new hat. I think he should wear one of those other hats he has."

By this time, knowing that the store in Merced was about to close, I interrupted and told her, "Mae, you're right. But I called Stefani's, they're open for another hour, and if you take him down there now, they have some nice hats for him. It will be charged to my credit card." When I interrupted her again, she agreed to help my father get the new hat. He picked out a beautiful dark brown hat that matched his suit.

I thought more about my father and began to understand him through that hat. It was a reflection of his pride and gave him a level of dignity and respect that he would not have, in his mind, without it. I think it made him whole as a black man. I recalled seeing pictures of Thurgood Marshall, in public settings when traveling, with a hat. Did it make Justice Marshall stand taller as a man? Did it confer dignity and respect on this great jurist? I recalled as well Dr. Martin Luther King, Jr., even in some of his more famous marches, wearing or carrying a hat. Was it a symbol of pride, not to mention the dominant fashion for that generation of black men? Did it suggest that a black man was a gentleman and was educated? Was it perhaps a way of conveying to whites that they were not threatening? Was it of some significance to them? I could not understand why the hat was so important to them. It certainly meant nothing to my generation or me. Or did it?

I was never conscious of owning or wearing a hat. I know I never discussed it with my father when I was growing up. However, in pictures of me in college and law school, I am invariably wearing a hat. Was this passed on without my being conscious of it? Does it symbolize or portray some ornament of critical importance to black men? I could not explain why I wore hats, but the pictures don't lie. That didn't seem important to my father. He had his new hat and was ready to fly. I couldn't have been more pleased.

My uncle arrived early the next day and accompanied my cousin and me to Dulles Airport to meet my mother and father. We met my parents in the baggage claim area. When my father saw his brother Robert walking toward him, he stopped, and his mouth opened, wordless. My uncle grabbed my father and held on to him as though everything in life depended on it. He cried without shame, and before long we were all crying. The words the two brothers uttered were largely incoherent, because neither had thought about what to say after forty years. One thing is clear: they both wore beautiful dark brown hats.

The swearing-in ceremony marked my second trip to the U.S. Supreme Court. I had been there for the *Bakke* protests the day before the argument and during the argument. This time, the Court promptly came to order, our boss, Frank Carter, introduced the PDS attorneys to the Court, and, in a matter of moments, we were sworn in as lawyers permitted to argue cases before the Supreme Court.

It was a remarkable day, but there was a nagging sensation I couldn't dismiss. As I looked at my father and Justice Thurgood Marshall in the Court that day, I was struck by the contrasts. They were my two heroes. They both influenced my interest in law, but in vastly different ways. My father had experienced his share of problems with the law, but felt powerless to change it. Marshall also experienced discrimination while growing up in Baltimore, but decided to fight back by going to law school, getting legal training, and fighting from within the system.

My father was a different person that day. He beamed and held his head high, visibly proud of his son's accomplishments. Marshall, by contrast, looked beleaguered, as if time and circumstances had taken their toll, and he seemed to lack the energy that I remembered from my visit to the Supreme Court five years earlier, during the *Bakke* argument, perhaps Justice Marshall's finest moment. *Bakke* was, in many respects, the test case to examine *Brown*'s legacy and continued relevance. Marshall was actively defending the principles of affirmative action, defending his lifework on a different level. But much had changed between *Brown* and *Bakke*.

The wrinkles on my father's face told a story of the impact of race on a black man outside the courtroom. The wrinkles on Marshall's face that day illustrated the cumulative impact of his efforts to fight to defend the powerless, while the power to decide important questions had shifted to his conservative colleagues. Marshall had become a critical part of the institution he had spent years trying to turn around, and it appeared that this institution was now perhaps getting the best of him.

I wondered where I fit in. My father had distrusted the system and its lack of fairness, while Marshall was committed to working within the system to make it work. Was it better to reflect my father's skepticism or Marshall's optimism? I had been a direct beneficiary of Marshall's optimism, and his path seemed the right one. Because of Marshall and the *Brown* decision, I was able to go to Stanford and Harvard Law School and become a lawyer. Perhaps it could have happened without the *Brown* decision, but I didn't believe so.

Thurgood Marshall opened the doors to places like Harvard that did not recruit talented African-American college graduates for most of the twentieth century but that aggressively sought students like me, largely because of his efforts in *Brown*, later on. On the other hand, watching my father that day reminded me how far my family had come. While the simple decision would have been to count my blessings, accept the generous progress that I had experienced in life, and follow the Marshall course of having faith in the system, that day I became conscious of the path that I would take: I would steadfastly challenge the system, and try to avoid being co-opted by it. I could see Marshall's bitterness increase from that day forward, while, in contrast, my father's pride soared.

My father sat in the courtroom that day, tall and angular, a proud black man, with a life of hard work behind him, though he had little formal education. I admired him for his perseverance and his determination to live life exactly as he wanted. He accepted life as it was, rarely tried to change it—just tried to find some joy, if not transcendence, in it. He was not impressed by degrees or prestigious positions. I knew there were countless African-Americans in my hometown of Merced who placed no greater value on these things than my father did. How would *Brown* and *Bakke* better their lives? The challenge was not to ponder the question but rather, in the spirit of the struggles that my father and Justice Marshall had endured, to find the answer.

PART II

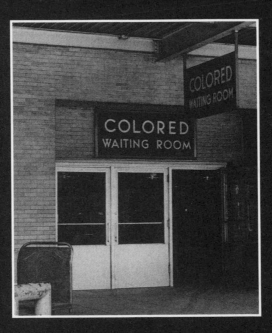

Bus station, colored waiting room. Memphis, Tennessee, circa 1960s.

CHAPTER 6

LIFE BEFORE *BROWN*

M uch of the significance of *Brown* flows not from what the opinion says, but from an appreciation of what it hoped to eliminate: an American social, political, economic, and legal system that had once treated African descendants as property, and after the end of slavery, erected an alternative system of subjugation that treated them as second-class citizens. It was the legal segregation system known as Jim Crow.

Jim Crow, a caricature of a black man created by a white minstrel in 1828 to entertain white crowds, had by late in the century come to symbolize a systematic political, legal, and social repression of African-Americans.[1] Blacks were subjected to judicially and politically sanctioned segregation, discrimination, and violence in a system Glenda Elizabeth Gilmore, a professor of history at Yale University, has called one of "white supremacy, a system that was established both through legislation and the courts, and through custom. It could mean anything from being unable to vote, to being segregated, to being lynched. It was part and parcel of a system of white supremacy. Sort of like we use the word apartheid as a codeword to describe a certain kind of white supremacy."[2]

Segregation grew out of white resistance to black emancipation in the wake of the Civil War. Leon Litwack has documented the ways in which southern whites resented and rejected African-American attempts to resist work conditions that simply replicated the forced labor of the plantation with an attendant social order of abject deference to whites.[3] The newly freed African-Americans sought inclusion in a wage labor system that respected their transformed status as laborers and citizens who had the same legal rights and privileges as whites. But southern whites clung to the old paternalistic myths justifying slavery, seeing themselves as protectors of southern blacks and regarding their former slaves as ignorant and now resentful children. Newly freed African-Americans were prohibited from participating on equal terms with whites in the labor market.

In the political sphere, additional barriers were erected to prevent recently freed slaves from enjoying many of the freedoms available to all citizens. In an 1873 decision in three cases known collectively as the *Slaughter-House Cases*, the Supreme Court effectively created two tiers of citizenship, by interpreting the Fourteenth Amendment to guarantee the "privileges and immunities" of citizenship nationally, as enforced by the federal government, but not locally in the individual states.[4] The states could now determine the citizenship status of those who lived within their jurisdiction, and many created a second-class citizenship for African-Americans. Ten years later, in an 1883 decision in a number of consolidated cases known as the *Civil Rights Cases*, the Court introduced the nonconstitutional concept of "state action" to undermine the Fourteenth Amendment's reach beyond governments into the actions of individuals.[5] Plaintiffs claiming a violation of this amendment were now required to assert that state officials had discriminated against them. The court also distinguished between social and civil rights,[6] declaring that racial discrimination was a social matter. Ultimately, the Court refused to outlaw private acts of discrimination, thus setting the stage for permissible segregation that became known as Jim Crow.

At the state level, private and public agents quickly seized on the two-tiered system of justice to disenfranchise African-Americans. Voting rights were removed by a variety of means, most notoriously by the "grandfather clauses" that required voters to be descended from individuals who were citizens of the states during slavery. That effectively removed most African-Americans from the voting rolls.[7]

Moreover, state officials and private citizens used a variety of legal and illegal means to steal land from African-American farmers. African-Americans removed from their property were forced to turn to sharecropping and the virtual peonage of service on white plantations in order to survive. Many of those plantations printed their own money, which could be used only in the plantation store. Other forms of fiscal servitude saw white towns prohibit African-Americans from purchasing farming tools except on credit at extortionate rates of interest, thus requiring them to sell all their produce to whites during the harvest. In this way, blacks' dependency on whites was continued from slavery into Jim Crow.[8]

African-Americans were excluded from jury service as well, paving the way for nullification of criminal prosecutions of whites for violence against blacks. African-Americans suffered not only economic and political oppression but also violent repression by whites, most notably through lynchings. As John Hope Franklin and Alfred A. Moss, Jr., have noted, the rise of the Ku Klux Klan marked a turning point in the increasing violence against African-Americans: "For ten years after 1867 there flourished the Knights of the White Camelia, the Constitutional Union Guards, the Pale Faces, the White Brotherhood, the Council of Safety, the '76 Association, and the Knights of the Ku Klux Klan."[9] The primary aim of these organizations was to exercise absolute control of blacks, drive them and their fellows from power, and establish white supremacy. They resorted repeatedly to intimidation and murder. Between 1880 and 1930, an estimated 3,220 African-Americans were lynched in the South alone, 7 in the Northeast, 79 in the Midwest, and 38 in the Far West.[10]

In addition to lynching, whites around the country, in the Midwest as well as the South, commonly engaged in "nigger drives," which aimed to remove African-Americans from towns and cities and claim their property for white people.[11] After African-Americans were driven out, cities established informal "sun down" laws. Notices in prominent places notified African-Americans that they could not remain in the city after dark. For example, signs in Norman, Oklahoma, in the early 1920s read, "Nigger, don't let the sun go down on you in this town."[12] At other times, the racial violence took the form of riots. These were coordinated, often officially sanctioned efforts to subjugate African-Americans who were then attempting to carve out lives for themselves in the shadow of Jim Crow. Riots broke out in Wilmington, North Carolina, in 1898; Springfield, Missouri, in 1906; Helena and Elaine, Arkansas, in 1919; and Sherman, Texas, in 1930.[13] Of particular importance were the Chicago riots of 1919, the last and bloodiest of the "Red Summer" riots following the end of World War I. Chicago's city government waited until the fourth day of rioting before deploying the state militia to restore order. In the end, the violence claimed the lives of 38 Chicagoans—23 blacks and 15 whites. Additionally, over 500 were injured, and hundreds of families lost everything when their homes were torched by rioters.[14] The growth of riots out of a pervasive atmosphere of discrimination and violence is now being documented. For example, the Oklahoma Commission to Study the Riot of 1921, a body created by the Oklahoma state legislature, linked the riot to racial violence throughout Oklahoma. Its report concluded,

> The root causes of the Riot reside deep in the history of race relations in Oklahoma and Tulsa which included the enactment of Jim Crow laws, acts of racial violence (not the least of which was the 23 lynchings of African-Americans versus only one white from 1911) against African-Americans in Oklahoma, and other actions that had the effect of "putting African-Americans in Oklahoma in their place" and to prove to African-Americans that the forces supportive of segregation possessed the power to "push down, push out, and push under" African-Americans in Oklahoma.[15]

In response to this Jim Crow segregation, blacks created something of a parallel country within America, what the scholar W. E. B. Du Bois called living "behind the veil" from whites. Leon Litwack and Darlene Clark Hine describe this creation of a parallel country as a way for blacks to draw inward, to create a black community quite separate from the white world.[16] In many towns, African-Americans had their own churches, social clubs, and fraternal organizations. Women played a critical role in the development of the communities. They "formed missionary societies and benevolent associations and cared for the orphaned young, the poor, the widowed, and the elderly. They formed sewing circles, literary groups, and community-reform groups. They created a cultural world of poetry readings, theater, and classical music concerts."[17]

One of the most successful institutions created by African-American women was the National Association of Colored Women (NACW), which attempted to promote and nurture the community and its history. Founded in 1896 by prominent black women, including Ida B. Wells, Harriet Tubman, and May Murray Washington, Booker T. Washington's wife, the NACW took as its motto "Lifting as we climb" and raised funds for kindergartens, vocational schools, summer camps, and homes for the elderly.[18] The 300-member club sponsored cultural events, including poetry readings, and campaigned for the right of black men and women to vote. In fact, it supported the women's suffrage movement two years before the General Federation of Women's Clubs, an organization for white women.[19]

Men, meanwhile, formed fraternal organizations, sporting teams, and volunteer fire companies—self-help associations that paralleled those in the white community. Du Bois observed, "The colored man wakes in his own house built by colored men, . . . he is insured by a colored insurance company, he patronizes a colored school with colored teachers, and a colored church with a colored preacher; he is buried by a colored undertaker in a colored graveyard."[20] Cornel West best captures the importance to African-Americans of institutions that preserve cultural integrity and the crucial role such institutions play in providing hope and meaning in the face of white supremacy:

> The genius of our black foremothers and forefathers was to create powerful buffers to ward off the nihilistic threat, to equip black folk with cultural armor to beat back the demons of hopelessness, meaninglessness, and lovelessness. These buffers consisted of cultural structures of meaning and feeling that created and sustained communities; this armor constituted ways of life and struggle that embodied values of service and sacrifice, love and care, discipline and excellence. In other words, traditions for black surviving and thriving under usually adverse New World conditions were major barriers against the nihilistic threat. These traditions consist primarily of black religious and civic institutions that sustained familial and community networks of support.[21]

Although they were confined within rigid boundaries, African-Americans improvised strategies to live normal lives under abnormal circumstances. Most tried to enjoy the personal and family experiences that life had to offer. Moreover, blacks in the South were often inclined to favor segregated schools, and particularly all-black colleges, because they promoted independence. Du Bois wrote, "Theoretically, the Negro needs neither segregated schools nor mixed schools. What he needs is Education." He concluded, however, that "either he will have separate schools or he will not be educated."[22] Like Du Bois, many other African-

Americans simply recognized that integration was not a realistic goal and that it would not serve as the panacea for racial subordination. They understood that, given adequate resources, blacks were perfectly capable of designing curricula and teaching their own children; moreover, trusting white decision makers to act in their best interests was often risky and seldom resulted favorably.

The 1899 Supreme Court ruling in *Cumming v. Richmond County Board of Education*[23] demonstrates that Du Bois's distrust in these decision makers was justified. A unanimous Court rejected a challenge to a county's closing of its black high school while keeping open its two white high schools.[24] Blacks who went to school (many did not) were confronted with small, decrepit classrooms and, in the South, an educational system separated by law from the more functional white schools. Franklin and Moss have observed that the "compliance in the South with the provision of equality in educational facilities was nowhere more than slight; and in most instances there was a studied disregard for the principle of equality."[25]

Communities attempted to ameliorate this situation as best they could. The Julius Rosenwald Fund assisted in the construction of more than five thousand Negro school buildings in fifteen southern states between 1913 and 1932. The number of predominantly black colleges also grew rapidly, from one in 1854 to more than a hundred in 1973. Their growth was swiftest in the thirty years following the Civil War; it slowed in the second half of the twentieth century, as blacks began to enroll in larger numbers in predominantly white colleges and universities. The increased enrollment in these institutions was caused in part by the lack of opportunities for graduate and professional training at the predominantly black institutions.[26]

Although the black community developed all the institutions it needed to survive during the Jim Crow era, its members disagreed on the question how blacks ought to conduct themselves and construct their lives during this time. There was no single, cohesive approach to combating Jim Crow, or even agreement on whether the Jim Crow laws should be resisted at all. In 1905, the issue of how most effectively to deal with Jim Crow came to a head in the debate between Booker T. Washington and W. E. B. Du Bois over the strategies for pursuing racial progress in a Jim Crow society.

Washington believed that working hard at farming and in community-based support groups would best enable southern blacks to avoid retributive and hateful violence. African-Americans, he held, needed to build an economic base from which to pursue political and social goals; as a result of this conviction, his interest in civil rights laws was considerably overshadowed by his concern with economic progress. Of the schools and colleges that he helped found and support, Tuskegee Institute, which educated blacks in agriculture and other vocations, was the most widely recognized.[27] He considered education to offer the best means of achieving a measure of economic security from which to challenge the Jim Crow system. He also organized the National Negro Business League in 1900 to promote black development and advancement in commerce, agriculture, education, and industry. Even though his goal was to have the league promote black businesses, he did network with white corporate leaders such as Andrew Carnegie and Julius Rosenwald in order to generate financial support for African-American enterprises. This desire to work with and accommodate whites has led some commentators to contend that Washington "sold out" to whites, while others suggest that he focused just as much on black solidarity.[28]

On the other side of this debate stood Du Bois, who more vigorously demanded full constitutional rights for African-Americans. He called for "full access to the American dream on terms not left to the caprice of a racist majority."[29] His demands included freedom of speech, education, "manhood suffrage," and "the abolition of all caste distinctions based simply on race and color." These tenets became the basis of the Niagara movement, founded by a small group of African-American intellectuals critical of Washington; it in turn spawned the NAACP in 1910. Du Bois implored African-Americans to make choices that benefited their community, such as supporting African-American merchants.[30] Despite the differences in Washington's and Du Bois's approaches, both men were deeply committed to making life better for African-Americans.

Throughout this period, the black press played a critical role in furthering the cause of equality. "The first Negro newspaper was born to protest," the historian P. L. Pratis observed. He also pointed out that the black press encouraged members of the black community to protest, by continually informing them about how they were being denied their rights as citizens, and that it strongly supported the efforts of organizations like the NAACP and the Urban League.[31] Black communities felt the need for their own newspapers, to provide the services most white newspapers could or would not provide. White newspapers rarely devoted space to news of interest to black readers, but rather limited their racial reporting to crimes committed by blacks.[32]

One of the most influential publications in the African-American community was Du Bois's *Crisis*. Du Bois saw the *Crisis* serving several functions: first, it would record the "very important happening and movement in the world which bears on the great problem of interracial relations and especially those which affect the Negro American"; second, it would include reviews "of opinion and literature" relating to the race problem; third, it would offer a forum for "a few terse" articles; finally, it would provide an editorial page, composed primarily by Du Bois, standing "for the rights of men, irrespective of color or race, for the highest ideals of American democracy."[33] The *Crisis* descended from Frederick Douglass's *North Star*, William Garrison's *Liberator*, and Samuel Eli Cornish and John Russwurm's *Freedom Journal*, the first newspaper in North America published by an African-American.[34]

By April 1916, the *Crisis* was reaching 45,000 readers, and its pages brought many disturbing stories. One issue, for example, counted and named the African-Americans lynched in each year between 1885 and 1914; another featured on its cover the body of Jesse Washington hanging from a tree. By contrast, a more uplifting segment of the magazine highlighted Talented Tenth firsts—a section devoted to successful African-American professionals.[35]

Just as African-Americans felt it necessary to create a paper by and for their community, many were motivated to establish their own businesses. In 1885, George Allen Mebane, a black newspaper editor, began work on a book called "The Prominent Colored Men of North Carolina," in which he intended to record "the progress of the race" from 1860 to 1885, by providing brief biographies of two hundred successful businessmen and politicians.[36] This ambitious attempt attests to the existence of many successful businessmen in the African-American community. As Wilmoth Carter has contended, black barbers, boot and shoe makers, butchers, hucksters, fish and meat dealers, and restaurant operators who had once served both black and white patrons in a city's

downtown "front streets" were relegated to upstairs and hidden loca-
tions after the passage of Jim Crow laws. The location of the businesses,
he contends, seemed always related to the racial and status group to
which the business catered. Carter also observes that as Jim Crow laws
were tightened and segregation was enforced, the black business world
began to contract to black customers and clients. With "Negro leaders
stressing work, thrift and education as the means of solving the Negro's
economic problems; and with the mounting number of professional
Negroes in the community without free social and economic opportunities, development of parallel institutions in a separate social world was
a necessary concomitant."[37] In 1898, John Hope, a professor at Atlanta
University, who said that the plight of African-Americans was due not
wholly to ignorance and incompetence but in part to competition with
whites for jobs in new fields, called on African-Americans to become
their own employers. The conference at which Hope made this proposal
adopted resolutions declaring that "Negroes ought to enter into business life in increasing numbers" and that "the mass of Negroes must
learn to patronize business enterprise conducted by their own race, even
at some slight disadvantage."[38] Booker T. Washington's formation of the
National Negro Business League, which by 1907 boasted 320 branches,
reflected these sentiments.

At the end of the century blacks owned and ran numerous businesses, as Franklin and Moss have recounted:

> They operated grocery stores, general merchandise stores, and drugstores;
> they were restaurant keepers, caterers, confectioners, bakers, tailors,
> builders, and contractors. Some operated shirt factories, cotton mills, and
> rubber good shops, lumber mills, and carpet factories. There were many
> cooperative businesses, such as the Bay Shore Hotel Company of Hamp-
> ton, Virginia; the Capital Trust Company of Jacksonville, Florida; the
> South View Cemetery Association of Atlanta, Georgia; and the Southern
> Stove Hollow-Ware and Foundry Company of Chattanooga, Tennessee.[39]

They have also recounted stories of flourishing African-American entrepreneurs, including Madam C. J. Walker, whose hair and skin preparation business gave rise to similar establishments over the ensuing fifty
years, and a North Carolina fish dealer worth more than $25,000.

Meanwhile, two black real estate agents in New York City were worth more than $150,000 each, and one in Cleveland owned property valued at $100,000.[40]

Blacks also developed financial institutions to support further business development. In 1888, Richmond's Savings Bank of the Grand Fountain United Order of True Reformers was organized as the first bank administered entirely by blacks, and the following year saw the foundation of the Mutual Bank and Trust Company of Chattanooga and the Alabama Penny Savings Bank of Birmingham. The number of black banks had reached fifty-five by World War I, but most suffered short life spans because of a lagging volume of trade and commerce. Nonetheless, as Franklin and Moss have argued, these efforts show that blacks were attempting to assimilate themselves by adopting the business and social ideals of the rest of America.[41]

Another example of a flourishing African-American business, recently cited by Richard Wormser, is the North Carolina Mutual Life Insurance Company, founded by John Merrick, C. C. Spaulding, and Dr. Aaron Moore. These men developed a $250 initial investment into a multimillion-dollar enterprise. They were able to do this partly because they provided the African-American community with an opportunity to receive respectful service from their agents and also reminded them that their patronage helped support their African-American neighbors. Spaulding believed that the best way to generate customers was to persuade them "to patronize a colored insurance company of standing. Tell them that every time a Negro takes a policy, it protects him and it employs another Negro."[42] The North Carolina Mutual created hundreds of jobs for blacks and encouraged others to start businesses; an agent described it as "one of God's ways through which he is reaching our people. His message to us is: 'Lower your buckets where you are.'"[43]

Apart from the organized, political, and personal resistance to Jim Crow, African-Americans attacked white supremacy by means of nonpolitical, but defiant, cultural expressions. Spirituals and other forms of music symbolized racial pride and helped to combat prejudice. The historian George Fredrickson has observed that in "pursuing their natural race genius, blacks would realize that segregation was not a system of racial oppression, but a benevolent service that protected both races from cultural annihilation."[44] It was this natural genius that gave voice to the spirituals, blues, and jazz.

In *The Souls of Black Folk,* Du Bois also recognized the importance of music to the black community. Throughout the book, he used the device of pairing Negro spirituals with European verse—by Browning, Byron, Swinburne, Symons, Tennyson—as epigraphs for each essay. The juxtaposition was intended to promote the novel ideal of creative parity and complementarity of white folk and black folk. Du Bois meant this to be "profoundly subversive" of the prevailing cultural hierarchy.[45]

The Harlem Renaissance was a time when "[n]ew poets and novelists gained national attention by giving voice to the ancient wrongs, the brooding sorrows, and the mounting indignation of their race."[46] Black protest literature had for some time resisted white supremacy, but the 1920s saw this resistance grow substantially. The movement was rooted in Harlem, where thousands of southern blacks had migrated. It produced essays, poems, and novels that "rejected sentimentality, romanticism, and escapism to focus directly on the root causes of the crippling plight of black America: white racism."[47] Du Bois encouraged talented artists to leave the South. Then the editor of the *Crisis*, he was at the height of his fame and influence in the black community. The *Crisis* published the poems, stories, and visual works of many artists of the period. Interestingly, the short stories that appeared there from 1910 to 1932 were in perfect harmony with the general attitudes of the African-American middle class during this period.[48] They were not, however, representative of the literature produced by the black "intelligentsia" after 1920. The members of this group, part of the second generation of educated blacks, rebelled against the lives their fathers and grandfathers had led, and they attempted to articulate new values and to replace them with values of their own. These rebels created the Harlem Renaissance, which subordinated racial protest to art. As Robert Bone has stated, "the Harlem Renaissance was prompted by a wave of Negro nationalism which swept over the colored community [after the disillusionment] of World War I."[49]

Although the Harlem Renaissance perhaps contributed to a certain relaxation of racial attitudes among young whites, arguably the greatest impact of this period was to reinforce race pride among blacks. James

Weldon Johnson poignantly articulated his thoughts about race and the times with his book *Fifty Years and Other Poems*. The title poem, which marked the fiftieth anniversary of the signing of the Emancipation Proclamation, "made it clear that African Americans were determined to remain in America and to enjoy the full fruits of their labors."[50] Along with this sort of serious and often introspective literature, the Harlem Renaissance also provided an outlet for African-American theater, music, and dance. In Harlem there was "a real African-American theater in which black actors performed before predominantly African-American audiences. It was no longer necessary for blacks to attempt only those roles that were acceptable to white audiences."[51] This time also produced black musical revues, such as *Shuffle Along*, which was written and produced by blacks. The Harlem Renaissance allowed for serious music as well, including the revival and reinterpretation of Negro spirituals. Franklin and Moss have summarized the Harlem Renaissance as a period that future historians will regard as merely the beginning of a long period of self-expression and self-revelation of the black in American life.[52]

Despite this progress, segregation dominated and was even judicially sanctioned with the 1896 decision in *Plessy v. Ferguson*. In this case, which concerned a Creole arrested for refusing to move from the white section of a train, the Supreme Court held that states could constitutionally require segregation. The lone dissenter, John Marshall Harlan, cautioned that the Constitution "neither knows nor tolerates classes among its citizens,"[53] but his warning fell on deaf judicial ears. *Plessy* crystallized the Jim Crow system within the American constitutional framework, and it stood for another fifty-eight years.

This legally sanctioned system designed to keep black folks in a subordinated position failed to achieve its goal in places like Tulsa Oklahoma. The success of segregated black communities in spite of Jim Crow fueled white hatred and unleashed unfettered violence and destruction.

In spring 1921, the Greenwood section of Tulsa was a vibrant African-American community, with a population of nearly eight thousand. Its professional class had become so prosperous by 1921 that the streets on which it conducted its business were collectively known as the Negro Wall Street.[54] The southern end of Greenwood Avenue, including the adjacent side streets, housed dozens of African-American-owned and -operated businesses—grocery stores and meat markets, clothing and dry goods stores, billiard halls, beauty parlors and barbershops, as well as a drugstore, a jewelry store, an upholstery shop, and a photography studio. Greenwood's diverse economy comprised businesspersons and professionals as well as skilled and semiskilled workers. Because of racial segregation, these businesses served primarily African-Americans. There were two African-American newspapers, the *Tulsa Star* and the *Oklahoma Sun.* Greenwood was also home to a local business league, various fraternal orders, a YMCA branch, and a number of women's clubs.[55]

On the evening of May 31, 1921, a white mob, many of whose members were drunk, gathered in front of the Tulsa jail and was rumored to be preparing to lynch an African-American man accused of attempting to assault a white woman. Some African-American men, including World War I veterans, came to the jail to prevent the lynching. During a scuffle between the white and black men, shots were fired and "all hell broke loose."[56] The mayor of Tulsa called out local units of the National Guard and deputized and armed them. The deputies were instructed to "go get . . . a nigger."[57] Over the next day, there was rampant violence and destruction of property in Greenwood. In the early hours of the morning of June 1, local units of the National Guard drove African-American residents from their homes and looted many buildings before burning Greenwood to the ground.

The riot, coming only sixty years after the end of slavery, was part of a much larger culture of discrimination against African-Americans. Many of the riot victims were former slaves. Many whites defended the riot, claiming that it was the result of increasingly aggressive attitudes of African-Americans, who sought "social equality" following their service in World War I.[58] One African-American property owner was characterized as a man who had "come back from France with exaggerated ideas about equality and thinking he can whip the world."[59] Greenwood never reclaimed its place as the Negro Wall Street, for hundreds of blacks lost their lives and property, and a number of residents moved to other states, vowing never to return to Tulsa.

By the end of the 1920s, African-American communities all around the country were beginning to rebound from the end of Reconstruction and decades of enforced segregation. Nonetheless, even in those communities that survived the prolonged violence against them, a newfound sense of determination emerged, and the NAACP began to plan new strategies to defeat Jim Crow. A legal challenge to *Plessy* was one of the selected options. A young African-American lawyer, graduating from Harvard Law School in 1922, would soon join the NAACP and develop the legal strategy to defeat segregation in the United States. His name was Charles Hamilton Houston.

CHAPTER 7

DEFEATING JIM CROW

There was little in Charles Hamilton Houston's childhood or early life that suggested that he would devote his talents to masterminding the legal battle against segregation. Even today Houston, unlike Du Bois, King, or Marshall, is rarely given credit in public or private discussions as the architect of the legal and political strategy that ultimately brought the reversal of the infamous "separate but equal" doctrine from *Plessy v. Ferguson*. Although Houston grew up in the segregated Washington, D.C., of the early twentieth century, his comfortable middle-class upbringing and supportive family life offset some of the harsher realities of being black in the Jim Crow South. His father was a successful and financially secure lawyer, well respected within the local black community. His mother was a schoolteacher who later took on a more lucrative career as a hairdresser for affluent whites in Washington. Seeking the best possible education for their son, the Houstons insisted that he reject a full academic scholarship to the University of Pittsburgh and instead accept the financially burdensome option of enrolling at Amherst College. He rewarded them, and himself, by earning top grades and election to the academic honor society, Phi Beta Kappa.[1]

Upon graduation, Houston was not certain whether he wanted to pursue a career in law, despite his father's dream of one day adding his son's name to the sign overhanging his law practice. The younger Houston initially preferred the idea of a career in music, diplomacy, or education. The United States' entrance into World War I and Houston's service in the military dramatically changed his plans. After having spent his entire life to date either among his family or on the predominantly white, all-male, but congenial Amherst campus, Houston experienced extreme and pervasive racism while in the military. For example, though he held the rank of officer, he nevertheless was required to live in segregated housing, arbitrarily denied the opportunity to serve in his trained field of artillery, constantly harassed and humiliated by white officers, and, in one disturbing incident on the streets of Vannes, nearly lynched by a mob of white soldiers. Houston was especially troubled by his work as an appointed judge advocate for the prosecution of infractions, in which he found himself powerless to stop several miscarriages of justice that were often racially motivated.[2]

Houston was honorably discharged in 1919, but on returning home to Washington he experienced a new assault on his middle-class upbringing: the nation was experiencing white racial resistance to even modest black progress, and the city he had grown up in was now besieged by race riots and endemic lynchings. Houston's resolve, developed during his army days, was clear: "I made up my mind that I would never get caught again without knowing something about my rights. . . . I would study law and use my time fighting for men who could not strike back."[3]

Houston applied to Harvard Law School and was accepted. One of only a very few blacks in his class, he earned top marks in his first year, especially in his classes in contracts and property. Thanks to his outstanding academic performance, he became the first African-American to be selected to the *Harvard Law Review*. Houston also attracted the attention and mentoring of eminent Harvard professors such as Joseph Beale, the future Supreme Court Justice Felix Frankfurter, and legendary dean Roscoe Pound. In 1922, Houston received his LL.B. and elected to remain at Harvard to pursue the doctorate of juridical science (S.J.D.), in the course of which he earned a straight A average and wrote his doctoral dissertation on administrative law, under the supervision of Professor Frankfurter.

Awarded the Sheldon Traveling Fellowship in 1923, Houston continued his legal studies in the civil law program at the University of Madrid, where he maintained a regular correspondence with Roscoe Pound. Frankfurter and Pound, the era's giants of legal scholarship, strongly influenced his thinking about legal doctrine, the role of the lawyer, and, most important, the ways in which the law could be utilized to achieve social progress. Throughout his career, Houston remained in contact with his two mentors, and they served as his advisers and confidants.[4]

Around the time that Houston was completing his legal training, the NAACP was making plans to challenge segregation. In the mid-1920s, the NAACP received the promise of a $100,000 grant from the Garland Fund, a foundation dedicated to the support of liberal and radical causes. Ultimately, the NAACP received only about $20,000, because of the Depression's effect on the fund's holdings and ideological disagreements between the NAACP and the fund's more radically class-minded board of directors. The NAACP's initial plan to fight segregation in education had its genesis in the development of proposals to effectively take advantage of the Fund's financial support.[5]

Walter White, acting secretary of the NAACP, prepared the first outlines of a legal strategy to counter educational segregation. White proposed filing taxpayer suits in the Deep South and seeking court orders to equalize municipal and state spending on black and white schools. He reasoned that forcing equal spending on black schools would make a dual school system prohibitively expensive and thus compel school districts to integrate. Moreover, the South's abhorrence of any notions of equalization made it likely that southern officials would appeal any cases they lost, and this would allow for higher-court decisions that covered more territory. White anticipated that successful NAACP suits would serve as a positive example, inspiring black families all over the South to bring similar suits, potentially leading to a grassroots movement of equalization litigation. Finally, even if the cases were not successful, they would at the very least serve to focus national attention on the overt discrimination in the apportionment of public school funds.

White hired Nathan Margold—another Harvard Law graduate and protégé of Frankfurter—to plan and coordinate the litigation campaign. Margold began by writing a 218-page strategic report, which would prove enduringly influential on the course of the NAACP's strategy leading up to *Brown*. The report found that it would be relatively easy to demonstrate the grossly unequal spending on black schools, but that the real difficulty would be in seeking a remedy. The problem with the equalization remedies of the earlier proposals, Margold held, was that the NAACP would have to bring an action for mandamus, a state court order directing compliance with the "separate but equal" requirement of the law, against each official responsible for expenditures. This would inevitably lead to finger-pointing and "not me" defenses, in which each defendant would claim that some other, unnamed official was responsible. Moreover, mandamus was retroactive, making it necessary to bring new actions every year, an impossible litigation load, given the NAACP's limited funds. Finally, because state law often required equal funding among counties, it would be easy for state officials to get around the order by equalizing money between counties while overlooking discrepancies between schools. Margold instead advocated suits that sought declarations of unconstitutionality in the unequal allocation of funds. Faced with those declarations, state officials could then choose whether to attempt the costly route of equalizing funds or simply to desegregate the schools.[6]

In 1933, Margold was appointed solicitor of the Department of the Interior and resigned his position at the NAACP. White replaced him with Houston, who had been extensively consulting with the NAACP on its developing campaign while serving as vice dean of Howard Law School. White was happy to appoint a black lawyer to lead the NAACP's legal campaign against segregation. In the early 1930s, the NAACP had begun actively recruiting black lawyers to stimulate and inspire membership activities in the branch offices, to demonstrate the advance of the race in areas previously open only to whites, and to respond positively to an increasingly held notion within the black community that the organization that represented the black community in court should also reflect that community's composition.[7]

Perhaps no figure at that time better represented and inspired the advancement of African-Americans into the professional ranks of the law than Charles Hamilton Houston. In 1924, he had joined the Howard Law faculty, which then consisted of only an evening program. He was highly regarded by his students and colleagues as an exceptional— though tough and demanding—teacher. Practicing law with his father by day, Houston brought a valuable practitioner's perspective to the classroom in addition to his world-class academic rigor, developed under the tutelage of Frankfurter and Pound. In 1927, Houston researched and prepared, at the request of Howard's board of trustees, surveys and studies examining the status and activities of black lawyers and law schools in the United States, as well as the "Survey of Howard University Law Students."[8]

On the basis of these studies, Houston drafted a twenty-page document, "Personal Observations on the Summary of Studies in Legal Education as applied to Howard University School of Law," in which he outlined his vision for the law school.[9] Houston was strongly influenced by the social realist legal philosophy of his mentor Pound, who viewed the law "as a social institution to satisfy social wants—the claims and demands and expectations involved in the existence of civilized society . . . in short, a continually more efficacious social engineering."[10] The time had come, Houston believed, to claim, to demand, and to expect equal protection under the law, and through litigation the social institution of the law could be utilized to challenge institutional racism effectively. Since well-trained lawyers would be needed to accomplish this, Houston envisioned Howard Law School as the institution that could create the select and talented corps of lawyers who would work to fulfill constitutional promises. Howard ought to produce not just lawyers but also social engineers who fought for a more advanced and enlightened society.[11]

In 1929, Howard University appointed Houston, who had recently recovered from a bout of tuberculosis, vice dean of the law school. Upon assuming supervision over the school's day-to-day operations, Houston began his campaign to upgrade the unaccredited Howard Law School to a top-flight institution of legal training. He persuaded the board of trustees to eliminate the dwindling evening program in order to focus resources on further developing the day program. He raised admission standards, improved and expanded the law library, hired new personnel, including more full-time law professors, lengthened the school year, made recruiting trips throughout the country to recruit talented applicants, and instituted a far more demanding curriculum. Houston's reforms did not go without criticism, especially from alumni who attributed their law licenses to the evening program and who decried Houston's "Harvardization" of Howard. But Houston remained confident in his reforms, and soon even his critics had to acknowledge that he had substantially improved Howard Law School, which was accredited by the American Bar Association in 1930 and elected to membership by the Association of American Law Schools in 1931.[12]

Having transformed Howard Law School into a serious institution of legal training, Houston sought next to prepare a generation of black lawyers who would file the claims and argue the cases that would bring down institutional racism. In his article "The Need for Negro Lawyers," he urged African-Americans to undergo the rigors of intense legal training so that they might join the fight to secure for an entire race real equality under the law. He maintained that "the social justification for the Negro lawyer as such in the United States today is the service he can render the race as an interpreter and proponent of its rights and aspirations."[13]

In regard to Howard, Houston wrote, "If a Negro law school is to make its full contribution to the social system it must train its students and send them into just such situations. This does not necessarily mean a different course of instruction from that in other standard law schools. But it does mean a difference in emphasis."[14] Accordingly, Houston recruited faculty who had been active in civil rights litigation and advised them to teach their courses with the goal of producing future civil rights litigators principally in mind. He demanded a great deal of his students, and his high expectations earned him the affectionate nickname Iron Shoes.[15] While students loathed the heavy workload and complained about his exacting pedagogical style, they respected him and shared his vision. They knew Houston was preparing them to undertake the task of bringing about the most significant legal and social reforms of the twentieth century.

Houston's appointment as special counsel to the NAACP presented him with the unique opportunity to bring black lawyers and citizens already out there into the fold while simultaneously leading the charge against institutional segregation. Upon taking over the helm of the NAACP's litigation effort, Houston began work on a three-prong strategy: first, to solidify a nationwide network of African-American lawyers to file "test case" litigation against segregation practices; second, to build precedential support for a direct constitutional attack against segregation through this carefully targeted litigation; and third, to organize local black communities in broad, unified support of legal, political, and social action against ongoing discriminatory practices. In his mind, the legal campaign was part of a greater national effort to mobilize the black community against segregation.[16]

At the NAACP, Houston marshaled his former students into a national network active in the fight against segregation. This tight-knit network of lawyers, who met semiannually at the National Bar and African-American Bar meetings, devoted their time and energy to helping Houston and the NAACP find plaintiffs, file suits, and bring cases under the general direction of his targeted litigation strategy. They formed an indispensable part of Houston's strategy, for they provided the NAACP largely pro bono assistance while serving as local militias—legal advocate foot soldiers in the national office's strategic campaign. Without this cadre of lawyers, the NAACP, with its limited staff and budget, could never have taken on the workload of the hundreds of cases that led up to *Brown*.

With his mind on establishing key precedents that would lay the groundwork for an eventual direct attack on segregation, Houston carefully selected a few target areas for the litigation campaign. He first resolved that he wanted to concentrate the litigation effort on segregation and inequities in education. Himself the product of a first-rate education, he saw quality education as the essential preparation for life and believed that poor, inadequate schools placed a lifelong handicap on many American blacks, both in competing economically and in seeking equal rights. To Houston, segregation and inequities in American schools represented the worst symptom of American racism: in addition to denoting that African-Americans were legally an inferior caste, school segregation reinforced and contributed to the perpetuation of that caste system. Houston decided that the NAACP should focus exclusively on three kinds of school desegregation cases: suits seeking the desegregation of state-run graduate and professional schools, suits seeking to equalize the salary discrepancies between black and white teachers, and suits seeking to equalize the disparate physical facilities for black and white elementary and secondary schools.[17]

Though neither the Garland Fund proposals nor the Margold report contemplated them, segregation suits against public graduate and professional schools had numerous strategic advantages. Graduate schools were an area where the South was most vulnerable: while most southern states had separate and unequal colleges for African-Americans, none of those colleges had any sort of training facilities for graduate students. Remedies in successful suits would force state university officials either to admit black applicants or to establish separate, equal facilities for the suits' plaintiffs. It was easy to find willing plaintiffs among the ranks of young, ambitious African-American students who wished to further their education but were denied the opportunity by their state university's discriminatory exclusion practices. The legal theory for such cases was simple, clear, and compelling and had easy application to a variety of factual situations, running the gamut of public, graduate, and professional training programs. Judges would more likely be receptive to such cases because they appreciated firsthand the value of advanced education and training beyond college.[18]

In Houston's mind, the true advantage of the segregation suits against graduate and professional programs was that they would most effectively advance the goals of community mobilization and precedent building. Successful suits would encourage more ambitious black students to consider applying to graduate programs and to bring additional segregation suits. The result would be the opening of the doors of elite educational opportunities to more African-Americans who wished to become community leaders and further support the fight for equality. Moreover, successful suits and the ensuing publicity would strengthen the black communities' resolve and the NAACP's membership—especially in the South, where it was needed most. Houston recognized that public support, both for political backing and for funding, was an essential ingredient of a successful litigation campaign.

Houston knew that segregation suits against graduate and professional schools could lead to victories for the NAACP and create precedents for a future direct attack on segregation without making waves. White opponents to integration were not going to fight the establishment of an in-state black pharmacy school or the admission of a sprinkling of black students to the law school, because their communities and, more especially, their young children would not be affected. Houston correctly anticipated that southern whites would not throw bricks or erect a blockade to protect the racial integrity of a graduate program, as they would to protect their children from the perceived threat of educational integration.

The salary and facility equalization suits had similar advantages and would serve similar purposes of community mobilization and "test case" precedent building. Successful equalization cases would force white officials to pay prohibitively high sums for the luxury of maintaining separate school systems and thus indirectly encourage them to consider integration. Also, equalization suits, as indirect attacks on segregation, could establish useful precedents enforcing the promise of equal separate facilities without the significant social upheaval that would follow a successful direct attack, which sought full integration as a remedy.

As part of their mobilizing efforts, Houston and his star pupil Thurgood Marshall went on proselytizing campaigns throughout the South, building organizational support while arousing interest in forming plaintiffs' classes. Houston wrote a number of articles and pamphlets instructing communities how to bring lawsuits, build community solidarity, and agitate for better schools. This literature also explained how the equalization lawsuits were part of a greater strategic plan to attack educational segregation specifically and fight institutional racism generally. Most of all, Houston emphasized that while "the NAACP stands ready with advice and assistance," ultimately "the decision for action rests with the local community itself."[19]

Though the NAACP sought any and all public support, when it came to actual suit filings, Houston proceeded with caution. He patiently waited for the best plaintiffs who were in the jurisdiction of the best possible forums. He elected to bring cases in the Upper South and border states, where segregation existed in full form, but judges and officials would be less defiant than their Deep South counterparts. Moreover, traveling to nearby forums in the Upper South was easier and less costly for Houston and his national staff. He was careful to enter litigation only where his staff had a solid grasp of the procedural quirks and substantive nuances of local law or was able to utilize local lawyers to aid with the particulars. Most important, Houston realized, largely from early failures, that it was essential for the national organization to retain central control. An outline of procedures for bringing equalization suits drafted by Marshall in 1939 insisted that the national office be informed of "all steps *before* they are taken."[20] It was vital that local lawyers could benefit from the experience gained at the national office. With the help of strong local community and professional support, Houston was running a nationally coordinated litigation assault on segregation.

The NAACP won a number of important victories, which would together lay the foundation for *Brown*. It successfully brought teacher salary equalization cases in Maryland, Virginia, Alabama, Tennessee, Kentucky, Arkansas, South Carolina, Florida, and Louisiana. As a result, black teachers went from earning 50 percent of what white teachers earned in 1930 to earning 65 percent in 1945. However, these victories, often secured through state court–endorsed settlements, had small precedential value, and state officials found ways to get around court orders by implementing purportedly objective merit rating systems that provided a pretext for discrimination. Moreover, gains in salary equalization were generally confined to urban areas; rural officials were confident that they could resist such suits because of the lack of willing plaintiffs, the prevalence of more biased judges, and the effectiveness of old-fashioned intimidation. Equalization suits also tended to be difficult to sustain since they often involved costly data collecting and plaintiffs' classes were easily bought off with small wage increases. Notwithstanding these shortcomings, the equalization suits placed sustained pressure on state discrimination practices and rallied public support behind the NAACP and its litigation efforts. Nonetheless, by the mid-1940s, the NAACP had abandoned equalization cases, because they were costly and unlikely to produce any major precedent-setting victories.[21]

Meanwhile, the NAACP won such victories in its suits seeking admission for plaintiffs to public graduate and professional programs. In 1936, Houston and Marshall won their first major victory in *Pearson v. Murray*, in which they obtained a state court order, affirmed by the Maryland Supreme Court, directing the University of Maryland Law School to admit Donald Murray despite Maryland's offer to pay Murray's out-of-state tuition.[22] Marshall savored this victory; having chosen not to apply to the Maryland Law School, because he was certain, despite his excellent credentials, that he would be turned down, he became the Howard-trained lawyer who turned the university's discriminatory program upside down.

This victory raises more questions about Marshall's strategy than it answers. One wonders, given his awareness of the powerful segregation practices in Maryland and other parts of the South in the early 1920s and 1930s, why Marshall did not himself seek to serve as the test plaintiff to integrate his hometown law school.

The NAACP won its first major federal victory in a case on behalf of Lloyd Gaines, an honors graduate from Lincoln University, who was denied admission to the University of Missouri Law School. Houston and Sidney Redmond, a leading black attorney from St. Louis, were not surprised to lose their case in the state trial court. On appeal, the Missouri Supreme Court ruled that Missouri's offer to supply Gaines with an out-of-state scholarship satisfied the state's obligation to provide equal graduate training for black students. In 1938, in *Missouri ex rel. Gaines v. Canada*, the Supreme Court provided Houston and the NAACP a major precedent setting victory.[23] Justice Hughes's decision found that the right to equal protection was a personal one, which one state could not pass off to another. The Court held that Missouri had an obligation to provide Gaines with a graduate education, and it ordered the admission of Gaines to the in-state law school.[24] A troubling postscript to the case is that Gaines disappeared just before he was supposed to enroll. Though different theories speculated that he was either paid off or killed, no one ever found out for sure what happened to him.[25]

After World War II, the number of black applicants seeking admission to state college and graduate programs increased substantially and provided the NAACP with a wealth of plaintiffs from which to choose. In one major postwar victory, *Sipuel v. Oklahoma*, a young black woman named Ada Louise Sipuel sought admission to the University of Oklahoma Law School.[26] In 1948, the Supreme Court, relying on *Gaines*, ruled that Oklahoma had an obligation to provide Sipuel with an education on the same basis as white students. The Regents of the University of Oklahoma tried to respond by hastily establishing a separate law school for black students in three rooms in the state capitol building. Marshall challenged this arrangement, but the Supreme Court neglected to take any action. Sipuel was admitted to the white law school in 1949 when prohibitive costs for maintaining a separate school for one student caused the state to close the black law school.[27]

In the late 1940s, Houston, Marshall, and the NAACP won two major victories that cleared the way for a direct attack on educational segregation. Heman Marion Sweatt was denied admission to the University of Texas Law School. When Marshall filed suit, the state legislature allocated $100,000 to construct a separate black law school. The state court ruled that the state had satisfied its obligation by using a substantial amount of money to construct this separate law school. At the same time, a sixty-eight-year-old professor at the black Langston College in Oklahoma applied to the University of Oklahoma's Graduate School of Education. The state allowed Professor McLaurin to attend the white school, but he was forced to sit in a room adjoining the main classroom roped off with a sign that read "colored section." The state courts held that Dr. McLaurin's admission with separate treatment satisfied the state's obligation.[28]

Both cases—*Sweatt v. Painter* and *McLaurin v. Oklahoma*[29]—were appealed to the Supreme Court, and decisions were handed down in 1950 on the same day. In *Sweatt*, the Court assumed that there was equality between the two physical plants, but found that this was not sufficient. It held that there was more to legal education than a physical plant and that Texas could not replicate in the black school the learning environment, the established reputation, and the alumni contacts of the white school.[30] In *McLaurin*,[31] the Court found that the University of Oklahoma's arrangement for separate treatment within the graduate school stigmatized Dr. McLaurin and handicapped him in his ability to pursue his education.

These two cases together—one stating that physical equality was still insufficient to meet the requirements of equal protection and the other finding that actual equality with separate arrangements imposed a stigma and was therefore unconstitutional—opened up the opportunity for a direct attack on segregation and paved the way to the *Brown* decision. Marshall reacted to the Court's rulings by declaring, "The decisions . . . are replete with road markings telling us where to go next."[32] Though Houston was not there to aid him, Marshall began his direct attack on segregation, aware that his mentor and teacher had fully prepared him to complete the strategy developed more than a decade earlier, and fully resolved not to waver until the job was done. The road map for the political dismantling of Jim Crow was complete, and now the strategists had found the legal route to bring an end to what Du Bois had described as "the problem of the color line." The only question that remained was whether the changed goal—complete integration of public education—would indeed turn out to be the serious impediment that some of Marshall's allies feared it would be. Was the Court, let alone America, ready to embrace the Declaration of Independence's self-evident "truth"—that all men are created equal—in fact and not just in principle?

CHAPTER 8

RESISTANCE TO *BROWN*

B*rown v. Board of Education* had a profound and indelible impact on the United States. Declared the "case of the century," it established that intentional segregation was unconstitutional. This ruling served to fuel the civil rights movement and to challenge the legitimacy of all public institutions that embraced segregation. However, there was significant political and legal resistance to *Brown*'s mandate, and some commentators assert that because the mandate was not bolstered by vigorous enforcement, political leaders opposed to *Brown* could easily thwart its promise. Given the *Brown* Court's lack of firm resolve, as evidenced in its express refusal to order an immediate injunction against segregation and in its "all deliberate speed" modification, public resistance was inevitable. The resistance that came from local, state, and federal executive branch officials, and the absence of a coordinated effort on either the state or the federal level to enforce desegregation vigorously, compounded the Court's failure.

Prior to the oral argument in *Brown*, the United States had filed an amicus brief stating that *Plessy v. Ferguson* had been wrongly decided and that if the Court should reach the constitutional question in *Brown*, *Plessy* should be overruled. Before the case was reargued, a new Republican administration, under Eisenhower, took office. Though Eisenhower personally contributed to the second government brief in support of desegregation, his position was significantly weaker than the preceding administration's. Although he said he favored desegregation in principle, he "waffled on when and how it might be accomplished in public schools."[1] While this did not mark a departure from the government's prior stance, it significantly decreased the possibility of effective, aggressive desegregation.

Brown II provided no judicial guidance on remedies; it merely signaled that southern school boards could move gradually, "with all deliberate speed." Faced with this instruction, school districts stalled until they were forced to choose one of two options, neither of which welcomed *Brown* with immediate integration through affirmative measures. The two options approved by lower courts—assignment on the basis of residence and freedom of choice—accompanied the repeal of de jure segregation. Even before residence assignments were struck down by the Court as "inevitably lead[ing] toward segregation,"[2] freedom-of-choice plans emerged as the most common response to *Brown*. These plans repeatedly failed to yield any significant desegregation.[3] Yet until 1968 they largely survived judicial review because courts interpreted *Brown* as requiring only that black and white children have the option of attending school together. Representative of this view is a federal district court's insistence that even after *Brown* the Constitution "does not require integration, it merely forbids [segregation]."[4] This statement reflects a troublingly narrow reading of *Brown*, adopted by several current justices, that the constitutional problem at issue was state-sanctioned segregation, not a lack of integration.[5] Thus, freedom of choice plans became the dominant judicially sanctioned mechanism of implementing a view of *Brown* that remedied the constitutional violation, but did not stop the segregation.

Supporters of *Brown* expected President Eisenhower to back the *Brown* mandate, because he was certainly the most powerful and commanding white leader and, as president, had the moral authority to influence the public debate on integration. Moreover, Eisenhower was very popular among white business leaders in the South and leaders of the armed forces who would hold the keys to community responses to *Brown*.[6] Eisenhower, like many whites, considered himself a racially tolerant man and issued a number of presidential decrees in support of desegregation of federal facilities and schools in the District of Columbia. The public view, though, was that these actions were more ceremonial than substantive. Eisenhower also grew up at a time when segregation was the general practice in America, and he was well aware of its deleterious effects on African-Americans.

As a military man, Eisenhower had directly witnessed what should have provided him with an obvious model for action. His predecessor, President Harry Truman, had made impressive strides in the 1940s by mandating the integration of the armed forces and by making the public aware of the public benefits of an integrated America. Eisenhower did not follow Truman's lead in promoting integration. When he served in the army, it was still under the framework of Jim Crow, and Eisenhower opposed Truman's moves to desegregate the army, deeming them too disruptive.[7] This view informed his approach to school desegregation as well, especially as he saw his popularity rise with southern voters and had no desire to let the desegregation issue diminish his high approval ratings.

When the Supreme Court issued *Brown* in May 1954, Eisenhower accepted the decision, as he was bound to, but did not endorse it. Publicly he stated, "The Supreme Court has spoken, and I am sworn to uphold their—the constitutional processes in this country, and I am trying. I will obey." Privately, however, he stated that the Court's decision had set race relations progress back fifteen years and that desegregation could lead to social disintegration.[8] Indeed, though the segregationists who were opposed to *Brown* made their voices heard on the floor of Congress, on national television, and in public forums, the president did not respond.[9] Senator Harry Flood Byrd of Virginia coined the phrase "massive resistance," and 90 percent of the congressional delegation from the South signed a "Southern Manifesto," denouncing *Brown* as a "clear abuse of judicial power" and vowing to reverse it by using "all lawful means" at their disposal.[10]

Senator Strom Thurmond, meanwhile, called for the impeachment of Chief Justice Earl Warren and other members of the Court. When Eisenhower did speak out, he emphasized that integration should happen slowly. His position thus made it appear that any school district or judge calling for an expeditious implementation of *Brown* was taking an extremist stand.[11]

During the oral arguments in the *Brown* cases, Thurgood Marshall continually asserted that if an unyielding Supreme Court issued a stern decree, and if the executive branch supported it, the American people would follow, and desegregation would occur without major social upheaval.[12] The unfortunate reality was that the Court did not issue a stern decree and that there was no immediate executive enforcement. In the *Brown II* decision, issued on May 31, 1955, the Court refused to grant the petitioner's request that all schools be enjoined to desegregate immediately. It instead took a cautious approach—perhaps it knew that it would not have the backing of the Eisenhower administration or Congress to effectuate a swift and stern mandate. Neither of the other two branches of the federal government had expressed much enthusiasm for actions that would support or enforce the Court's order. Thus, the Court sent the school desegregation cases back to the federal district courts with directions to desegregate the schools "with all deliberate speed."[13]

The ruling did not ask the federal district courts to mandate that school districts formulate desegregation plans within any set time frame, and it did not set any time at which segregated schools would no longer be permitted. The only instruction the Court gave to the lower courts was to "require that the defendants make a prompt and reasonable start toward full compliance" with *Brown*.[14] In the District of Columbia, Missouri, Oklahoma, West Virginia, and Maryland, most school districts were able to work toward integration without any orders from a judge.

Brown II gave much of the discretion on how to carry out desegregation to federal district judges, but for more than a decade neither the Supreme Court nor the federal government gave them clear direction regarding desegregation.[15] Additionally, though the federal judges were supposed to be protected from political pressures, the district courts were located in communities in which "the segregated way of life was deemed very close to godliness."[16] Moreover, one could hardly expect these federal district courts to order immediate desegregation when the Supreme Court could not. As a result, many federal courts in the South delayed desegregation cases for long periods and then ordered only limited changes.

In the eleven states of the Deep South, the judges had the job of forcing compliance on unwilling school boards. Because President Eisenhower followed a policy of nonintervention on desegregation, the judges were less likely to act. Though the federal judges may have been politically insulated by lifetime appointments, they were still fearful of taking what could be perceived as an aggressive stance on integration, especially without the full backing of the federal government. Thus, if a judge could imagine a legitimate reason to delay, he would delay; in this way, "the most recalcitrant judge and the most defiant school board were allowed to set the pace."[17]

In the absence of strong leadership by the federal government, local officials did their best to thwart court orders of desegregation. They rushed to build schools before *Brown* came down to ensure that, while segregated, they were "equal." When the *Brown* decision overturned *Plessy*, most communities decided to wait and see what the decision really meant.

In many places, the decision did not pay any immediate dividends. Ten years after *Brown*, in fact, less than 3 percent of all black children in the South attended integrated schools. Northern segregation, meanwhile, was not chipped away at until the mid-1970s.[18] Some states, such as North Carolina, practiced token integration and positioned themselves to be somewhat conciliatory, thereby escaping judicial scrutiny of their public educational systems and actually experiencing less integration than those states that more fiercely resisted integration.[19]

From the White House to the city councils of the smallest towns, those in power found ways to either subtly defer or defiantly oppose desegregation. Thus the words "all deliberate speed" effectively lost their meaning. Several states—namely Alabama, Virginia, and Georgia—tried to deactivate the *Brown II* order by passing laws that forbade local authorities to desegregate, whether or not it was in compliance with a federal injunction.[20]

When the *Brown* decision was handed down, political leaders of several states denounced it. Senator James Eastland of Mississippi rebuked the justices, accusing them of perpetrating a "monstrous crime." Though many other southern states, such as Arkansas and Virginia, at first reacted more moderately, political leaders soon found that vocal opposition to *Brown* was an easy way to win support among white voters.[21] In fact, several notable southern political figures, including George Wallace and Orval Faubus, began as moderates on race issues, but later found that the key to success lay in vehemently opposing integration. Wallace, attributing his failure to win the 1960 Democratic gubernatorial nomination in Alabama to his moderate stance on race issues, declared that he would never be "outniggered" again. Following a racist campaign that awarded him the governorship, he affirmed this position in his 1963 inaugural address: "I draw the line in the dust and toss the gauntlet before the feet of tyranny, and I say, 'Segregation now! Segregation tomorrow! Segregation forever!'"[22]

Similarly, Governor Faubus of Arkansas chose the segregation issue as the cornerstone of his campaign for a third term. And on September 3, 1957, he called out the National Guard to prevent the integration of Central High School in Little Rock. When a federal district judge enjoined Faubus from keeping the black students from attending, Faubus sent the troops away and left the students to deal with the angry mob alone. President Eisenhower ultimately intervened, sending in army troops and federalized Arkansas National Guardsmen to protect the students, who finally attended a full day of classes on September 23.

The Little Rock school board reacted by stating that the disorder proved that desegregation had to be delayed further. This led to litigation, spearheaded by Thurgood Marshall, that turned into the landmark case of *Cooper v. Aaron.* In February 1958, the school board sought permission from the district court to suspend the court-approved integration plan. The board's position was that, because of extreme public hostility, the maintenance of a sound educational program at Central High School, with the Negro students in attendance, would be impossible. It therefore proposed that the Negro students already admitted to the school be withdrawn and sent to segregated schools, and that steps to implement the board's desegregation program be postponed for a period it later suggested should be two and one-half years.[23]

The district court granted permission after a hearing, but the Eighth Circuit reversed. The Supreme Court, infuriated that Arkansas was openly violating *Brown,* met in a special term to hear the case. The justices stated that the conditions in Arkansas were "directly traceable to the actions of legislators and executive officials of the State of Arkansas, taken in their official capacities, which reflect their own determination to resist this Court's decision in the *Brown* case and which have brought about violent resistance to that decision in Arkansas."[24] The Court proclaimed that the state could not deprive the black children of their constitutional rights in the face of the violence and disorder that the state had brought upon itself. It went on to affirm the basic principles of constitutional law and reminded the governor and legislature, "It is emphatically the province and duty of the judicial department to say what the law is."[25] Furthermore, the Court's interpretation of the Fourteenth Amendment in *Brown* was the supreme law of the land and had to be obeyed. Though the Court's pronouncement was a victory for the students in Little Rock and for all supporters of *Brown*, Governor Faubus went on to win four more campaigns for governor because of his resistance to the Court. He ordered the four high schools in Little Rock to be closed for the 1958–59 school year and became a hero to many whites across the South.[26]

As early as July 1955, the mettle of *Brown* was tested in the courts in the case of *Briggs v. Elliott*. In South Carolina, Judge James Parker, speaking for a three-judge federal district court, issued a ruling that threatened the force of *Brown*. The panel stated that the Supreme Court did not mean that "states must mix persons of different races in the public schools. . . . What it has decided and all it has decided is that a state may not deny any person on account of race the right to attend any school that it maintains. . . . The Constitution, in other words, does not require integration. . . . It merely forbids the use of governmental power to enforce segregation."[27] The panel also gave a clue as to how states could maintain segregation: "[I]f the schools which it maintains are open to children of all races, no violation of the Constitution is involved even though the children of different races voluntarily attend different schools, as they attend different churches. Nothing in the Constitution or in the decision of the Supreme Court takes away from the people freedom to choose the schools they attend."[28]

In November 1955, James Kilpatrick, editor of the *Richmond News Leader*, began to promote the doctrine of "interposition." Eleven states took part in the interpartisan movement, "interposing" their own authority to protect their citizens from unjust actions by the federal government. These states organized committees to promote segregation and blatantly flout the directives of *Brown*. Efforts included the burning of crosses and other forms of violence, legal action to enjoin segregation, and a media front. When a Louisiana-sponsored committee was criticized by the NAACP for attacking desegregation in a *New York Herald Tribune* advertisement, the newspaper responded that it had published the ad in the "best tradition of the free press."[29]

When blacks filed suit to bring about desegregation, they found that even though the law was on their side, their opponents had many of the advantages. For example, school boards would change the rules of the game during the middle of litigation. The recalcitrant states knew that even though many of their laws defying segregation would eventually be struck down, each law meant "another round of motions, briefs, hearings, rulings, and appeals." This in turn meant further delay of desegregation. As one segregationist stated, "As long as we can legislate, we can segregate."[30]

Southern cities soon learned that they had a tremendous arsenal in preventing desegregation. The most powerful weapon was actually closing schools when faced with a court order mandating desegregation. Several southern states, including Virginia and North Carolina, passed laws, often by referendums, either requiring the closure of integrated public schools or threatening to abolish public education altogether if the courts ordered desegregation.[31]

Like the students who bravely integrated schools in the South, those judges who took the mandate of *Brown* seriously faced violent opposition. Judge Richard Rives ruled in favor of blacks in Montgomery against the segregated city bus system in 1956. Following his order, he found that his son's gravesite had been desecrated, and many of his erstwhile friends abandoned him. Prior to the *Brown* decision, local whites threatened Judge Waties Waring, who had supported the plaintiffs in *Briggs v. Elliott*, by throwing a large lump of concrete through his window, barely missing him and his wife.[32]

Local governments found that the strategies they used to keep school desegregation at bay could be applied to preserving segregated neighborhoods as well. Many cities raced to rezone, rebuild, and redevelop in order to isolate black populations. Political appointment systems in some southern towns ensured that the influence of liberals was minimal. In Georgia, for example, 121 rural counties, accounting for only one-third of the state's population, were entirely responsible for nominating a governor.[33]

As the civil rights movement gained speed, President Kennedy started to pay attention. Partly in reaction to Governor Wallace's attempt to prevent integration at the University of Alabama, Kennedy introduced a civil rights bill in 1963, aimed at abolishing Jim Crow in public accommodations. After Kennedy's assassination, President Johnson became a supporter, albeit at times a reluctant one, of Kennedy's civil rights bill. In 1964, advocates of integration in Congress strengthened the bill; Congress passed it after Senator Hubert Humphrey of Minnesota guided it through the longest filibuster in Senate history. The

Civil Rights Act was the first major civil rights law in ninety years. Because discrimination was rendered illegal in all schools and other institutions receiving federal dollars, the real changes envisioned by *Brown* were now possible. The attorney general was authorized to bring suits against officials, including school administrators who perpetuated systems of de jure discrimination.[34]

Under President Johnson, the federal government vigorously enforced desegregation, and rapid and dramatic changes were realized in the South. The federal rules implementing the legislation became effective in 1965, and Justice Department civil rights lawyers began filing suits. The sanctions imposed by the law and the cutoffs to federal aid were effective tools to regulate school districts that refused to desegregate. One observer has noted that "just a few years of intensive enforcement was enough to transform Southern schools and to create much stricter and clearer desegregation standards."[35] However, this commitment lasted for only about three years, until President Nixon took office in 1969. During his presidential campaign, Nixon curried favor with white voters by attacking early busing policies. He believed that the Court had tried to force integration "too far too fast," and he wanted to be a leader in working to undo its decisions.[36] It is notable that Nixon expressed the view that desegregation was happening "too fast" in 1970, a full fifteen years after *Brown II*.

Nixon vehemently opposed the Court's decision in *Swann v. Charlotte-Mecklenburg Board of Education*,[37] finding post-*Brown* busing schemes an appropriate means of achieving desegregation. Nixon's antipathy to these measures went so far as to include support of a constitutional amendment to limit them.[38] Not coincidentally, he was to appoint to the Court the year that *Swann* came down the staunchly conservative William H. Rehnquist. The now–Chief Justice would become the Court's most apparent opponent of desegregation initiatives; in 1970, prior to his nomination, he had helped author for the White House the potential anti-busing amendment. Rehnquist's appointment by Nixon signified that president's rightward emphasis on the Court.[39]

In their book *Dismantling Segregation: The Quiet Reversal of Brown v. Board of Education*, professor Gary Orfield and Susan E. Eaton provide a compelling analysis of the political resistance to *Brown*. They track the role the Republican administrations played in appointing conservatives to the Supreme Court, helping to narrow the scope of *Brown*'s reach in desegregating public schools. They demonstrate that, even though a full decade passed before *Brown* began to be enforced, the 1960s saw great progress in the desegregation of public schools and other public accommodations. In 1974, however, the momentum stopped with the decision in *Milliken v. Bradley*,[40] which represented the first major Supreme Court move against school desegregation. In *Milliken*, the Court was faced with the most basic barrier to school desegregation, especially in northern urban areas—white suburbanization. In many districts, there were not enough white students for a sustainable program of desegregation. The lower courts thus approved a plan of desegregation that would go beyond the city (Detroit, in this case) and into the surrounding suburbs. Five justices—four of them appointed by Nixon—found that the plan unfairly punished the suburbs and contradicted longstanding principles of local control over schools. Without any discriminatory suburban or state action, relief that had a punitive effect on the suburbs could not be granted.[41] Detroit could desegregate only by mixing its few remaining white students with the black majority.

Chief Justice Warren Burger had asserted that local control of school districts was a "deeply rooted tradition." It was just this tradition that undermined *Brown* and that school districts were able to exploit in order to avoid *Brown*. The *Milliken* decision effectively meant no desegregation at all in Detroit. This suited the Nixon administration very well, fitting nicely with Nixon's attacks on busing and on efforts to open up suburban housing to black families. Nixon believed that compulsory desegregation measures were not crucial and that Congress should stop courts from compelling local districts to comply with "complicated plans drawn up by far-away officials in Washington, D.C."[42] His desire to allow desegregation to be dealt with on the most local of levels allowed communities to escape the mandate of *Brown*. As white suburbanization increased, the desegregation envisioned by *Brown* moved farther out of reach.

The *Brown* strategy was challenged, on the one hand, by officials in the executive and legislative branches who thought that the effort to desegregate the schools was moving too quickly and, on the other, by civil rights leaders who regarded the progress as far too slow. Thurgood Marshall would soon realize that the *Brown* strategy was not only vulnerable to attacks in the courts but also subject to questioning by the African-American community. While Marshall continued to press for legal reform, an effort was under way to fight segregation through political channels—an effort led by a Morehouse College–educated minister from Atlanta named Martin Luther King, Jr.

CHAPTER 9

MARSHALL AND KING:
TWO PATHS TO JUSTICE

In 1950, Thurgood Marshall faced new challenges in the effort to dismantle Jim Crow segregation. His mentor Charles Hamilton Houston had passed away, and he was left to lead the campaign for integration. By 1950, a young minister from Atlanta, Martin Luther King, Jr., was beginning to be recognized as a gifted leader of nonviolent efforts to end segregation through direct political action. The courses taken by Marshall and King were different, but complementary; *Brown* and its legacy might not have been possible without the contributions of both of these men. They followed separate paths to power and disagreed about the best strategy to further racial equality, but in the end both played a pivotal role in the civil rights movement in the 1950s and 1960s.

Thurgood Marshall was born in Baltimore, Maryland, in 1908, to Norma Arica Williams, a schoolteacher and one of the first blacks to graduate from Teachers College at Columbia University, and William Marshall, a dining steward at an exclusive white club and a railroad porter. Named for his paternal grandfather, a former slave, who changed his name to Thurgood when he joined the army during the Civil War, Marshall was first drawn to the law by the efforts of his father, who took him and his brother to the courthouse to watch trials.

In 1925, Marshall entered Lincoln University, the nation's oldest black college, in Chester, Pennsylvania. There he quickly got involved in the fight against racism, participating in a sit-in in a segregated theater the same year. Although Marshall also took advantage of the great social life at Lincoln, he did well academically, graduating cum laude in 1930. His classmates included Langston Hughes, a Harlem Renaissance writer and poet, and Kwame Nkrumah, later the first president of Ghana once it became the first African nation to gain independence from colonial rule, in 1957. Marshall wanted to attend the University of Maryland Law School, which was only ten minutes from his home, but did not even bother to apply, because of its segregationist policies—Maryland had graduated only two black students in its entire history. A disappointed Marshall was forced to commute forty miles to Howard University Law School, in Washington, D.C. This was, nonetheless, a fortunate turn of events that would alter the course of race relations in America. It was at Howard that Marshall met his future mentor Charles Hamilton Houston. Marshall graduated at the top of his law school class in 1933. Oliver Hill, a native of Richmond, Virginia, was second in the class, and their friendly academic rivalry created a formidable tag team of civil rights lawyers.

After graduation, Marshall opened his own law practice in Baltimore in the bleakest years of the Great Depression. He accepted cases even though his clients often could not pay him, and he used his legal skills to fight for equality. For example, in one of his earliest cases, he brought suit against the state of Maryland, which had been paying black teachers the same salary as janitors. He won the case and obtained raises for black teachers and principals.

Marshall also tackled segregation in higher education. As we saw in chapter 7, he brought suit against the University of Maryland Law School and even helped choose the man, Donald Murray, who would become the plaintiff in this case. Despite his credentials, Murray was denied admission twice, and the school suggested that he attend Howard Law School instead. Marshall successfully argued that the school's "separate but equal" policy violated due process of law under the federal Constitution, and the trial court ruled in his favor. On January 15, 1936, the Maryland Court of Appeals, the state's highest court, affirmed the trial court's decision—a case that Marshall later called his "sweet revenge"—and found that Murray would have to be admitted to the law school.[1]

Marshall's career showed early signs of remarkable promise. In 1936, he became assistant special counsel to the NAACP. Two years later, he became chief legal counsel, and in 1939 the NAACP created the Legal Defense Fund, which became a separate nonprofit organization under Marshall's direction. He led the legal battle against racial segregation and discrimination and successfully brought suit against the U.S. military, eventually forcing it to allow black soldiers to become officers and pilots after World War II. Marshall's work also contributed to Truman's 1947 establishment of the President's Committee on Civil Rights.

Marshall fought for racial equality in other contexts—for example, after the supreme court of Texas struck down the state's attempts to exclude black voters by statute and the state delegated control over primary elections to private organizations, which then discriminated against blacks. Marshall brought suit on behalf of Louis E. Smith, against S. W. Allwright, who was an election judge. In 1944, the Supreme Court found the white primary system unconstitutional in the case of *Smith v. Allwright*, and thus made it unconstitutional to deny the right to vote in primary elections on the basis of race.[2] Instrumental in ensuring the right of blacks to vote in the South, this case led to an increase in black voter registration. Marshall later called the case his "most significant victory—not excepting the *Brown v. Board of Education* decision."

In 1946, Marshall won *Morgan v. Virginia*, which prohibited segregated seating in interstate transportation, and in 1948,[3] he helped win *Shelley v. Kraemer*, a landmark decision in which the Supreme Court found that court enforcement of racially restrictive covenants, the clauses in housing contracts and deeds used to exclude blacks from white areas, violated the equal protection clause.[4] He also won numerous criminal cases in southern states, utilizing innovative legal arguments. Marshall attributed his success in all of these cases to the careful tutelage offered by Houston.

A growing number of victories paved the way and served as a preamble to the *Brown* decision. In 1953, Marshall began final arguments for *Brown v. Board of Education* before the U.S. Supreme Court. That year he attacked the "separate but equal" doctrine that had also played a central role in his suit against the University of Maryland, setting the stage for a legal victory that remained one year away.

By 1955, Marshall and other civil rights leaders had already begun assessing their victory in *Brown I* and *Brown II*. Featured on the cover of *Time* magazine, he was the most famous lawyer in the United States, a recognized champion of desegregation. He was well respected within the legal community and immensely popular in the black community. Meanwhile, Martin Luther King, Jr., was quickly gaining visibility as the leader of a local civil rights movement. Whereas Marshall believed that the best way to end segregation was through the court system, King advocated a strategy based on moral conviction and nonviolent political protests. King believed that nonviolence, in the face of angry response from whites, provided a more compelling story for the news media than did court decisions.

Although King began his fight for equality more than twenty years after Marshall, he quickly became a leading figure in the civil rights movement. He was born twenty-one years after Marshall, in 1929, in Atlanta. His father, the Reverend Martin Luther King, Sr., and mother, Alberta Williams King, recognized early on the importance of education, for they enrolled him in school at the age of five, although the legal age was six for his elementary school. When his age was discovered, he was not allowed to continue to attend school until he turned six.

Like Marshall, King was a gifted student. He skipped both the ninth and the twelfth grades and was admitted to the prominent historically black Morehouse College because of his high scores on the college entrance exams, even though he was only fifteen. Graduating from Morehouse in 1948, King enrolled in the Crozer Theological Seminary in Chester, Pennsylvania, where Marshall had attended Lincoln University in the 1920s. Eventually elected president of the senior class, he won an award for being the "most outstanding student," as well as a fellowship for graduate study. He earned his divinity degree in 1951 and then chose to study theology at Boston University and Harvard University, receiving a Ph.D. in 1955 from Boston University.

King was catapulted to national prominence by the Montgomery bus boycott. On December 2, 1955, Mrs. Rosa Parks, a seamstress and former secretary to the president of the NAACP, was arrested in Montgomery, Alabama, for refusing to give up her seat on a segregated bus to a white passenger. King, then a pastor of the Baptist church in Montgomery to which Parks belonged, called a meeting at his church in response to the incident. A large crowd attended, and King stated that the only way to respond was to boycott the bus company. The boycott began just three days later, on December 5, with very few blacks still riding the buses. King helped form an organization, called the Montgomery Improvement Association, to oversee future action, and was elected president. The boycott lasted for over one year. Not until the U.S. Supreme Court struck down Alabama's public transportation segregation laws and issued federal injunctions did the boycott end, and the young Georgia native became the leader in the civil rights movement. He was arrested thirty times for his efforts to further the movement.

Despite Marshall's apparent success in employing his integration strategy, King's extrajudicial efforts took center stage in the media. King received acclaim when he was awarded the Nobel Peace Prize, in 1964, at the age of thirty-five, and notoriety by becoming the FBI's most investigated public figure. By all accounts, King reached the pinnacle of his extraordinary career on August 28, 1963, when he led the March on Washington. Over 200,000 Americans gathered near the Lincoln Memorial, and although many other civil rights activists also spoke, it was King's "I Have a Dream" speech, calling for the end of segregation and envisioning the benefits of an integrated society, that remains memorable. Many people shared his hope that his children, in a future integrated and equal America, would be judged not by the color of their skin but by the content of their character. What few remember is the part of King's speech that resonated with a frustrated black population, impatient with the slow progress in race relations:

> But one hundred years later, the Negro still is not free; one hundred years later, the life of the Negro is still sadly crippled by the manacles of segregation and the chains of discrimination; one hundred years later, the Negro lives on a lonely island of poverty in the midst of a vast ocean of material prosperity; one hundred years later, the Negro is still languishing in the corners of American society and finds himself an exile in his own land.
> So we've come here today to dramatize a shameful condition.[5]

In 1965, King helped lead a fifty-mile march from Selma to Montgomery, protesting racially discriminatory voting practices. This march faced violent opposition and drew national attention, which aided the passage of the Voting Rights Act just months later. King actually met with President Johnson and conveyed his views about the provisions the act should contain.

King has also been credited with being one of the early proponents of affirmative action. Speaking in 1968 for the last time at the National Cathedral in Washington, D.C., King declared, "They say the Negro must lift himself by his own bootstraps. . . . The people who say this never stop to realize that the nation made the black man's color a stigma; but beyond this they never stop to realize the debt they owe a people who were kept in slavery 244 years."[6] President Johnson later appeared to adopt this view in his famous 1965 commencement speech at Howard University, in which he attempted to provide a philosophical justification for the eradication of discrimination, arguing that equal opportunity was "not enough" because we need "[n]ot just equality as a right and a theory but equality as a fact and equality as a result."[7]

As King rose to prominence as the civil rights leader, Marshall took on the role of jurist. In 1961, after winning twenty-nine of the thirty-two cases he argued before the Supreme Court, he was appointed by President Kennedy the first African-American to serve on the Court of Appeals for the Second Circuit. In 1965, President Johnson appointed him the first black solicitor general and, later, the first black Supreme Court justice. Johnson subsequently referred to the latter appointment as "the right thing to do, the right time to do it, the right man and the right place."[8] However, Marshall's voice was to be muted because on the Court he faced a resolutely conservative majority, and he began to lose influence in the civil rights movement.

Although my parents never mentioned the name of Thurgood Marshall, the young Baltimore lawyer who won the *Brown* case, they were quick to praise Dr. Martin Luther King, Jr., the young Baptist preacher who was leading the effort to organize marches and demonstrations in order to strike a blow against segregation. Dr. King became a household name in the late 1950s, even in the Ogletree home. When my parents found his picture in the newspaper, they placed it in the living room, next to the pictures of Jesus Christ, a staple in nearly every black home of that generation.

Less than one year after Marshall's historic appointment, on April 4, 1968, King was struck down by an assassin's bullet in Memphis. Almost immediately, black rage exploded throughout America. Riots erupted in Washington, D.C., Baltimore, Chicago, and many other urban communities. Strangely enough, these riots provided the major

A class photograph of Charles Ogletree's virtually all African-American and
Latino third-grade class at Galen Clark Elementary School in Merced, California.
Ogletree is in the top row, third from the right. (November 1961)

A class photograph of Charles Ogletree's all African-American and Latino fifth-grade
class at Galen Clark Elementary School in Merced, California. Ogletree is in the front
row, second from the left. (October 1963)

Mr. Willie Reed, son Charlie Reed, and wife, Essie D. Reed.
(1965)

Picture of Essie D. Reed, grandmother, and Nadine Reed
Washington, daughter of Essie D. Reed. (1967)

Ogletree presiding over a meeting as the first elected African-American student body president at Merced High School. (October 1970)

Ogletree is one of two African-American students to receive state scholarships at Merced High School. Ogletree is in the front row, third from left. (March 1971)

Denise Schnyder and Lynn Vitero, two Stanford undergraduates, raising funds for Angela Davis's defense. (December 1971)

Dr. St. Clair Drake, Ogletree's mentor at Stanford. (Spring 1973)

Ogletree leads Stanford student demonstration promoting affirmative action and recruitment of minority faculty. (Spring 1975)

Black students at Sanford march out of graduation where Daniel Patrick Moynihan was the commencement speaker. (June 15, 1975)

Attorney Theodore Landsmark assaulted with an American flag during the Boston busing crisis. ("Violence in Boston," courtesy Stanley Forman, Pulitzer Prize, 1977)

Charles (left) with Charles Ogletree, Sr. (right), and Robert Ogletree, Sr. (center), at Supreme Court swearing-in ceremony. (May 31, 1983)

Charles (back row, second from left) with his mother, Willie Mae Ogletree (front left), and sisters and brothers at his mother's sixtieth birthday party. (March 1984)

Photograph of the District of Columbia Public Defender Service attorneys and staff. (1984)

Charles Ogletree's daughter, son, and other friends congratulate him after he argued the death-penalty case *Ford v. Georgia* before the Supreme Court. The Supreme Court issued a unanimous decision reversing Ogletree's client's death-penalty conviction. (November 6, 1990)

Anita Hill legal team during confirmation hearings. From left to right: (standing) Sonia Jarvis, Warner Gardner, John Frank, Charles Ogletree, Kim Taylor, Shirley Wiegand; (seated) Kim Crenshaw, Janet Napolitano, Emma Jordan, Anita Hill, Susan Deller Ross. (October 1991)

Charles and Pam on their twentieth wedding anniversary on Martha's Vineyard. (August 1995)

Pamela Ogletree, Scott Darling, Kathy Reddick, and Caroline Hunter, founders of the Benjamin Banneker Charter School, during painting and repair work prior to opening of the school in Cambridge, Massachusetts. (July 1996)

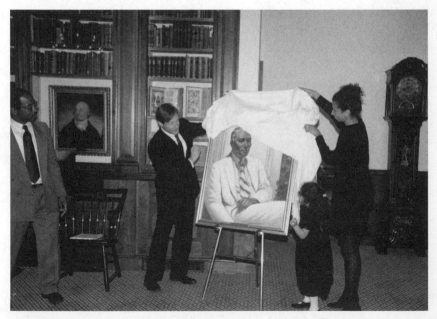

Charles Ogletree, Dean Robert Clark, and members of Charles Hamilton Houston's family unveil Houston's portrait on the seventy-fifth anniversary of his graduation from Harvard Law School. (Fall 1998)

A Celebration of Black Alumni at Harvard Law School on September 22–24, 2000.
Professor Ogletree is in the front row on the left.

Ogletree presents a $50,000 check in honor of his mentors in Merced to initiate the Ogletree Scholarship Fund for Merced students in the Juneteenth celebration on June 16, 2002. (Marci Stenberg)

Kaiser Family Foundation's celebration of the AIDS-HIV initiative in South America, with former president Clinton and Nelson Mandela. (September 2002)

Photo of Otis Clark (second from right), a hundred-year-old client in the Tulsa reparations case, with his attorneys Charles Ogletree (right), Johnnie Cochran (second from left), and Dennis Sweet (left) on February 27, 2003, the day before the filing of the 1921 Tulsa race riots reparations lawsuit. (James Kavin Ross/ *The Oklahoma Eagle*)

The Reparations Coordinating Committee files the Tulsa reparations lawsuit on behalf of the survivors of the 1921 Tulsa race riot, February 28, 2003. (James Kavin Ross/*The Oklahoma Eagle*)

Professor Ogletree meets with one of his clients in the Tulsa race riot reparations case, the legendary historian Dr. John Hope Franklin. (December 16, 2003)

impetus for the enactment of the Civil Rights Act of 1968 and the Fair Housing Act, and for the acceleration of other reforms.

Now, decades later, it appears that Marshall's contributions to the civil rights movement, which have been extensively discussed within the legal community, have been largely overlooked by the American public. Marshall is more widely known for his role as the first African-American Supreme Court justice than for his contributions to the civil rights movement. In contrast, King has become something of a legend, and his name is everywhere—on streets, libraries, schools, scholarships, and awards. Martin Luther King Day, which became a national holiday in 1986, was the first new holiday created since Memorial Day in 1948. Still, though Marshall currently receives less recognition than either King or Malcolm X, some observers, including the late Justice Lewis Powell, have concluded that he did more to further equality under the law than any other individual.

The civil rights careers of Marshall and King illustrate two different approaches to the rule of law, and two different philosophies of democratic action. Marshall's approach was to reform the law by means of the law; King's appeal, most fully developed in his famous "Letter from Birmingham Jail," was that the rule of law must give way to the higher law of justice and that civil disobedience—action contrary to the law of the land—was not only an acceptable but a necessary reaction to an unjust law.

In "Letter from Birmingham Jail," King explained his impatience with the normal course of legal change and the continued role that morality played in the efforts to promote integration:

> We know through painful experience that freedom is never voluntarily given by the oppressor; it must be demanded by the oppressed. Frankly, I have never yet engaged in a direct action movement that was "well-timed," according to the timetable of those who have not suffered unduly from the disease of segregation. For years now I have heard the word "Wait!" It rings in the ear of every Negro with piercing familiarity. This "Wait" has almost always meant "Never." . . . We must come to see with the distinguished jurist of yesterday that "justice too long delayed is justice denied."[9]

These two conflicting approaches were played out throughout the federal legal system, from the Supreme Court to Judge Frank M. Johnson's district court (where King litigated some of his most famous issues, including the Montgomery bus boycott and the Selma-to-Montgomery march). For example, in his dissenting opinion in *Walker v. City of Birmingham*, Chief Justice Earl Warren appeared to endorse King's view: "[I]t shows no disrespect for the law to violate a statute on the ground that it is unconstitutional and then to submit one's case to the courts with the willingness to accept the penalty if the statute is held to be valid."[10] However, the majority, led by Justice Hugo L. Black, appeared to equate civil disobedience with anarchy, and King's taking to the streets seemed comparable to the massive resistance he sought to oppose. Much more preferable, according to Black, was the litigation strategy then pursued by the NAACP:

> [W]e are asked to hold that this rule of law, upon which the Alabama courts relied, was constitutionally impermissible. We are asked to say that the Constitution compelled Alabama to allow the petitioners to violate this injunction, to organize and engage in these mass street parades and demonstrations, without any previous effort on their part to have the injunction dissolved or modified, or any attempt to secure a parade permit in accordance with its terms. . . . [W]e cannot accept the petitioners' contentions in the circumstances of this case. . . . The rule of law that Alabama followed in this case reflects a belief that in the fair administration of justice no man can be judged in his own case, however exalted his station, however righteous his motives, and irrespective of his race, color, politics, or religion. This court cannot hold that the petitioners were constitutionally free to ignore all the procedures of the law and carry their battle to the streets. One may sympathize with the petitioners' impatient commitment to their cause. But respect for judicial process is a small price to pay for the civilizing hand of law, which alone can give abiding meaning to constitutional freedom.[11]

Both Marshall and King emphasized the place of law in an unjust society, and both sought to determine acceptable responses to an unjust law. Their differences were both philosophical and political and set the stakes for the first part of the civil rights movement, presaging the mass riots in the late 1960s. But their debate was also about who bears the burden of racial progress and racial reconciliation. King's view that it was the task of African-Americans to redeem the country from its racist past was an integral part of his politics. Given the strong moral nature of his appeal, and his insistence on a nonviolent movement, in contrast to whites' violent resistance to integration, his strategy generated extensive media coverage, and national attention on civil rights, making him the public face of civil rights progress. Although Marshall and King disagreed about the right course to end segregation, both of their strategies were correct and necessary. The importance of their dual roles was evident even after the 1954 *Brown* decision. Both men increased their efforts to win the integration battle, in the courtrooms and on the streets, respectively.

It was perhaps inevitable, given their differing ideologies, that privately Marshall would express disapproval for King. Marshall firmly believed in a system of laws and working within the legal system in order to effect change. He disapproved of "lawless" direct action, even if nonviolent. It was counterproductive, he held, to break the law as King did. He was particularly horrified by King's use of children in the Birmingham march. In view of the riots and unrest that often accompanied King's demonstrations, it is not surprising that Marshall called him a "first-rate rabble-rouser" and a "boy on a man's errand" and complained about always "saving King's bacon."[12]

Nevertheless, although Marshall did not support King's strategies, he insisted on providing legal representation and bail money to King and others who were arrested in their protests. This relegated Marshall and the NAACP's legal teams to a support role in these civil rights developments. Furthermore, King's efforts sometimes even had extreme negative consequences for the NAACP legal team. For example, it was the NAACP legal team that actually brought the suit that ended segregation in the Montgomery bus system, but King received much of the credit for the victory. Yet the state segregationist leaders blamed the NAACP for the boycott and succeeded in obtaining an injunction that prevented the NAACP from operating in Alabama for the next eight years.

Just as the NAACP litigated many of the cases brought against King and other civil rights leaders, King's political protests benefited the legal battles. Without them, "all deliberate speed" might have been no speed at all.

PART III

Clifton Graves and other black law students at a
1977 protest in Washington, D.C., the day before
Bakke was argued.

CHAPTER 10

REVERSING THE *BROWN* MANDATE: THE *BAKKE* CHALLENGE

I n the years following *Brown*, the Supreme Court moved from simply prohibiting segregation to stating that school districts bear "an affirmative duty to take whatever steps might be necessary to [achieve an integrated system] in which racial discrimination would be eliminated root and branch."[1] Put differently, the Court recognized that providing the opportunity for integration was not enough: some positive, remedial steps needed to be taken to ensure that black citizens and students were not denied equal benefit of the laws. President Johnson's "Great Society" was but the political expression of this goal.

Although in the South, colleges, universities, and graduate schools had been the site of the initial battle over equalization, by the 1970s many of these establishments had become engines for integration. Many of this country's colleges and universities recognized that it was part of their mission to create the leaders of the future. For example, W. J. Bender, then the Harvard College dean of admissions, claimed that "if scholarly excellence were the sole or even predominant criterion, Harvard College would lose a great deal of its vitality and intellectual excellence and that the quality of the educational experience offered to all students would suffer." In a report addressing fears similar to those articulated by the provost at the time, Paul Buck, Dean Bender expressed his worry about the balance between "democratic selection" and "aristocratic achievement."[2] There was a concern about the homogeneity of students who, though intelligent, came from the same social, cultural, and economic backgrounds.

Wilbur J. Bender, a Harvard graduate originally from the Midwest and from poor origins, wanted a student body that comprised diverse talents and backgrounds.[3] When faced with the assertion that Harvard was losing its appeal, he said that this was inconsequential if the person who was losing interest was the "well-dressed polite, Nordic blonde from a family with an income of $20,000 a year and up, living in a swanky suburb." His primary concern was to "keep some kind of balance among the diverse groups needed to make a healthy student body." In attempting to achieve this balance, Bender developed an elaborate plan to place greater weight on nonacademic factors. This was done in part, according to Bender, to combat "the notion that [Harvard is] just a grind factory full of goggle-eyed bifocal geniuses or precious effeminate types none of whom speak to each other, have any juice in their veins or give a damn about normal, healthy aspects of life."[4]

Of course, Harvard had never been just a college for the goggle-eyed. Its reputation for liberalism had always been overstated, given its policies of denying admittance to women, its tendency to discriminate against racial minorities and especially Jews, its reliance on the legacy admissions system, its focus on attracting a variety of athletes, and its concentration on men from northeastern United States. But a diverse student body promised more than increasingly diverse pools of excellence in which Harvard could fish for America's brightest students; it provided a means of exporting the Harvard mystique to a much greater segment of the population, and a correspondingly greater pool of alumni and alumnae from which to garner funds for the university. Producing leaders in different segments of the community directly benefited Harvard, financially and institutionally; thus, for Harvard—and for all the other educational institutions that made diversity one of their goals—diversity was not so much backward looking, but it rested on the contribution an individual's personal history could make to the classroom and to academic discussion. Harvard, like many other colleges and universities, was diversifying its sources of future income and, secondarily, engaging in a massive project of social engineering that benefited not only African-Americans but, even more, the many white women now permitted to attend these formerly all-male bastions of education, privilege, and power.

The court system in general, insofar as it acted as a mechanism of social (and particularly racial) reform, faced a choice in the methods of accomplishing that reform. Should the Constitution be read in a color-blind manner, as Justice Harlan (grandfather to the Warren Court justice of the same name) had counseled in his famous dissent in *Plessy v. Ferguson* in 1896? Or should the law attempt to combat racial injustice in a color-conscious manner, as did the Civil Rights Act of 1866 (commonly referred to as "Section 1981," after its position in the U.S. Code)? Many whites viewed the race-conscious approach in the manner of the Supreme Court at the height of its dismantling of Reconstruction:

> When a man has emerged from slavery, and by the aid of beneficent legislation has shaken off the inseparable concomitants of that state, there must be some stage in the progress of his elevation when he takes the rank of a mere citizen, and ceases to be the special favorite of the laws, and when his rights as a citizen, or a man, are to be protected in the ordinary modes by which other men's rights are protected.[5]

During the 1960s, the courts and other institutions came to realize that much more was needed to remedy the inequalities produced by centuries of racial discrimination. Racially neutral programs had thus yielded to programs that gave a preference to members of groups that had been the victims of past discrimination. Affirmative action programs were becoming standard in educational institutions and government programs. They began in the federal government and were given their name by President Kennedy.[6]

NEARLY TWENTY-FIVE YEARS after the landmark *Brown* decision, a major challenge to its underlying principles of equality in education was emerging. The timing was significant for me in that I was among the large wave of first-generation African-Americans going to college and graduate school. Even though *Brown* paved the way by removing the barrier of segregated educational systems, it remained to be seen who would now have the opportunity to attend the prestigious institutions that had been substantially, if not completely, closed to African-Americans. While the battle for integration continued in the courtrooms around America, the shocking assassination of Martin Luther King, Jr., in April 1968, triggered a chain reaction of nationwide black protest; it also forced many institutions to open their doors much faster than they had contemplated. Harvard Law School was no different. A private institution, it claimed that its doors had always been open to people regardless of color (although women were not admitted until 1953), and it could point out that George Lewis Ruffin, an African-American, had graduated from the law school in 1869 (which, coincidentally, was the year that Howard Law School was founded), but there was still no real effort to seek out and admit African-Americans.

As late as 1965, Conrad Harper, who subsequently served with the NAACP Legal Defense and Education Fund, was the only African-American in his graduating class. Although Harvard did little to recruit and admit African-Americans before King's assassination, the school did organize a legal preparatory institute in 1965, bringing African-American women and men on campus for a summer institute to prepare them for the study of law. Harvard made it clear that this program, distinctive at the time, was not a road to admission to Harvard, but simply a benevolent effort to introduce aspiring students to the study of law. It enabled Harvard to attract some young students who ultimately made a powerful impact on the legal profession. Reginald Lewis, the billionaire entrepreneur, made a $3 million gift to Harvard Law School in 1993 (after first giving Howard Law School $1 million, even though he did not attend Howard) and is viewed as one of Harvard's most successful graduates. Rudolph Pierce, a native of Roxbury and a former state court judge, was in the same summer institute and is now a prominent practitioner in Boston. James McPherson also attended the institute and Harvard Law School, but rather than practicing law went on to write a Pulitzer Prize–winning book. Many of the others who attended the institute, such as A. C. and Ruby Wharton, did not attend Harvard Law School, but became successful practitioners—back in their home state of Tennessee, in the Whartons' case. By all accounts, Harvard's early attempts to expose African-Americans to the possibility of legal careers reaped immediate dividends.

When I arrived in the fall of 1975, Harvard Law School was admitting fifty to sixty African-American students each year, nearly 10 percent of its entering class. Harvard was, in fact, admitting more African-American students than any of its peer institutions and, with the exception of Howard Law School, was at the top of all law schools in the number of minority students enrolled. Some twenty-five years after *Brown*, diversity appeared to be a permanent part of Harvard's educational mission. Our sense of comfort was nearly shattered, however, when Allan Bakke, a white student who had applied to the University of California at Davis Medical School and been rejected, filed a suit challenging an admissions program that affirmatively recruited and admitted African-American and Chicano applicants. The lawsuit called the *Brown* case into question, and squarely raised the issue of what public institutions could do, or not do, to increase the deplorably low representation of minorities in their universities and graduate schools.

Already less than twenty years after *Brown*, the modest success of the NAACP began to show signs of eroding. By 1970 Earl Warren was gone as chief justice and, by 1978, so were many of the great judges of the Warren Court. Throughout the 1960s, the Supreme Court had ratified almost every lawsuit brought by the NAACP to end discrimination. Justices Hugo Black, William O. Douglas, John Harlan, Arthur Goldberg, and Abe Fortas had all left the bench. President Nixon's and, later, President Ford's more conservative appointees, including Chief Justice Warren Burger and Justices John Paul Stevens, William Rehnquist, and Harry Blackmun, replaced them. With this changing of the guard, the Court's receptivity to the old civil rights agenda began to wane, until even the stalwart of the NAACP's litigation strategy—graduate education—came under attack.

In 1971, Marco DeFunis, Jr., brought an action against the University of Washington Law School, contending that its admissions process violated the equal protection clause by discriminating against him as a white applicant. The trial court agreed with DeFunis's claim and ordered his admission to the law school—an order that the University of Washington reluctantly followed. The judgment was reversed on appeal, but by this time DeFunis was in his second year of law school. The Supreme Court determined that since DeFunis was in law school, the matter did not raise an issue that was ripe for a decision, and declined to accept the case. The issues the case raised, however, would not be so easily dismissed. A white applicant to medical school a few years later would find fertile ground to renew the challenge.

Allan Paul Bakke was born in 1940, in Minneapolis. In 1958, he graduated from high school as a National Merit Scholarship Finalist. He subsequently attended the University of Minnesota, where he majored in mechanical engineering. During college, he maintained a

3.51 grade point average.[7] After his graduation, he served in the marines for four years, achieving the rank of captain.[8] He then worked as an engineer with the NASA Ames Research Center,[9] while simultaneously completing a master's degree at Stanford University.[10]

In 1972, after working with NASA for six years, Bakke began applying to medical schools.[11] He was thirty-two at the start of his application process (he would be thirty-three when he brought his lawsuit). Over a two-year period, Bakke applied to eleven medical schools, including Northwestern, the University of Southern California, UCLA, the University of California at San Francisco, the University of Minnesota, Mayo Medical School, Wayne State University, Georgetown, the University of Cincinnati, Bowman Gray Medical School at Wake Forest University, and the University of California at Davis.[12] He was rejected by all of them despite "[high] undergraduate grades . . . laudatory recommendation letters, proven motivation and professional background, and medical school admissions test scores substantially higher than those of the average medical student admitted to Davis that year."[13]

Disappointed with his first rejection from UC Davis, Bakke wrote a letter to its admissions committee, expressing his views against racial quotas, and indicated that he was considering the possibility of suing for admission.[14] Peter Storandt, assistant to the dean of admissions at Davis, answered Bakke's first letter, informing him that he came very close to being admitted and encouraging him to reapply for the early admissions program that fall. He also suggested that Bakke continue to look into the use of racial quotas in the UC Davis "special admission process," which set aside sixteen out of one-hundred places for individuals, particularly members of minorities, who had suffered economic or educational disadvantage. He even gave Bakke the names of two attorneys who were well versed in challenges to racially motivated admissions policies.[15] Because of his advice, Storandt has been regarded as an instrumental figure in Bakke's ultimate decision to bring suit against the university.

In the spring of 1974, Bakke received his second rejection letter from the UC Davis School of Medicine. He also received rejection letters from the other medical schools that he applied to. The Davis admissions committee told Bakke that his age worked strongly against him: "The committee believes that an older applicant must be unusually highly qualified if he is to be seriously considered." Dr. Theodore West, who interviewed Bakke for Davis, wrote that he was "a well-qualified candidate for admission whose main handicap is the unavoidable fact that he is now 33 years of age." Another admissions committee member described Bakke as a "rigidly oriented young man, who has the tendency to arrive at conclusions based more upon his personal impressions than upon thoughtful processes using available sources of information." As a result, the faculty interviewer recommended Bakke as an "acceptable, but certainly not an outstanding candidate."[16] Bakke's second application was rejected in both the early decision pool and the general application pool.

Bakke's assertion that the affirmative action program denied him a seat in the entering class at UC Davis has not gone unchallenged. As Goodwin Liu has noticed, while Bakke presented his case as one that should compare his score with those of the minority students who were admitted through the special program, the real question is why a candidate whose scores were better than that of the average white students who were admitted through the regular admissions process was himself denied admission. In fact, Bakke's scores were not better than all of those students who benefited from the special admissions process; and that process was not, at least on paper, focused on race. Over one hundred *white* students in each of 1973 and 1974 were considered for the places set aside for the special admissions process. Bakke was not so considered, because he did not fit the criteria for economic or educational disadvantage. Furthermore, white students with lower scores than Bakke's were considered and admitted through the normal process.

After receiving his rejection letter, Bakke retained legal counsel, Reynold H. Colvin, an established San Francisco lawyer. Prior to taking any legal action, Bakke discussed his intentions with Storandt, who expressed sympathy with Bakke's situation and offered him advice on litigation strategies. On June 20, 1974, Colvin brought suit in the Yolo County California Superior Court in front of Judge F. Leslie Manker, a sixty-seven-year-old asked to come out of retirement to hear the case because of the heavy backlog of the other sitting judges.

Colvin's theory was that the equal protection clause of the Fourteenth Amendment, the California constitution's article I, and Title VI of the 1964 Civil Rights Act prohibited a public state university from setting aside sixteen of the one hundred seats in the entering class for "economically and/or educationally disadvantaged" applicants from one of four minority groups: "black, Chicano, Asian, and American Indians." According to Colvin's complaint, Davis's separate consideration of minority applicants for sixteen spots was an unconstitutional quota—regardless of the benevolence of the social goals that the admission policy promoted—that served to reduce, by virtue of race alone, the number of spots for which Bakke could compete. The complaint alleged that "the sole reason [Bakke's] application was rejected was that he was of the Caucasian race." It also alleged "that all students admitted under the special program were members of racial minorities, that the program applied separate, i.e., preferential, standards of admission as to them, and that the use of separate standards resulted in the acceptance of minority applicants who were less qualified for the study of medicine than Bakke and other nonminority applicants not selected."[17]

The complaint sought mandatory, declaratory, and injunctive relief to compel by court order Bakke's admission to Davis. This placed the burden of proof on Bakke to show that he would have been admitted to Davis had it not been for the racial quotas of the admissions program. Davis filed a cross-claim asking the court to declare its special admissions program constitutional and not in violation of Title VI. The university argued that it considered the minority status of an applicant as only one factor in admissions decisions, and that the purposes of the special admissions program were to promote diversity in the student body and the medical profession and to expand medical education opportunities to persons from economically or educationally disadvantaged backgrounds.[18]

In November 1974, the trial court ruled that the special admissions program involved a racial quota, because minority applicants in that program were rated only against one another and because sixteen places in the class of one hundred were reserved exclusively for them. Although Judge Manker ruled that Bakke was entitled to have his application reviewed without consideration of his race or the race of other applicants, he did not order Bakke admitted to Davis, since there was no clear way to show that he would have been admitted in the absence of the program.[19] In May 1976, Bakke appealed Judge Manker's decision, and the University of California appealed the portion of the decision holding that its special admissions program was unlawful.

In September 1976, the California Supreme Court declared the Davis special admissions program unconstitutional by a vote of 6 to 1. Chief Justice Stanley Mosk's opinion, applying the strict scrutiny standard, found that although integrating the medical profession and increasing the number of doctors willing to serve minority patients were valid and compelling state interests, the special admissions program was not an appropriate way to achieve those ends. The court held that the program violated the equal protection clause, and directed the trial court to order Bakke's admission to Davis.[20] Justice Matthew Tobriner, the sole dissenter, filed a fifty-seven-page dissent maintaining that the special admissions program was constitutional.[21]

In December 1976, the University of California appealed to the U.S. Supreme Court. The *Bakke* case generated significant public debate and national interest. More than fifty groups, including several universities and organizations such as the NAACP and ACLU, submitted amicus curiae briefs. The vast majority of the briefs supported the University of California's special admissions program.

Among the amicus briefs filed was one by Harvard University, defending "race sensitive" admissions on the grounds that diversity of background enriched the exchange of ideas among students. Derek Curtis Bok, president of Harvard since 1971, supported the brief and countered the objections by a few faculty members that Harvard's intervention was an inappropriate political statement.[22] Formerly professor and dean of Harvard Law School, Bok as president was preoccupied with exploring "the proper nature of [Harvard's] social responsibilities."[23] Many believed that when he departed, in 1991, he left behind a more worldly Harvard, responsive to both the needs and the dictates of the outside world.

Another Harvard Law School professor, former Supreme Court law clerk, former solicitor general of the United States, and the independent prosecutor selected to investigate President Nixon's Watergate actions also played a prominent role in the *Bakke* case. Archibald Cox was in 1978 widely viewed as one of the nation's foremost constitutional law scholars. UC Davis hired him to argue on its behalf and defend the admissions program before the Supreme Court. Having enjoyed considerable success in arguments before the Court, he was the right man for the job.

In my second year at Harvard Law School, I was elected national chairman of the Black Law Students Association. In that capacity, I asked Professor Cox to meet with me to discuss the *Bakke* case. To my utter surprise, he agreed. I explained the importance of this case to the future of affirmative action and asked whether we could do anything to help him. Cox, with whom I had not taken any classes, listened intently, even taking notes on his legendary yellow pad, and was incredibly respectful. I don't know what he was thinking at the time, but when I left his office, which was in the stacks of Langdell Hall near our library, it dawned upon me that I was trying to give legal advice about a Supreme Court argument to perhaps the most brilliant Supreme Court lawyer of all time! But *Bakke* was so important to me that I was unwilling to let my status as a mere law student keep me from doing everything I possibly could to prevent a wrong decision by the Court.

I did not stop with Cox. We went to Washington with other civil rights leaders to make the same appeal to another Harvard Law School graduate who would play a pivotal role in the case, Wade McCree. Surprisingly, McCree seemed less forthcoming about the government's commitment to affirmative action than Cox. I regarded McCree as a "race man," who would sympathize with our plight. At that time, however, McCree considered himself the government's top lawyer, as solicitor general, and his constituency was the American people; his boss was the president of the United States; his allegiance was to the Court, to offer his objective view of where the law should lead the Court in the *Bakke* case. This battle, I soon realized, would be more difficult than I had imagined.

Wade McCree, an African-American who served on the *Harvard Law Review* while attending law school, was appointed solicitor general by President Jimmy Carter and was expected to argue the case in front of the only other black man who had held the post of solicitor general before him, Justice Thurgood Marshall. McCree had attended the exclusive Boston Latin School, which would, in subsequent years, be the subject of a lawsuit to dismantle an affirmation action program designed to attract more minority students to this college-preparatory school.[24] Upon graduation he had intended to attend the University of Iowa to earn his undergraduate degree, but when he learned that black students were denied space in the residence halls, he opted instead for Fisk, a historically black college. In 1942, McCree entered Harvard Law School with a scholarship and graduated twelfth in his class. It is important to note that, when McCree came to Harvard, there were no programs focused on recruiting qualified minorities to the law school. Perhaps his own experiences of succeeding as an individual, before *Brown* and before *Bakke*, intuitively influenced his subtle thinking about the value of a race-based admissions policy. Of course, his judicial experience might well have affected his thinking on the subject of race and integration as well. In 1961, John F. Kennedy appointed him to the U.S. District Court for the Eastern District of Michigan, where he served until 1966, when President Johnson named him to the U.S. Court of Appeals for the Sixth Circuit, the first black to hold the position.[25]

Although McCree's formal role was that of solicitor general, he was also viewed as President Carter's spokesman in the Supreme Court. His role, however, took on additional significance in the *Bakke* case. McCree rejected the suggestion that he should be true to "the black community," responding that he had to be true to himself.[26]

Like many African-Americans, I felt that a political solution should also be pursued. As a result, black law students, labor unions, civil rights groups, and women's groups, among others, started to organize rallies around the country in defense of affirmative action. I was able to attend a conference in Philadelphia, organized by the dean at the University of Pennsylvania Law School, Louis Pollak, whose law school joined Harvard and other schools in supporting affirmative action in admission to graduate schools. Coincidentally, Pollak was a lawyer who had worked on the *Brown* case. Marches were held around the country, culminating in a massive demonstration on the steps of the Supreme Court the night before the argument started. I spent the night outside with others, near the Supreme Court, and wanted to be in the line of those seeking one of the limited seats available for the *Bakke* argument. My overnight wait paid off, and I was able to hear the argument.

The Supreme Court was all that I imagined—and more. The justices seemed larger than life, and like the Socratic dialogue in law school classes, the questioning was intense and relentless. When the justices questioned McCree and Cox, it seemed clear that they had decided that the plan of affirmative action was hopelessly unconstitutional. When they questioned Bakke's lawyer, Reynold Colvin, it also appeared that the Court was quite skeptical of his claim that the UC Davis plan amounted to reverse discrimination and that Allan Bakke deserved to be admitted to the medical school. If they wished to conceal how they intended to decide the case, the justices succeeded in doing so.

Cox's argument was elegant, and he exhibited the same manner that he used in teaching his classes at Harvard: controlled mastery of details, quick references to cases, and use of analogy to make his points. McCree's oral argument corresponded to the Justice Department brief but went further, stressing that discrimination was so pervasive in American life that it made remedial programs necessary.[27] McCree stated, "Many children born in 1954, when *Brown* was decided, are today, 23 years later, the very persons knocking on the doors of professional schools, seeking admission, about the country. They are persons who, in many instances, have been denied the fulfillment of the promise of that decision because of resistance to this Court's decision that was such a landmark when it was handed down." In such a situation, he added, "to be blind to race today is to be blind to reality."[28]

The *Bakke* arguments must have been particularly poignant for Justice Marshall, who had been the lead attorney in *Brown*. Now a member of the Court, he desired to carry *Brown* to the next logical step. In his view, the principle of color-blindness could not yet work, because for too many years the laws had specifically disadvantaged African-Americans on account of their race. In his April 13 memorandum to the conference he wrote, "For us now to say that the principle of color-blindness prevents the University from giving 'special' consideration to race when this Court, in 1896 licensed the states to continue to consider race, is to make a mockery of the principle of 'equal justice under law.'"[29] Marshall then attempted to show that many more years would have to pass before African-Americans were on equal footing with whites. He knew that this was a result of racial discrimination that had been upheld and promoted at every level of society between *Plessy* and *Brown*. He thus saw no need for a specific showing of past discrimination at Davis, because the discrimination was endemic in the nation and intrinsic to its institutions. He went on to assert, "If you view the program as admitting qualified students who, because of this Nation's sorry history of racial discrimination, have academic records that prevent them from effectively competing for medical school, then this is affirmative action to remove the vestiges of slavery and state imposed segregation by 'root and branch.'"[30]

To Justice Brennan, the Davis program mirrored Marshall's concerns. Supported by three colleagues, Brennan focused on the students admitted to the Davis program who would not otherwise have been admitted. This focus on the previously disadvantaged group was very much in line with the Court's prior decisions in *Brown* and the cases that followed. In *Brown, Green,* and *Swann,* the Court had shown an increasing recognition that significant steps needed to be taken to rectify the effects of discrimination, which had endured for centuries.

The justices who wanted to strike down the Davis program focused on the lack of evidence that the school had discriminated against people of color in the past. Chief Justice Burger and Justice Powell concluded that, in the absence of such evidence, the use of race in the Davis program violated equal protection. In doing this, they interpreted the Court's prior cases as remedying very specific past wrongs instead of as removing the effects of broad societal discrimination. Such a narrow focus allowed them to strike down the Davis program and ignore the stark realities of the overwhelming consequences that years of racial discrimination had produced.

To the remaining justices, however, the exclusion of white students without more justification was simply going too far. Indeed, Chief Justice Burger and the ultimate swing voter, Justice Powell, did pinpoint their focus on who was being kept out of Davis. This was not surprising, since Bakke himself was a very sympathetic character. For this very reason, Brennan was strongly against granting certiorari in the *Bakke* case. He feared that a majority of the Court would be offended by the existence of a "quota" and strike down any use of race in admissions programs.[31] Additionally, Burger and Powell might have found it easy to focus on the excluded white student, because there was no one to represent the minority students' interests. This factor also separates *Bakke* from much of the prior litigation.

Sadly, the sentiments expressed by Justice Marshall, before the decision was issued, did not persuade the other members of the Supreme Court. Marshall began by noting, "If only the principle of color-blindness had been accepted by the majority in *Plessy* in 1896, we would not be faced with this problem in 1978." He continued,

> As a result of our last discussion on this case, I wish also to address the question of whether Negroes have "arrived." Just a few examples illustrate that Negroes most certainly have not. In our own Court, we have had only three Negro law clerks, and not so far have we had a Negro Officer of the Court. On a broader scale, this week's U.S. News and World Report has a story about "Who Runs America." They list some 83 persons—not one Negro, even as a would-be runnerup. . . . The dream of America as a melting pot has not been realized by Negroes—either the Negro did not get into the pot, or he did not get melted down. The statistics on unemployment and the other statistics quoted in the briefs of the Solicitor General and other *amici* document the vast gulf between white and black America. That gulf was brought about by centuries of slavery and then by another century in which, with the approval of this Court, states were permitted to treat Negroes "specially."[32]

Marshall's strong appeal to his colleagues during the *Bakke* case fell upon largely deaf ears. He was right about *Plessy*, *Brown*, and *Bakke*, but his pleas did not command a majority on the Court.

In *Bakke*, Justice Powell asserted that Title VI of the Civil Rights Act of 1964 proscribed only racial classifications that would be unconstitutional if used by a state. He applied strict scrutiny and concluded that, although achieving a diverse student body constituted a compelling state interest, the California program was not narrowly tailored to meet that end.[33] He upheld the aspect of the UC Davis plan as that allowed the consideration of diversity, as articulated in the Harvard plan, as one factor, in selecting a class of students to pursue higher education. Justices Brennan, White, Marshall, and Blackmun coauthored an opinion concurring with Justice Powell in the dissolution of the lower court's injunction against all consideration of race but then dissenting from the invalidation of California's program. They considered Davis's interest in remedying past societal discrimination sufficiently important and found that the program neither stigmatized a discrete group or individual nor used race unreasonably in light of the program's objectives.[34] Thus, though applying strict scrutiny, they did not apply the typical "'strict' in theory but fatal in fact" version.[35] Justice Stevens, joined by Chief Justice Burger and Justices Stewart and Rehnquist, concluded that the question whether race could ever be considered was not before the Court, and he concurred in Justice Powell's opinion insofar as it held that Title VI invalidated the program and compelled admission of Bakke.

When I read the *Bakke* decision and its conclusion that race, as one factor among many, was appropriate for a university to consider in selecting from among qualified applicants, I was euphoric. All of our marching, protests, and my visits with the lawyers arguing the case, and attendance at the Supreme Court argument seemed to have been vindicated. Not only had we won the right to consider racial diversity as a constitutional principle, but also Harvard University had submitted a brief, with other elite universities, that Justice Powell and the Supreme Court found persuasive. It seemed to be good news all around. However, I then read Justice Marshall's dissent in the case; it immediately caused me to reassess whether we had indeed prevailed in the *Bakke* case. Perhaps my glee was premature. Perhaps the modest concession that the Harvard plan was okay was not a real victory for the vast majority of black and brown students who could not attend Harvard or Stanford. Perhaps the victory was largely symbolic, benefiting only the Talented Tenth. I read Marshall's words very carefully and learned a lot about myself that day.

Marshall filed a dissenting opinion arguing, "It must be remembered that, during most of the past 200 years, the Constitution as interpreted by this Court did not prohibit the most ingenious and pervasive forms of discrimination against the Negro. Now, when a State acts to remedy the effects of that legacy of discrimination, I cannot believe that this same Constitution stands as a barrier."[36] Marshall went on to recount the long and shameful history of American racism, including the Court's role in affirming the status of slaves as noncitizens and later in emasculating the Civil War amendments.[37]

Marshall then discussed the continuing effects of that long history. "The position of the Negro today in America is the tragic but inevitable consequence of centuries of unequal treatment. Measured by any benchmark of comfort or achievement, meaningful equality remains a distant dream for the Negro."[38] He detailed the many disparities between blacks and whites and concluded, "In light of the sorry history of discrimination and its devastating impact on the lives of Negroes, bringing the

Negro into the mainstream of American life should be a state interest of the highest order. To fail to do so is to ensure that America will forever remain a divided society."[39] It was ironic, in some respects, that I was graduating from a premier law school, on my way to a job I desperately wanted, and Marshall was signaling to me, and others like me, that our modest success paled in comparison with the closing of the doors of opportunity for other blacks, Native Americans, and Hispanics throughout the country. It was not enough that the Harvards and Stanfords were doing well, if the public institutions of higher education were starting to shut their doors. Marshall was issuing a warning, and I wondered, despite the protests that I had organized and participated in, whether I really heard his plea.

Justice Marshall went to great lengths to develop the rationale for affirmative action in the *Bakke* case, reviewing the history of both the Fourteenth Amendment and Title VI, and he concluded that neither was intended to prohibit actions aimed at remedying past discrimination:[40]

> While I applaud the judgment of the Court that a university may consider race in its admissions process, it is more than a little ironic that, after several hundred years of class-based discrimination against Negroes, the Court is unwilling to hold that a class-based remedy for that discrimination is permissible. In declining to so hold, today's judgment ignores the fact that for several hundred years Negroes have been discriminated against, not as individuals, but rather solely because of the color of their skins.[41]

Professor Derrick Bell has argued that if minority groups had been directly represented in the litigation, "they would have brought sorely needed realism to litigation that has been treated more like a law school exam or an exercise in philosophy than a matter of paramount importance to black citizens." Bell also suggests that if minorities had played a greater role in *Bakke*, they would have been able to marshal evidence showing past discrimination in California schools and the UC Davis Medical School.[42]

Marshall realized that the *Bakke* decision was the beginning of the end of his efforts to meet the promise of *Brown*. This was obviously a painful experience for a man who had dedicated his career to ending segregation and creating an integrated society that fostered equality. His judicial colleagues thought he had gone too far. Marshall knew, however, that he had not gone nearly far enough.

The mixed blessing of the *Bakke* opinion was most eloquently captured in the concurring opinion of Justice Harry Blackmun, who stated,

I yield to no one in my earnest hope that the time will come when an "affirmative action" program is unnecessary and is, in truth, only a relic of the past. I would hope that we could reach this stage within a decade at the most. But the story of *Brown v. Board of Education*, 347 U.S. 483 (1954), decided almost a quarter of a century ago, suggests that that hope is a slim one. At some time, however, beyond any period of what some would claim as only transitional inequality, the United States must and will reach a stage of maturity where action along this line is no longer necessary. Then persons will be regarded as persons, and discrimination of the type we address today will be an ugly feature of history that is instructive but that is behind us. . . . I suspect that it would be impossible to arrange an affirmative-action program in a racially neutral way and have it be successful. To ask that this be so is to demand the impossible. In order to get beyond racism, we must first take account of race. There is no other way. And in order to treat some persons equally, we must treat them differently. We cannot—we dare not—let the Equal Protection Clause perpetuate racial supremacy.[43]

The new era would focus on diversity and color-blindness and significantly slow the process of reaching the goal of actual equal treatment under the law that *Brown* had promised.

The school desegregation cases not only reveal how courts have interpreted *Brown* but also provide a backdrop for analyzing the Court's decision in *Bakke*. Perhaps the most obvious example of symbiosis between *Brown* and *Bakke* involves the repeated emphasis in each decision on the exceptionality of education. As Akhil Amar has written, "*Bakke* builds squarely on the rock of *Brown. Brown* held that education was *sui generis* and that even if racial segregation could be tolerated in other spheres, the school was different."[44] It is further pointed out that in the same way that *Brown* did not wholly overrule *Plessy, Bakke* concluded that even if affirmative action in some contexts was unconstitutional, universities fulfilled such a critical role in American society that their employment of race-conscious remedies was socially necessary.[45] Powell's *Bakke* concurrence rejected broader justifications, including the counteracting of "societal discrimination," that would have spilled over to justify remedies in other spheres, and instead invoked diversity as the justification for affirmative action in education.

What differentiates *Brown* from *Bakke* is the forced abandonment of a legal and intellectual justification of integration based on remedying past discrimination. *Bakke* placed the legitimacy of affirmative action in universities squarely on educational diversity rather than on remedial aims. In so doing, some commentators argue, Powell's conception of diversity poorly articulated the integrationist ideal that motivates affirmative action:

> The early rationale for affirmative action, whether in the initial Philadelphia Plan formulation or in its academic counterparts, was clearly integrationist. Society was taking responsibility for minorities' past subordination. Based on this moral authority, a forward-looking claim emerged about the necessity to improve the status of minorities, with blacks as the overwhelming case in chief, so as to promote their integration into mainstream American society.[46]

A number of arguments have been made about the deficiencies of the diversity rationale. First, it is a poor justification for affirmative action because it becomes less persuasive as the percentage of minority students grows—there are diminishing marginal returns in terms of racial diversity once the number reaches a certain point. This disjunction between how many minority students represent a critical mass, in contrast to the modest allowance that was envisioned by *Bakke*, makes post-*Bakke* policies look more like a commitment to getting to a certain number of minority students for each class than like loyalty to diversity. This is not really troublesome on its own, but it has certainly complicated recent efforts to argue that post-*Bakke* programs are narrowly tailored. Additionally, it is suggested that the diversity rationale is internally incoherent because if diversity of the learning group is the real justification for affirmative action, then why is it restricted only to those groups that have suffered historical oppression? This is a particularly difficult question in a time when there is a disconnect between the past injustices

and oppression faced by blacks and the experience of current generations of whites, whose only exposure to racial classifications is their use
in providing benefits to minority groups.

Professor Charles Lawrence argues that promotion of the "liberal
defense of affirmative action," or more precisely the diversity defense
first articulated by Powell in *Bakke*, has crowded out "more radical
substantive defenses."[47] He holds that not only must defenders of affirmative action question how traditional admissions standards continue
to perpetuate racial and class-based privilege; they must also emphasize
how past and current discrimination makes affirmative action necessary.
Lawrence characterizes the diversity defense as essentially conservative
because it only seeks to integrate existing black elites into current power
structures as opposed to centering the project of racial justice at the
forefront of the university's mission. He emphasizes, "Liberalism's focus
on fair process and bad actors and its agnosticism toward continuing
conditions of subordination allow the liberal defender of affirmative
action to champion racial justice without confronting the moral question of whether he can define as just a society still significantly separate and unequal."[48] For Lawrence, blind reliance on SAT scores and the
extra weighting of Advanced Placement courses in university admissions
represents "systemic, institutional racial preferences."[49] He does admit,
however, that much as the diversity defense understates the vast advantage whites have in university admissions, these types of preferences
become insurmountable obstacles without affirmative action. To those
who would criticize him for abandoning the diversity defense, Lawrence
replies that an alternative approach that looks beyond individual legal
or political battles is necessary: "Transformative politics also seeks to
change the political consciousness of those privileged by systems of subordination. The task is to help the privileged comprehend the profound
costs associated with inequality—the public costs of prisons, crime, illit-
eracy, disease, and the violence of an alienated underclass. . . ."[50]

Similarly, Professor Lani Guinier argues that proponents of affirmative action need to reclaim the debate by directly contesting the mis-
conception that "affirmative action is a departure from an otherwise
sound meritocracy."[51] She believes that traditional admissions criteria
disadvantage not only women and people of color but also the poor and
working class. Put simply, *Bakke* marked the end of the radical chal-

lenges to the status quo. Before *Bakke*, the Supreme Court recognized that the playing field was not level, but had been skewed in favor of whites and consistently took steps to remedy the inequality. After *Bakke*, it abandoned its attempts to rebalance the playing field by lifting African-Americans, women, and others to the same level as white men.

I share the concerns of both Lawrence and Guinier. The Supreme Court's failure to accept the University of California's efforts to remedy the dearth of minorities in professional schools was unwise and unfortunate. With one decision, the Court accelerated the process of undoing *Brown*.

CHAPTER 11

THE LEGACY OF THURGOOD MARSHALL

Justice Thurgood Marshall's unerring commitment to the rights of the ordinary citizen was articulated in opinions he wrote during the twenty-four years he served on the Supreme Court. In the thousands of decisions that he participated in while on the Court, his clarity and conviction did not change, whether he was writing for the majority, concurring in a judgment of the majority, or dissenting in opinions. Whether in the area of civil rights or in that of criminal justice, his voice was always strong and unwavering.

From the time Marshall joined the Court, in 1967, until his retirement, in 1991, he left an indelible mark on its jurisprudence in many important areas. In the First Amendment context, for example, Marshall joined the *Buckley v. Valeo* majority in striking down expenditure limits as unconstitutional (showing his libertarian streak),[1] but he later came to revise that view when he saw that the campaign finance regime was undermining the constitutional ideal of equal citizenship. In *Austin v. Michigan Chamber of Commerce*, Marshall's opinion upheld a prohibition against the use of corporate treasury money in election campaigns, on the grounds that dominance in the economic marketplace should not translate into dominance in the political marketplace.[2] Marshall would promote the broadest interpretation of the First Amendment, but at the same time limit its ability to dilute the fundamental principle of one person, one vote. Similarly, while Marshall obviously believed strongly in the affirmative duty of states to remedy past discrimination, he wrote the majority opinion in *Linmark Associates, Inc. v. Willingboro*, which struck down a local ordinance seeking to stem the tide of white flight by forbidding the posting of "For Sale" and "Sold" signs.[3]

In the context of race, Marshall's jurisprudence had several components. First, he believed in a broad conception of state action. For example, in desegregation cases, where other justices considered racially isolated neighborhoods to be a private matter, Marshall recognized the role of the state in both facilitating and encouraging the attitudes that promoted racial segregation. His experiences as a lawyer for the NAACP made him familiar with the way racism could be subtle, but debilitating. Marshall also firmly believed that the government should be required to take remedial measures to correct constitutional wrongs.

Marshall was particularly concerned about inequality in resources to address educational issues. In *San Antonio Independent School District v. Rodriguez*, the Court examined the financing of local school districts.[4] A conservative majority of the Supreme Court held that Texas's system of financing school systems primarily through local property taxes did not violate the equal protection clause, ruling that public education is not a fundamental right protected by the Constitution. Thus, the Court held that, so long as the state can provide any justification, no matter how minimal, for its policy, then wealth-based classifications would be permissible.[5] Justice White, joined by Douglas and Brennan, dissented on the grounds that the Texas system failed to provide a meaningful option for poor districts to increase their per-pupil expenditures.[6]

Marshall, joined by Douglas, argued that "the majority's holding can only be seen as a retreat from our historic commitment to equality of educational opportunity and as unsupportable acquiescence in a system that deprives children in their earliest years of the chance to reach their full potential as citizens."[7] He declared that "the right of every American to an equal start in life, so far as the provision of a state service as important as education is concerned, is far too vital to permit state discrimination on grounds as tenuous as those presented by this record," and he showed how logic and the actual history of the controversy demonstrated that the political process was ill suited to remedy the gross inequities inherent in the system.[8] While acknowledging that the Constitution did not guarantee a right to public education, he argued that because education "directly affects" children's exercise of

First Amendment rights, adequate public funding was essential to the concept of quality education.[9] Marshall's inability to persuade a majority of his colleagues to join him in the *Rodriguez* case was a telling sign of *Brown*'s demise. Unfortunately for Marshall, *Rodriguez* was simply the beginning of what would prove to be tough times in attempting to advance the educational equality envisioned in *Brown*.

Marshall fervently believed that discrimination on the basis of group wealth is even more invidious than discrimination based on individual wealth, because an individual has no control over the former.[10] He asserted that localities should not be allowed to control how much is spent on education, because to do so takes educational choice, and with it the ability to ensure a quality education, out of the hands of the poor individual and concentrates it in those of the wealthy. While the other justices focused on the broader theoretical application of the Constitution, Marshall saw the children of San Antonio, like the children in *Brown,* as the victims of a local power structure that did not designate education as the highest priority.

Marshall was similarly concerned about an indirect tax imposed by North Dakota, which allowed certain school districts to charge fees for students who rode the bus to school. He viewed the bus fee as tantamount to a fee for education and an excessive burden on a poor person's interest in receiving an education.[11] Drawing on his real-life appreciation of the abuse of power against the powerless, he questioned whether these fees for busing, similar to the fees used as poll taxes for blacks during the Jim Crow years, were designed to deny fundamental protection to the least powerful in our society. Memorably, he said, "The intent of the Fourteenth Amendment was to abolish caste legislation."[12]

After Marshall joined the Court, the legacy of *Brown* still held firm in cases like *Green v. County School Board of New Kent County, Virginia,*[13] decided one year after his arrival. In *Green* the Court unanimously held that the freedom-of-choice plan adopted by New Kent County, Virginia, did not fulfill the affirmative duty to eliminate the vestiges of school segregation. The issue that the Court examined was the county school system's sponsorship of white children's attendance of all-white schools while black children attended public schools that remained segregated. Three years later, in *Swann v. Charlotte-*

Mecklenburg Board of Education,[14] after Warren Burger succeeded Earl Warren as chief justice, a unanimous Court affirmed district courts' remedial powers in implementing *Brown*'s mandate. Under *Swann*, federal courts were permitted to adopt wide-ranging remedial orders to ensure that segregated or "dual" systems were eliminated and replaced by a unified system. In *Keyes v. School District. No. 1, Denver, Colorado*, the Court was nearly unanimous in holding, "Where plaintiffs prove that the school authorities have carried out a systematic program of segregation affecting a substantial portion of the students, schools, teachers, and facilities within the school system, it is only common sense to conclude that there exists a predicate for a finding of the existence of a dual school system."[15]

In endeavoring to define the parameters of a quality education, Marshall brought a level of humanity to the law that none of his colleagues could match. His voice in the Court's deliberations was critical. In fact, Justice Brennan suggested, "Although Justice Marshall did not write any of these three important opinions, his strong statements during the Court's conferences—drawing on his familiarity with the problems—sharpened the Court's resolve to strive for unanimous decisions."[16]

The real turning point came in 1974, with *Milliken v. Bradley*, which prohibited federal courts from using multidistrict remedies to ameliorate segregation that was endemic in one district only.[17] In *Milliken*, white flight from the city—out of Detroit—led to increasingly minority urban areas and white suburbs. The suburban areas had no history of segregation; they were small areas that might not even have had a school before white flight. The more and more conservative Supreme Court concluded that the white families that moved to the suburbs should not be penalized, through remedial measures, even though their actions led to segregated, uniform schools.

For Marshall, *Milliken* was a stark reminder of the unfilled mission of *Brown*, and he wasted no time letting his colleagues know that their decision was contrary to everything that was right about ending a segregated education system. *Milliken* is one of the pivotal decisions in the re-creation of Marshall's new role as a dissenter. His opening paragraphs illustrate his unequivocal view of the danger of moving away from the mandate of *Brown*:

After 20 years of small, often difficult steps toward that great end, the Court today takes a giant step backwards. Notwithstanding a record showing widespread and pervasive racial segregation in the educational system provided by the State of Michigan for children in Detroit, this Court holds that the District Court was powerless to require the State to remedy its constitutional violation in any meaningful fashion. Ironically purporting to base its result on the principle that the scope of the remedy in a desegregation case should be determined by the nature and the extent of the constitutional violation, the Court's answer is to provide no remedy at all for the violation proved in this case, thereby guaranteeing that Negro children in Detroit will receive the same separate and inherently unequal education in the future as they have been unconstitutionally afforded in the past. . . .

The rights at issue in this case are too fundamental to be abridged on grounds as superficial as those relied on by the majority today. We deal here with the right of all of our children, whatever their race, to an equal start in life and to an equal opportunity to reach their full potential as citizens. Those children who have been denied that right in the past deserve better than to see fences thrown up to deny them that right in the future. Our Nation, I fear, will be ill served by the Court's refusal to remedy separate and unequal education, for unless our children begin to learn together, there is little hope that our people will ever learn to live together.[18]

Marshall first chided the majority for ordering the district court to eliminate the segregation in Detroit city schools, after prohibiting what the district court had found to be the only possible avenue to that goal. He insisted that the district court chose its remedy on the basis not of "some perceived racial imbalance either between schools within a single school district or between independent school districts" but of "a systematic program of segregation affecting a substantial portion of the students, schools . . . and facilities within the school system."[19] The district court had determined that the state had taken actions contributing to segregation in Detroit schools, that the Detroit Board of Education was an agency of the State, and that "under Michigan law and practice, the system of education was in fact a state school system, characterized by relatively little local control and a large degree of centralized state regulation, with respect to both educational policy and the structure and operation of school districts."[20]

Marshall deemed it irrelevant whether the state was directly responsible for the concentration of Negro students in Detroit; what mattered was that state action had led to school segregation, and if an interdistrict remedy was the only way to cure that problem, then such a remedy was within the district court's equitable powers. He found support for this contention in earlier cases that had not only permitted but also required district courts to account for the risk of white flight in designing remedies.[21] He laid heavy emphasis on the idea that continuation of racially identifiable schools constituted both a vestige of past discrimination and evidence of continuing discriminatory intent.[22]

Despite this obvious setback, when *Milliken* returned to the Court in 1977 (*Milliken II*),[23] Marshall and like-minded justices were sometimes able to cobble together a majority and uphold the imposition of remedial education programs for past segregation victims. Brennan later noted, "Justice Marshall's [*Milliken I*] dissent may well have made the Court more responsive to the plight of Detroit's schoolchildren when the case returned before us in [*Milliken II*]."[24]

Marshall was increasingly in the minority in the years following *Milliken I* and sometimes found himself alone in dissent.[25] He was the sole dissenter in *Crawford v. Board of Education of City of Los Angeles* (1982), which upheld California's Proposition I, a state constitutional amendment that barred the state judiciary from imposing busing remedies.[26] Marshall argued, "Proposition I works an unconstitutional reallocation of state power by depriving California courts of the ability to grant meaningful relief to those seeking to vindicate the State's guarantee against *de facto* segregation in the public schools."[27] He found it "beyond reasonable dispute" that the passage of Proposition I was racially motivated.

Marshall's influence on the Court in race matters reached its lowest point in *Board of Education of Oklahoma City v. Dowell* (1991), in which Justice Souter did not participate and Justices Blackmun and Stevens joined Marshall's dissent. The Court concluded that if the district court found that the Oklahoma City School District was being operated in compliance with *Brown*, and if the school board was not likely to return to its segregative ways, the desegregation decree should be dissolved. Marshall angrily responded,

I believe a desegregation decree cannot be lifted so long as conditions likely to inflict the stigmatic injury condemned in Brown I persist and there remain feasible methods of eliminating such conditions. Because the record here shows, and the Court of Appeals found, that feasible steps could be taken to avoid one-race schools, it is clear that the purposes of the decree have not yet been achieved and the Court of Appeals' reinstatement of the decree should be affirmed. I therefore dissent.[28]

Marshall then recounted the history of Oklahoma City's school segregation, demonstrating "nearly unflagging resistance by the Board to judicial efforts to dismantle the City's dual education system." In 1985, the school board adopted an attendance zone plan, the result of which was that 44 percent of the black children went to nearly all-black schools. The Court, and the country, would rue that day when Marshall's worst fear, the resegregation of the public schools integrated by *Brown*, came true.

Marshall's frustration with his colleagues' narrowing interpretation of racial justice extended to employment discrimination cases. He found the battle to achieve racial justice difficult in *Fullilove v. Klutznik* (1980), which upheld a requirement in a congressional spending program that localities use 10 percent of any federal public works grant money to hire minority-controlled businesses.[29] Chief Justice Burger's opinion for the Court, joined by Justices White and Powell, stated that the program would survive under either of the tests urged in the *Bakke* opinions. The chief justice emphasized "appropriate deference to the Congress" and stated that Congress need not compile the kind of "record" that a court or administrative agency would require in order to justify such a program.[30]

Marshall's concurrence upheld the act applying the version of strict scrutiny outlined in the four-justice joint opinion in *Bakke*. Marshall concluded, "Today, by upholding this race-conscious remedy, the Court accords Congress the authority necessary to undertake the task of moving our society toward a state of meaningful equality of opportunity, not an abstract version of equality in which the effects of past discrimination would be forever frozen into our social fabric."[31]

Despite cases like *Fullilove,* as Marshall began his second decade on the Supreme Court, he witnessed broader assaults on *Brown*. The issue was not simply the disparity in educational resources. As in *Fullilove*, the targets were often remedies to address disparities in employment opportunities. In *City of Richmond v. J. A. Croson Co.* (1989),[32] the Court struck down a plan that required contractors working for the city to set aside 30 percent of the contract amount to hire "Minority Business Enterprises." Writing the majority opinion, Justice O'Connor concluded that Richmond had not made sufficient findings to justify the set-aside plan as appropriate remedial action. The Court held that, in the absence of any consideration of race-neutral alternatives, the only goal to which a 30 percent quota could be narrowly tailored would be "outright racial balancing."[33]

Marshall decried this "deliberate and giant step backward in this Court's affirmative-action jurisprudence" and pointed out the irony in the majority's assertion that Richmond had not made sufficient findings of past discrimination, given "the city's disgraceful history of public and private racial discrimination."[34] He also criticized the majority's suggestion that, because blacks are the dominant racial group in Richmond, Richmond's action required particularly strict scrutiny. He argued that the majority's view "implies a lack of political maturity on the part of this Nation's elected minority officials that is totally unwarranted. Such insulting judgments have no place in constitutional jurisprudence."[35] The *Croson* decision was a major setback for Marshall and others who felt that existing measures to address employment opportunities for minorities were inadequate.

WHILE MARSHALL IS BEST REMEMBERED for his work on the civil rights front, he was similarly concerned with criminal rights and procedures. Perhaps most important was his focus on a criminal defendant's rights to a fair jury trial. In *Batson v. Kentucky*, for example, a black defendant was convicted in a case in which the white prosecutor had challenged black jurors on the basis not of any evidenced bias but of their race alone. The Court held that the equal protection clause forbade the prosecutor from challenging solely on the basis of race or racial stereotype, and that a defendant could make out a prima facie case of discrimination if he established that the prosecutor had excluded members of his race and that facts and circumstances permitted an inference that he had done so on racial grounds.[36] The Court reaffirmed the long-standing principle that, although defendants have no right to a jury composed in whole or part of their race, they do have a right to juries chosen impartially. Marshall's concurrence went further and urged that racial discrimination in jury selection could be eliminated only by doing away with peremptory challenges altogether.[37]

Marshall also pressed for the broadening of the Fourth Amendment's safeguard against impermissible searches and seizures and the Fifth Amendment's protection against compelled confessions. In these areas, he was a frequent dissenter. *United States v. Robinson,*[38] a case in which the majority found constitutional a police officer's removal and search of a crumpled cigarette packet from the coat pocket of a man arrested for a mere traffic offense, exemplifies Marshall's occasional indignation at the Court's Fourth Amendment jurisprudence. Searches incident to arrest are permissible, Marshall noted, in order to check for evidence or weapons incident to that particular arrest. Since no further evidence of a traffic offense could possibly have been found in the cigarette pack, he argued, the defendant's Fourth Amendment rights were clearly violated.[39]

Finally, Marshall was a zealous opponent of the death penalty. His concurrence in *Furman v. Georgia,*[40] a case that temporarily suspended the death penalty, stressed that capital punishment was excessive and unnecessary and that it violated the Eighth Amendment's prohibition against cruel and unusual punishment because a better-informed public would find it morally reprehensible.[41] When the Court four years later in *Gregg v. Georgia*[42] set forth procedural criteria under which the death penalty could be reinstated by the states, Marshall went further and urged that the two supposed justifications for capital punishment were no justifications at all: the penalty's deterrent effect was illusory and its retributive purpose an illegitimate government objective.[43] Immediately after *Gregg,* Marshall began filing a dissent in every single capital case in which the Court denied certiorari. However, when Marshall realized that the more conservative Court was unlikely to heed his absolutist advice, he began to focus on the slightly narrower issue of arbitrariness and discrimination in death sentences. He never abandoned his view, however, that the need to eliminate arbitrariness in sentencing, coupled with the need for some measure of judicial discretion, produced an unresolvable conflict that was reason enough to abandon capital punishment altogether. Marshall also pushed for greater procedural protections and occasionally proved victorious. *Ford v. Wainwright*, for example, held unconstitutional the execution of the insane.[44]

Nonetheless, in both criminal and civil rights cases, Marshall often found himself on the dissenting side of the divide, particularly in later years. While his first decade on the Court with a majority of liberal justices brought about the preservation of the *Brown* mandate, the second decade showed a dramatic shift in the Court's ideology. Marshall's views in the second decade did not change, but his role, as the conscience of the Court, was virtually eliminated. The great civil rights lawyer became the great Supreme Court dissenter. It was a role that Marshall could not have anticipated and one that, in the end, he could not sustain.

By the end of the 1990–91 term, Marshall had finally reached the point where there was no more fight in him. After spending seven decades as a fierce advocate for racial justice as a lawyer, judge, and Supreme Court Justice, Thurgood Marshall announced his retirement on June 27, 1991. It was a painful day for me, although I knew, given his failing health, that it was inevitable. Feeling as if I had lost a parent, I could not believe the reports I was hearing in Washington. I said a prayer for Justice Marshall and thanked God for bringing him unto this earth—and allowing him to do so much for so many people, so well, for so long. There would not be another one like him.

In his letter of retirement to President George H. W. Bush, Marshall indicated that, after serving twenty-four years, it was time to step down from the Court. He further informed Bush that he would remain on the Court until a replacement could be found.

I had naïvely hoped that Justice Marshall would be able to remain on the Court until a Democrat occupied the White House and increased the chances that someone with a liberal disposition would replace him. I was not alone in this hope. Many civil rights groups, legal scholars, and members of the special-interest groups he invariably supported as a justice wanted him to remain forever.

No one took Marshall's tenure on the Court more seriously than the justice himself. Marshall indicated that a Supreme Court justice was appointed for life and that he intended to fulfill that appointment.

When he was ill and hospitalized in the early 1970s, the rumor circulated that President Richard Nixon, a Marshall nemesis, inquired about his health. When a Nixon associate inquired how he was feeling, Marshall wrote a note on a piece of paper that made his point clear: "Not yet!" Years later when asked whether he would retire, Marshall retorted, "I plan to serve until I'm 108 years old and I will leave then when I'm shot by a jealous husband."

I wish it had been so. Unfortunately, by June 27, 1991, Marshall's closest friend on the Court, Justice Brennan, had already retired. It was a monumental personal loss for Marshall, since he and Brennan had been viewed for decades as the twin towers on the liberal end of the Court. Marshall did not retire, however, without leaving a strong message for the new conservative majority in his final dissent. In *Payne v. Tennessee*,[45] a 1991 decision that reversed decades of Supreme Court jurisprudence prohibiting victims' ability to offer comments in criminal cases designed to enhance the punishment of those convicted of crimes, Marshall chastised the Court, stating,

> Power, not reason, is the new currency of this Court's decisionmaking. Four Terms ago, a five-Justice majority of this Court held that "victim impact" evidence of the type at issue in this case could not constitutionally be introduced during the penalty phase of a capital trial. . . . Neither the law nor the facts supporting [those cases] underwent any change in the last four years. Only the personnel of this Court did.
>
> Today's decision charts an unmistakable course. If the majority's radical reconstruction of the rules for overturning this Court's decisions is to be taken at face value—and the majority offers us no reason why it should not—then [this decision] is but a preview of an even broader and more far-reaching assault upon this Court's precedents. Cast aside today are those condemned to face society's ultimate penalty. Tomorrow's victims may be minorities, women, or the indigent. Inevitably, this campaign to resurrect yesterday's "spirited dissents" will squander the authority and the legitimacy of this Court as a protector of the powerless.
>
> I dissent.[46]

Even though many conservatives were undoubtedly cheering Marshall's retirement, his colleagues seemed genuinely saddened. In his book *Thurgood Marshall: American Revolutionary*, Juan Williams records that, when Marshall announced his retirement to his colleagues on the Court, Justice O'Connor cried and Chief Justice Rehnquist hugged him.[47] Such was the breadth of Marshall's appeal that even those who disagreed with him were sad to see him go. Some of his intellectual adversaries on the Court offered unconditional praise in law journal tributes following his retirement.

Many of those adversaries were happiest to comment on his abilities as storyteller and raconteur. It was certainly true that after Rehnquist was named chief justice and O'Connor was appointed to the bench, Marshall's influence on the Court had become more circumscribed and his ability to persuade his colleagues more infrequent. Although the Court continued to be receptive to his amazing personal charm, its members did not support his judicial philosophy. When Rehnquist shared his thoughts on Marshall's retirement in the *Stanford Law Review*, he described Justice Marshall as a man only of the "common touch . . . dedication, and . . . insightful perspective on key issues of our time." Rehnquist lamented, "We will of course miss his wise counsel in our future deliberations, but we will equally miss his personal charm, and the innumerable 'tall tales,' based upon his extraordinary experiences, with which he often delighted us."[48]

For his allies on the Court, or even those who were most often "on the fence," no other justice could bring such practical real-world experience to the Court. Brennan said that Marshall "was a voice of authority: he spoke of first hand knowledge"[49]—knowledge, moreover, that was most often deployed with a particular purpose in mind. Part of his wily cantankerousness was to make verbal jabs at his opponents to force them to think and to debate—a virtue in the deliberative process, but one that became less pronounced with the Rehnquist Court's ideological disdain of consensus. O'Connor in her tribute said, "Marshall imparted not only his legal acumen but also his life experiences, constantly pushing and prodding us to respond not only to the persuasiveness of legal argument but also to the power of moral truth."[50] Kennedy admired Marshall's powerfulness on his opinions concerning "the citizen's right to privacy from government intrusion, the morality of the death penalty, and the need to combat the inequities born of poverty."[51]

Above all else, Marshall was a witness to the manner in which the majority will had the potential to silence and marginalize all Americans.

His special concern before his ascent to the Court had been the discrete minorities identified by race, particularly African-Americans. Once he was on the Court, his genius was to recognize that we are all potentially minorities and that forces beyond our control can place any one of us under the "tyranny of the majority." Judge A. Leon Higginbotham commented, "To laud Thurgood Marshall *solely* for improving the options of African-Americans would be too simplistic a tribute for a person who has touched so many lives. Most Americans . . . have benefited from the extraordinary catalytic and ripple effects of [his work]."[52] Marshall "spoke for those who might otherwise be forgotten," Brennan remarked.[53] He "knew the anguish of the silenced and gave them a voice," observed O'Connor.[54]

Marshall's special legacy is, perhaps, empathy as a jurisprudential principle: the ability to see ourselves as others see us, and to see them too. O'Connor elaborated on his distinctive perspective, noting, "His was the eye of a lawyer who saw the deepest wounds in the social fabric and used law to help heal them. His was the ear of a counselor who understood the vulnerabilities of the accused and established safeguards for their protection."[55] Brennan, who of all the justices knew him best, emphatically proclaimed, "Of no other lawyer can it so truly be said that *all* Americans owe him an enormous debt of gratitude."[56]

At the press conference following the announcement of his retirement, Marshall was asked what his reason for retiring was. In his trademark fashion, he was blunt and clear, "I'm old. I'm getting old and falling apart."[57] Marshall's retirement was a major disappointment, but the selection of his replacement would be devastating.

After his retirement, my wife Pam and I visited Marshall at the Supreme Court in 1992 and conducted a long interview concerning his mentor Charles Hamilton Houston. I was amazed both at the clarity of Marshall's mind concerning stories that were sixty years old and at his comfort in sharing dirty jokes in our presence. It was a memorable occasion and left me feeling even more proud to know this great man.

By the time Marshall announced his retirement from the Supreme Court, I had joined the Harvard Law School faculty and was teaching full-time. In the fall of 1992, the appointments committee at the law school informed me that I would be coming up for a vote on tenure in the spring of 1993. I was looking forward to 1993. On January 18,

1993, we celebrated what would have been Dr. Martin Luther King's sixty-fourth birthday. Three days later came a national news flash that broke my heart. Justice Thurgood Marshall, "the eighty-four-year-old retired Supreme Court Justice, died at 2:00 p.m. today at Bethesda Naval Hospital." The nation had lost a giant and I had lost the greatest role model one could ever have as a lawyer. I traveled to Washington, D.C., several days later to view Marshall's body, lying in state at the Supreme Court. I saw many friends and familiar faces of prominent people. Thousands of tourists who were in Washington despite the cold weather also came to view his body. I was particularly struck by the number of elderly black women and men who walked around his casket whispering and telling stories about the "colored lawyer" whom they all remembered fighting for justice when they were much younger. It was not the judges, lawyers, or celebrities who stood out that day. It was the common, everyday, voiceless, and powerless African-Americans who came to mourn the death of a legal giant.

I attended Marshall's funeral at the National Cathedral. Many people spoke that day, but one voice was particularly eloquent. Vernon Jordan, a prominent African-American lawyer, confidant of President Bill Clinton, and someone mentored by Marshall, gave a eulogy that resonated with everyone who attended the service. As we sat there, painfully aware that Marshall would be gone forever, Jordan reminded us that we should not mourn his death but celebrate his life and continue in his giant footsteps.

PART IV

Ogletree confers with Anita Hill during the 1991
Clarence Thomas confirmation hearings.

CHAPTER 12

THE RISE OF
CLARENCE THOMAS

On Sunday, June 30, 1991, I was invited to appear on *Face the Nation* to discuss Justice Thurgood Marshall's retirement and speculate about his possible replacement. The additional guests that Sunday were Professor Stephen Carter, a colleague of mine from Stanford, also a professor at Yale Law School and former law clerk for Marshall; and Richard Thornburgh, the former governor of Pennsylvania and the attorney general for President George H. W. Bush. Robert Schieffer, the news magazine host, asked me whether it was necessary that Justice Marshall be replaced by an African-American. My response was swift and unequivocal. The president, in my view, had to appoint an African-American in Marshall's place. Anything short of an African-American nominee would be strongly condemned by the African-American community. Professor Carter was more circumspect. He said that President Bush should appoint someone who was moderate, but did not think that race was an essential attribute for the nominee. Attorney General Thornburgh, a central player in finding candidates for President Bush to consider, argued that no litmus test was being applied, that the president was considering a variety of candidates, and that an outstanding choice would be forthcoming soon.

When I left the CBS studios that afternoon, I was pretty optimistic. Thornburgh, whom I knew through a variety of meetings on criminal justice matters at the Department of Justice a year or two before this event, did not seem overly hostile to my insistence that an African-American be appointed.

I failed to notice Thornburgh's smugness that day, but the reason for what in retrospect I recognize was smugness soon became clear. Two days later, there was a press report that President Bush would be announcing his choice to fill Justice Marshall's seat and that he and the nominee would both be speaking from Bush's summer home in Kennebunkport, Maine. I hoped to see the face of Harry Edwards, a distinguished African-American justice who served on the D.C. Circuit Court of Appeals, or that of Amalya Kearse, a distinguished African-American jurist who served on the Second Circuit Court of Appeals. Both of these circuit courts were considered ideal steppingstones for judges being considered for Supreme Court vacancies.

My first choice was unfortunately too old, too liberal, and too controversial to be appointed by Bush. That person was A. Leon Higginbotham, Jr., a distinguished scholar, law professor, and chief judge of the Third Circuit Court of Appeals. Judge Higginbotham also had uncanny connections both to Marshall and to Bush's eventual nominee. When President Lyndon Johnson was considering the vacancy created by the retirement of Justice Tom Clark in 1967, one of his aides suggested that he consider appointing Higginbotham to the Court. On the merits, the nomination of Higginbotham made sense. Higginbotham was a graduate of Antioch College and one of the first African-Americans to graduate from Yale Law School. He was the youngest appointee to the Federal Trade Commission, and he served on the federal district court in Philadelphia. He had also worked with President Johnson in developing responses to the civil rights rebellions in the 1960s and was considered a talented and respected jurist.

When the name was mentioned, Johnson responded in his usual colloquial style saying, "The only two people who ever heard of Judge Higginbotham are you and his momma. When I appoint a nigger to the bench, I want everybody to know he's a nigger."[1] Johnson's point was that Marshall was known in the black community, had attended predominantly black schools, and after the *Brown* case, was associated with the most important case in civil rights history. Marshall, not Higginbotham, would give the politically calculating Johnson the support he needed in the black community, in the event that he sought a second term as president. Higginbotham would also have a very public series of exchanges with Bush's eventual nominee. None of my predictions regarding that nominee were correct. In fact, they weren't even close.

Standing slightly behind President Bush that afternoon was a person I knew, but had not for a moment considered as a potential nominee.

Bush's nominee was Clarence Thomas, an African-American who had served just over a year on the D.C. Circuit Court of Appeals, but was best known for his harsh criticism of the NAACP, civil rights, and affirmative action. When I saw Thomas about to be introduced as the replacement for Justice Thurgood Marshall on the U.S. Supreme Court, I viewed it as a bad omen. Thomas was an African-American, but he was not what I had in mind as a replacement for Justice Marshall. Thomas's critics began to appear quickly, attacking his lack of qualifications to serve and his lack of candor on some issues concerning judicial philosophy. Ultimately, it was his character that generated the greatest amount of opposition to his candidacy. Although Marshall and Thomas had had no real interaction before Thomas was nominated to the Supreme Court, their careers intersected in Washington, D.C., in the 1980s, as Thomas strengthened his connections to conservative Republicans in politics and Marshall's power on the Court began to decline. Change was in the winds in the 1980s, and the transfer of power from those who supported Marshall's views to those who opposed them was unmistakable.

Since the Supreme Court prefers to have all nine justices available to start its term hearing cases on the first Monday in October, President Bush wanted to initiate Judge Thomas's hearings right away. He urged the Senate Judiciary Committee chairman, Senator Joseph Biden, to schedule the hearing in July 1991, so that the Senate could consider his appointment before the end of the summer or, at worst, early in the fall. At the same time Bush and the Republicans were pushing to advance Thomas's hearing, liberal groups were looking for any evidence to keep Thomas, a known conservative, from being confirmed. The Democrats were feeling quite confident about challenging Thomas's conservatism and perhaps even keeping him off the Court. A well-organized campaign in 1987 had succeeded in defeating President Reagan's effort to place the conservative judge Robert Bork on the Court. The word in Democratic circles, emboldened by the 1987 victory, was that Thomas would be "Borked" as well.

Little did I know that I would be drawn into the Thomas affair.

Those were busy times in my life. I had been appointed an assistant professor of law at Harvard in 1989 and was halfway through the process of being promoted to full professor. I was completing an article about a Supreme Court case for the *Harvard Law Review,* and it was due in October. I had opened up the Criminal Justice Institute at Harvard Law School, a program focusing on teaching, research, and practice related to criminal justice matters. I was also the founder of the Saturday School Program, a lecture series created to explore a wide range of legal issues through frank and often provocative presentations by judges, lawyers, activists, and law professors, with the list ranging from Fred Korematsu, a Japanese American placed in an internment camp during World War II, to Harry Blackmun, then a recently retired Supreme Court justice. This was hardly a time to take on additional responsibilities. However, as a result of my comments about Marshall's replacement on the national news a few weeks earlier, the Leadership Conference on Civil Rights asked me to be one of the academic panelists to testify about Thomas's qualifications to serve on the Supreme Court. I was originally eager to do so, because I knew Thomas to be something of a conservative ideologue. He was a favorite of President Reagan's, having served in the Civil Rights Office of the Equal Employment Opportunity Commission (EEOC) and being the frequent choice of conservatives when they needed someone black to take a stand on race issues.

Still, I respected his intellectual honesty as a conservative. Thomas was well known to those of us active in Washington politics, as was Clarence Pendleton, another conservative black Republican. Thomas and Pendleton would often take the conservative position at any gathering of black professionals and defend their views effectively in rooms dominated by liberal Democrats. I admired their willingness to come into an environment where they were the underdogs and to fight for their point of view. Having felt like an underdog all my life, I also had to admire the confident way they handled themselves.

When asked to testify against Thomas, I started reading his recent public statements. I was surprised to see in the newspapers and in public appearances on Capitol Hill a different Clarence Thomas from the one I knew. He was smiling, humble, and easygoing. In the usual political settings, he had been serious, arrogant, and even somewhat tense. He proudly wore his conservatism during the years I had known, seen, and heard him, and he was a constant critic of civil rights, the NAACP, and even Justice Marshall. The Thomas I saw and heard in July 1991 was a different man. For example, his opening statement at his confirmation hearing suggested a more nuanced and respectful view of Marshall, the NAACP, and the civil rights movement. He said:

> So many others gave their lives, their blood, their talents. But for them I would not be here. Justice Marshall, whose seat I have been nominated to fill, is one of those who had the courage and the intellect. He's one of the great architects of the legal battles to open doors that seemed so hopelessly and permanently sealed and to knock down barriers that seemed so insurmountable to those of us in the Pin Point, Georgias of the world.
>
> The civil rights movement, Reverend Martin Luther King and the SCLC, Roy Wilkins and the NAACP, Whitney Young and the Urban League, Fannie Lou Hamer, Rosa Parks and Dorothy Height, they changed society and made it reach out and affirmatively help. I have benefited greatly from their efforts. But for them there would have been no road to travel.[2]

Thomas's confirmation transformation sounded sincere, and it seemed possible to me that, partisan as Thomas had been during his days as a political appointee in the executive branch, he might become more moderate as a Supreme Court justice. As long as Thomas meant what he said, it did not much matter whether he had been moderate all along, but forced into partisanship by President Reagan, or whether his moderation stemmed from experience on the bench, considered reflection upon learning of his nomination, or something else. The freedom from political influence that Supreme Court justices enjoy would ensure that Thomas could fulfill his duties consistently with this more nuanced philosophy.

I found myself increasingly unwilling to oppose Thomas's nomination, not only because of my doubts as to whether Thomas was really as bad as I had once thought he was, but also because I found his personal story so compelling. I believed that his experiences would not merely lead him to reasonable decisions but also provide a much needed minority perspective on an otherwise all-white Supreme Court.

Admittedly, I found it unsettling that the confirmation hearings focused so much on Thomas's character, rather than on his intellect, as the central feature of his candidacy. The Republicans portrayed Thomas as the Horatio Alger of the black community, who had made it from Pin Point, Georgia, a poor rural southern community, to the Supreme Court and was deserving of deference as a black man who had come so far from his roots. Still, knowing my father's roots in Birmingham, Alabama, and my mother's roots in Little Rock, Arkansas, I found the Thomas story to be a powerful one. He actually presented an amazing contrast to Thurgood Marshall, my hero. Marshall surely came from a family with humble roots, tracing his grandfather's connections to slavery, but he grew up with both of his parents and lived in comfortable surroundings in middle-class Baltimore with a free and successful black population. Thomas, by contrast, did not grow up with his mother and father; he was raised by his grandparents, in a dirt-poor but proud community. Thomas related how his grandfather taught him many things about life and responsibility.

His reflections resonated with me as I recalled the critical role my grandparents had played in my life. I remembered the great influence of my grandmother, a wise woman, though she had had no formal schooling. Big Mama took me under her wing and taught me a few things. She taught me how to make rice pudding with coconut and raisins; she taught me how to iron my clothes; ultimately, she taught me how to survive, no matter what challenges I faced in life. Behind all of her instruction was one overarching lesson: always be able to take care of yourself, since there is no promise that anyone will take care of you. As I heard Thomas describe his grandfather's tough love, I remembered Big Mama's for me.

How could I oppose a black man who, like me, had come from the same low valley to get to the mountaintop? His views and demeanor now seemed as reasonable as could be expected of a conservative nominee. Moreover, I considered it sufficiently important to have a black person on the Court that I was unwilling to oppose Thomas unless it was clear he would be a reactionary. Thus, I could not testify against Thomas, and I declined the invitation of the civil rights groups to do so.

I was by no means the only person in the progressive community who felt torn between the desire to resist the confirmation of any conservative justices, on the one hand, and to support the elevation of blacks to high office whenever possible, on the other. Delegates at the annual convention for the National Bar Association, a professional association for black lawyers, voted 128 to 124 to oppose Thomas's nomination.[3] Opinion polls taken in August 1991 showed that about 57 percent of blacks supported his nomination.[4]

President Bush thus successfully divided the black community, without whose firm opposition it would be difficult to defeat Thomas's confirmation. Thomas's expressions of admiration for civil rights heroes and the things they stood for, and his focus on his powerful life story, added to that division. They allowed him to escape the fate of Robert Bork, who entered his confirmation hearings with a longer paper trail and was unapologetic about his conservative views.

At this point, I thought that my connection with the Thomas nomination would end for good and that I would get back to my work at Harvard. It was not to be. I received a call from Wade Henderson, the NAACP's legal director. Wade and I had been friends in the 1970s, particularly during our days of activism during the *Bakke* case. He asked a small favor: Would I be willing to write a short analysis of Thomas's legal speeches and writings, for a report he was preparing for Benjamin Hooks, the NAACP president, and their board? I told him of my reluctance to take on any project, since I was not tenured yet and had work to do at Harvard. Wade promised me that if I wrote the report, it would not require any testimony and would be used only for the internal deliberations of the NAACP board. Like many black and civil rights organizations, the NAACP was reluctant to oppose Thomas. Some feared losing the "black seat" if Thomas was not confirmed. Some thought he would actually be a positive influence on race issues, given his humble background. In any event, Wade wanted the divided membership to be fully informed about Thomas before the organization took a public position on his candidacy. I don't know why I took on this added burden in 1991, but I agreed to research Thomas's background. I told Wade, however, that I would call it as I saw it, with no preconceived notion as to whether Thomas should be confirmed or opposed. Perhaps Wade knew more about Thomas than I did, because he did not oppose my insistence on offering an objective review of the body of work.

In 1991, Thomas had a modest record of writings, including speeches and, as a result of his very recent appointment to the D.C. Circuit Court, his judicial opinions. I searched all of the usual legal venues to find published articles, speeches, opinion editorials, or other reviews that might offer some inkling of Thomas's potential judicial philosophy. The danger in such an effort is that a small body of work may not reveal any sense of someone's political or judicial philosophy. Nevertheless, there was enough material to give me a glimpse of the man and of his peculiar views on certain subjects.

In July 1991, Thomas's previous litigation experience was minimal, and having served as a judge for only a year, he had few published opinions. The cases in which he participated were interesting in and of themselves, but not very revealing. For example, the first case I reviewed was *Farrakhan and Stallings v. U.S.*,[5] where the D.C. circuit panel that Thomas sat on remanded a case to the trial court for further hearings. The case was a well-publicized event, involving Minister Louis Farrakhan's and Bishop William Stallings's appearance in court during the high-profile trial of the Washington, D.C., mayor Marion Barry. The trial judge removed them, fearing that they would, by their presence, have an impermissible influence on the jurors. On appeal, a per curiam court, which included Thomas, remanded so that Farrakhan and Stallings could present their claims to the district court, which ultimately let them appear. Nothing of Thomas's opinion could be gleaned from the per curiam opinion. The second case shed no light on his judicial philosophy at all. In *Boyd v. Coleman*,[6] an unpublished disposition, Thomas and his colleagues concluded that entry of summary judgment in a jury trial was harmless error, despite a possible violation of the defendant's Seventh Amendment right to trial by jury. It was clear to me that these opinions were of little value in understanding Thomas's thinking about the law.

I embarked on an examination of the writings of Clarence Thomas, the public intellectual and darling of conservatives. I looked beyond law reviews and court reports and found a fairly large and varied body of material, including articles, speeches, and interviews. None of it was particularly long or detailed. But a careful analysis revealed an incredibly complex man, with fairly radical thoughts about law and the legal system.

I was fascinated by what I described in the NAACP report as "Judge Thomas's world view." My research revealed that Thomas had given careful thought to the application of legal principles to various problems, and to alternative ways of resolving matters when the law was imperfect or underinclusive. I felt that his clearly articulated philosophical views strongly suggested that his judicial approach would be quite conservative; I also recognized that it was important for a judge to have clearly defined philosophical views. Additionally, before being appointed to the federal bench, Thomas had repeatedly given talks on issues relating to race, the rights of individuals, and the role of government in addressing the problems of those seeking relief from the claims of race and sex discrimination. My conclusion was that Thomas's writings, speeches, and decisions revealed some fairly well-developed judgments, which in turn suggested what shape his judicial philosophy would take.

The materials suggested to me that Thomas was conservative yet independent. He quoted Malcolm X, Du Bois, and Frederick Douglass and placed his own views in the context of phrases they had uttered. He did not want to follow the traditional path of most blacks, whose political identity would be moderate to liberal (often the latter). Thomas came from a far different place and was on a mission to go in a radically different direction. I remember finding examples of his praise for Colonel Oliver North, a controversial military leader during the Reagan administration. North was considered a loyal soldier by a military standard, but political leaders regarded him as a dangerous operator. He was at the center of claims that the United States was covertly involved in providing arms to rightist Nicaraguan rebels during the Iran-Contra conflict. Thomas admired North's dedication to President Reagan and his willingness to express absolute commitment to his belief, without fear of the consequences.[7]

I discerned three powerful pillars that supported his thinking. First of all, he was a devotee of rugged individualism, which informed his views on the proper relationship between government and individuals in such areas of legal interpretation as affirmative action and legal assistance to the poor. According to this radical individualist philosophy, individuals, and not the state, needed to take the lead in overcoming hardships and barriers.[8]

Second, and relatedly, although Thomas was very conscious of his race, he fiercely opposed any attempt to stereotype him as a black man who would think a certain way. He refused to be typecast in roles deemed suitable for blacks or to be seen as focusing on "black issues" and was, by his own account, a self-made man in the model of his mentor and grandfather.[9] Moreover, he did not appear to appreciate the irony of his profiting from being an African-American conservative.

A striking example of this appears in remarks Thomas made at a gathering of African-American conservatives at the Fairmont conference in December 1980. He told an interviewer, "If I ever went to work for the EEOC or did anything directly connected with blacks, my career would be irreparably ruined. The monkey would be on my back again to prove that I didn't have the job because I am black. People meeting me for the first time would automatically dismiss my thinking as second-rate."[10] Thomas's actions conflicted with his heartfelt views. Thomas accepted an appointment by President Reagan as the assistant secretary of education for civil rights in 1980, and two years later he accepted the position of chairman of the EEOC. His acceptance of these positions suggests to me that, while Thomas found such positions, in theory, to be typecasting for blacks, he had no qualms about taking them when conservative whites offered them to him.

Third, Thomas admired the concept of natural law and expressed a more than passing interest in it. His brand of natural law mirrors the writings of theologians and philosophers such as Thomas Aquinas. Put simply, law is rooted in the divine. Thomas does not subscribe to this theory because he believes it is morally right; rather, he believes that the Constitution and Declaration of Independence themselves were intended to embody divine law. In other words, because the framers intended to incorporate natural law into the law of the land, judges should look to natural law to resolve cases.[11]

My report pointed out just how worrisome Thomas's willingness to look to natural law sources to resolve cases that came before him in the Supreme Court would be. I reminded the NAACP board of directors about Thomas's courtesy visit to the office of Senator Howard Metzenbaum, a member of the Judiciary Committee, during the confirmation process. These visits are a routine part of that process; they give Supreme Court nominees an opportunity to meet informally with the individuals responsible for approving or rejecting his nomination. The subject of natural law came up during their chat, in the following way. Senator Metzenbaum asked Judge Thomas to elaborate on his view of natural law. "Well, Senator," Thomas reportedly asked, "do you think it's proper for a human being to own another human being?" Metzenbaum said no. "The reason you think that's wrong is because we all have natural rights," Thomas explained. That did not end the discussion, however. "What about a human being owning an animal?" the senator said. "Is that part of natural law?" Thomas said he would have to check his own and other writings on natural law for an answer.[12]

Thomas's writings demonstrated how the abstract principles in his personal philosophy would have concrete consequences for many of the NAACP's primary areas of concern. He consistently employed notions of individual rights to criticize affirmative action policies and a range of progressive judicial moves. The word "individual" appears repeatedly in Judge Thomas's opinions and writings. In his essay in *Assessing the Reagan Years*, Thomas expressed his understanding of the purpose of an insulated judiciary: "The judiciary was protected to ensure justice for individuals."[13]

I gained similar insight into Thomas's likely future behavior as a judge from his actions as chairman of the EEOC and from the sizable record he had amassed in that role. Thomas's tenure as chairman saw a dramatic reduction in the number of class action suits filed to remedy claims of racial and other forms of discrimination. I reported the trend to the NAACP, with the reminder that in evaluating Thomas as a nominee to the Supreme Court, one should carefully examine his record in handling discrimination cases to get a reading on his likely judgments on similar matters as a justice.

The NAACP had reason to be concerned about Thomas's approach to employment discrimination law. African-Americans, particularly African-American women, have fewer employment options and are particularly vulnerable to downturns in the economy.[14] At the time of my report, the *Washington Post* carried a story about gender and race issues in the employment arena; it identified a disturbing trend that suggested the need for vigilance on the part of civil rights groups: "white women have more job mobility because they are more often seen by management as sisters, daughters, or wives, but black women are seen as outsiders. So white women get to be patronized, and black women get nothing."[15]

In reviewing Thomas's opinions as EEOC chairman, I found areas of concern that I wanted the NAACP to consider carefully. An opinion rendered under his leadership in 1985 gave disturbing evidence of governmental acquiescence in forms of gender discrimination. In that case, three female sales clerks filed a Title VII complaint after losing their jobs as clerks in a women's fashion store. Each had been fired after refusing to wear swim attire while at work during a swimsuit promotion. The women charged that, unlike other promotional outfits, swimsuit attire would have subjected them to sexual harassment and left them vulnerable to unwanted sexual remarks and conduct. They complained that even when dressed in their normal working attire of jeans and a blazer, they were subjected to recurring instances of young men whistling and knocking on the store's windows to get their attention. The women also noted that they regularly had to venture outside the store to use common mall facilities because the store had no restroom or eating facilities of its own. Almost four years after the women lost their jobs, the EEOC ruled against them. According to the commissioner's decision, the evidence was not sufficient to support a finding that the outfits would have subjected them to unwelcome sexual conduct or harassment. The EEOC noted, however, that in certain circumstances a requirement that employees wear sexually provocative outfits could violate Title VII.[16]

It should surprise no one that Thomas's EEOC was reluctant to intervene in the conflict between these women and their employer. His belief in radical individualism was inextricably bound up with a conception of limited government. Thomas firmly believed—and his judgments reflected the belief—that affirmative action policies and other forms of government assistance reduce individual motivation and foster dependence on government interference in matters that are best regulated by market forces. In this regard, I questioned whether he would exacerbate the conservative Supreme Court's already disturbing unwillingness to assist those who came to the Court seeking various forms of relief from race discrimination. During this period, women won most of their equal protection cases, although they did less well in employment law. One of the reasons that women fared better was that Justice O'Connor, having suffered from gender discrimination herself, could more easily sympathize with gender discrimination victims than with racial discrimination victims. Also, Chief Justice Rehnquist became a moderate on gender issues, whereas he remained quite conservative on race issues. Thomas, not a fan of "government interference" in these matters, warned of the inherent risks associated with government regulation: "Maximization of rights is perfectly compatible with total government and regulation. Unbounded by notions of obligation and justice, the desire to protect rights simply plays into the hands of those who advocate a total state."[17]

Distressing as I found some of Thomas's views, I did respect the ideas underlying his advice to African-Americans on how to handle the burden of succeeding in a society where racism constantly intensifies the challenges they face. The theme of self-help pervades his autobiographical recollections, where he discusses his opinion of government assistance programs to disadvantaged people. His commencement speech at Savannah State College in 1985 also bore ample witness to his faith in self-help. Judge Thomas's speech was passionate and eloquent. He exhibited genuine humility and spoke in personal terms about racial discrimination. He returned to the familiar theme that anyone can overcome discrimination through hard work and dedication:

> Over the past 15 years, I have watched as others have jumped quickly at the opportunity to make excuses for black Americans. It is said that blacks cannot start businesses because of discrimination. But I remember businesses on East Broad and West Broad that were run in spite of bigotry. It is said that we can't learn because of bigotry. But I know for a fact that tens of thousands of blacks were educated at historically black colleges, in spite of discrimination. We learned to read in spite of segregated libraries. We built homes in spite of segregated neighborhoods. We learned how to play basketball (and did we ever learn!), even though we couldn't go to the NBA.[18]

I found Thomas's speech to be oblivious to the complex structural effects of racism. His statement of blacks' courage and resourcefulness in the face of discrimination was accurate enough, but his omission of this country's historical pattern of discriminatory practices that denied full opportunity and his suggestion that discrimination was primarily a private problem to be worked out among private individuals struck me as disingenuous. For example, Thomas failed to address the systemic exclusion of blacks from venture capital, or the contemptible practices of predatory lending to blacks seeking mortgages to finance home purchases, or the debilitating effects of overcrowded and underfunded public schools, and the resulting problems of high dropout rates and limited opportunities for educational advancement. In the reality that Thomas described, the problems of racism had been solved, and we black people only needed to pull ourselves up by our bootstraps and move forward. Thomas spoke of an America that did not exist. His worldview left little or no role for a vigilant civil rights movement to protect the rights of women or blacks and other ethnic groups.

Clarence Thomas's logic, as reflected in his practices, speeches, and writings, told a story of an America that Dr. King had dreamed about, but not one in which his children, or I, or Thomas lived in 1991. Thomas created a liberal straw man of sorts, suggesting that blacks have tried to abdicate all responsibility for their own liberation because of prejudice, and then knocked it down by citing some anecdotes about the few who had overcome the legacy of past discrimination and the barriers of continuing discrimination. He inferred, from the few, that everyone could make it and that the unevenness of the playing field was not a matter for governmental concern.

Even more disturbing, however, was the way in which this logic led to blaming the victim. By Thomas's logic, if some blacks made it in the face of discrimination, then surely *all* blacks can, and if *all* blacks can make it in the face of discrimination, how does one account for the fact that so many don't make it? The obvious answer is that there is something wrong with them—they just don't work hard enough.[19] Why don't they work hard enough? Thomas offered an answer to this question as well: "In 1964, when I entered the seminary, I was the only black in my class and one of two in the school. A year later, I was the only one in the school. Not a day passed that I was not pricked by prejudice. But I had an advantage over black students and kids today. I had never heard any excuses made. Nor had I seen my role models take comfort in excuses."[20] The obvious implication is that somehow, in reminding the African-American community of systemic racism, white and black progressives had disabled the community. It is not difficult to extend this logic to a generalized opposition to affirmative action. Perhaps more difficult to see, yet critical to the NAACP's assessment of Thomas, was the subtle but profound message that civil rights organizations are themselves to blame for the black community's continuing misfortunes.

Given the troubling implications of Thomas's individualism and commitment to limited governmental attempts to prevent and remedy discrimination, I worried that his enthusiasm for natural law might lead him to a similarly narrow conception of the constitutional right to privacy.[21] Women would be particularly vulnerable if the Court limited or abolished abortion and contraception rights, and poor people and minorities would be the first to come under the microscope if the Court narrowed constitutional protections for family privacy. That Thomas had praised Lewis Lehrman's article on a fetus's right to life was well known.[22] Lehrman argued that a fetus should have an inalienable right to life (thus precluding states from allowing even therapeutic abortions). This was even more radical than what the conservatives on the Court maintained at the time: rather than arguing that the Constitution forbade abortion, they held that the Constitution had nothing to say about the matter and that the decision whether to limit or prohibit abortion should be left to state policy. In numerous public statements, Thomas had shown hostility toward the two decisions most fundamental to Americans' privacy and reproductive freedoms of Americans: *Griswold v. Connecticut*,[23] right to use contraception, and *Roe v. Wade*,[24] right to obtain an abortion. My concern in 1991 was that, despite Thomas's assertion (almost certainly false) that he had never discussed or thought about these decisions, there were suggestions in his philosophy that these hard-won rights would be vulnerable if he ascended to the Supreme Court.[25]

In the 1980s, Thomas frequently recited the prose of prominent African-American heroes, characterizing them as supporters of his point of view. For example, he twisted the logic and text of Frederick Douglass's writings and public pronouncements to provide support for his arguments against *Brown v. Board of Education* (or at least against an expansive reading thereof) and other civil rights measures in ways that raise serious doubts about his credibility.

In his 1987 article in the *Howard Law Journal*, Thomas would have the reader believe that Frederick Douglass and Thomas were intellectual soulmates. According to Thomas, we should regard "the Constitution to be the fulfillment of the ideals of the Declaration of

Independence, as Lincoln, Frederick Douglass, and the Founders understood it."[26] Douglass, of course, believed one could argue for the abolition of slavery by claiming that the Constitution was an antislavery document, but imagine his surprise if he had learned that Thomas attributed to him the belief that the Declaration of Independence was also an antislavery document.[27] Thomas takes Douglass's comments about the Declaration of Independence, which Douglass lambasted because its promises of life, liberty, and the pursuit of happiness did not apply to blacks, out of context to suggest that Douglass in fact believed that it applied to African-Americans. Yet Douglass lamented,

> What, to the American slave, is your Fourth of July? I answer: a day that reveals to him, more than all other days in the year, the gross injustice and cruelty to which he is the constant victim. To him, your celebration is a sham; your boasted liberty, an unholy license; your national greatness, swelling vanity; your sounds of rejoicing are empty and heartless; your denunciation of tyrants, brass fronted impudence; your shouts of liberty and equality, hollow mockery. Your prayers and hymns, your sermons and thanksgivings, with all your religious parade and solemnity are, to him, mere bombast, fraud, deception, impiety, and hypocrisy—a thin veil to cover up crimes that would disgrace a nation of savages. . . .[28]

Douglass begged white Americans to interpret the Constitution so as to remove the blot on the nation made by the Declaration of Independence's hypocrisy. When Thomas argues that "we should put the fitly spoken words of the Declaration of Independence in the center of the frame formed by the Constitution"[29] and claims that Douglass agrees with him, he sullies Douglass's name and falsifies the history of his fuming speech in 1852. Thomas's distortions of Douglass's views and history did not end with the *Howard Law Journal* article, nor did my critique of Thomas end there.

My conclusion in my report to the NAACP was straightforward. Though the record of Clarence Thomas's judicial opinions was slim, I wrote, there was ample evidence to piece together the political philosophy that had animated his career. Even more important, the record persuaded me that Thomas would embrace few, if any, of the NAACP's core principles. Indeed, I was convinced that he would be hostile to them.

The NAACP had my report, and it took the opportunity to examine Thomas's record carefully. There was much to fear from Thomas, but the fear of opposing a black man's appointment to the highest court of the land was perhaps even greater. By nominating Justice Thomas, a conservative African-American, to serve on the Supreme Court, President Bush had achieved a remarkable feat: he had divided the black community throughout the country and had left those opposed to Thomas powerless to do anything.

Thomas's nomination proceeded without interruption until October 1991. His focus on character, rather than intellect and legal ability, carried the day. The civil rights groups could find little to fault in his character, and they had all but conceded that his nomination would be approved. Some staff members on the Senate Judiciary Committee, however, began to hear some rumors of Thomas's role in some sexual discrimination matters while in the Reagan administration. It created a buzz in Washington, and the Thomas hearing, scheduled to conclude, took a new turn in the national spotlight.

CHAPTER 13

WHO'S GETTING LYNCHED?: HILL V. THOMAS

Justice Marshall's retirement was a major blow to the civil rights movement. It would be virtually impossible to find a voice to replace his on the Supreme Court. With Clarence Thomas as the likely candidate to join the Court, there was even greater concern among members of the civil rights community about his voice on issues of race and civil rights. No one had anticipated, however, that race would not be the primary issue during Thomas's confirmation hearing. As it turned out, the nation would focus not on Thomas's controversial race views but on whether he had been involved in a variety of incidents involving sexual harassment a decade earlier. For me, a greater surprise was that I found myself drawn into the public debate over Thomas's fitness to serve on the Supreme Court.

After Thomas's nomination to the Supreme Court, a number of people familiar with his background, and not involved in his confirmation process to date, took a keen interest in his candidacy. Susan Hoerchner, a workers' compensation judge in California, remembered that a friend of hers, Professor Anita Hill, had worked with Thomas when she was a young lawyer and had told her privately that Thomas was the man who, ten years earlier, had sexually harassed her. A few weeks later, Hill phoned Gary Liman Phillips, a Yale Law School friend, to inform him that she had left the EEOC because Thomas sexually harassed her. Soon thereafter, word of Thomas's involvement with Hill reached Nan Aron and George Kassouf of the Alliance for Justice, a public-interest organization that actively participated in the judicial nominations process and had been critical of Thomas's candidacy. Aron passed the tip on to a member of the Senate Judiciary Committee, who was on the staff of Senator Howard Metzenbaum, a liberal Democrat. Rumors of other possible claims against Thomas were also reported to Aron and others. In early September, Gail Laster, with whom I had worked earlier in her career as a public defender in D.C. and who was now working for Senator Metzenbaum, decided to follow up on the claims. When asked whether there was sexual harassment during her service as an employee under Thomas at the EEOC, Hill told Laster to look into it, but did not discuss her own personal history with Thomas. Laster never thought to ask Hill directly whether she had been harassed. At the same time that the Alliance for Justice and others were trying to determine the validity of the claims, the staff of Senator Ted Kennedy, another Judiciary Committee member, contacted Hill to see whether her claims could be verified. After some resistance, Hill agreed to cooperate, but only if she could be assured that the information would be kept confidential and that she would not have to reveal anything publicly. Hill provided a statement to the staffers, which was distributed to several of the Democrats on the committee.

When the Thomas hearings started, on September 10, 1991, another friend of Hill's, James Brudney, who also worked for Senator Metzenbaum, contacted Hill and told her that the information about her relationship with Thomas was circulating through the halls of Congress and that she needed to respond. Brudney assured her that she could testify confidentially. After Hill gave her statement to the Senate Judiciary Committee members, a strange thing happened. It was ultimately dismissed as irrelevant and was neither placed in the record nor discussed by any of the committee members.

Of course, I had no knowledge of any of these events and little knowledge of Professor Hill. I knew her from occasional brief social interactions at law teacher conferences. I also knew her as the faculty coach of the University of Oklahoma Law School's Frederick Douglass moot court teams. Most black students at law school would prepare a team to participate in an annual moot court competition, and Hill had a reputation for preparing one of the best teams each year. After the committee called her to testify, she telephoned two of her Yale Law School classmates, Kim Taylor and Sonya Jarvis, seeking advice and possibly counsel to guide her. Both are black women whom I knew well. Sonya and I were Stanford undergraduates together and participated in a lot of campus activism. Kim was one of the people I worked with as a public defender in D.C. It is amazing what a small world we live in.

After Hill explained to her Yale classmates what was going on, they called me. They were very vague, giving me nothing solid to proceed on. They indicated that they knew that someone had provided the Senate Judiciary Committee with information concerning some form of sexual misconduct by Judge Thomas, and that the committee had ignored it. I probed further, to determine whether it involved a sexual assault, and whether it involved a child or an adult. Hill's friends refused to tell me any of these details, concerned about the privacy of their source. They wanted to know whether I could get the committee to look at this information, which they described as critical to the issue of Thomas's suitability to serve on the Supreme Court. I pressed for more information to no avail. I really didn't think that I had enough information to contact the Judiciary Committee, but I decided to consult my colleague Professor Larry Tribe, who knew many of the senators, having been a key witness for the Democrats during the successful challenge of Judge Bork for a Court vacancy. I told Tribe about the critical call I had received, and he asked me for the same details I had sought. When he understood that I had little more to offer, other than the plaintive plea of two people whom I greatly respected, he called Ron Klain, who was a former student of Tribe's and a legal counsel to Senator Edward Kennedy, and reported, as I suggested, "There is some sensitive information, of a sexual nature, that the Senate Judiciary Committee has, about Judge Thomas, and it is important that they consider it." This communication by Tribe had an impact, and within a day the report that Hill provided was distributed to all committee members, and there was an immediate interest in having Hill appear before the committee to verify her assertions.

The day Hill was contacted by the committee members to follow up on the report, she called me and revealed, for the first time, that she was the person referred to in my cryptic conversation with her classmates. She wondered whether I could discuss the next steps with her. She was pleased that my call to Tribe had led the committee to look at the material, and hoped that no more would be required of her. Now, however, the committee wanted the FBI to talk to her, and she wondered what to do. I advised her to be truthful with the agents and suggested she should probably have counsel with her when she talked to them. As

it turned out, Hill met the agents without counsel, and they took a statement, while also asking her, curiously, whether she would be willing to
take a lie detector test to verify her claims. They also informed her that
she might be called as a possible witness against Judge Thomas in his
confirmation hearings.

Shortly thereafter, Hill's confidential FBI report was leaked to Nina
Totenberg, and her name and identity were revealed on National Public
Radio. Hill called me to report this, and I advised her to avoid making
any statements and probably to get a lawyer. She also said that the press
was at her home and at her office at the law school, and was trying to
talk to her friends and family about her work for Thomas and about the
claim of sexual harassment. At the same time, she received a subpoena
to testify before the Senate Judiciary Committee and had to report
within a few days. There were dozens of reporters at the law school, and
I suggested that she read a prepared statement, indicating that she
would comply with the subpoena, but I urged her not to respond to the
barrage of questions coming from the press about the incidents. Hill
attended the press conference, refused to respond to the shouts for more
commentary, and called me back to determine whether she had handled
it well.

I saw the press coverage and thought she had handled the aggressive press questioning well, and I told her so. I wished her well in Washington and imagined that my involvement was finished. I was wrong.
That same evening, I got a call from Professor Emma Coleman Jordan,
a Georgetown law professor who was also the first black president of
the Association of American Law Schools. She told me there was a
problem. Hill was heading to Washington to testify against her former
boss, Clarence Thomas, but she did not have a lawyer to represent her.

I told Jordan that I had assisted Hill earlier and assumed that she
would get local counsel as the matter progressed. Jordan said she and
others were going to volunteer to assist Hill and wanted to know
whether I would continue to help. I declined, without telling her that my
main reasons were that I had substantial work to do in preparing for
tenure and that I had already been involved in this matter. Jordan persisted and asked whether I could at least spend a few hours with her and
her volunteer legal team, to help her get ready for the hearings. I
thought that this made no sense and told Jordan as much. Still, she was

relentless, saying that if I just flew to Washington the morning before and offered Hill a few suggestions, it would then be okay for me to return to Boston and continue with my work. This would be my modest contribution, I thought, and then I could get back to my responsibilities at Harvard Law School. I did not worry that my actions so far would affect the tenure process, because neither my conversations with Professor Tribe nor my advice to Professor Hill before the press conference had made public my involvement in the case.

On the shuttle flight from Boston to Washington, I saw an old friend, and occasional nemesis, William Bradford Reynolds, on the plane. Reynolds was the former chief of the Civil Rights Division of the Department of Justice under President Reagan and, in my view, was instrumental in turning back the clock on civil rights during his tenure. During the flight, we chatted about my law review article on *Miranda*, which was in draft form, and his enthusiasm about being back in private practice in D.C. He asked whether I would be there long, and, without indicating why I was going there, I told him it was a day trip for business. When I saw Reynolds months later, he recalled our chat and, as a Thomas supporter, was not surprised that I had not shared more with him. On that Thursday, my involvement was so minimal that I did not see any reason to mention it at all. That would change.

My agreement with Hill and with Jordan was straightforward: my role would be confidential and limited. I would fly to Washington, meet with Hill, help prepare her testimony, and then return to Cambridge to finish my article. It was more than I wanted to do, but I did not want to turn down my friends, or this person in a jam not of her own making.

By the time I arrived in Washington, several female law professors who knew Hill had also volunteered to assist her. Additionally, two senior volunteers on the team, Warner Gardner and John Frank, had longstanding ties on Capitol Hill and wanted to work with the Senate Judiciary Committee staff in negotiating the process for the hearing. We met in the law offices of a friend of one of our team members and started preparing Hill for her expected testimony. I arrived after several other lawyers had spent some time working with her and reviewing her prepared testimony. We now expressed differing views about how specific and graphic her testimony should be, though all of us were loyal to Hill. Her women supporters saw her testimony in a broader context and wanted to focus on Thomas's strong interest in pornographic material and his persistent efforts to date her while she was an employee under his supervision. I was interested in Hill as a client, who needed to be protected from her adversaries, as well as from well-intentioned friends who might not have her best interests in mind. I thought that the additional details were necessary and appropriate. Despite our disagreements, we were able to form a unified force and prepare her for what would be a brutal process. One of the areas of contention was Hill's prepared testimony.

When writing her statement, she revealed many of the details of her involvement with Thomas, including details that had not been explored in her earlier brief questioning by the FBI. She discussed his interest in pornography in her statements, and the sexual jokes he had told her when they chatted in his office. Interestingly, the older white men on the team were troubled by her graphic testimony, as both the pro-Thomas and anti-Thomas white men in the Senate would later be. The women thought that, since it was all true, she should present it as she had experienced it. I agreed with the women. In fact, I had decided to help Hill precisely because I felt that it was imperative for her to tell the truth, no matter what, and for her to bring out all the details in her direct testimony, rather than allow the Senate to think she had left out potentially critical details. Before preparing Hill for her expected cross-examination, I decided to check with a friend, Jeff Robinson, who knew something about the senators who would be questioning Hill. He was able to learn that Arlen Specter, the senator from Pennsylvania, would be the principal cross-examiner, but that we should also expect tough questioning from Senator Orrin Hatch from Utah.

I used Jeff's information to focus my questioning of Hill, including asking her some questions about things that I knew were not true. This was a tactic I had used in hundreds of cases as a lawyer, to see how a witness responded to surprises. Hill found my questions to be offensive, accusatory, and false. I appeared to be accusing her of lying about Clarence Thomas. She seemed troubled by my bold, false allegations. She was right to be angry, but I wanted her to know that my questioning was mild, compared with what the senators would ask. I reminded her that these questions were simply a small sample of what I expected her to face the following day on Capitol Hill.

In addition, our team worked cooperatively with members of the Senate Judiciary Committee staff to ensure that Hill would be able to submit a written statement to the committee and able to call witnesses to corroborate her accusation that Thomas had engaged in sexually harassing behavior when she worked for him in the 1980s. After several hours of preparation, I was convinced that Hill was ready to testify. I gave her and her voluntary team of legal assistants my best wishes and prepared to head back to Cambridge. We had a commitment that Hill would begin her testimony shortly after the hearings opened on Friday morning and would then be allowed to call her witnesses, even though we were sure that the committee members would have questions for her. We also worked with her to arrange for her family members to arrive in Washington on Thursday night, to be there with her during her testimony on Friday.

As it turned out, I had lost track of the time and could not get a flight back to Boston that night. I planned to take the first flight back Friday morning. I spent the night at the Washington Marriott and explained to my *Harvard Law Review* editors some of the changes to the draft of my article. Later that night, Hill called to thank me again for helping out and to express how valuable the experience had been in preparing her for what would be a highly publicized and politicized event the next morning. We talked for a while, and she shared with me some information about common friends.

Trying to ease the tension that was in the air as we both contemplated the historic nature of her testimony scheduled for Friday morning, I joked with her about her success as the coach for the Oklahoma Law School Black Law Students Association (known by the acronym BLSA) moot court team and urged her, as consideration for my volunteer time preparing her, to give the Harvard team a break in the upcoming competition. She laughed and said that there was nothing she could do, since the Oklahoma students were more talented. I had to laugh at the confidence she had in her students, and quietly hoped she would have the same confidence in her own efforts a few hours later. She told me about her life, about her parents' farming business in Oklahoma, and that she was the youngest of thirteen children. I took comfort in hearing about a black family in the South still involved in farming. Having read about the enormous loss of property by black families in the South, through discriminatory and unjust practices by local authorities, I was pleased to learn that her family had managed to thrive as farmers. Their story provided a critical balance to Thomas's humble beginnings and illustrated that Hill, too, had overcome poverty to be, by 1991, a tenured law professor. I wished her well, and then called my wife to tell her about the session with Anita Hill and said I would be on the morning flight back home. Pam was pleased to hear that I was able to help Hill get prepared, but happy that I was heading home and not getting further involved in "this Thomas thing." She knew how wringing the summer involvement had been for me, and knew that, with a law review article due and tenure at Harvard Law School on the horizon, my focus needed to be elsewhere.

At five the next morning, I was on the phone dictating some changes for my law review article. There was banging at my door. My first instinct was to assume that there was a fire and that either I had been too tired to hear it or the alarm system was not working. I decided it was a mistake and ignored it. Whoever it was persisted. I went to the door and found Emma Coleman Jordan, the Georgetown law professor who had led the effort to organize Hill's volunteer team, and Susan Deller Ross, another member of the team. I was not expecting to see either of them. Coleman said that there was a critical matter involving Hill and that they needed to catch me before I left for the airport. They explained they had been trying to reach me by telephone, but it had been busy all morning. Coleman told the person at the front desk a lie, saying that my line was busy and that they had to get some emergency information to me. The front desk gave her my room number, and she came up to find me.

They told me that, given my involvement the day before and Hill's confidence in me, I could not leave her at that critical moment. They talked about the historic hearing about to happen: a black woman coming forward to accuse a black man of sexual harassment. Hill's team had white men on it and black and white women. What it lacked, they argued, was a respected black man, who would not be fearful of publicity or politicians and who knew how to protect a client's interests. I was reluctant, until they made one more point: having no black male on Hill's team could send a message that black men doubted her credibility. They played the race card, and it grabbed my attention.

I called Pam to try to explain to her that I would not be coming home as expected, since Hill and her team insisted that I stay to assist her in the hearing. Pam's initial response was silence. I was familiar with this response. It always got more attention from me. The message was clear: she did not think this was a good idea. She was solidly behind Hill and strongly believed that she needed help in this important event that was about to occur, but Pam's concern was about me and our family. Why can't someone else represent her, she asked, particularly with all of those lawyers in Washington? She was right to be concerned.

She believed that since July the White House and the Republicans had made it clear that they would allow nothing to stand in the way of Thomas's confirmation, and that anyone who interfered would risk getting crushed. She was not concerned about a bitter disagreement among people who were ideological opponents. She was concerned about the powerful weapons, legal and illegal, available to the government to make people pay for opposing its agenda. She feared that FBI agents might find a reason to place us under surveillance. It was hard to disagree with her, and my only response was that Hill had asked me to help her and that I felt it difficult, under all of the circumstances, to turn her down. Pam found my response unsatisfactory, but not surprising. There were always causes, and I always seemed to get in the middle of them.

After obtaining Pam's tepid approval, I called my confidant John Payton to see whether he thought getting in the case was a good idea. John, in his usual Socratic way, asked me more questions, leading me to the answers that I wanted. He thought that, though my concerns about tenure at Harvard were valid, they should not be the overriding factor. He knew that this would be controversial at Harvard, but that it should not influence my ultimate decision. John's final question was "Why not?"

It was early Friday morning, and I had no way of reaching anyone in this rapidly developing chain of events. I could not even reach my secretary, but I did leave her a sheepish message, saying that I would not be in the office that morning. As the intensity grew, the prospect of sitting behind Professor Anita Hill within an hour or two and advising her as needed loomed as more of an obligation than I had planned on. I had hoped to reach two colleagues in particular, both of whom had an interest in these hearings. Both were also familiar with Thomas, though neither knew Hill.

After thinking about Coleman's persuasive argument and Payton's approval of the idea, I decided to accept the invitation to rejoin and lead Hill's team. Professors Hill, Jordan, and Ross were pleased with my decision, but they had left out one critical detail. The senior lawyers on our team of volunteers, John Frank and Warner Gardner, had not been told that I was going to stay on the team and, more important, that I would be Hill's lead lawyer. They wanted me to get dressed quickly, come downstairs for the scheduled breakfast meeting, and join them in sharing this news with these legendary lawyers.

At breakfast, John Frank started to review the plans for the morning. He was surprised to see me, but said nothing of it. Jordan stopped his review of the day's plans and announced that there were some changes in the plans. She spoke emphatically but respectfully to the two gentlemen, telling them that she had been in contact with Hill and that Hill wanted me to be her lead attorney. Jordan explained that all of Hill's lawyers had to be selfless and that it did not make sense for Hill to have white men or women lead her representation. Jordan also thought that she, as a black woman, should not lead the representation. Ross, too, felt that it should not be viewed as being led by what would be perceived as a feminist legal team. Frank was somewhat flustered to hear this, since he had worked through the night on aspects of the hearing, and he and his law partner, Janet Napolitano, now the governor of Arizona, had flown from Arizona to provide pro bono assistance to Hill. He had to check with his firm to see whether they should stay in Washington.

When I had a chance to speak, I told Frank and Gardner of my own reluctance to play the role of lead counsel, and just as I had almost persuaded myself not to stick with the team, Jordan jumped in, refocused the conversation, and said that the deal was done. I then agreed to serve as lead counsel for Hill and reviewed our plans for the day.

Friday, October 11, 1991, was the first day of one of the most challenging and disappointing events in my life. Hill was scheduled to testify at 10 a.m., to be followed by her corroborating witnesses. Then, on Saturday, the Senate Judiciary Committee would hear from Thomas, and any witnesses he chose to call to corroborate his denials. I sent the other team members to the hearing room and went to the hotel where Hill was staying, just blocks from Capitol Hill. I wanted to talk to her in person one more time before her testimony and to prepare her for what I assumed would be an ugly day of cross examination and recriminations. She seemed prepared.

Waiting in her room with a few of her friends, we noticed that every television channel was covering the hearings live. Among the friends were her law school colleague Professor Shirley Wiegand, who was a settling force and a staunch supporter throughout the confirmation hearings, and Judge Susan Hoerchner, someone with whom Professor Hill had discussed the Thomas harassment charges soon after they occurred. Hoerchner became a witness at the hearing on Hill's behalf. After they returned to Oklahoma, Wiegand felt harassed by her colleagues and ultimately left the university of Oklahoma Law faculty.

As we were about to leave for the Hill, Senator Biden made a shocking announcement that set the tone for the next few days. Biden, the chairman of the Judiciary Committee, announced that the committee would grant Judge Thomas's request to speak to the committee before the hearings started. This was a change for us, and we assumed that Thomas was going to announce that he would be withdrawing from consideration and would acknowledge that something did happen, without necessarily giving the details. As I listened to him, I was certain he would withdraw. He said, "It is not worth it." But then he categorically denied the accusations; we then realized that we had been duped. Anita Hill had been subpoenaed to be a witness, and contrary to any sense of procedural regularity, the committee allowed the accused to respond to allegations from the accuser, before the accuser had spoken. I picked up the phone and called Senator Biden's chambers, screaming at the poor legislative intern, demanding that Biden leave the Senate right then and take my call. I threatened to keep Hill from appearing that day, even though she was under subpoena, because the Democratic-led Senate had just capitulated to the White House's pressure and unjustifiably given Thomas an opportunity to deny the charges to the nation, on live television, before they had even been made.

The intimidated intern found someone higher ranking to speak to me. After some delay and a break, Senator Biden did take my call and explained that the decision was not a partisan one and that he simply wanted to give Judge Thomas the right to defend himself. Biden's comments were utterly unpersuasive. He gave Thomas national exposure, put Hill on the defensive as the accuser, and enabled the Republicans to start their spin machine with Thomas's presentation of his denial, without a single senator asking him any questions about the substance. In effect, he was a witness allowed to testify with impunity, since he was not being subjected to any cross-examination, and his testimony would have an uncontested quality that Hill's cross-examined testimony could not possibly achieve, even in the best of circumstances. This was unprecedented in my practice. Unfortunately, this bout of favoritism by Biden and the Judiciary Committee toward Thomas, the White House, and the Republicans was only the beginning of our difficulties in the hearings.

Once we were ready to have Hill testify, we encountered problems of our own. We were looking forward to having her parents, who were in their late seventies, and her siblings sit behind her in the hearing room, to give her a boost of confidence. Since Thomas had unexpectedly been allowed to speak first, Hill's family members did not know when, or if, they should attend the hearing. By the time it was clear that she would be testifying, we had to arrange for them to come from several miles away to join us. Having to improvise so that Hill would not be alone, I then called our team of volunteer lawyers, up to ten people that morning, into the hearing room, and had them take the Hill family seats. The committee seemed a little puzzled, because the people behind Hill were not her family, but rather a group of black and white lawyers, male and female, young and old. The family arrived just as Biden reconvened the hearings, and Hill introduced her family and lawyers to the committee.

Hill's testimony was graphic, describing in detail Thomas's casual conversations about pornography, and his attempts to date her, even visiting her apartment unannounced. The Republicans, unhappy with her testimony, seemed anxious to cross-examine her. She testified for hours; during each break, I insisted on a process that would ensure time and opportunity for brief moments of reflection and preparation. First, she would have a few minutes alone, to gather herself. Then she would have a few minutes to chat with her family. Finally, the lawyers would give me their various updates to share with her, and Jordan and I would review information and options with her. For example, someone would have notes from the Democrats, who were supposed to be helpful. Others would overhear what the Republicans were saying. Still others would summarize the comments made by Nina Totenberg on radio or television, and others would be reading faxes coming in, listing ideas about what to do next, other possible witnesses to support Hill's account, or critics who called her a liar. I, along with other team members, thought that these outrageous statements from Thomas supporters should be disregarded, and that our focus should be on the actual facts, something that was being ignored by the senators and press.

At the end of the day, we were quite pleased with Hill's testimony. Not only had she told her story clearly and convincingly, but she had also answered the senators' questions with confidence and clarity. As we started preparing the corroborating witnesses to testify on her behalf, we experienced the second shock of the day. We were well into our preparation for Saturday when word circulated that Judge Thomas was going to return to the hearing. My early suspicion was that he would, in light of Professor Hill's full testimony, withdraw from consideration. Instead, Thomas did something extraordinary. Accused of sexually harassing a black woman, he played the race card. It was a powerful moment in the hearings, and his performance, whether credible or not, was impressive. He was an angry black man, and he accused the all-white, all-male Judiciary Committee members of engaging in a "high-tech legal lynching, of uppity blacks, who would deign to speak for themselves, to do for themselves, to have different ideas, and it is a message that unless you kowtow to an old order . . . you will be lynched, destroyed, caricatured by a committee of the U.S. Senate rather than hung from a tree."[1] I was particularly disappointed that Thomas attacked the committee members directly and that neither Senator Ted Kennedy, who had led the Democratic defeat of Judge Bork's nomination four years earlier, nor Senator Patrick Leahy of Vermont, nor any of the other Democrats responded when Thomas presented the most dramatic testimony of the entire hearing.

There was an incredible mood shift in the room after Thomas's speech. The irony of his use of the lynching metaphor was lost on the committee. The term has such a special meaning coming from an

African-American male, given this country's ugly history of lynchings. Moreover, no one seemed to reflect on the fact that it was Hill, not Thomas, who was being lynched, as committee members accused her of lying, being infatuated with Thomas, or suffering from some mental illness. She was caricatured, vilified, and demeaned by the Republicans on the committee and by others who voluntarily made public statements about her to any reporter willing to listen. A lynching occurred that weekend, but the actual victim was Anita Hill, not Clarence Thomas.

Thomas's late-night appearance was another violation of the procedures that John Frank had negotiated with the committee. Thomas was allowed to speak again and to refute Hill's testimony without being questioned. He was given a second appearance on television, which in turn gave the public a chance to sympathize with him. He was able to blunt the effect of Hill's testimony, by refuting it while it was still fresh in the minds of the senators and the viewers. It was time for us to go on the offensive. We told Biden that we had witnesses ready to corroborate all of Professor Hill's testimony, and that they would be ready to start Saturday morning. We also learned, through some modest but helpful leaks from the Democrats, that the Republicans planned to go after some of our witnesses on personal issues unrelated to anything involving Hill, so we chose to call a select few witnesses. We prepared the witnesses in advance, and they were scheduled as factual witnesses. They corroborated the many essential details of Hill's testimony. The Republicans, receiving no serious opposition from the Democrats, cross-examined these fact witnesses about Hill's character, in line with their theory that she was a lying jealous woman. These questions were well beyond the scope of what was agreed upon, but, thankfully, our witnesses had been prepared for this. Their testimony about her character was even stronger than their testimony about the facts.

At the end of the day on Saturday, we knew that we had succeeded in convincing many people that Anita Hill was truthful. We felt that we had done our job in presenting a truthful witness to the Senate Judiciary Committee and that our mission was accomplished. Saturday would be Thomas's time to testify, and panels of his supporters, lining up to call Professor Hill a liar, a jealous woman, and a Thomas groupie, would follow him. We knew by Saturday that the Republicans were going to skewer Hill. The first surprise came from their principal interrogator,

Senator Specter, who, after his questioning, went from the role of fact finder to that of prosecutor. He suggested, falsely, that Professor Hill had committed perjury during her testimony. Senator Hatch implied that her testimony was not credible; he read from a passage in *The Exorcist* that he suggested was similar and perhaps the source for her fabrication. Senator Alan Simpson had warned that she would be chewed up as a witness, and he tried his best to keep his promise.

Most of the skepticism about Hill's testimony came not when she was testifying but as a result of questions that Republicans put to other witnesses. The Democrats were only mildly helpful. Senator Kennedy was ineffective. Biden, playing the role of the objective chair, was not very tough on Thomas or his supporters. Senators Metzenbaum of Ohio and Howell Heflin of Alabama did a good job of questioning Thomas's witnesses, and Senator Leahy was pretty consistently vigorous.

Throughout the hearings, which were brutal, we sought to protect Hill. We wanted to keep her from the press, which salivated for any comment she might make; from critics, who hated her for testifying against Thomas; and from interest groups, including feminists, who wanted her to be a poster child for women's rights. The Anita Hill we knew was neither an ideologue, nor a feminist, nor a politician. She was a law professor, who grew up in Okmulgee, Oklahoma, and enjoyed writing articles about the uniform commercial code and discussing statutory construction and remedies in contract law. She had no political agenda, and we wanted to preserve her innocence.

During the hearings, we were the victims of typical Washington grandstanding by the Republicans who supported Thomas, and of the ineffectiveness of the Democrats who opposed him. I was convinced that she was telling the truth and that Thomas was lying. I thought we needed a way to clear her name, but feared it would not come through the politicized confirmation process. President Bush and the Senate Republicans wanted Thomas confirmed, and they would resort to anything to make that happen.

It seemed that we had to do something dramatic to prove Hill's innocence. After the second day of the hearing, a staff member for one of the Democratic senators approached me. The question was a blunt one, with no room for equivocation. Would Professor Hill be willing to take a lie detector test, to back up her allegations? I thought it was an outrageous request. Lie detector tests were often used in law enforcement exercises, security checks, and in screening for government positions to detect deception. They were generally inadmissible in courts, in large measure because there was no proof that they were sufficiently reliable to serve as evidence. I asked why this request was being made; the Senate aide reported that her senator had read Professor Hill's report to the FBI, where she responded positively when asked to take the test, but the FBI had never followed through.

I knew enough about lie detector tests from my work as a lawyer, and had used them in practice on occasion, to get charges dismissed when the prosecutor accepted them and to convince clients that their insistence on testifying might not be such a good idea. I also knew that if Hill agreed to do this, it would become our strongest statement of her truthfulness, in this otherwise highly politicized process. I asked her whether she would take a lie detector test and submit to questions concerning the truth of her allegations against Thomas. Without blinking an eye, she said yes.

Now I had to find a polygraph examiner. I talked to John Payton, who was always able to help me see matters with such clarity, and to Lani Guinier, a civil rights lawyer and a professor at the University of Pennsylvania Law School. Guinier, who in 1993 had her nomination to head the Civil Rights Division of the Justice Department pulled by President Clinton, and in 1998 became the first African-American woman on the faculty of Harvard Law School, gave me the names of some polygraph examiners she knew from her days as a litigator with the NAACP Legal Defense and Education Fund. These were good suggestions, but my problem was time. It was Saturday night, and we had to do the test, if at all, on Sunday and have the results while the hearings were still in session. I decided to try one other source for names of polygraph examiners and to approach someone who could not be accused of partisanship by either Republicans or Democrats on the Judiciary Committee.

I called a dear friend, former U.S. Attorney Charles Ruff, to ask for the name of the toughest polygraph examiner he knew, since the results would be widely scrutinized. I knew a lot of examiners, but realized that if I used the typical defense polygraph examiner, no matter how credible the person proved to be, the White House and the Senate Republicans would find a way to challenge his or her objectivity. I knew that

Ruff was a tough but fair prosecutor and would know a tough but fair polygraphist. Ruff recommended Paul Minor, who had actually helped establish the FBI's polygraph lab in Washington, D.C., before retiring and setting up a private practice.

After I spoke to Minor on Saturday night, and he agreed to perform the examination in Ruff's office early Sunday morning, I tried to take a nap. It was impossible to sleep. I was too worried about the test, wondering whether the senator who suggested the idea had perhaps duped me. The senator had nothing to lose, but if Hill failed the test, there would be no way to recover. I used the time to chat with friends who were my confidants during the hearing, and I usually called them well after midnight. During those late-night sessions, I would chat with three colleagues at Harvard—Larry Tribe, Susan Estrich, and Kathleen Sullivan. Minor agreed to meet with Hill and me in Ruff's law office Sunday morning, so that he could administer the test. He made two troubling statements to me privately. First, he told me that, like the rest of the world, he had been watching the hearings and that Thomas's denial was persuasive. Second, he asked that I pay him in advance for the test, since, as often happens, an unhappy result could lead to a dispute about the fees. Hill and I had never discussed the cost of a polygraph test; given her need to focus on other things, I wrote Minor a check for $1,000. I later learned that he deposited it the same day I gave it to him. He certainly was not going to take any chances.

Hill took the polygraph test and passed it for every question that Minor raised regarding her relationship with Thomas, the statements she had made about it, and the truthfulness of what she was offering. After the test was complete, Minor met with Hill and me and informed us that she had passed the test completely and that there was no indication of deception in any of her responses. It was a precious moment for Hill's defenders, and I asked Minor and Ruff to join me at the Senate Judiciary Committee hearing building. There, at a hastily called press conference, we announced the results. Hill went back to her hotel room on Capitol Hill, because we wanted to protect her from another press spectacle. We were ecstatic, and the Republican senators called a recess to denounce our decision to announce the polygraph results. Senator Orrin Hatch of Utah was not at all pleased; he labeled my decision to have Professor Hill take the polygraph test as the work of a "cheap,

two-bit lawyer." The words stung, but only momentarily. We had succeeded in showing the world that Anita Hill was truthful, no matter
what decision the Judiciary Committee made.

During the three days of the hearings, I did not get any sleep. I
would meet with Hill early and avoid subjecting her to a lot of questions, even from her team of lawyers and supporters. I would also meet
with the witnesses we called, to cross-examine them in preparation for
the hostility they would experience from the senators. Finally, I would
spend the hours after midnight (the hearings typically ended around two
each morning and resumed at nine) talking to friends around the country who had ideas, or interviewing witnesses who claimed they had
some light to shed on the hearings. About six in the evening, I would
prepare to take a nap, but would find that questions raised earlier in the
day required some additional work. A quick shower and too much cof-
fee were the staples of my existence.

On Tuesday, October 15, the Senate approved Thomas's nomination. The next day, I went with Hill to the airport. She returned to Oklahoma and I to Cambridge. Thomas had survived all of the challenges to
his confirmation, and he took his seat on the Supreme Court that week.
Once he was on the Court, it did not take him long to show his true col-
ors.

The NAACP leadership opposed the nomination of Thomas, but
the Senate, by a vote of 52 in favor and 48 opposed, nonetheless confirmed him. Clarence Thomas became a justice by the slimmest margin
of any nominee in the history of the U.S. Supreme Court. It was ironic
as well that senators like Strom Thurmond, who had opposed Thurgood Marshall's confirmation in 1967, were staunch supporters of
Thomas in 1991. It was not race, but ideology, that mattered. Conservatives found Thomas's judicial philosophy to their liking, and he has not
disappointed them.

CHAPTER 14

JUSTICE THOMAS:
A NEW ERA IN RACE MATTERS

Shortly after Thomas was appointed, he received a letter from a legal giant of quite a different judicial mind-set. Judge A. Leon Higginbotham had been considered a possible selection to the Supreme Court in 1967, but the choice fell on Marshall. Having led a distinguished life as a jurist, he was deeply concerned about the Court's ideological response to race issues with Marshall's resignation, and he wanted to make sure that Thomas was acutely aware of the Court's seminal role in promoting equal justice under law. Higginbotham's open letter to Thomas was published in the *University of Pennsylvania Law Review*, and portions of it also appeared in the *Philadelphia Inquirer*.

Knowing Thomas's penchant for judicial restraint, Higginbotham reminded him that the reason *Plessy* came down the way it did was that the justices "had the wrong values" and that Thomas himself owed much of his position in life to persons in the legal community who possessed the *right* values: "I suggest, Justice Thomas, that you should ask yourself every day what would have happened to you if there had never been a Charles Hamilton Houston, a William Henry Hastie, a Thurgood Marshall, and that small cadre of other lawyers associated with them. . . ." Higginbotham proceeded to give Thomas a history lesson, taking him through the work of Hastie and the early battles fought by Houston and Marshall in the incremental progress toward *Brown*.[1]

Thomas was selected to promote an extreme and activist conservative judicial agenda, and he has done exactly that. While his public statements before, during, and after the confirmation process reveal a side of his complex personality, his judicial opinions offer a much clearer sense of his judicial philosophy. The opinions he has written, frequently in dissent, demonstrate a dramatic difference between his view of the Constitution and that of Justice Marshall. Although it is all too easy to label him a conservative, his views on race, like those on other matters, are complicated. He fits into some comfortable conservative judicial schools of thought, but to understand him, one must take a deeper look at the text and context of his judicial writings.

To be sure, Justice Clarence Thomas is not alone in espousing his conservative ideology on the Supreme Court. Chief Justice Rehnquist, in his more than thirty years on the court, has made his conservative ideology into an art form and has generated substantial critiques from many observers.[2] I have written a fair share of critiques of Chief Justice Rehnquist as well.[3] By the same token, Justice Scalia has often been described as a staunch conservative and criticized for what appears to be ad hominem attacks on his judicial colleagues.[4] In light of my involvement with Justice Thomas during the confirmation process and his appointment to fill the seat held by Justice Thurgood Marshall, much of my critique of the Supreme Court's jurisprudence on matters of race focuses on Thomas's opinions.

Justice Thomas is the most consistent and conservative adherent of "originalism" on the Court. According to this doctrine, the Constitution contains only those rights that existed when this great nation was founded. This view necessarily ignores that the Constitution has changed a number of times to accommodate the major changes experienced in modernizing our society: the Civil War, the Lincoln justification of government of the people, by the people, for the people, and the Civil War amendments; and the New Deal and the massive centralization of government and the delegation of power to regulatory authorities designed to make sure that capitalism survived through the creation of a welfare state.

Originalism could include, but generally chooses to ignore, these major historical political and governmental changes. As a historical matter, the Thirteenth, Fourteenth, and Fifteenth Amendments were enacted to alter the relationship between state and federal governments dictated by the Constitution and the Bill of Rights. They quite straightforwardly undermine the power of the state to endorse discrimination against citizens on the basis of race and seek to empower minorities against the majority population of the country. Originalists, however, do not like to acknowledge the transformative character of the Civil War amendments; they instead wish to recast the relationship of state and federal government to the citizens as if those amendments did not exist. In so doing, they all too quickly dismiss this nation's history of slavery and its deference to the powerful and wealthy. They ignore the transformation in the years leading up to and including the New Deal that forever altered the treatment of women and the poor.

The ideals of the originalists are those of the justices who decided the *Civil Rights Cases* during Reconstruction, and who recognized the import of the Fourteenth Amendment's reconstitution of the government and sought to eviscerate it. The promise of the civil rights amendments was destroyed within two decades of their enactment by a revisionist and reactionary Supreme Court that used its own brand of originalism to permit the states to undermine the rights of its poor, black, and female citizens in derogation of the promises made by President Lincoln at Gettysburg and at the close of that war. They attack the final realization of those promises during the Warren Court era of the 1950s and 1960s as activist judicial overreaching, and adopt an activist agenda to interpret the Constitution to contain only those rights available in a pre-*Brown* era.

Although Thomas himself personally benefited from affirmative action programs as a student, he has consistently condemned similar race-conscious programs and, in the recent affirmative action case *Grutter v. Bollinger,*[5] evinced his suspicion of the value of the integration mandated by *Brown*. Put simply, Thomas attacks the very decisions that made it possible for me to go to Stanford, and for him to go to Holy Cross, and for us later to attend law school at Harvard and Yale, respectively. Thomas is rarely alone in this view of the Constitution. His frequent companions are Chief Justice Rehnquist and Justices Scalia and Kennedy. Though Thomas and Scalia vote together about 90 percent of the time, there are occasions when even Scalia is not willing to go as far as Thomas.[6]

Nonetheless, Thomas should not be understood as an intellectual purist pursuing a theoretically rigorous agenda. Where originalism cuts against the conservative grain, he is only too happy to abandon it and finds ways to reach the result he wants when the dogma of originalism collides with his conservatism. Many decisions that would benefit from a close and consistent reading of history are insupportable for conservative justices. So, where it suits, he acknowledges the importance of stare decisis, and in some instances he has openly embraced positions that are almost certainly inconsistent with the "original understanding." As one might expect, these tend to be in areas where modern-day conservative ideology and the original understanding part company.

Supporters of originalism present it primarily as a doctrine of interpretation. It holds that the best way to interpret the Constitution is to ground the language used by the framers in the common uses or understandings prevailing at the time the document was drafted. As practiced by Thomas, it focuses on narrowing the power of the federal government, expanding the power of state government in certain instances, and placing an extreme value on individual rights in others.

Thomas's originalism entails a number of principles:

- The power of government to interfere with private conduct is limited to that which is consistent with the conceptions of liberty and equality current at the time of the framers.
- The powers of the national government are strictly limited in nature and extent to those expressly provided in the Constitution, as understood at the relevant time.
- The relevant rights protected by the Constitution are those of individuals, not groups.
- The rights of individuals are confined to those clearly delineated in the Constitution, as understood in light of traditional practice and the core rights of liberty and property embodied in the Declaration of Independence.
- All individuals possess the same rights, and, except in compelling cases of national emergency, any governmental action that involves racial classifications to burden the rights of others is invalid.
- The meaning of the Constitution does not change, so courts should not rely on social science, which is often divided, subject to change, and, in any case, unnecessary to demonstrate clear constitutional truths.
- The separation of powers must be strictly preserved; in particular, the judiciary should not step beyond the limits of its defined role, either in declaration/creation of law or in prescription of remedies.

The Constitution has, however, been amended at different times during America's history, most comprehensively at the end of the Civil

War. These changes are embodied in the Civil War amendments, the Thirteenth, Fourteenth, and Fifteenth Amendments, which declared slavery unconstitutional, guaranteed equal protection and due process, and protected against abridgement of the right to vote. Thus, a thoroughgoing originalism would question how the "re-framers" of the Constitution understood the Civil War amendments, and whether these changed the Constitution and the Bill of Rights. The short answer, appearing on the face of the Fourteenth Amendment, is that the Civil War amendments extended the social and political opportunities hitherto enjoyed only by the majority—what the amendment calls the "privileges and immunities" of citizenship—to the rest of the population, and, in particular, to African-Americans. It provides a means by which individuals can enforce their rights against the states, and authorizes Congress to create new rights, should it choose to do so.

Originalists like Thomas, however, do not adopt the understandings of Lincoln and the "re-framers" of the Constitution. Thomas's originalist conservatism instead owes much to the anti-Reconstruction Court of the 1870s and is a strongly reactionary attempt to limit the substance and procedure of the Warren Court's rights revolution during the 1960s. The Warren Court's view of constitutional interpretation was primarily propounded by the Court's intellectual leader, Justice Brennan, and his greatest ally, Justice Marshall. Marshall certainly viewed the Constitution as a "living document" setting out the basic values necessary to govern American society, but also as containing procedures through which those values could be changed and expanded if necessary. The most important of those procedures, Marshall believed, were contained in the Fourteenth Amendment, itself the product of the constitutionally created power to expand the document by amendment to adapt to new and unforeseen circumstances.

A major feature of the Civil War amendments, the New Deal, and the Warren Court (especially through the judicial philosophy of Brennan and Marshall) was their attempt to constrain the ability of the majority of the population to undermine or destroy the rights of a minority of the population. Put differently, a prominent aspect of American history since the creation of the Republic has been a fear of the "tyranny of the majority," and the effort to use the Constitution and the doctrine of "separation of powers" to constrain the will of "the people." Time and again, the majority has voted to mistreat identifiable groups—whether through enacting segregation during Jim Crow or engaging in union busting and other anti-union legislation during the New Deal. From the Fourteenth Amendment until *Bakke*, a recurring feature of liberal politics has been an effort to rectify the balance by empowering minorities.

Thomas and I have very different views of the Constitution. Like Marshall, I believe that the Constitution could not remain as it was when it was drafted, because we as a nation have changed. Most obviously, the original Constitution authorized the slave trade in the United States and counted blacks as three-fifths of a person for the purpose of legislative representation, notions that our nation does not countenance today. Even though important and often valid, the doctrine of individualism, when pushed to extremes, empowers the majority at the expense of the minority. The "tyranny of the majority" understands that a slight majority suffices to eviscerate the rights of large groups of individuals. Throughout American history, one of the most significant of those groups has been African-Americans; another has been women. Segregation was created by the dominance of a relatively slim white majority in the southern states and directed not at individuals, but at a whole race identified only by membership in the group. White-only and colored-only fountains were aimed at groups. Racial profiling is aimed at groups. One should not simply focus on the harm of racism in an individual case and ignore its profound impact on the group.

Thomas's originalism, however, ignores the text of the Fourteenth Amendment and understandings of the re-framers of the Constitution, instead adopting the views of the deeply reactionary Court of 1873, which quickly moved to limit the rights conferred under the Civil War amendments.

There are two possible interpretations of the purposes of emancipation and the Civil War amendments that followed the declaration of freedom from slavery in the southern states. One understands the Civil War amendments—freedom from slavery, citizenship for all African-Americans, equal protection of the laws for all citizens, and universal suffrage for men—as ensuring freedom from certain forms of racially discriminatory state interference. In this view, emancipation created a series of "negative" rights enforceable against the government, preventing them from interfering with individual rights in certain ways. This view is close to, but stops short of, the more radical emphasis on individual rights endorsed by the originalists. The more plausible version focuses, however, on the reinterpretation of citizenship as the most important outcome of the Civil War. Citizenship suggests a much loftier aspiration than simple freedom from interference: it invokes the "positive" rights to participate in a community—what Booker T. Washington was to call "a blotting out of sectional differences and racial animosities and suspicions, in a determination to administer absolute justice, in a willing obedience among all classes to the mandates of law."[7] Hundreds of thousands of Americans of all races had fought and died over the character of the polity and the quality of membership and participation in American society itself. The great goal of the Union became not just the preservation of the country, or the end of slavery, but nothing less than the construction of a nation that practices racial equality.

The promise of the Civil War amendments was that the country, reconstituted in a new union, would no longer rely primarily on the good faith of the states in protecting the rights of its individual citizens. To secure this claim, the fathers of this new Constitution enacted the Civil Rights Acts of 1866,[8] 1871, and 1875 to ensure the full equality of all citizens regardless of race by protecting African-Americans from the violent reaction of whites and by creating a remedial regime to redistribute the benefits of the privileges and immunities of citizenship to the former slaves.

The debate surrounding the Civil War amendments was not limited to race but, like the modern originalist arguments, included an attempt to define the relationship between the federal government and the states, the scope of federal power, the limits of judicial power, and the appropriate means to interpret the Constitution. In 1873, the scope of the Fourteenth Amendment was settled in a series of cases filed in Louisiana that reached the Supreme Court under the name of the *Slaughter-House Cases*,[9] which eviscerated the privileges and immunities clause of the Fourteenth Amendment, a clause that was intended to ensure a broad protection of fundamental rights to all citizens of the United States.[10] The Court held that the Fourteenth Amendment did not alter the role of the federal and state governments in securing civil rights generally but was instead intended solely to emancipate slaves.[11] In fact, the Court, like Thomas, adopted a much more restricted view of the role of the federal government than Madison advocated during the Constitutional Convention. Furthermore, the *Slaughter-House Cases* rested on a rationale of separating citizenship of the United States from citizenship of individual states; the Constitution and its amendments protected only federal rights, and the federal government protected very few rights, if any.[12] Put simply, the *Slaughter-House Cases* recognized, if they did not create, a dual system of government, federal and state. In the federal system, which was sharply confined despite the Civil War amendments, African-Americans perhaps had equal citizenship rights; in the state system, African-Americans had only those rights (if any) that the states were willing to give.

The Court of that era also introduced a number of doctrines, neither imagined by the framers nor having any basis in the text of the Constitution, to limit severely the rights of individuals against the state government. The Court declared, in the 1883 *Civil Rights Cases*, that the Civil Rights Act of 1875, which prohibited discrimination in public places, was unconstitutional.[13] Some plaintiffs had been excluded from inns, theaters, and (in a claim that presaged *Plessy v. Ferguson*) the "ladies' car" of a train. The Court, in developing the new doctrine of "state action," held that these cases involved a "social right," rather than a civil right, and that unless the discriminatory acts could be traced to agents of the state, rather than private citizens, it was not the business of the courts to interfere.[14] These judge-created limitations on the reach of the federal government and the protections of the Civil War Constitution clearly eviscerated the equalizing power of the Civil War amendments and were contrary to the text and understandings of the Fourteenth Amendment.[15]

Thomas's originalist legal approach emerges in his Supreme Court decisions. A particularly troubling opinion came within the first year of his appointment to the Court. In *Hudson v. McMillian* (1992), a case that involves the mistreatment of an African-American prisoner, only Thomas, joined by Scalia, dissented from the 7-to-2 decision majority opinion, which was supported by the conservative justices Rehnquist, O'Connor, and Kennedy.[16]

One of the major features of the originalist agenda, I have suggested, is the curtailment of the power of the federal government and the federal courts to regulate and supervise the state governments. Thomas's emphasis on deference to state decisions at the expense of federal regulation has had some of its most profound impact in the realm of prison reform. State prisons, especially in the South, in the era before the Warren Court's rights revolution, were directly modeled on slavery and even called "plantations." The most famous of these, Parchman State Farm, in Mississippi, was fairly typical.[17] The state prisons were generally understaffed, and the guards used brutal, frequently fatal, methods to control the prisoners. Guards delegated authority to inmates, called trusties, who tended to be mentally unstable. Nonetheless, these trusties were armed and invested with much of the authority of the guards themselves. Corporal punishment and treatment amounting to torture were rife. Nothing was done about such conditions until the 1960s.

The justification for interfering in the running of state prisons was the extension of the Eighth Amendment's prohibition of "cruel and unusual" punishment. Before the 1960s, the theory was that "punishment" meant the sentence delivered by the court, rather than the conditions of confinement in state and federal prisons. Thus, a question would arise only when a new form of punishment, such as the electric chair, was to be employed. Under the Warren Court's rights revolution, however, the Court recognized that prisoners were sentenced not in the abstract but to particular places of confinement. The conditions within those facilities were as much a part of the sentence as the length of the sentence—as much a means of executing the sentence as was the electric chair. The Court therefore enabled a vast array of new cases to be filed challenging prisoners' conditions of confinement and, incidentally, the manner in which states ran their prisons.[18]

Thomas certainly does not subscribe to the Warren Court's interpretation of the Eighth Amendment. His emphasis on the relation between the federal and the state governments requires that the states be left alone to regulate their prisons as they see fit, free of federal interference. Harking back to the days when the only inquiry was whether the sentence violated the "cruel and unusual" clause, Thomas would permit any behavior condoned by prison policy or undertaken by prison officials so long as it did not involve an "unnecessary or wanton infliction of pain." He would permit even "sadistic" behavior so long as it did not rise to a sufficiently serious level of injury. This understanding of the Eighth Amendment leaves the state unfettered discretion in obtaining its penal objectives, no matter what the consequences for the individual prisoner.

This consequence was particularly apparent in *Hudson*. The late Judge Higginbotham describes the case as follows:

> In *Hudson v. McMillian* . . . a cuffed and shackled black prisoner was beaten by two guards, his eyes blackened, his teeth loosened, his dental plate broken and his lips burst. Seven justices declared that the beating amounted to cruel and unusual punishment under the Eighth Amendment. Only Justice Thomas, joined by Justice Antonin Scalia, dissented. After the opinion came down, the New York Times called Justice Thomas "The Youngest, Cruelest Justice."[19]

But if Thomas puts his thumb on the scales of justice to tip it in favor of the states against the federal government, the most profound difference between Thomas and Marshall concerns their view of how the Constitution organizes the relationship between the majority and the minority, the group and the individual. Marshall clearly thought the major constitutional evil consists in the tyranny of the majority over a minority group of citizens. The Constitution exists to protect the minority and redress the balance. For Thomas, the prime constitutional evil is the infringement of any individual right. Marshall's view allows for— even requires—redistributive justice. Thomas's does not, or does so only to the extent that redistributions are consistent with the noninfringement of individual rights to be free from racial discrimination. As a practical matter, Thomas's views prevent redistributive efforts designed to ameliorate racial injustice because, by its nature, redistribution takes from some to give to others. Thomas characterizes redistributive racial justice as a form of stigmatizing "paternalism" that has no place in a color-blind society.

Thomas has written opinions, concurrences, and dissents in a number of important cases, often providing a much needed vote for the conservative agenda in a closely divided Court. Even where his vote makes no difference, however, in the context of racial discrimination, he has often chosen to follow a path that, though generally in line with the conservative orthodoxy of modern originalism, sounds a unique voice in the Court's jurisprudence. For him, the basic harm that befalls individuals under the antidiscrimination provisions of the Fourteenth Amendment is government-sponsored racial identification of any kind in the awarding of benefits or burdens.

A developing theme in Thomas's jurisprudence begins with an objection to the unforeseen effects of benign race-based redistributions and culminates (at least for now) in a position that comes close to suggesting that any consideration of race when determining state or federal entitlements is, by itself, intolerable. Originally, his objection seemed to be that the effect of awarding benefits to discriminated-against minorities on the basis of race created unpredictable consequences that were likely to undermine the self-esteem of African-Americans. For Thomas, one consequence is that the recipients of redistributive benefits based on efforts to remediate historical discrimination are no longer free to believe that their achievements belong to themselves as individuals, rather than stemming from some collective benefit awarded to their group as a whole.

The problem with this reasoning is that it is inherently ahistorical, taking the playing field as level when it is in fact skewed in favor of the majority race. Thomas's view ignores the collective benefit accruing to whites from membership in the majority group and enforced over years of slavery and Jim Crow. It is as easy to claim that whites do not deserve the preferences currently accruing to them from their historically inflated social status (which can include membership in certain professions or trades, educational privileges, and the ability to live in areas or join clubs still denied to African-Americans and often to women as well) as to claim that the beneficiaries of remedial efforts do not deserve the benefits belatedly directed at them. The argument cuts both ways. Thomas, however, takes a fairly hard view of individual responsibility for these acts and considers whites who have not engaged in intentional discrimination but are simply the "accidental" beneficiaries of racial discrimination, as subject to a windfall and not required to surrender the rights or benefits obtained through the wrong of discrimination. For Thomas, African-Americans must, in the words of Booker T. Washington's "Atlanta Exposition Speech," "[c]ast down your bucket where you are."[20]

Thomas also appears to maintain that the combination of group identification and malign stereotype (which he does not address as perpetuated by the majority white population) causes an intolerable burden for individual successful African-Americans. The others, those who fail to shake off the shackles of discrimination or fail to achieve success in American society, are characterized as freeloading victims seeking to become, in the words of the *Civil Rights Cases*, the "special favorites of the law"—to jump the queue to the American Dream. His current position seems to suggest that the attempts to undo the effects of segregation and to engage with the goal of integration and to redress it are so harmful to the meritorious few that manage to make it in American society that integration itself may be too great a price to pay in terms of white rights and black self-esteem.

An important decision that illustrates how Thomas differs from Marshall is his opinion in *Adarand Constructors, Inc. v. Pena* (1995), which struck down "the Federal Government's practice of giving general contractors on Government projects a financial incentive to hire subcontractors controlled by 'socially and economically disadvantaged individuals,'" as identified according to race-based presumptions.[21] This case affirmed the difficult hurdle that those attempting to address racial disparity in employment had to clear to justify remedial measures. *Adarand* established strict scrutiny as the standard to be applied to all racial classifications, benign or otherwise, imposed by any level of government.[22] Thomas provided the crucial fifth vote for the Court's new standard to support even benign race-based remedies. He argued that there is no "racial paternalism exception to the principle of equal protection" and "that there is a 'moral [and] constitutional equivalence' between laws designed to subjugate a race and those that distribute benefits on the basis of race in order to foster some current notion of equality." Thomas's view was that government "cannot make us equal; it can only recognize, respect, and protect us as equal before the law."[23] Thomas cited the Declaration of Independence as authority for "the principle of inherent equality that underlies and infuses our Constitution" and concluded,

It is also true that "remedial" racial preferences may reflect "a desire to foster equality in society[.]" But there can be no doubt that racial paternalism and its unintended consequences can be as poisonous and pernicious as any other form of discrimination. So-called "benign" discrimination teaches many that because of chronic and apparently immutable handicaps, minorities cannot compete with them without their patronizing indulgence. Inevitably, such programs engender attitudes of superiority or, alternatively, provoke resentment among those who believe that they have been wronged by the government's use of race. These programs stamp minorities with a badge of inferiority and may cause them to develop dependencies or to adopt an attitude that they are "entitled" to preferences.[24]

As he often does, Thomas either ignores or dismisses the well-documented history of racial discrimination in employment law and trivializes the continuing harm of such practices.

Adarand was a difficult decision for many in the civil rights community to swallow. It clearly marked the end of the antimajoritarian redistributivism that characterized Marshall's judicial philosophy and a turn to an aggressive, ahistorical individualism that has characterized Thomas's judicial philosophy. Worse was yet to come.

Chief Justice Warren considered the most important decision of his tenure to be not *Brown* but *Reynolds v. Sims*,[25] a case that enshrined the principle of "one-person, one-vote" in the American constitutional system. By the extension of the vote to every person, Warren believed, those individuals would have the power to guarantee that their voice was heard in the halls of government.

Reynolds, however, was just the start and not the answer. In order to perfect the voting system, the 1965 Voting Rights Act provided mechanisms to ensure that the widespread voter fraud perpetrated in the southern states and, incidentally, in New York would be curtailed by federal court scrutiny of redistricting plans. The act also imposed a mechanism to ensure the creation of districts in which African-American votes could make a difference and return the candidate of their choice. The most direct effect of these "majority-minority" districts was to ensure a rapid rise in the number of African-American members of the House of Representatives. As yet, the act has made little difference in the Senate, which has had only two African-American members, Edward Brooke of Massachusetts and Carol Moseley Braun of Illinois, since the end of Reconstruction.

For conservatives, including Thomas, the Voting Rights Act and the federal enforcement of statewide redistricting plans marked an unconscionable interference by the federal government in state affairs. Worse, that interference was explicitly race-based. The solution that emerged during the 1990s was that although the redistricting mandated by the decennial publication of the census (redistricting is required by the *Reynolds* mandate that the district borders be realigned to ensure a parity of population between each voting district) was to include a certain number of majority-minority districts where the state's minority population reached a certain threshold, those district lines could not be drawn with regard to race.

Interestingly, in the 1990s the most avid foe of race-based redistricting was the Bush Justice Department. Knowing the composition of the Court, it wished to bring the issue of race-based districting to a head. It succeeded in 1993, in *Shaw v. Reno*, a 5-to-4 decision in which O'Connor wrote the majority opinion and Thomas joined.[26] In that case, the voting district was multisided and oddly shaped. It just looked strange. Clearly, it was possible to redistrict a state from scratch by means of regular shapes (where natural boundaries permitted) and not produce the kind of crazy-quilt effect of the district in *Shaw*.

The harm in *Shaw* was the stigma of being placed in a voting district on the basis of race alone. One can prove that district lines were drawn primarily on the basis of race by demonstrating that the district shape is sufficiently bizarre as to be otherwise unexplainable or by showing that the government "disregard[ed] traditional districting principles such as compactness, contiguity, and respect for political subdivisions."[27] The Court argued that drawing district lines to include people "separated by geographic and political boundaries" and sharing little more than their skin color "bears an uncomfortable resemblance to political apartheid"; it reinforces stereotypes that members of a race "think alike, share the same political interests, and will prefer the same candidates at the polls." It also suggests to representatives that "their primary obligation is to represent only the members of [the majority-minority] group."[28]

Shaw mirrors Thomas's concurrence in another voting case, *Holder v. Hall* (1993),[29] that challenged the enforcement of the Voting Rights Act. In *Holder*, Thomas was upset that the act could be used to alter the manner in which districts were apportioned and that federal courts could determine the manner in which citizens were grouped, even taking race into account. He remarkably claimed that the act was a "remedial mechanism that encourages federal courts to segregate voters into racially designated districts to ensure minority electoral success."[30] His concern, as expressed in the case, was that the courts' promotion of "political apartheid" in establishing racially constructed voting areas "can only serve to deepen racial divisions by destroying any need for voters or candidates to build bridges between racial groups or to form voting coalitions."[31] In short, Thomas's view reflected by his opinion in *Holder* and his vote in *Shaw* is that districting based on race is tantamount to segregation for purposes of voting. It stigmatizes African-Americans (and others) who are forced into voting districts based on stereotypes over the manner in which they will vote and the assumption that they will return a candidate able to "represent the race."

There are certainly problems with the Voting Rights Act and with the principle of "one person, one vote" as applied in the current system of elections. Unfortunately, experiments with other systems have tended to promote the disenfranchisement of minority populations by a process known as vote dilution, either by splitting a community into different districts (a practice known as cracking) or concentrating a diverse population in a single district (packing). The Voting Rights Act prohibits such practices and requires that each state create sufficient districts within the state to represent the minority population living there. The percentage of majority-minority voting districts must, within certain limits, mirror the percentage of minority citizens within the state. *Shaw* requires that such districts respect "traditional" districting criteria. That is easier in urban areas, but difficult in rural areas, where communities may be spread out, and conditions of discrimination have spread minority communities along highways or railroads or in other areas on the fringes of the majority community. The attempt to ensure that these individuals are represented produces strange and convoluted-looking districts.

The conservative criticism of the Voting Rights Act is that it stereotypes all African-American voters as voting the same way and does not account for diversity within minority communities. According to this view, the act disvalues the individuality of the citizens within the majority-minority communities. In fact, the act is neutral in respect to individual preferences: it simply suggests that groups of people come together at voting time to agree on a candidate, that there are many majority white places in which that happens, and that there should therefore be some majority-minority places as well. This is all the more true since one of the traditional districting practices ignored by O'Connor and Thomas is the "packing" and "cracking" used to disenfranchise African-Americans since the end of Reconstruction.

Thomas is particularly worried about the use of stereotypes to predict voting outcomes. Like the lone African-American invited to an all-white party to speak "on behalf of the race," Thomas mistrusts the view that African-Americans have only one point of view on social and political issues: in fact, he is the greatest living proof to the contrary. The harm suffered in the voting rights cases is, therefore, more direct than in *Adarand*. It is not some speculative stigma associated with redistributive benefits, but the stereotype upon which the redistribution itself is based, that Thomas finds so objectionable in the context of voting rights. Unfortunately, his concerns do nothing to address the reality that, prior to the Voting Rights Act, no African-American had been elected to Congress from the South since the end of Reconstruction. Like Marshall, I am not willing to gamble that attitudes are so changed that we can dismantle the act until majority white communities start electing African-Americans. The experience of the U.S. Senate offers little hope in that regard.

The final place in which Thomas has worked through the problem of racial stereotyping is the arena of education. Here he has reached his most far-reaching conclusions. The difference between the judicial philosophies of Marshall and Thomas was quite evident in the Kansas City school district case *Missouri v. Jenkins* (1995),[32] a 5-to-4 decision where Thomas joined the majority opinion and wrote a separate concurrence. The Court struck down a district court decree and held that orders designed to make the district more attractive to whites living outside it constituted a remedy beyond the scope of the identified harm. Additionally, in determining whether the district has complied with *Brown*, the district court should look not to whether students in the district were performing at or below national norms but rather to "whether the reduction in achievement by minority students attributable to . . . segregation has been remedied to the extent practicable."[33]

In his opinion, Thomas complained,

> It never ceases to amaze me that the courts are so willing to assume that anything that is predominantly black must be inferior. . . . First, the court has read our cases to support the theory that black students suffer an unspecified psychological harm from segregation that retards their mental and educational development. This approach not only relies upon questionable social science research rather than constitutional principle, but it also rests on an assumption of black inferiority.
>
> I do not doubt that Missouri maintained the despicable system of segregation until 1954. But I question the District Court's conclusion that because the State had enforced segregation until 1954, its actions, or lack thereof, proximately caused the "racial isolation" of the predominantly black schools in 1984. . . .
>
> In effect, the court found that racial imbalances constituted an ongoing constitutional violation that continued to inflict harm on black students. This position appears to rest upon the idea that any school that is black is inferior, and that blacks cannot succeed without the benefit of the company of whites.[34]

Thomas cites studies criticizing the studies *Brown* relied on and undermining claims that desegregation has improved black achievement or "remedied any psychological feeling of inferiority black schoolchildren might have had."[35] He sees "no reason to think that black students cannot learn as well when surrounded by members of their own race as when they are in an integrated environment"; indeed, the experience of historically black colleges suggests to him that primarily black institutions may be better places to learn.[36]

In some respects, Thomas's views about learning environment are right. One of the strongest critiques of the manner in which *Brown* has been enforced concerns the practice of undermining African-American institutions and forcing African-Americans into white ones without considering the worth of the African-American experience and the possibility that *all* Americans would benefit from exposure to it. Integration resulted in the loss of too many African-American institutions, too much African-American social capital, for it to be considered an unmitigated good in the manner the majority of America embraced it.

But the *Brown* challenge was not to environment alone; it was also to equal resources. Whether you are in an all-black or an integrated setting, equal resources and integration of differing ideas are essential to a well-rounded education. Thomas ignores what I believe to be the central goal of *Brown* and its progeny, with little regard for the impact these decisions will have on the African-American children struggling in the underresourced schools. Furthermore, he seems not to recognize the obvious impact of cutbacks on decisions that try to implement the *Brown* mandate. The effect is unconscionable: the resegregation of the very same schools that Marshall and others fought so hard to integrate, upgrade, and bring within acceptable constitutional standards.

Thomas's second objection is to the enormous expansion in the powers that *Brown* and its progeny spawned, which, though intended as justifiable temporary expedients to address massive resistance, became more urgent necessities as the resegregation of urban schools took root. Such broad equitable remedies, Thomas argues, are out of tune with historical practice and separation of powers and federalism values.[37] Perhaps the most glaring example of Thomas's originalism philosophy is in his concurring opinion in *Zelman v. Simmons-Harris*,[38] the school vouchers case decided June 27, 2002. In an opinion written by Chief Justice Rehnquist, five members of the court concluded that vouchers provided to religious and nonreligious schools did not violate the Establishment Clause of the Constitution. Justice Thomas's concurrence struck a particularly defiant tone in that he quoted Frederick Douglass and continued on to say, "Today many of our inner-city public schools deny emancipation to urban minority students. Despite this Court's observation nearly 50 years ago in *Brown v. Board of Education,* that 'it is doubtful that any child may reasonably be expected to succeed in life if he is denied the opportunity of an education,' urban children have been forced into a system that continually fails them."[39] Thomas went further, "While the romanticized ideal of universal public education resonates with the cognoscenti who oppose vouchers, poor urban families just want the best education for their children, who will certainly need it to function in our high-tech and advanced society."[40]

Thomas concludes, "As Frederick Douglass poignantly noted, 'no greater benefit can be bestowed upon a long benighted people, than giving to them, as we are here earnestly this day endeavoring to do, the means of an education.' "[41]

Thomas has provided a reliable vote to reverse the import of *Brown* and its progeny. While *Brown* continues to survive, despite some justices questioning its relevance, Justice Thomas has found additional grounds to attack it. Fortunately, some of his criticisms are unpersuasive, even among his conservative allies.

PART V

Law professors participate in a 2003 protest rally
during the Michigan affirmative action case.

CHAPTER 15

THE MICHIGAN CASES: MIXED SIGNALS

I routinely discuss legal, personal, and social issues with my friend John Payton, and in 1997, John called with some exciting news. His law firm had been approached by the University of Michigan to represent it in a lawsuit filed by some white applicants who had unsuccessfully applied to Michigan's law school and undergraduate program. The white applicants were represented by the Center for Individual Rights (CIR), a conservative Washington, D.C.–based organization. By 1997, the CIR had already been successful in challenging the consideration of race in higher education. The Center filed suit on behalf of several white students in the *Hopwood* case against the University of Texas, and the Fifth Circuit agreed with its central criticisms of the university's program; the circuit court caught the attention of the civil rights community when it ruled that the *Bakke* decision was not binding law.[1] On the basis of its 1996 victory in *Hopwood*, the CIR decided to use the same strategy a year later in Michigan. This strategy was frighteningly similar to that employed by Charles Hamilton Houston and Thurgood Marshall, leading up to the *Brown* decision. Find those institutions with programs that draw distinctions on the basis of race, target them, get a victory, and parlay it into a larger strategy to challenge the entire consideration of race. A further similarity is that the CIR chose a southern state to launch its offensive and then applied the successful strategy to other targets.

The Michigan lawsuits demanded, among other things, the end to any program that considered an applicant's race, the immediate admission of those whites who were allegedly qualified and denied admission, and money damages. In choosing Payton to lead the defense against these claims, the University of Michigan made a very wise decision.

John Payton, an outstanding litigator, was operating in familiar territory, for he had argued a critical affirmative action case before the Supreme Court in 1985, involving a voluntary program developed by the city of Richmond to create employment opportunities for minority contractors, in order to reverse the city's acknowledged history of discrimination against minorities. Although the Supreme Court ruled 5 to 4 against his clients, the city of Richmond, in a rather extraordinary rejection of a voluntary program to address past discrimination in Richmond, John was recognized as a brilliant lawyer who just happened to run up against a conservative, defiant Court.

It did not take John long to get immersed in the Michigan cases. He and others recognized right away that the cases would likely lead to the Supreme Court's first consideration of the highly controversial issue of diversity in higher education since its highly fractured consideration of the issue in *Bakke* in 1978. The task facing John was daunting. Since *Bakke*, the lower courts had questioned whether *Bakke* was still good law, and the Supreme Court's refusal to accept any lower-court case challenging *Bakke*'s continued validity led many to suspect that a majority of the justices, on a virtually new Court over the twenty-five-year period, felt the same way.

John Payton, being also a student of the Houston/Marshall strategy, realized immediately that, in order to challenge these conservative forces, every aspect of the Michigan program had to be examined, and the arguments for the programs had to be supported by credible and highly influential experts, so that a comprehensive record could be developed to defend the Michigan diversity plan. John carefully reviewed the *Bakke* case, the decades of analysis of that decision since it was issued, and the possible vulnerable aspects of the Michigan plan. He took a page out of the Houston/Marshall strategy book by first presenting expert testimony to support Michigan's program and by having data to show the value of race as a factor in admissions. John's timing could hardly have been better.

Harvard's former president Derek Bok, who had been instrumental in submitting a brief in *Bakke* outlining the Harvard diversity plan found acceptable by Justice Powell, had just published, with the former

Princeton president William Bowen, a book analyzing the success of diversity programs in highly selective universities. The book, *The Shape of the River,* would prove to be very influential throughout John's handling of the cases. The historian and sociologist Thomas Sugrue, the historian Eric Foner, and the psychologist Claude Steele joined Bok and Bowen, among others. Payton developed an extensive record of information in both cases and, after presenting the material to the district court judges, successfully argued the case before the Sixth Circuit Court of Appeals. The stage was set for the case to proceed to the Supreme Court.

On April 1, 2003, I was fortunate to receive one of the coveted seats to hear the argument held there. Justice Stephen Breyer invited me as one of his guests, and I was pleased to see, as well, three of my former students, Robin Lenhardt, Kitanji Jackson, and Russell Robinson, all African-Americans who had served as law clerks to Breyer.

Much had changed since the time I witnessed the *Bakke* argument. Now I participated in a panel discussion the weekend before the argument, led by some of my former Harvard law students, who organized it, and a group of Howard law students, who hosted it. This time was also different in that two Ogletrees were attending the argument. My daughter, Rashida, a first-year law student at New York University, had joined other law students who took an overnight bus to D.C. to participate in the protests outside the Supreme Court. For me, it was a moment of joy to see my daughter, who was born one year after the *Bakke* decision, fighting for the future of affirmative action and participating in a protest march with her dad at the Supreme Court. I also worked closely with the presidents of my alma maters, Stanford and Harvard, to make sure that they planned to submit briefs in support of the Michigan cases. Both submitted terrific and compelling briefs. I also wrote an op-ed piece in the *Boston Globe,* on why it was reasonable for the Court to stand by the precedent of *Bakke* set twenty-five years earlier.

The argument went along the expected ideological lines, with my hope that Justice Sandra Day O'Connor, who held the swing vote, would support the Michigan plan. O'Connor and I had many points of contact. We were both Stanford graduates, and both served on Stanford's board of trustees. Her law school experience at Stanford, where she was one of only a few women, made her aware of the changes in the world and at Stanford in fifty years. I knew she was proud that Stanford had a woman as dean, Kathleen Sullivan, and a diverse faculty and student body. O'Connor and I had participated in Ninth Circuit judicial conferences, and she came to Harvard to speak at my Saturday school program the year before the Michigan decision. At that time, I asked her about her former, and now deceased, colleague Justice Thurgood Marshall, and she praised him for his contributions to the Court's sense of mission. She also attended a dinner in my honor in Washington, D.C., with a small group of close friends, when I decided to accept an appointment to chair the University of the District of Columbia board of trustees.

The civil rights community and those private and public universities committed to maintaining a diverse pool of applicants for their institutions learned some painful lessons from the *Bakke* case, and they decided to develop a more focused effort this time around. More than 150 groups filed briefs in support of the Michigan diversity plan; they included law schools, universities, members of Congress, and corporations. Retired members of the armed forces, reporting that the military could not have credibility without an affirmative action plan that recruited minority officers into its ranks, filed a highly influential brief. Their brief caused a stir, in that it went against the public position of President George W. Bush, who filed a brief opposing the Michigan plan and labeled it a quota. There were further splits within the Republican ranks, as the highest-ranked and best-known African-Americans in the Bush administration, Colin Powell and Condoleezza Rice, also supported diversity and, in Powell's case, supported Michigan explicitly. Despite all of this external agitation, only nine votes counted, and I was carefully counting to see whether we could muster five votes.

I focused that Tuesday morning on Justice O'Connor. Her questions to the lawyers suggested that she might decide in favor of Michigan's programs, even though she was concerned about how long such programs would be necessary. I was seated next to an African-American woman who also was a member of the Michigan Board of Regents, who bet me that Justice Thomas, as was his custom, would not speak. I thought the occasion was too significant for him to remain silent. With less than a minute left in the two-hour argument, Thomas finally asked a question about diversity in black colleges, and the argument ended. I felt confident of a victory in at least the law school case, and a strong statement in support of the diversity rationale. Two weeks before the *Grutter* and *Gratz* decisions, a Federal District Court judge upheld a voluntary desegregation plan adopted by the Lynn Public Schools near Boston, Massachusetts. In a compelling opinion, Judge Nancy Gertner concluded that the Lynn initiative was critical to establishing a racially diverse educational system in Massachusetts.[2] On June 23, the Court issued the decisions. That John O'Connor, Sandra Day O'Connor's husband, was in the courtroom, suggested that Justice O'Connor would have something significant to say. She did.

In *Gratz v. Bollinger* and *Grutter v. Bollinger*,[3] the Supreme Court answered the central question, debated since Bakke, of the propriety of university or college affirmative action programs. The results were, at best, a moderate success for affirmative action. They remain, in the context of the Court's jurisprudence on race- and economic-based educational programs, an important setback to the mission established in *Brown*. By a vote of 5 to 4, the Court upheld the Michigan Law School's affirmative action plan. By a vote of 6 to 3, it held that the undergraduate program was tantamount to a quota system, and unconstitutional. Despite this relative disappointment, it was a day to celebrate, largely because a contrary decision in the law school case would have been unfathomable.

In *Grutter*, O'Connor presented a robust endorsement of the principle of diversity as a factor in university admissions. Justice O'Connor not only endorsed Justice Powell's broad mandate in *Bakke*[4] but went even further in embracing the significance of diversity in the *Grutter* decision:

> Justice Powell emphasized that *nothing less* than the "nation's future depends upon leaders trained through wide exposure to the ideas and mores of students as diverse as this Nation of many peoples."[5]

So long as the admissions program does not constitute the type of quota system of "racial balancing" outlawed by *Bakke*, it may admit a "critical mass" of minority students in an effort to obtain a racially diverse student body. Educational institutions are permitted to use race as a factor (in the words of *Bakke*, quoted in *Grutter*, as a "plus") in minority admissions, so long as the decision to admit the student is "flexible enough to ensure that each applicant is evaluated as an individual and not in a way that makes an applicant's race or ethnicity the defining feature of his or her application."[6]

In the *Gratz* opinion, Chief Justice Rehnquist, writing for a 6-to-3 majority, found the undergraduate admissions program unconstitutional. He was joined by the conservative justices Scalia, Kennedy, O'Connor, and Thomas. The centrist justice Breyer concurred in the judgment of the Court while not joining the chief justice's opinion. The chief justice found that awarding a blanket score—in this case, 20 points, or just over 13 percent of the maximum 150 points used to rank applicants—ensured that the university would admit all qualified minority applicants.[7] He held that the scoring system, "by setting up automatic, predetermined point allocations for the soft variables [including race], ensures that the diversity contributions of applicants cannot be individually assessed."[8] The university's failure to consider individualized features of the diversity of each applicant rendered its affirmative action plan unconstitutional and required the Court to strike it down.

Grutter held that attainment of the educational benefits flowing from diversity (such as promoting cross-racial understanding that breaks down racial stereotypes) constitutes a compelling interest, and deferred to the university's determination that diversity is essential to its educational mission. The law school's position was further bolstered by numerous expert studies and reports, as well as the experience of major American businesses, retired military officers, and civilian military officials. Finally, universities and, more especially, law schools are training grounds for future leaders, and "the path to leadership must be visibly open to talented and qualified individuals of every race and ethnicity."[9]

Moreover, the individualized consideration, the absence of quotas, and the recognition of diversity stemming from sources other than race (all of which resemble the Harvard approach that Justice Powell praised in *Bakke*) render the plan narrowly tailored. However, affirmative action must be limited in time, and the Court expects it will no longer be necessary twenty-five years from now.

O'Connor's opinion in the law school case, written on behalf of five justices, was breathtaking in its scope. O'Connor began, "Today we endorse Justice Powell's view that student body diversity is a compelling state interest that can justify the use of race in university admissions."[10] She went further, however, in describing the scope of the Court's ruling, as well as its intent: "We have never held that the only governmental use of race that can survive strict scrutiny is remedying past discrimination. . . . Today, we hold that the Law School has a compelling interest in attaining a diverse student body."[11] In reaching this decision, O'Connor noted the importance of briefs submitted by retired military officers and leaders in corporate America as well. Her conclusions did indeed embrace a wide range of common interests.

Although O'Connor's opinion rests on an unequivocal endorsement of diversity as a goal in university selection, it quietly rejects another three possible justifications that were touted in *Bakke* but rejected there by Justice Powell. According to O'Connor, it is impermissible to use affirmative action solely to reduce a historical deficit of traditionally disfavored minorities in various occupations or professions or to remedy general societal discrimination (because such measures would risk placing unnecessary burdens on innocent third parties who did not cause and are not responsible for that discrimination) or, it seems, to increase the number of individuals who will practice their profession in minority communities that are underserved by that profession.

Furthermore, remedying past discrimination may afford a justification for race-based governmental action if it is narrowly tailored to a particular harm. None of the universities that submitted amicus briefs in *Grutter*, or the University of Michigan itself, was willing publicly to acknowledge its history of discrimination to the extent of having to admit students to remedy that harm. Nor is it clear that such an admission would carry the university very far. Instead, O'Connor rested her decision on the claim that education occupies a special place in the constitutional scheme, that the Court should therefore defer to the law school's judgment that diversity is essential to its educational mission, and that Michigan may take race into account to accomplish this mission.

Collectively, *Grutter* and *Gratz* preserved the institution of affirmative action in American higher education and, to that extent, are important. Nonetheless, both cases—*Grutter* by what it did *not* say and

Gratz by what it *did* say—are troubling in that they will likely fail to be the catalysts for dispensing with the "all deliberate speed" mentality adopted in *Brown*. With the decisions, the Court did not erect a further barrier in the path of the struggle to true integration and equality; it also did little to promote that struggle.

Initially, there is an obvious dissonance between *Grutter* and *Gratz*. Justice O'Connor's opinion in the former placed the burden of remedying diversity failures on educational institutions alone, while Chief Justice Rehnquist in the latter struck down just such an attempted remedy. After *Brown* and before *Bakke* minority communities could demand that state schools place people in professions that traditionally do not serve or represent them. They could earlier point to their historical exclusion from institutions of higher learning and demand some form of inclusion as a remedy and expect the university to gear programs to training individuals from the community to serve the community. That power is now removed. The future of diversity after *Bakke*, reinforced in the Michigan cases, is dependent on the goodwill of educational institutions.

The program struck down in *Gratz* is one manifestation of that goodwill, one example of an institution's attempting to do something about the history of segregation in higher education. It is worth emphasizing that the University of Michigan's admissions policy did not require it to admit any underqualified applicants. All students admitted to both the law school and the undergraduate college, including those admitted pursuant to the university's affirmative action policy, were qualified applicants. The debate in *Gratz* was not about whether the university admitted African-Americans who were below its educational threshold. On the contrary, Rehnquist's opinion makes clear that race was not used to push underqualified applicants into the university. Rather, the problem, as the Court and the petitioners saw it, was this: "The university has considered African-Americans, Hispanics, and Native-Americans to be 'underrepresented minorities,' and . . . admits 'virtually every qualified . . . applicant' from these groups."[12]

The defendant in that case, the former University of Michigan president Lee C. Bollinger, had stated, "All students admitted to the University of Michigan meet threshold requirements establishing that they are fully qualified to do the work of a demanding undergraduate program."[13] That policy is not limited to Michigan, but extends country-wide. Gerhard Casper, former president of Stanford University, has said, "Affirmative action does not require, and does not mean, quotas or preferment of unqualified over qualified individuals."[14]

In one sense, then, *Gratz* was a setback after *Grutter* because it struck down the solution precisely envisioned by *Grutter*—a university-initiated program intended to give qualified minority applicants access in order to ensure that the incoming class was sufficiently diverse. In another sense, however, *Gratz*'s outcome is not surprising, given the strict scrutiny for all racial classifications applied by the Court in the past and repeated in *Grutter*. Justice Ginsburg's dissent in *Gratz* is on point: "[T]he Court once again maintains that the same standard of review controls judicial inspection of all official race classifications. . . . This insistence on "consistency" . . . would be fitting were our Nation free of the vestiges of rank discrimination long reinforced by law. . . . But we are not far distant from an overtly discriminatory past, and the effects of centuries of law-sanctioned inequality remain painfully evident in our communities and schools."[15] Moreover, as the NAACP argued in its *Grutter* amicus curiae brief, the Fourteenth Amendment was enacted to "secure the constitutionality of race conscious legislation. . . . [The] Court should not, therefore, interpret this Amendment to bar the very kinds of race-specific remedial measures it was designed to authorize and legitimate."[16]

Additional troubling signals emanate from the otherwise important victory in *Grutter*. Justice Scalia, in dissent, suggested that future litigation can and should challenge the institution's express commitment to the educational benefits of diversity. He commented, "Tempting targets, one would suppose, will be those universities that talk the talk of multiculturalism and racial diversity in the courts but walk the walk of tribalism and racial segregation on their campuses—through minority-only student organizations, separate minority housing opportunities, separate minority student centers, even separate minority-only graduation ceremonies."[17] Scalia's dissent rests on the traditional refusal to recognize that affirming one's ethnic diversity is not the same as separatism or segregation.

Justice O'Connor's opinion provided more than an answer to the mere question of *whether* the Michigan diversity plan was constitutional. She and a majority of her colleagues agreed that it was, but she went on to suggest *when* the diversity rationale would no longer find support from the Court: "It has been 25 years since Justice Powell first approved the use of race to further an interest in student body diversity in the context of public higher education. Since that time, the number of minority applicants with high grades and test scores has indeed increased. We expect that 25 years from now, the use of racial preferences will no longer be necessary to further the interest approved today."[18]

O'Connor's message in *Grutter* seems clear: the Court's decision does not solve the problem the Court addressed; it merely prolongs it. Although her support for the concept is unmistakable, her tolerance of long-term reliance on almost any rationale that focuses on race is limited. Her twenty-five-year sunset clause on diversity can properly be viewed as a challenge to the institutions of higher education, as well as the actual beneficiaries of such policies, to a make a serious effort to reach the goal of a color-blind society. For civil rights advocates and supporters of affirmative action, her sunset provision, eerily similar to Justice Powell's equally limited commitment to the diversity principle, holds the potential of being at once the most problematic and the most promising aspect of her opinion. Her challenge is problematic in that the opinion effectively dictates that affirmative action policies be considered merely temporary and in that it sets a window for achieving the elimination of affirmative action that is, when considered in the context of the centuries of de jure and de facto discrimination that preceded (and even followed) *Brown*, relatively short in time. On the other hand, the sunset provision can be viewed as aspirational and promising because it forces civil rights advocates and others to use this as the needed mandate to focus their work on structural changes in our society. These include the necessary push for substantial and sustained investments in elementary and secondary education and, at the same time, meaningful and comprehensive public policy initiatives to eliminate racism from such areas as housing, lending, employment, and health care, if the goal of permanent solution is to be achieved. Civil rights advocates must regard O'Connor's twenty-five years not as a deadline but as a call to arms—a mandate to attack the pervasive societal discrimination that has made "affirmative action" a dirty word in the twenty-first century.

Furthermore, the Court's adherence to strict scrutiny for benign racial classifications itself contributes to the unrealistic nature of the twenty-five-year mark. Some civil rights activists, including Harvard professor Gary Orfield, see in *Grutter* and *Gratz* a solid framework in which universities can successfully pursue the goals of diversity and integration. One of my colleagues at the law school, Lani Guinier, recently published a *Harvard Law Review* article in which she argued that the Michigan decisions provide leeway and incentives for universities "to engage the public in a larger conversation about what type of society we want to live in and what higher education institutions must do to bring us closer to that goal."[19] If universities heed that challenge, she thinks, the sunset goal might prove workable. While I concede that the decisions could have been much worse, my optimism does not reach that level. Lamenting the Court's adherence to strict scrutiny and the nation's sorry history on integration, Justice Ginsburg is again on target:

> It is well documented that conscious and unconscious race bias, even rank discrimination based on race, remain alive in our land, impeding realization of our highest values and ideals. . . . However strong the public's desire for improved education systems may be, . . . it remains the current reality that many minority students encounter markedly inadequate and unequal educational opportunities. . . . From today's vantage point, one may hope, but not firmly forecast, that over the next generation's span, progress toward nondiscrimination and genuinely equal opportunity will make it safe to sunset affirmative action.[20]

While the clock has already started running out on the future of affirmative action, Ginsburg reminds us that all of society must contribute to the change required to meet that deadline—and it will not be met without significant investment and effort toward the achievement of equal opportunity.

The *Gratz* dissent by Justice Ginsburg and the *Grutter* dissent by Justice Thomas offer alternative visions regarding the future of affirmative action. Although the conclusions reached by the two dissents are markedly different, Ginsburg in particular presented a stark indictment of how public education fails minorities. It is a painful irony that *Brown*, which was intended as a race-conscious remedy for the educational disparities inflicted through segregated education, is now used to justify strict scrutiny of any measure aiming to benefit African-Americans and to perpetuate an unequal system of primary and secondary, but also college, education.

The Ginsburg and Thomas opinions actually address the core question underlying this book: whether integrated education and other opportunities really benefit minorities. Each provides an alternative remedy for the failure of our education system. In this manner, we should regard the problem of affirmative action as more broadly the problem of integration[21]—whether we, as a community, wish to live together, under what conditions we can properly do so, and who has the moral authority to decide these questions. It is clear that as a society we have consistently abandoned attempts to remedy discrimination through broad-based programs to help minorities even when those programs, driven by diversity concerns, benefit whites as well.

Ginsburg addresses head-on the problem of changing the system from the bottom up, starting with primary school education. She notes that the various majority opinions have essentially adopted Powell's one-person holding in *Bakke*,[22] endorsing the use of race so long as it did not harm the majority population. Ginsburg, however, goes further and mounts a scathing attack on the failure of the education system adequately to prepare poor children for higher education. As she notes in *Gratz*,

> In the wake "of a system of racial caste only recently ended," large disparities endure. Unemployment, poverty, and access to health care vary disproportionately by race. Neighborhoods and schools remain racially divided. African-American and Hispanic children are all too often educated in poverty-stricken and underperforming institutions. Adult African-Americans and Hispanics generally earn less than whites with equivalent levels of education. Equally credentialed job applicants receive different receptions depending on their race. Irrational prejudice is still encountered in real estate markets and consumer transactions. "Bias both conscious and unconscious, reflecting traditional and unexamined habits of thought, keeps up barriers that must come down if equal opportunity and nondiscrimination are ever genuinely to become this country's law and practice."[23]

In *Grutter*, Ginsburg relied on data from the Harvard Civil Rights Project to demonstrate that public education in this country is still predominantly segregated and that "schools in predominantly minority communities lag far behind others measured by the educational resources available to them."[24] Nonetheless, some of these students do succeed and pass the required thresholds. Affirmative action is especially appropriate under these circumstances.

Conspicuous in Ginsburg's opinion is my view that America continues to be two nations, separated by race, income, and opportunity. As she notes, affirmative action does little to change this—it holds open the door for a privileged few while shutting it to the many. She—along with Justices Stevens, Souter, and Breyer—is a member of the centrist wing of the Court: there are no liberals on the current Supreme Court. Nonetheless, she appears to assume the mantle of Justice Marshall, one of the great liberal justices.

Thomas's dissent (virtually all of which Scalia joined) has received much attention and generated considerable controversy. He reaffirms his belief that strict scrutiny of racial classifications would be fatal in virtually all cases, except those involving national security and the like and those where a governmental institution is remedying past discrimination for which it is directly responsible.[25]

Calling diversity a "fashionable catch-phrase" and a matter of "racial aesthetics," and treating it as a covert form of unlawful "racial balancing," Thomas dissects the state's interest and finds that it has two elements, *both* of which must be compelling to pass strict scrutiny. The state wishes to achieve a marginally better education *and* to remain an elite institution. From this argument it follows that a state has no compelling interest in establishing a public law school (five states do not even have one), much less an elite law school (the only states with top-fifteen law schools are Michigan, Texas, California, and Virginia).[26]

Thomas also finds that the program is not narrowly tailored; he points to the various state universities, in particular the University of California at Berkeley's Boalt Hall's experience, to demonstrate that race-conscious policies are not necessary to keep minority admissions up. In addition, he maintains that switching to a certificate system or some other system that relies less on the SAT and makes less room for merit exceptions (such as preferences for legacies) could also achieve higher minority admissions.

Finally, in what is probably his most perplexing observation in his dissenting opinion, Thomas suggests that there is no evidence that minority students learn better at elite institutions than they would at less competitive institutions, and there is in fact evidence to the contrary. He faults affirmative action programs for "tantalizing" students to enter environments where they "cannot succeed." Moreover, it engenders feelings of superiority or resentment among the nonbeneficiary races and of dependency or entitlement among beneficiaries.

Thomas's dissent in *Grutter* asserts that integrated education negatively impacts African-Americans. The claim that affirmative action stigmatized these individuals' achievements seems more a function of white prejudice than a result of affirmative action. Many of the nation's leaders today—in top business, educational, and local and state government posts—are beneficiaries of their undergraduate and professional schools' affirmative action programs, and they do not find these opportunities stigmatizing at all. They are judged today, as they should be, on their performance rather than on their skin color.

Thomas makes clear his belief that the University of Michigan Law School faced the Hobson's choice of admitting underqualified minorities or maintaining its elite status: to admit minorities, he suggests, would require Michigan to forgo its ranking as one of the top five law schools in the country. He implies that admitted African-American candidates are somehow underqualified and are dragging down the university's status in a manner other students are not.[27]

Thomas's argument is essentially that the University of Michigan Law School must admit all qualified applicants by grades alone. Given that most elite law schools receive applications from many more candidates than they can possibly accommodate, the real question is not whether to be selective but what sorts of selection criteria are appropriate. In the crafting of a class, individually tailored selections on the basis of race, ethnicity, geography, or social class, have long been tolerated, so long as they do not perpetuate social injustice.

Thomas's first major school desegregation case was *United States v. Fordice* (1992).[28] In addition to joining the majority opinion (only Scalia did not join it in full), Thomas wrote a separate concurrence. The majority held that in determining whether Mississippi's university system had met its obligations under *Brown*, even if the relevant policies appear to be neutral, the district court should find a violation. More specifically, the Court said,

> If the State perpetuates policies and practices traceable to its prior system that continue to have segregative effects—whether by influencing student enrollment decisions or by fostering segregation in other facets of the university system—and such policies are without sound educational justification and can be practicably eliminated . . . even though the State has abolished the legal requirement that whites and blacks be educated separately and has established racially neutral policies not animated by a discriminatory purpose.[29]

What appeared in *Fordice* to be a defense of the value of African-American cultural educational institutions has now been revealed as Thomas's belief that the only space in which African-Americans can thrive is in a separate community surrounded by its own cultural institutions that inspire African-American self-esteem. Integration itself is seen as the evil, because the price of the ticket admitting African-Americans into white society—the cost of redistribution of resources to African-Americans—is revealed to be the negative stereotype that none of us made it on merit and thus are unworthy of our place. Thomas's solution is to cede that place to whites who are untroubled by the fact that they may get there thanks to a historical preference that is the legacy of racial discrimination from slavery and Jim Crow.

One of the paradoxical aspects of Thomas's jurisprudence is that he bolsters this unsettling acceptance of the stereotypes of white supremacy with an odd reliance on the wisdom of black philosophers, all of whom would probably disapprove of his role on the Supreme Court. He has quoted W. E. B. Du Bois and Frederick Douglass, with particular vigor, in race cases. His quotations of these race men are invariably out of context and used to serve his narrow, ideological agenda.

For example, Thomas begins his concurrence with a quotation from Du Bois: "We must rally to the defense of our schools. We must repudiate this unbearable assumption of the right to kill institutions unless they conform to one narrow standard."[30] He approves of the majority's standard because, given that "it does not compel the elimination of all observed racial imbalance, it portends neither the destruction of historically black colleges nor the severing of those institutions from their distinctive histories and traditions."[31] He sees "sound educational justification" for maintaining historically black colleges, which "have survived and flourished" in spite of "the shameful history of state-enforced segregation," and have even expanded as blacks have gained greater access to historically white institutions.[32] Citing various sources, Thomas argues that these institutions have historically played a central role in creating opportunities for blacks, and continue to do so, as "a symbol of the highest attainments of black culture."[33]

Du Bois's vision of political and social action by blacks was strongly interlinked with education: he famously advocated the creation of a Talented Tenth of African-Americans through elite-style college education and was himself the product of Harvard and the University of Berlin. He therefore thrived at these most elite of majority white institutions and was not content to confine himself to the historically black Fisk College, where he earned his undergraduate degree. Moreover, for Du Bois, individual success was nothing without a recognition of community obligations. The point of success was to help those less fortunate. His vision for the Talented Tenth depended upon a strong sense of racial kinship, urging the most successful African-Americans to recognize that racism lumped them in with the least successful, all of them standing as representatives of their race, rather than the "trickle-down" theory of success whereby the goods accruing to the most talented and successful would come to be shared by the rest of the African-American community.[34] Du Bois's notion of activism through education is therefore the very antithesis of Thomas's robust individualism.

That individualism reaches its apogee in the *Grutter* dissent, where Thomas begins with the words of Douglass to support the plea to end remedial or redistributive justice. According to Thomas, Douglass stated,

> Do nothing with us! Your doing with us has already played the mischief with us. Do nothing with us! If the apples will not remain on the tree of their own strength, if they are worm-eaten at the core, if they are early ripe and disposed to fall, let them fall! . . . And if the Negro cannot stand on his own legs, let him fall also. All I ask is, give him a chance to stand on his own legs! Let him alone! . . . [Y]our interference is doing him positive injury.[35]

This appears to be the plea of a man at one with Thomas in distrusting remedial schemes. Douglass, however, was no foe to social redistribution. On the contrary, he was an avid proponent of the need for reconstruction after the Civil War. During this speech to Abolitionists in Boston, Douglass castigated those who would undermine African-American efforts to assert their citizenship. The lines that Thomas omits are these:

> Let him alone. If you see him on his way to school, let him alone, don't disturb him! If you see him going to the dinner table at a hotel, let him go! If you see him going to the ballot box, let him alone, don't disturb him! If you see him going into a work-shop, just let him alone,—your interference is doing him positive injury.[36]

Clearly, it is not redistribution or remediation to which Douglass objects, but the manner in which America had prevented, and would continue to prevent, African-Americans from asserting their rights. As Derrick Z. Jackson noted in the *Boston Globe*, Thomas dropped "the sentences where Douglass held America accountable . . . [and] white America collectively kept interfering, keeping black children out of schools, restaurants, ballot boxes, and good jobs for another century" after Douglass gave his speech.[37]

Marshall viewed the Constitution as an inherently flawed document that contained the means of subjugating millions of Americans: the silent endorsement of slavery; the treatment of African-Americans as three-fifths of a white person; the continuance of the slave trade for twenty-one years after ratification; and the endorsement of the southern states' fugitive slave acts. Such a document could not command the assent of moral men and certainly not the secular deification of its framers. But Marshall's view cuts against originalism, which raises the Constitution, unamended, along with its framers, to the pinnacle of moral authority. Turning a blind eye to the need for our Constitution to develop—as it did almost immediately through the Bill of Rights and continues to do today—has been the worst vice of American intolerance. In Thomas's hands, the fine words of Du Bois and Douglass are deflected away from their meaning, then and now. The Constitution is ossified, no longer a living document. And with it goes the challenge of integration.

Integration remains a challenge for America. For Thomas, the burdens of integration are insupportable, and he has now turned away from them. For Marshall, the burdens of integration were worth the fight because the reward was an America that could shake off the sham it tolerates as the embodiment of the words of the Declaration or the Constitution. Our Union will never be perfect, only more perfect, and it is our daily task to see that it becomes so. That is Marshall's lesson—that even a document as flawed as our Constitution can be redeemed in time.

It is in some ways sad to note that the general response, at least from supporters of affirmative action, to the Supreme Court's companion decisions in the University of Michigan affirmative action cases has been a collective sigh of relief. If affirmative action is safe for the moment, it is so by the narrowest of margins and for reasons that retain, rather than eliminate, the problems of a system geared toward an attempt to remedy educational inequality that occurs too late to do any good to the majority of the population. Justice Ginsburg's persuasive analysis makes that crystal clear.

It is also clear not only that Justice Thomas has offered a point of view on matters of race that is 180 degrees different from that of Justice Marshall but also that, with the reckless bravado expressed in his University of Michigan Law School dissenting opinion, he has an unparalleled comfort in eliminating all that remains from the vision of equality articulated in *Brown*. My fear that *Brown*'s vision is being accomplished only with "all deliberate speed" is now supplanted by my greater fear that resegregation of public education is occurring at a faster pace. While we celebrate the Michigan decision as a vindication of the principles articulated in *Brown*, we must also be vigilant to make sure that the progress of fifty years is not compromised any further.

PART VI

Ogletree and other Reparations Coordinating Committee lawyers meet with survivors and descendants of the Tulsa race riots and their supporters in 2003.

CHAPTER 16

MEETING THE EDUCATIONAL CHALLENGES OF THE TWENTY-FIRST CENTURY

The problem of racially integrating our schools has changed its structure over the fifty years since *Brown*. At first, massive resistance in the South imperiled the integrationist ideal. After the southern courts of appeal in the Fourth and especially the Fifth Circuits won the struggle for desegregation as a political ideal, the nationwide battle for integration began. The Boston busing crisis was just one of many conflicts between poor whites and African-Americans over the struggle for quality education. At the same time, middle-class whites fled urban education wholesale to suburbia and its racially homogenous public education systems. The challenge of equalizing schools thus assumed a class-based as well as a race-based aspect, as poor whites were left behind with poor African-Americans, and both felt they were fighting for the same scarce resources.

In large part, responsibility for this depressing trend falls on the shoulders of a Supreme Court that has meekly enforced its *Brown II* mandate. In his powerful book *What* Brown v. Board of Education *Should Have Said*, Professor Jack M. Balkin takes note of this hollowing of *Brown* through a number of subsequent and unfortunate Court decisions[1]—decisions that have rendered integration initiatives nearly impotent. Of particular consequence, for example, was *Milliken v. Bradley*,[2] which in 1974 excused white suburban neighborhoods from desegregation programs involving inner-city Detroit.[3] With that exemption, African-American students in metropolitan Detroit schools had few white counterparts with whom to integrate, further stemming the tide of desegregation.

Even before *Milliken*, and despite the progressivism of the Warren

Court, race-based decisions some years after *Brown* accelerated the process of judicial ignorance of de facto segregation and, in turn, helped halt affirmative integration projects. *Loving v. Virginia*[4] and *McLaughlin v. Florida*,[5] vital and progressive decisions in their own right, nonetheless both classified the *Brown* decision as concerned with de jure discrimination against suspect classes[6] and not as about the affirmative process of integration. By the time of the Burger Court, those decisions and others were in turn used to justify *Washington v. Davis*,[7] a seminal discrimination case and one that confirmed the Court's lack of concern with discriminatory *effect*. Small wonder, then, that *Brown*, while today seen as the most important of a long line of equal rights cases, has veered far from the course of actual integration. While we laud the Court's and the nation's progress in ending mandated segregation, antimiscegenation laws, and other important roadblocks to equal rights, we forget that *Brown II* promised more.

Representative of this judicial back-turning is the replacement of Justice Marshall by Justice Thomas, who very much does not see a role for the courts in enforcing *Brown II*. Where Marshall pushed for integration in his *Milliken* dissent and felt a powerful responsibility to increase educational opportunities for all children, Thomas urges restraint and militates against the benefits of integration. In his dissent in *Missouri v. Jenkins*,[8] Thomas focuses on *Brown I* and argues it was concerned solely with de jure, and not de facto, segregation. He notes that as a result, *Brown II* was "extraordinary" in its scope and that such powers should have been temporary and used only to overcome the "widespread resistance" to desegregation.[9] For Thomas, the de jure/de facto split is paramount, and it leads him to characterize *Brown II* as not a promise of integration but as an anomaly, designed to deal with initial "widespread resistance" and nothing more. One could not get much farther from Justice Marshall's understanding of the case—a case that he himself litigated, a case that helped put Justice Thomas where he is today.

Beyond Thomas, the Supreme Court as a whole has increasingly professed a lack of concern with the *Brown II* mandate. Particularly damaging has been its retrenchment from enforcing existing desegregation orders, cemented in the 1991 case of *Board of Education of Oklahoma City v. Dowell*.[10] In *Dowell*, the Court found that good faith attempts at compliance with *Brown II* were sufficient to escape from under desegregation orders,[11] regardless of the resegregative impact such escapes would have. In *Jenkins*, four years later, the Court struck down a district court–ordered school plan for Kansas City that required increased funding for both educator salaries and remedial education programs. The plan, designed to attract white students to inner-city schools, was found an abuse of the lower court's discretion to end desegregation.[12]

With decisions like *Dowell* and *Jenkins*, schools remain segregated, and they remain unequal. And the problem facing education in America is no longer simply one of racial parity but of economic equality. The Michigan affirmative action cases held out the hope that diversity can serve as a rationale for promoting integration in college education. Achieving diversity would end the need for special programs of race-based assistance. Yet that diversity is increasingly missing in our public schools and has been promoted by a combination of private and public decisions taken by the rich at the expense of poor urban communities to abandon the goal of an equal and quality education for all. Regretably, education in America is not, and never has been, a fundamental right. Indeed, education of any quality is now becoming a privilege. Funded primarily by states reluctant to spend their diminishing budgets on communities that are disenfranchised in myriad ways, America is on the verge of creating an uneducated underclass defined predominantly by race. As Professor Balkin notes, "[a]t the start of the twenty-first century, the principle of *Brown* seems as hallowed as ever, but its practical effect seems increasingly irrelevant to contemporary public schooling."[13]

Indeed, the United States has been in a period of resegregation for some time now. Resegregation is strongly correlated with class and with poverty. Today, white children attend schools where 80 percent of the student body is also white, resulting in the highest level of segregation of any group. Only 15 percent of segregated white schools are in areas of concentrated poverty; over 85 percent of segregated black and Latino schools are.[14] Schools in high-poverty areas routinely show lower levels of educational performance; even well-prepared students with stable family backgrounds are hurt academically by attending such schools.

U.S. public schools as a whole are becoming more nonwhite as minority enrollment approaches 40 percent of all students, nearly twice the percentage in the 1960s. In the western and southern regions of the country, almost half of all students are minorities. In today's schools, blacks make up only 8.6 percent of the average white student's school, and just over 10 percent of white students attend schools that have a predominantly minority population. Even more striking is the fact that over 37 percent of black and Latino students attend 90–100 percent minority schools.[15]

This trend has led to the emergence of a substantial number of public schools where the student body is almost entirely nonwhite, including a very rapid increase in the number of multiracial schools where three different racial groups comprise at least one-tenth of the total enrollment. However, these schools are attended by only 14 percent of white children. Most of the shrinking white enrollment occurs in the nation's largest city school systems.[16]

Minority segregated schools have much higher concentrations of poverty and much lower average test scores, lower levels of student and teacher qualifications, and fewer advanced courses. They are often plagued by limited resources and social and health problems. High-poverty schools have been shown to increase educational inequality for the students who attend them because of such problems as a lack of resources, shortage of qualified teachers, lower parent involvement, and higher teacher turnover. Almost half of the students in schools attended by the average black or Latino student are poor or nearly poor. By contrast, less than one student in five in schools attended by the average white student is classified as poor. As Gary Orfield, co-director of the Civil Rights Project (CRP) at Harvard University, and Susan E. Eaton, researcher at CRP, note, "Nine times in ten, an extremely segregated black and Latino school will also be a high-poverty school. And studies have shown that high-poverty schools are overburdened, have high rates of turnover, less qualified and experienced teachers, and operate a world away from mainstream society."[17]

BOSTON, WHICH HAS A NATIONWIDE reputation for being a center of liberalism, is viewed by many African-Americans as "a cold, segregated city." In Boston, the average black resident lives in a neighborhood that is 75 percent black, compared with the average white person, whose neighborhood is less than 30 percent minority.[18] More and more smaller neighboring cities are also experiencing an increase in their resident minority population.[19] Boston's minority percentage of the population grew from 9.8 percent in 1960 to 40.8 percent in 1990; its black population increased from 67,873 in 1960 to 145,993 in 1990. In the same period, the white population dropped to 360,920. In the last decade of the twentieth century, Boston neighborhoods were increasingly segregated, with the majority of blacks living in Mattapan and Roxbury. This was also true for the minority population at large, which found itself concentrated mostly in five of the city's neighborhoods.[20]

Boston's suburbs continue to house an overwhelmingly white population. Such a disparity has increased segregation in the suburbs of Boston, and very little progress has been made to reduce such patterns. Even as minority populations rise in the suburbs, segregation rates between these groups and whites increase. Segregation levels remain much higher in the city of Boston than in outlying areas. While blacks continue to experience the highest levels of segregation in Boston, the level of segregation among Latinos increased in Boston in the 1990s. These high levels can be attributed to two main factors. Redlining, the denial of home loans in areas seen as undesirable because of a large minority population, has forced many minorities together into alternative communities. White flight, the movement of white residents out of the inner city and into the suburbs, has also contributed to the increasingly segregated neighborhoods.[21] Social scientists who have studied these patterns conclude that "the exclusion of minority children from suburban schools is the most significant key to racial inequality in the Boston region."[22]

Despite the perceived advances made by the courts, Boston schools are falling back into a pattern of segregation. In the past decade, thousands of white students have left the Boston public elementary schools. The percentage of white students in the schools reached an all-time low in 2000. In 1990, the student enrollment was made up of 76 percent nonwhites; ten years later, that figure stood at 86 percent.[23] This development reflects white flight into the surrounding suburban neighborhoods, and middle-class families who are choosing to send their children to private and parochial schools.[24]

As a result of these trends, the city of Boston's schools are becoming places for the poor. In 2000, the average white student attended an elementary school where 78 percent of the students received free or reduced lunches, a measure of poverty. For blacks and Asians it was 81 percent and for Latinos 83 percent.[25] The schools left with the largely minority population have fewer educational resources than the others but still are held to the same standards—the Massachusetts Comprehensive Assessment System and college entrance exams.[26] While many cultural and ethnic groups choose to live among one another in order to form a better sense of community and to enjoy other benefits, for too many minority Bostonians, segregation concentrates poverty in minority neighborhoods.[27] Often without a base of economic and political power, these neighborhoods lose investment and important resources.

Communities have responded to the failure of *Brown* in a number of ways. Many individuals and groups have assumed the responsibility of creating an alternative educational system that meets the needs of children. The idea of self-determination took root with some vigor in the post-*Brown* period. From Harlem to Watts, efforts were made to build institutions that gave the black community greater control of its children's education and that reflected the community's values. Some of these programs were considered controversial, largely as a result of their sponsors.

A sampling of the institutions created during the past fifty years is instructive. Bob Moses, a civil rights veteran, believed that teaching our children math, and in particular algebra, was one way to prepare them to be competitive in the twenty-first century. He began the Algebra Project in Cambridge, Massachusetts, which is now popular in many cities and states. Dr. Jeffrey Howard took a different approach in establishing the Efficacy Institute; it emphasizes, among other things, training and retraining teachers to understand and teach minority children, with the goal of imparting to them, at an early age, the value of intelligence and knowledge. In Washington, D.C., Peggy Cooper Cafritz started the Duke Ellington School of the Arts, to give urban children some exposure to the arts and to use their artistic ability as a tool for engaging their intellectual abilities. Meanwhile, Benjamin Banneker High School in Washington is dedicated to academic excellence and preparing minority children for the challenges that lie ahead. In New York City, the Boys Choir of Harlem, founded by Dr. Walter Turnbull, teaches young men the qualities of self-respect, discipline, and motivation, making them great performers onstage and successful students in the classroom. In Chicago, Marva Collins opened the Westside Preparatory School in 1975, to serve the children in Garfield Park, an inner-city area neglected and underserved. Collins, a former schoolteacher, wanted the school to educate the children who others said were "unteachable." Through her various programs, she has educated a generation of urban children who might otherwise have landed in a life of crime and poverty. Today her former students are doctors, lawyers, and, most important, teachers. These are just a few of the examples illustrating the black community's broad responsiveness to the needs of children.

Such models also found a ready community in Cambridge. In the early 1990s, as parents of two children in the Cambridge public school system, Pamela and I got involved in programs designed to address the undereducation of minority children in our community. We benefited from the earlier work of black parents and teachers living in Cambridge. In the late 1980s, a group of concerned black staff in the Cambridge public school system decried the quality of the education received by black and Hispanic children. Specifically, their research revealed that black students were placed in less competitive classes, received little mentoring, and had no real opportunity to pursue an academic track that might have increased their chances of going to college and beyond. The report was the brainchild of two people deeply involved in the Cambridge school system and frustrated with its system's failure properly to educate black and brown children.

Dr. William McLaurin was a science teacher by training, but served as the assistant principal of Cambridge Rindge and Latin High School. Doc, as he was known, was deeply religious and also deeply devoted to children. His wife, Joyce, an elementary school teacher, made endlessly creative use of paper, scissors, tape, paint, and glue to create an exciting and educational classroom. At the same time, Caroline Hunter, also a science teacher and administrator, brought a critical eye to the education of Cambridge's minority children. Unlike Doc, whose children were in college in the 1980s, Caroline and her husband, Ken Williams, had a school-age daughter, Lisette, attending Cambridge public schools. Caroline and Doc would attend Cambridge School Committee meetings and present data about the underperformance of minority children and their neglect in the school system. Caroline and Ken were no strangers to confronting injustice. A decade earlier, Ken had worked as a photographer and Caroline as a chemist at the Polaroid company in Cambridge. Ken noticed that many of the photos they were processing were for black people, but they did not appear to be Americans. Caroline determined that the photos were of black South Africans, to be used as identity cards in South Africa. They confronted Polaroid with this information, but the company denied it. When they proceeded to obtain proof of and publicize this practice, which was against the policy of sanctions against South Africa, they were promptly fired. The momentum, however, made them heroes, and eventually Polaroid had to admit its error and stop making the passbook photos of black South Africans.

The reports authored by Caroline and Doc found that black students were three times more likely to be suspended from elementary school than white students, and that Hispanics were twice as likely to be suspended as whites. They also determined that while minority students constituted the majority of enrollment in Cambridge schools, whites were still more than 7.5 times more likely to be enrolled in Advanced Placement classes than black or Hispanic students. In addition, black and Hispanic students were over 1.5 times more likely to fail at least one academic course at the high school level than white students. Perhaps the most troubling statistic was that four out of five low-income high school students failed at least one course.[28]

The real difference came not because of the efforts of these progressive educators, whom we must applaud, but because parents in Cambridge, who were rightly frustrated, took matters into their own hands. A key player of that effort was a dear friend of ours, Kathy Reddick. Kathy grew up in Cambridge, attended its elementary schools, and later moved to the neighboring community of Medford, where she graduated from high school. Her husband, Clark, also went through the Cambridge public schools. They are the proud parents of five children, including a set of triplets, who all attended the Cambridge public schools. Both parents worked hard to provide for their family and took an active role in their children's education. They nonetheless realized that their children were not getting the skills or the guidance they needed to excel. Kathy did not accept this situation. She advocated for her children, went to school committee meetings, and, no matter what the topic of the day was, used the time allowed for public comment to lambaste the system for undereducating and misadjusting minority children. Kathy discovered that she was not alone in her concern about the school system. She met Angela Garraway, a single parent who felt the same way. She discussed the problem at length with Laurie Haynes, another single mother whose child was being labeled as developmentally challenged and not getting the services she needed to get out of her educational rut. She spent hours comparing notes with Lynette Riley, yet another single parent who expressed frustration with her child's placement in unchallenging classes. She commiserated with Sharon Reid, whose extraordinarily talented daughter was not reaching her potential. In short, she found a community whose members, nearly forty years after *Brown*, were not realizing its promises and who were seeking another solution. Ironically, Cambridge had voluntarily desegregated its schools after *Brown*. It had a complex system in place to balance students racially at every school. Yet, even in their integrated classroom, black, Latino, and poor students lagged behind other students. Parents therefore met with Caroline Hunter and Doc McLaurin and discussed what, collectively, they could do.

While the educators and parents were organizing a strategy to address the problems their children faced in the public school system, a young, dynamic African-American minister, the Reverend Jeffrey Brown, was engaged in a similar effort. The Reverend Brown was one of the founders of the Ten Point Coalition, a group of young black ministers concerned about Boston's high rate of juvenile murders, largely among black men. Instead of simply complaining to the police, a strategy they had tried and found unsatisfactory, they did something extraordinary. At midnight, they patrolled the streets where the young gang members gathered, and literally put their lives on the line to keep one brother from killing another. They were not trying to preach the gospel at two in the morning; they were teaching self-respect and praying for peace. Their collaboration with community members, police, and public officials produced a strategy that virtually eliminated gang violence.

Others who joined the effort included my Harvard Law School colleague Charles Nesson and his wife, Fern, state representative Alvin Thompson, community activist Scott Darling, and Wayne Williams, a Harvard graduate student at the time. The founding committee submitted a proposal to start a charter school for their neglected children; they called it, in light of their mission, the Bread and Roses Charter School. The idea of a charter school was their way of addressing the pervasive problems of neglect and of taking personal responsibility for the education of their children. It was an ambitious proposal, but the state did not approve it. The members of this group would not be deterred, though. Seeking out additional allies in their efforts, they approached my wife and me and asked whether we could support the idea. We did not hesitate to join the effort.

In pursuing our idea of establishing a model charter school focused on the needs of African-American children and dedicated to the attainment of the highest academic skills, we tried to think of someone who embodied the ability to overcome barriers to education. After some discussion and research, we named the school the Benjamin Banneker Charter School. It could hardly have been a more appropriate name, given our goals.

Benjamin Banneker, whose father and grandfather were slaves, was born in Maryland in 1731. His astonishing accomplishments, despite his humble beginnings, made him a perfect model of someone our children could emulate. In 1753, for example, Banneker borrowed a pocket watch, decided to take it apart, made a drawing of each component, and, on reassembling it, got it to work as well as before. He subsequently built a wooden clock that kept accurate time for over fifty years. As a surveyor, he later made a significant contribution to the District of Columbia's unique design. In 1791, he published the first of a series of almanacs. To illustrate the intellectual prowess of African-Americans, he sent a copy to Secretary of State Thomas Jefferson, who had declared that African-Americans were inferior in areas of mathematics.

Banneker also wrote the slave owner and future president a twelve-page letter, asking him to recognize the mental endowments and achievements of African-Americans, notwithstanding the burden that race imposed upon them:

> I suppose it is a truth too well attested to you, to need a proof here, that we are a race of beings, who have long labored under the abuse and censure of the world; that we have long been looked upon with an eye of contempt; and that we have long been considered rather as brutish than human, and scarcely capable of mental endowments. . . . I apprehend you

will embrace every opportunity, to eradicate that train of absurd and false ideas and opinions, which so generally prevails with respect to us; and that your sentiments are concurrent with mine, which are, that one universal Father hath given being to us all; and that he hath not only made us all of one flesh, but that he hath also, without partiality, afforded us all the same sensations and endowed us all with the same faculties; and that however variable we may be in society or religion, however diversified in situation or color, we are all of the same family, and stand in the same relation to him.[29]

Jefferson replied, in part,

No body wishes more than I do to see such proofs as you exhibit, that nature has given to our black brethren, talents equal to those of the other colours of men, & that the appearance of a want of them is owing merely to the degraded condition of their existence both in Africa & America. I can add with truth that no body wishes more ardently to see a good system commenced for raising the condition both of their body & mind to what it ought to be, as fast as the imbecility of their present existence, and other circumstance which cannot be neglected, will admit.[30]

Because Banneker never went beyond the eighth grade and nonetheless found ways to excel as an astronomer, mathematician, and scientist, he seemed an example of great significance to African-American children who had been told they could not analyze and solve problems. The Benjamin Banneker Charter School was dedicated to the proposition that children must do well in math and science and that technology should be an integral part of their educational plan. It would defy the prevailing view that African-Americans lack the ability to excel. The founders envisioned an urban school, kindergarten through the eighth grade, that emphasized math, science, and technology and was committed to excellence. We believed that all children had the capacity to excel as learners and as citizens when provided with a rich, supportive, and stimulating educational environment. Our school would not only teach its students well but make sure that community leaders, parents, educators, and others shared the common vision of excellence, and that we could provide young people with role models, mentors, and challenging educational opportunities to ensure that they would succeed.

When we originally submitted the proposal for a charter school to the state of Massachusetts, we lacked many things. We had no building, no teachers, and no students. We had a kernel of an idea, but it eventually bore fruit.

The Banneker School is one example of a black community's response to the unmet promises of *Brown*. Another example is Building Educated Leaders for Life (BELL), a wonderful effort to give back to the community by a group of my black law students at Harvard. Two of them, in particular, Kobi Kennedy Brinson and Earl Martin Phalen, who were co-chairs of the Harvard Law School Black Law Students Community Affairs Committee, recruited law students to tutor in Cambridge and Boston public schools and community centers. Their goal was to raise the bar on community service by offering their intellect as black law students, the best and the brightest, to local children of Cambridge and Boston, who desperately needed role models. The Black Law Students Association was concerned, rightly, about the lack of African-American students from the Boston area admitted to and attending Harvard. Kobi, Earl, and a third black law student, Cathy Hampton, wanted to work with local kids to show them that they were loved and valued and to inspire them to reach for academic excellence. Earl and others began to volunteer at the Roxbury Boys and Girls Clubs. Kobi and Cathy started tutoring at a Cambridge public school, where they met Kathy Reddick, the parent of three children in the school. At Kathy's urging, they expanded the program and called it Black Butterflies. They were all young, gifted, and black—students and teachers—and that identity was crucial to the success of their strategy. When I asked Kobi why she started the Black Butterflies, she replied, "We just wanted to help. We hoped that if the children got excited about learning after school, they would be inspired to work hard in school despite the less than optimal atmosphere they were subjected to in the Cambridge school system. My personal motto is *noblesse oblige*. Absolutely every person at Harvard is privileged to be there. Community service is owed; it is not optional. I came up with the name Black Butterflies because of the lyrics of Deniece Williams's 'Black Butterfly.' " Kobi explained to me that she was inspired by the song because it motivated youths to reach toward greater heights.

In 1991, Earl Martin Phalen came to visit me in my office to discuss his career plans after graduation. Earl, a graduate of Yale College, had the intellect and training to work for any corporate law firm, be a leader in public-interest law, or be appointed to the bench. He told me he wanted to use his talents not on Wall Street but in Cambridge, not to make money for corporations but to raise money to educate the next generation of children. He wanted to build on the community service activities he and Kobi had started and create an after-school program for children, beginning with black children as early as kindergarten. It would be based in Cambridge, operate within the public schools, and strengthen children's academic performance by focusing on math and reading skills. He saved the best part of his plan for last. He wanted me, his mentor at Harvard Law School, to serve as the chairman of the board of this new group, which he planned to call the BELL Foundation. At that moment, I thought Earl was naïve and maybe even out of touch with reality, but I did not want to dismiss his proposal out of hand.

Many students come to me with naïve ideas and then, on reflection, settle for more sensible ideas. Earl returned a few weeks later, even more committed to the idea. I asked a few questions: "Do you have an office for BELL?" "No." "Do you have any money to start a program?" "No." "Do you have any schools that have approved your proposal to start a tutorial program in their schools?" "No." A little perturbed, I asked, "How do you plan to start an after-school tutorial program, with no building, no schools, and no money?" I felt bad about being so blunt with one of my favorite students, but thought it better that I, rather than someone else, expose the holes in his plan. Earl collected himself and answered, "I have some black parents who want this, I know some children who need it, and I can raise the money to make this happen." I was doubtful, but could not dissuade him. Besides, agreeing to be the chairman of the board of an organization that would never exist added no burden to my already overburdened schedule.

Earl came back two weeks later, with stationery listing him as the president and me as the chairman of the board, and he had recruited

Kathy Reddick to be the parent representative on the Board. He had me sign a slew of letters addressed to my Harvard Law School colleagues, Harvard black alumni, Boston business leaders, and others, asking for money to start an organization dedicated to educating the next generation of children. Like Dr. King, he dreamed that the children would be judged by the content of their character rather than by the color of their skin.

In 1992, BELL opened its doors as an after-school program founded by Earl and one of his closest friends, Andrew Carter. It responded to challenges that were not otherwise being met in the public school system. BELL quickly evolved into a rigorous tutoring and mentoring program for elementary school children who lived in low-income, underresourced communities. All the BELL children were called "scholars" from the moment they arrived and were constantly reminded that they would not be allowed to fail. The program features a rigorous curriculum delivered by positive adult role models, a variety of educational and cultural activities, and year-end evaluation and continuous improvement.

Today, BELL has two core programs: the BELL After-School Instructional Curriculum (BASICs), a thirty-week tutoring and mentoring program that operates Monday through Friday; and the BELL Accelerated Learning Summer Program, a six-week academic summer program. BELL's measurable success is built on its supportive, achievement-based approach, which targets underperforming students with the greatest academic and social needs; selects a tutoring staff of knowledgeable young people and adults who reflect the scholar group demographics and who are committed to serving as mentors for their development; implements a literacy and math curriculum focused on core skills, personal integrity, and better self-image; is linked to national and state learning standards; and requires parental involvement in all elements of their children's academic lives and social development.

BELL now serves nearly 1,500 scholars a year in Boston, New York City, and Washington, D.C., and, over the past decade, has tutored over 6,000 students. The high quality and success of its programs were recognized by former President Bill Clinton, who awarded BELL the 1997 President's Service Award, selecting it as one of 16 organizations from the national pool of 3,600 nominees.

Perhaps the most successful effort of this nature is the Metropolitan Council for Educational Opportunities Program, known as METCO, a voluntary school desegregation program that was created in 1966. METCO buses minority children from Boston's urban neighbor- hoods to predominantly white suburban schools. The benefits of METCO include the fact that when METCO students complete their four years at suburban high schools, they attend four-year colleges at twice the rate of their peers attending the Boston city schools. These students also perform at a much higher rate on state-mandated achievement tests.[31]

The BELL and Banneker experiences have convinced me that, although the battle for racial justice must continue in the courtrooms and although we must never lose sight of the goal of achieving racial equality in education through the legal system, we must also have an alternative strategy of taking responsibility for educating our children and determining their fate. All of these community-driven efforts provide critical opportunities to students but do not address fully the long-term challenge of eliminating the persistent inequality at the core of our society. There are other measures being debated today that seek to end racial inequality "root and branch." One of those efforts is the call for reparations for descendants of African slaves.

CHAPTER 17

ADDRESSING THE RACIAL DIVIDE: REPARATIONS

There should be no mistaking the fervor of the reparations movement. The claim that America owes a debt for the enslavement and segregation of African-Americans has had historical currency for over 150 years. Occasionally, the clamor for repayment of that debt has intensified, particularly in the period following the Civil War. Although the civil rights strategy of Dr. King did not focus on reparations, the rhetoric he used at the March on Washington, about America's giving blacks a check marked "insufficient funds," certainly has the sound of a claim for reparations.[1] I have to believe that if King were alive now, he would come to the same conclusion I have reached. Today, in America and worldwide, we again face one of those historically significant moments when the clamor for reparations increases, and arguments that seemed morally and legally precluded are certain now to become part of the political mainstream. The voices of reason and passion have subsided and been replaced by a consensus demanding justice, and demanding it now. The movement has moved from the courts, and from the churches, to urban America. The call for reparations has moved to those blacks who did not relocate to the suburbs as a result of integration and who were not lifted up as a result of affirmative action. The masses who were left behind feel comfortable in shouting slogans like "No justice, no peace!" These voices demand their reparations. The collective failure to embrace *Brown* may now cost us all a lot more.

As we lament the manner in which the nation's highest court, and lower courts, have addressed the urgent needs of quality education raised in *Brown*, with all deliberate speed, we are forced to consider other strategies to address the growing disparities between blacks and whites in America. One inevitable conclusion is that those who are restless as a result of this country's failure to address *Brown*'s modest goals have turned to more strident demands to achieve racial justice in America. The clarion call is now not just for quality education for all but reparations for African-Americans, as payment for an oppressive past. Those battle cries have been heard the loudest in Tulsa, Oklahoma, and Chicago, Illinois. Their intensity has increased in 2005 to unprecedented levels, and is unlikely to be abated.

The strength of the reparations movement can be attributed to the absence of judicial and political leadership in addressing racial disparities in America. Thurgood Marshall articulated a plan to promote equality in education, both in his cases as a civil rights lawyer and in his clarion voice as a member of the Supreme Court. The louder he seemed to shout, the more he was dismissed as out of step with reality. Political leadership can also be blamed. We have had ten presidents in the White House with the political authority to move the *Brown* mandate forward. In many respects, they have failed. President Eisenhower was not committed to the notion and did little to further the goals of *Brown*. We do not know what President Kennedy would have done had he not been assassinated, but his administration saw little progress on *Brown*. Ironically, President Johnson, a southerner from Texas, embraced *Brown* in more concrete terms than all of his predecessors. His actions were both symbolic and substantive.

Johnson's symbolic efforts included using his 1965 commencement address at Howard University to address the thorny issue of racism in America in the twentieth century. Speaking to the graduating class eleven years after *Brown*, he directly admitted America's failure to do what needed to be done in promoting racial equality:

> [F]reedom is not enough. You do not wipe away the scars of centuries by saying: Now you are free to go where you want, and do as you desire, and choose the leaders you please. You do not take a person who, for years, has been hobbled by chains and liberate him, bring him up to the starting line of a race and then say, "you are free to compete with all the others," and still justly believe that you have been completely fair. Thus it is not enough just to open the gates of opportunity. All our citizens must have

the ability to walk through those gates. This is the next and the more profound stage of the battle for civil rights.[2]

Johnson was aware that there were many "subtle" and "complex" reasons for the failure of African-Americans to achieve equality in America. But there were also two "broad basic reasons" for this lack of equality. One was poverty, which affected all races. The other, "much more difficult to explain, more deeply grounded, more desperate in its force," the president identified as "the devastating heritage of long years of slavery; and a century of oppression, hatred, and injustice."[3] Johnson did not mince words in describing the devastating impact of racial injustice on African-Americans:

> For Negro poverty is not white poverty. Many of its causes and many of its cures are the same. But there are differences—deep, corrosive, obstinate differences—radiating painful roots into the community, and into the family, and the nature of the individual. These differences are not racial differences. They are solely and simply the consequence of ancient brutality, past injustice, and present prejudice. They are anguishing to observe. For the Negro they are a constant reminder of oppression. For the white they are a constant reminder of guilt. But they must be faced and they must be dealt with and they must be overcome, if we are ever to reach the time when the only difference between Negroes and whites is the color of their skin.[4]

Johnson eventually called for the creation of an affirmative action program, to address the persistence of racism as a barrier to racial progress in America. His words were powerful, and generated great hope for change. What followed was the passage of many civil rights laws to meet the demands of *Brown*. In 1967, he appointed Thurgood Marshall to the Supreme Court. Despite these historic events, *Brown*'s hope for equal educational opportunity went largely unmet.

As a result of this failure, a movement that was long dismissed as marginal and not credible is now being discussed with increasing frequency in national newspapers, on television and radio, and in conversations in the office and over dinner tables. The failure to pay the debt of slavery and discrimination by offering quality education has given momentum to the call to pay blacks trillions of dollars for this country's role in using slaves to build a powerful economy.

The level of reparations litigation alone is extensive, with an increasing number of cases being presented in state and federal courts throughout the United States. A focus on reparations for African-Americans[5] reveals that suits have been filed in Illinois,[6] Texas,[7] New York,[8] New Jersey,[9] Louisiana,[10] California,[11] and Oklahoma.[12] These reparations lawsuits have been brought by different groups of attorneys in different jurisdictions asserting different theories on behalf of different classes of clients. Many of the suits were consolidated before a court in the Northern District of Illinois, but Federal District Court Judge Charles Norgle dismissed the complaint on July 6, 2005.[13]

At least four statutes addressing reparations for African-Americans have been passed at the state and municipal level, most notably in Rosewood, Florida,[14] but also in California,[15] Oklahoma,[16] and Chicago.[17] Representative John Conyers's bill, H.R. 40, demanding an investigation of slavery and recommending appropriate reparations, has again been presented to Congress.[18]

These legal and legislative initiatives can be analyzed from two perspectives. One model of reparations litigation includes the multidistrict litigation consolidated in Chicago as well as H.R. 40 and the California Slavery Era Insurance statute and the Chicago ordinance. These actions focus on injuries inflicted during and through the institution of slavery. Other models, such as the Tulsa, Oklahoma, case and the Rosewood, Florida, legislation, address injuries inflicted during the Jim Crow era. Some of the most vocal critics of the reparations movement in general are more supportive of the Jim Crow cases than of the slavery era cases.

Understanding the historical roots of the reparations movement is essential to understanding its current prominence. It is often believed that the reparations effort on behalf of African-Americans is based on the recent successful litigation in the Holocaust reparations movement[19] or on the successful reparations claims approved by Congress on behalf of Japanese Americans interned during World War II.[20] Neither is a basis for African-American reparations claims, which date back much farther. The historical precedents of African-American reparations efforts actually confirm that elements of the Holocaust and Japanese American cases derive from the African-American experience.

The first reported demand for African-American reparations dates back to the nineteenth century.[21] Vincene Verdun details the history of reparations efforts covering four distinct periods. These waves, as he describes them, were "inspired by the tension between the Union and the Confederacy and the attendant desire to restructure the South in order to enhance the Union's military advantage."[22] In the first wave, a broad coalition of white and black activists sought to use reparations not only to complete the emancipation of slaves but also to engage in compensatory (as opposed to distributive) justice by tying the award of property to freed slaves to the disenfranchisement of the former slave owners.

Verdun identifies the attempt by African-Americans to escape the South and achieve a semblance of freedom and economic parity in the North as the second period of reparations pursuit; it included an effort to force "Congress to pass legislation appropriating economic relief to freedmen." This, like subsequent reparations initiatives, contained a strong "black nationalist" element. During World War II, Senator Theodore Bilbo of Mississippi proposed to appropriate newly acquired territories for colonization by African-Americans, and his proposal was supported by another reparations advocate, Marcus Garvey, founder and leader of the United Negro Improvement Association.[23]

The most recent model of reparations efforts came during the 1960s and 1970s, at the height of the civil rights movement.[24] Dr. King's "I Have a Dream" speech can be seen as containing the seeds of a request for reparations, though this interpretation would be questioned by those who do not associate King with such a request. The central focus of his speech was not his dream for a color-blind society but his frustration with the deplorable state of race relations in America. King came to Washington to declare that America had defaulted on "a promissory note in so far as [America's] citizens of color are concerned."[25] Other reparations claims were raised in those years, including a demand by the Nation of Islam that the federal government provide African-Americans with several states located in the regions with large African-American populations as compensation for the work provided by slaves.[26]

One of the most widely publicized and controversial reparations events occurred in 1968, when the activist James Forman interrupted a Sunday morning service at Riverside Church in New York City to introduce the "Black Manifesto," which demanded $500 million in reparations for African-Americans. Interestingly, Forman demanded payment from the churches, synagogues, and other "racist institutions," rather than from the federal government, and he explained how the funds would be used to further the cause of African-Americans in the United States.[27]

During the last quarter century, many law review articles have dealt with reparations.[28] The national reparations effort has been promoted, most notably, by NCOBRA, the National Coalition of Blacks for Reparations in America. Without its continued activism, the movement would have little chance of remaining viable.

Interest in reparations in the twenty-first century has been spurred by two timely events. One was the publication in 2000 of Randall Robinson's book *The Debt: What America Owes to Blacks*, which argued, "No race, no ethnic or religious group, has suffered so much over so long a span as blacks have, and do still, at the hands of those who benefited, with the connivance of the United States government, from slavery and the century of legalized American racial hostility that followed it."[29] While not suggested as a legal brief on the issue, the book admirably states the case for reparations, in light of the history of black misery in America and the disenfranchisement of African-Americans:

> Race is and is not the problem. Certainly rac*ism* caused the gap we see now. The discriminatory attitudes spawned to justify slavery ultimately guaranteed that, even after emancipation, blacks would be concentrated at the bottom of American society indefinitely. . . . [However,] the use of *race* by itself as a general category for comparison is a dangerously misleading decoy. . . . [African-American children] fail [educationally and socially] for the same reasons that Appalachian children fail. Grinding, disabling poverty. Unfortunately, blacks are heavily overrepresented among the ranks of America's disabling poor. Owing to race and only race, it was American slavery that created this bottom-rung disproportion.[30]

The second major reparations event was the effort by Congressman John Conyers, who closely watched a united Congress pass the Civil Liberties Act of 1988[31] in support of Japanese Americans who were forced to live in internment camps, and decided that it was time for a similar legislative study to determine whether African-Americans had a viable claim against the government. Conyers's H.R. 40, in contrast to the Civil Liberties Act of 1988, generated limited support and stiff opposition. Indeed, some African-Americans,[32] including a majority of the members of the Congressional Black Caucus,[33] remain opposed to reparations.

The first known reparations lawsuit, *Johnson v. MacAdoo*,[34] was filed in 1915. In *Johnson*, the plaintiff, Cornelius J. Jones, sued the U.S. Department of the Treasury, claiming that the government's taxation of raw cotton produced by slave labor constituted an unjust enrichment from the labor of African-Americans. The D.C. Circuit Court of Appeals ruled against him, concluding that the government was immune from suit on sovereign immunity grounds.

In a broader lawsuit, *Cato v. United States*,[35] filed in the early 1990s, an African-American woman brought an action for damages against the U.S. government, alleging the kidnapping, enslavement, and transshipment of her ancestors, as well as continuing discrimination on the part of the government. It sought acknowledgment of the injustice of slavery and Jim Crow oppression, in addition to an official apology from the U.S. government.[36] The *Cato* lawsuit was also dismissed.[37]

My involvement in the reparations movement has had three different phases. The first occurred when I attended the Black National Convention in Gary, Indiana, on March 10–12, 1972, where there was a solidarity movement of African-Americans to seek a third political party, not tied to the Democratic and Republican parties. The conference was hosted by Gary's black mayor, Richard Hatcher, and included a wide range of radical political perspectives. Black nationals and black Muslims, black Hebrews and black Communists, black ministers and black politicians—all were present in Gary.

The most striking person there, though, was Queen Mother Audley Moore, a Black Nationalist who struck a powerful chord with me. While this Gary conference focused on black political power, Moore raised an issue unknown to me at the time. She argued that people of African descent in the United States are entitled to billions of dollars because of the slave labor of their ancestors in building this country. She made an urgent plea for reparations.

Queen Mother Moore was born in New Iberia, Louisiana, in 1898. Her grandparents were slaves who suffered greatly. Her great-grandmother was raped by her owner, and her grandfather was lynched in front of his wife. Moore attended segregated public schools through the third grade and then traveled across the South, experiencing the virulent racism of the Jim Crow period in America. During World War I, she went to Anniston, Alabama, my father's hometown, and helped establish a center to aid black veterans of the war, who were denied meaningful assistance by the Red Cross. In the early 1920s, she met Marcus Garvey, the leader of the Universal Negro Improvement Association, an organization planning to relocate people of African descent in the United States back to Africa. In 1931, she joined the movement, led by the Communist Party, to stop the lynching of the Scottsboro boys, nine black teenagers falsely accused of raping a white woman and scheduled to be executed. Her focus on the harm to Africans, at home and abroad, led her to push, in 1955, for reparations for African-Americans. In 1963, she organized the Reparations Committee of Descendants of U.S. Slaves, demanding reparations from the government. Incredibly, she was able to gather over one million signatures from citizens supporting this demand; even more remarkably, she managed to present the signatures to President Kennedy, along with the demand. She finally moved to Harlem, where she became a household name, thanks to her commitment to fighting discrimination practices against blacks and other poor people.

Despite her success in raising consciousness about slavery in 1963, many participants at the Gary convention in 1972 were scarcely aware of her great legacy. That would change, though. Moore was a powerful speaker, and, in an African and African-American gathering where men normally dominated the speaking roles, and black women were in subservient roles, she stood out as a powerful orator, and a leader. When she spoke, everybody listened. I did not learn much about her in Gary, but by the time we both were boarding a charter plane for Africa a year later, I had made it a priority to find out about this advocate for reparations.

The second phase of my involvement with the reparations movement came in 1973, when I was a student at Stanford and traveled to Africa for the first time. My intellectual mentor, a noted Pan-Africanist, Dr. St. Clair Drake, had hired me as a research assistant to work on one of his many projects focusing on the end of neocolonial rule in Africa.

Dr. Drake advised me to study the progress of colonial rule and how colonialism by European countries in particular led to the underdevelopment of Africa. I read Sir Walter Rodney's classic book on the topic, *How Europe Underdeveloped Africa,* as well as works by Ghana's first president following independence, Kwame Nkrumah, and by the great leader of Tanzania, President Julius Nyerere. I was struck by the number of African leaders who were educated in Europe and the United States. Drake's constant reminder to me, and others, that there should be an unbroken chain linking Africa and the black diaspora, which included people of African descent living in the Caribbean, South America, and North America, also resonated with me.

When I gave Drake, who had traveled to Africa and the Caribbean, memos based on my research, he would respond by sharing stories of his personal involvement with these African leaders. He wanted to expose Stanford students to a world beyond our imagination. When he offered me the opportunity to attend the Sixth Pan-African Congress, I jumped at it. Professor Tetteh Kofi, a Ghanaian economist teaching at Stanford, accompanied me.

I flew from San Francisco to New York, where we were to take a charter flight to Africa. Given that we were all people of African descent on this charter and that it was in a sense our pilgrimage to Mecca, or return to the homeland of Africa, we wanted to make sure that our trip had a serious Afrocentric focus. Many of the delegates, who came from throughout the United States, wore dashikis and other African clothing and carried African artifacts with them. Professor James Turner led the delegation from the Africana Studies Department at Cornell University. Courtland Cox, a policy analyst in Washington, D.C., who had extensive ties with Africa, was there. The delegation also included a number of people I had met a year earlier, at the Black National Convention, in Gary, Indiana. Among these was Queen Mother Moore. The Ashanti people of Ghana had named her Queen Mother while she was in Africa to pay her respects to Kwame Nkrumah. As we boarded the plane, many of us were focused on the need to end colonial rule in Africa and to ensure that the new African leaders did not become neocolonial rulers. Moore told us that, while we needed to fight for African liberation on the continent, we also needed to fight for the liberation of descendants of Africa in the United States, by keeping the pressure up for reparations.

My most recent involvement in the reparations movement, as a lawyer, was largely accidental. When I was in Washington in the early 1980s, I met Randall Robinson, also a Harvard Law School graduate and the founder of Transafrica, a black American think tank that lobbied for economic and political development in Africa and the black diaspora. I served on the board of Transafrica, but had been retained by Randall to represent him and others who chose to violate Washington's trespass laws by protesting apartheid at the South African embassy. Randall's goal was simple: get arrested in front of the embassy and then bring the issue of South Africa's apartheid system before the court. Our defense theory in these cases was called the necessity defense. It is a rarely successful, but generally applied, defense in political cases. The strategy is straightforward. While admitting that trespassing is against the law of the land, protesters argued that the continuation of the racist apartheid system in South Africa, as symbolized by the embassy in D.C., was an even greater crime against humanity. Thus, the protesters did not deny that they broke the law, but held that they did so in order to address the larger crime of apartheid.

Using this strategy, thousands of ordinary citizens from D.C., national elected officials, and other dignitaries were also arrested. The U.S. attorney, not wanting to get into this political hotbed, dropped all of the charges against my client, Randall Robinson, and the thousands arrested later. As momentum against South Africa grew, we also pushed Congress to impose economic sanctions against South Africa. The increasing pressure for sanctions, nationally and internationally, and widespread internal protest, eventually led to the dismantling of the apartheid system. On February 2, 1990, Nelson Mandela, the leader of the South African resistance movement, was released after serving twenty-seven years in prison. For me, this was a lesson that pressures outside the narrow parameters of the law can lead to fundamental changes in society.

Randall Robinson was convinced that the use of political pressure to bring national and international attention to issues could make a difference. Reparations for African-Americans was the campaign he pushed onto the national scene in 1999. His book *The Debt* made the case for reparations, and he called a group of scholars in law and the humanities, and reparations activists, as well as Congressman Conyers, to Washington in 2000, to discuss the subject. Randall arranged for the meeting to be covered live on C-Span, and we all gave our views about the importance of reparations. After the meeting, in response to press questions, Randall was asked whether he planned to sue anyone in particular for reparations and, if so, how he would proceed. Randall responded forthrightly, telling the press that a suit would be filed against the federal government and against corporations that had been involved in the slave trade. He went on to say that the leader of this effort would be Charles Ogletree, the legal scholar from Harvard Law School, a Transafrica board member, and a dear friend. There was one problem with this announcement: Randall had never mentioned the possibility of lawsuits to me, nor had he asked me to chair the Reparations Coordinating Committee. It was an enormous challenge. But I remembered Queen Mother Moore's advocacy for reparations decades earlier, all the way up to her death, in May 1997. She had carried the movement on her back for nearly fifty years, and it was now time for her followers to carry it forward.

I agreed to co-chair the Reparations Coordinating Committee with Randall Robinson; later on, Adjoa Aiyetoro, the legal counsel for NCOBRA, joined us as a third co-chair. We began to research possible grounds for a reparations lawsuit. As it turned out, we did not have to look far.

In September 2002, I was invited to give the Buck Colbert Franklin Lecture at the University of Tulsa Law School and to discuss reparations. I learned two important points that night. First, Mr. Franklin was a lawyer who was involved in a historic event in Tulsa, Oklahoma. He represented black residents in one of the most horrific eruptions of racial violence in our country's history. Second, he was the father of John Hope Franklin, the legendary scholar of African-American history at Duke University. I knew Dr. Franklin well and soon got to know him even better. While in Tulsa giving the Franklin Lecture, I learned about the city's history with Jim Crow segregation and about a reparations case waiting to be filed by some committed lawyers. The story was over eighty years old, but I was not intimately familiar with it.

The community in Tulsa called Greenwood comprised about thirty-five square blocks. W. E. B. Du Bois called it the Negro Wall Street in America. That name surely seemed appropriate. Greenwood was developed by blacks, for blacks, because local white segregationists did not want blacks to be a part of their community. As a result of segregation, Greenwood built its own thriving, sustainable community. That all changed in 1921.

On the night of Tuesday, May 31, 1921, a rumor spread through the black community in Tulsa that there was going to be a lynching. Dick Rowland, a nineteen-year-old African-American man, was arrested for having assaulted seventeen-year-old Sarah Page, who was white. In reality, Rowland accidentally stepped on her foot in an elevator, and she slapped him. The black community of Greenwood grew more anxious as the evening wore on, and eventually about fifty Greenwood residents went down to the jail to see whether they could do something to stop the lynching.[38]

Rumors circulated in the white community as well. Someone made a speech stating that black men were wandering around with high-powered pistols. When a group of whites confronted the blacks at the courthouse, there was a melee, and a gun went off. Then the shooting started in earnest. The police department's reaction to the fast-developing events was to deputize and arm hundreds of white men. The police commandeered a local gun shop and a pawnshop, stripping them of firearms. At about the same time, the mayor of Tulsa called in local elements of the National Guard. The guardsmen mounted a machine gun on the back of a truck in an attempt to flush out African-Americans from their defensive positions. Some reports indicate that the mob killed up to three hundred African-Americans, and many bodies were never recovered.[39]

At 5:00 a.m. the next day, a whistle blew and "the invasion of Greenwood began."[40] The National Guard, called in to restore order, only succeeded in making things worse. At 6:30 a.m., it moved in to transport the Greenwood residents to the state fairgrounds and McNulty Ball Park on the outskirts of town and held them there in "protective custody."[41] Then the white mob began burning the empty buildings. Over twelve hundred were destroyed, and the property damage was more than $20 million in 2003 dollars.

In the immediate aftermath, the white citizens of Tulsa accepted that reparations for the riot were required. For example, in the June 15, 1921, issue of the *Nation*, the chair of the emergency committee stated, "Tulsa weeps at this unspeakable crime and will make good the damage, so far as it can be done, to the last penny."[42] At about the same time, the mayor of Tulsa promised to compensate the victims of the riot for the losses they had suffered. He declared that a claims commission would be established to compensate the victims of the riot. Finally, the Tulsa Chamber of Commerce stated that as "quickly as possible rehabilitation will take place and reparation made. . . . Tulsa feels intensely humiliated."[43] Some eighty years later, a commission created by the Oklahoma state legislature to investigate and report on the riot, as well as to make recommendations for further action, reiterated, "Reparations are the right thing to do."[44]

Despite this compelling evidence that the black Tulsa residents were entitled to receive reparations for their loss of life and property, their claims were largely ignored. I was asked to meet with members of the Tulsa Reparations Coalition, a multiracial community group organized to fight for reparations for the Tulsa survivors. I listened to their pleas for help and decided that I couldn't say no. I contacted a number of my friends and mentors in the legal profession, many of whom had not been involved with the Reparations Coordinating Committee, and made two requests: join the reparations lawsuit on behalf of the survivors of the 1921 Tulsa race riot, and, more important, agree to represent these clients, without charging them a fee. The second point, in my view, was critical.

All we needed now was clients. Surprisingly, they were not hard to find. The Tulsa Reparations Coalition, led by the remarkable Mrs. Eddie Faye Gates, had interviewed many of these survivors from the 1921 riot, and they were eagerly seeking lawyers to represent them. Gates and Mark Stodghill have been major figures in organizing the battle for reparations in Tulsa. Gates served on the Oklahoma Commission to Study the Race Riot of 1921 and was responsible for compiling the record of those riot survivors who were still alive and entitled to reparations. She managed to find in excess of 130 survivors and many more descendants. Quite remarkably, she set about collecting an oral history of every African-American who survived that riot, along with photographs of them. Finally, and most important for our purposes, she asked all of them whether they would consent to the filing of a lawsuit on their behalf. Over 60 survivors had signed a provisional agreement. By the time I arrived in Tulsa, she and Stodghill had tried and failed to persuade a number of attorneys to take the case. Both of them were waiting for me when I came to deliver my lecture.

Eric J. Miller, a former student of mine, and at that time the Charles Hamilton Houston Fellow at Harvard Law School, prepared a memorandum outlining potential strategies for reparations litigation, and Michele Roberts, a former colleague from the Public Defender Service (PDS), reviewed the draft and agreed that Tulsa provided a compelling opportunity to advance the case for Jim Crow reparations.

Joining us in Tulsa in helping to draft the complaint was Suzette Malveaux, an associate at the law firm of Cohen, Milstein, Hausfeld and Toll. Suzette worked extraordinarily hard in putting together the first complaint, and is now a professor of law at the University of Alabama School of Law.

Michael Hausfeld and Agnieszka Fryszman of Cohen, Milstein, Hausfeld and Toll played an instrumental role in the district court hearings in Tulsa and in preparing the appeal to the Tenth Circuit and, ultimately, to the U.S. Supreme Court.

Several of us prepared a draft complaint, which contained the essence of the lawsuit. Everyone was impressed with the case, and especially surprised to hear that over 130 clients were waiting for representation. The task was then to assemble the legal team to represent them.

The best known member of our Tulsa team was Johnnie Cochran. Although he rose to national prominence as lead counsel for the defense during the trial of O. J. Simpson, Cochran enjoyed significant legal success for over twenty years in California. Until his death in April 2005, he was a strong advocate for and supporter of civil rights, filing dozens of lawsuits and winning tens of millions of dollars to compensate the victims of police brutality in California.

On the team, too, was Adjoa Aiyetoro, legal counsel not only for NCOBRA but also for the National Conference of Black Lawyers and the International Association of Black Lawyers. She has obtained injunctive relief and damages from both the federal government and the states for prisoners suffering disgraceful and unconstitutional conditions of confinement.

Michele Roberts, whom *Washingtonian* magazine rated the best lawyer in all of Washington, D.C., for 2002, was widely recognized as one of the country's best litigators. Michele has also been on the team of lawyers and judges whom I invite to Harvard Law School every year to train my students in trial advocacy. She is like family to me.

Willie Gary, one of the country's most successful tort lawyers, became an integral member of the team. Based in Florida, Gary is general counsel to the Reverend Jesse Jackson, but is best known for record-setting victories in the areas of personal injury, product liability, wrongful death, and medical malpractice law. His firm recently won a $240 million judgment against Walt Disney and in the 1990s won a $500 million jury verdict against the Loewen Group.

Dennis Sweet, a prominent tort lawyer, was my colleague at the PDS before moving into private practice. We tried cases together as public defenders in D.C. and are like brothers. He has won a number of substantial judgments, including a $400 million one against American Home Products for injuries sustained through use of its Fen-Phen diet pill.

We were also able to attract a highly regarded litigator, Michael Hausfeld, who successfully represented Holocaust victims in lawsuits against German, Austrian, and Swiss banks, and who brought to us his reparations litigation experience.

Rose Sanders and J. L. Chestnut, both from Selma, Alabama, have successfully litigated a number of voting rights and civil rights cases, including the "black farmers" litigation against the Department of Agriculture, which resulted in a $2 billion settlement. They are also founders of the National Voting Rights Museum in Selma.

In addition to this great national team, we were joined by some excellent local lawyers. Jim Goodwin, who was also the publisher of the *Oklahoma Eagle*, the Tulsa black newspaper, and Leslie Mansfield, a wonderfully talented clinical instructor at University of Tulsa Law School, joined our team. Another expert on local affairs who was essential to ensuring the quality and accuracy of the complaint was Professor Alfred L. Brophy. A member of the Oklahoma Commission on the riot, he literally wrote the book on Oklahoma reparations, and his help was pivotal throughout the litigation.

We have also received strong support from the sociologists, historians, and politicians on the Reparations Coordinating Committee.

Among the public officials who are members of the committee, the most prominent is Representative John Conyers, himself a lawyer and the ranking Democrat on the House Judiciary Committee. Representative Conyers, a supporter of the reparations movement for more than a decade, is the principal sponsor of H.R. 40, legislation designed to study the issue of reparations. One co-chair of our research committee is Manning Marable, professor of history and political science and founding director of the Institute for Research in African-American Studies at Columbia University. The other co-chair is Dr. Ronald Walters, director of the African-American Leadership Institute and Scholar Practitioner Program, Distinguished Leadership Scholar at the James MacGregor Burns Academy of Leadership, and professor in government and politics at the University of Maryland.

Serving with them on the Reparations Coordinating Committee are some distinguished academics. Cornel West, Class of 1934 University Professor of Religion at Princeton University, has championed racial justice for much of his life and is the author of the best-selling book *Race Matters*. Dr. Johnnetta B. Cole is the former president of Spelman College, which under her leadership became the first historically African-American college to receive a number-one ranking in *U.S. News and World Report*'s annual college issue. Formerly the Presidential Distinguished Professor at Emory, she currently serves as president of Bennett College. Richard America, an economist, is a lecturer at the McDonough School of Business Administration at Georgetown University. He has published two books on reparations: *Paying the Social Debt: What White America Owes Black America* and *The Wealth of Races: The Present Value of Benefits from Past Injustices*. Finally, James P. Comer is the Maurice Falk Professor of Child Psychiatry at the Yale University School of Medicine's Child Study Center. He founded in 1968 the Comer School Development Program, which promotes the collaboration of parents, educators, and community to improve social, emotional, and academic outcomes for children, has served as a consultant to the Children's Television Workshop (which produces *Sesame Street* and *Electric Company*), and has been awarded thirty-nine honorary degrees and been widely hailed for his extensive work with disadvantaged children.

We had an outstanding team of lawyers, public officials, and scholars organized and ready to put the complaint together. The next step was to meet the clients, explain our case, and flesh out their claims through personal interviews. I arranged for Michele, Eric, Johnnie Cochran, Dennis Sweet, and myself to travel to Tulsa to meet with Leslie Mansfield, Eddie Faye Gates, Mark Stodghill, and as many of the clients as we could.

When we eventually met our prospective clients, we were overwhelmed. Every client was at least 87 years old, with the oldest 105. One of the clients, Otis Clark, turned 100 on February 13, 2003. Mr. Clark was 18 during the riot, and his mind is as sharp now as it was then. He described the events in great detail, including being sent to a holding camp at the fairgrounds for all blacks from Greenwood and later fleeing to California, where he worked as a chauffeur for Douglas Fairbanks and other celebrities in Hollywood. Remarkably, at 100, Mr. Clark still drives and visits California often. I told him that this case, like all reparations cases, is exceedingly difficult. He looked me in the eye and said, "Professor, I have been through the Depression, two world wars, and Korea. I think that I can hold on to see this case through." His words were inspiring, as I looked at the confidence and pride of this centenarian.

We also intended to bring a claim on behalf of the descendants of victims who were no longer alive. There was one descendant who was not in the lawsuit, but I wanted to see whether he would consider joining it. I had earlier written Dr. John Hope Franklin about reparations; while mildly curious about the claim, he did not seem particularly interested. I discussed his father's role in representing the original clients in Greenwood in 1921, and how his father's law office was destroyed during the riots. Dr. Franklin clarified my report to him, by reminding me that his father had written an autobiography, completing it even though he was blind and seriously ill. Furthermore, Dr. Franklin informed me that he and his son finished his father's biography and had it published, as a tribute to his enormous contributions to the Tulsa race riot victims.

On February 27, 2003, I called Dr. Franklin, full of hope that he might join the lawsuit. After some conversation about the case, he agreed. I thanked God. I admired Dr. Franklin and was convinced that his joining the lawsuit would be nothing short of providential.

On February 28, 2003, we filed a 200-page complaint, on behalf of

150 survivors and nearly 200 descendants of the 1921 Tulsa race riot. Present at the filing were most members of the legal team. In the Oklahoma lawsuit, the complaint identifies four state actors: the governor of the state of Oklahoma; the city of Tulsa; the city of Tulsa Police Department; and the chief of Police for the City of Tulsa. The harms are ascertainable and ascertained in the body of the complaint.[45] So this style of Jim Crow lawsuit avoids the modern critique of reparations lawsuits.

On Friday, February 13, 2004, we presented our case before Judge James Ellison of the United States District Court for the Northern District of Oklahoma. On March 19, 2004, Judge Ellison granted the city and state's motion to dismiss the Tulsa case, although he wrote about the litany of injustices suffered by the victims in the 1921 Tulsa race riot. Judge Ellison observed that "there is plenty of evidence . . . to support the premise that African-Americans would have, and did have, an extremely difficult time pursuing their legal rights in the aftermath of the Riot."[46]

Judge Ellison was unequivocal as well in his conclusion that the Tulsa race riot victims had legal standing to bring the lawsuit, and that their claims were on sound legal footing:

> The Court agrees that the political question doctrine does not apply to federal-state relations, which are at issue here. . . . The State also argues that the reasoning of the Court in In Re African-American Slave Descendants Litigation is applicable here. The analysis in that case was that since Congress has addressed the injuries of slavery in a comprehensive manner, the Court should not address these issues. It is important to note that no federal law addresses the Tulsa Race Riot or provides any compensation to its victims. Moreover, the Oklahoma legislature has not rejected the notion that judicially ordered relief for legal wrongs could or would be appropriate. The Court concludes that the political question doctrine does not apply in this case.[47]

Judge Ellison also concluded that, given the extraordinary circumstances that existed in Tulsa in 1921, it was appropriate to toll the statute of limitations in favor of the plaintiffs:

> Plaintiffs assert extraordinary circumstances in a legal system that was openly hostile to them, courts that were practically closed to their claims, a

City that blamed them for the Riot and actively suppressed the facts, an era of Klan domination of the courts and police force, and the era of Jim Crow. There is no question that there are exceptional circumstances here. Both the Commission Report and the Legislative Findings and Intent resulting from that Report catalog the horror and devastation of the Riot as well as the intimidation, misrepresentation and denial that took place afterward. The political and social climate after the riot simply was not one wherein the Plaintiffs had a true opportunity to pursue their legal rights. The question is not a factual question of whether exceptional circumstances existed. They did. It is a legal question of the effect, with respect to the issue of statute of limitations, of those exceptional circumstances.[48]

Even in the ultimate decision to deny the plaintiffs' claim, Judge Ellison validated the appropriateness of the Tulsa race riot lawsuit, the seriousness of the claims raised by the plaintiffs, and concluded that he did not take comfort in ruling the way that he did:

There is no valid argument that bringing these claims constitutes sanctionable conduct. In fact, the filing of the motion for sanctions is more troubling than the filing of the Complaint. The contentious attitude of Defendants in this case has been destructive and wasteful of judicial resources. Plaintiffs brought serious claims against Defendants, and Defendants should have, and did, defend themselves vigorously against those claims. However, the contentious attitude that led to the filing of a motion for sanctions, in effect belittles the decision to bring this lawsuit, and only fuels the belief that the State and City are ignoring their moral responsibility for the Riot. Such conduct is, indeed, unfortunate particularly in light of the findings of the Legislature based on the Commission Report....

The Commission Report is a valuable tool in understanding and documenting the Race Riot of 1921. It also brings needed attention to an extremely tragic event in our City's and our State's history, and, hopefully, will be a tool for healing and uniting communities. Although Plaintiffs urge that it should also be the foundation for the application of equitable doctrines to prevent the barring of claims by the statute of limitations, the Court is unable to find any legal basis for using the Report in this way. There is no comfort or satisfaction in this result, and there should be none to Defendants. That Plaintiffs' claims are barred by the statute of limitation is strictly a legal conclusion, and does not speak to the tragedy of the Riot or the terrible devastation it caused.[49]

After Judge Ellison's ruling, we appealed to the Tenth Circuit Court of Appeals and were turned down again. Our request for a rehearing en banc before all active judges on the Tenth Circuit was also denied, but not without a stinging dissent from Judge Carlos Lucero, which was joined by three of his colleagues. Judge Lucero concluded:

> No case in my tenure on the court could be more compellingly described as meeting the Rule 35 en banc standard of presenting a "question of exceptional importance" deserving the attention of the entire court than this. In one of the more shameful events in our nation's history, over two hundred African-Americans were slaughtered and a whole section of the City of Tulsa was burned in an uncontrolled riot in 1921. Official government action by the City of Tulsa and the State of Oklahoma fueled this carnage by deputizing and arming the mob, and authorizing the National Guard to detain the victims while their forty-two square block community was razed to the ground. . . . All subsequent claims raised by the victims fell upon the deaf ears of the courts at the time, and most languished without even a cursory glance at the merits. None of the over one hundred lawsuits filed were successful. In a perversion of justice, a grand jury commissioned by the state exonerated the city and state, and all white rioters, and blamed the victims for the atrocity. This history alone raises a "question of exceptional importance"—the laudable recent investigation of this tragedy by the State of Oklahoma compels us to confront it.[50]

Neither the state of Oklahoma, nor the city of Tulsa, nor the Tulsa Police Department has ever compensated any of the African-American victims of the Tulsa race riot for the injuries they suffered at the hands of state and municipal officers. There is ample evidence of state action in the instigation and execution of the riot, with members of both the local police and the National Guard among the rioting mob. More than that, the guardsmen and police were present as part of a state and municipal policy decision to invade Greenwood and attack the citizens there.[51]

The state and municipal action was plainly discriminatory. Greenwood was razed to the ground because its inhabitants were black. To that extent, the Tulsa riot was simply one of many "nigger drives" taking place around Oklahoma in the 1910s and 1920s, designed to force black people from desirable towns and valuable land.[52] Our goal in this lawsuit is to set a benchmark for claims by those still alive and their immediate descendants to enable them to receive compensation for the violent and discriminatory treatment meted out to them during Jim Crow.

The Tulsa riot marks not only a pivotal moment in America's history of race relations but also a seminal case in African-American reparations litigation. Because the state's and municipality's acts were so violent and so plainly discriminatory, the merits of the case are stark: the state of Oklahoma and city of Tulsa participated in a race riot that outstrips even the 1923 massacre in Rosewood, Florida, in its ferocity. The Rosewood case involved fewer deaths and less destruction of property, and the Florida legislature, to its credit, did pay survivors reparations. The Tulsa case presents none of the problems traditionally associated with reparations lawsuits: a number of the victims are still alive and still uncompensated; the appropriate institutional defendants are clearly identifiable; and there is a manifest, constitutional basis for suit. As with other successful reparations litigation, the only real issue is the statute of limitations.[53] We are pursuing resolutions to this obstacle through a number of means.

Ironically, the *Tulsa World*, Tulsa's largest daily newspaper, which had consistently been critical of the lawsuit, made an observation with which I agree: "The last word on the riot has not been written."[54]

It is worth noting that these efforts to find forms of compensation for those who can raise valid reparations claims are beginning to bear fruit.

The new face of the reparations movement is none other than Chicago alderman Dorothy Tillman, a native of Montgomery, Alabama, and a protégé of Dr. Martin Luther King, Jr. Alderman Tillman, who also worked closely with former Chicago mayor Harold Washington, has been instrumental in ensuring that corporations that do business in the city of Chicago have disclosed their prior connections to slavery.

The ordinance has already begun to produce results. In January 2005, JPMorgan, which had initially denied any connection, was forced to admit that two banks affiliated with JPMorgan had served as banks to plantations and thereby helped facilitate the slave trade.[55] In an effort to make amends, the bank donated almost $5 million to a scholarship fund for descendants of slaves in the state.[56] Although the $5 million may seem like a paltry sum for such a large bank, the gesture is significant because it is will also make a real difference for the lives of the scholarship recipients. Moreover, the fact that JPMorgan Chase chose to create a scholarship fund is indicative of a forward-looking type of reparations.

In May 2005, the Chicago ordinance forced Wachovia to make a confession similar to JPMorgan's.[57] As of the writing of this book, Wachovia has yet to announce how or if it will attempt to make amends, but they will follow JPMorgan Chase's lead in, at the very least, making an important symbolic, reparatory gesture.

In February 2005, we filed a petition requesting that the Supreme Court hear the Tulsa race riot case. Given that the Supreme Court receives thousands of requests like ours every year but accepts fewer than a hundred, we knew we were facing long odds from the outset. We were hopeful when the Court asked us to prepare a brief outlining the reasons our case should be heard.

On March 9, 2005, 102-year-old Otis Clark, four other survivors, and a group of students from Harvard Law School traveled to Washington, D.C., to help us file the brief. As much as I thought the filing was an important educational event for the law students, I also wanted the survivors to understand our commitment to their cause. As we helped the survivors up the Supreme Court steps, petitions in hand, I wanted them to understand that no matter the outcome, the students and their generation would assume the burdens of the survivor's struggle.

In the end, the Supreme Court denied our petition, and the Tulsa riot litigation did not result in monetary reparations.

I wish we could have prevailed in the courts, but if the ever-unwinding legacy of *Brown* has taught us anything, it is that justice cannot be encapsulated in the form of a single case or a court order, not even in the form of a decree from the nation's highest court. Hence, our struggle for justice for the riot survivors continues. Even if the litigation did not produce the outcome we had hoped for, it created momentum for legislative action that could finally bring justice to the survivors. In fact, our litigation team, the riot survivors, and the group of Harvard Law students all met with the Congressional Black Caucus while we were in Washington filing our petition to promote the Tulsa Race Riot Survivors Bill, a bill recommending appropriate reparations for the riot survivors. In May 2005, we traveled back to Washington with the survivors to hold a hearing in Congress. As I write, several members of Congress are preparing to visit Tulsa as part of continued fact-finding mission, and the Congressional Black Caucus will honor the survivors at its fall 2005 legislative weekend.

The idea of raising reparations as a response to the failure to realize fully the promise of *Brown* is not one I arrived at easily. Like many who patiently believed that the problems of racial discrimination and disparity would be solved in the twentieth century, I now doubt that there is a commitment at the highest level of government, or in America's neighborhoods, to accept and embrace black people as an integral part of America. No group has worked harder or is more deserving (other than, of course, Native Americans, to whom we all owe the greatest debt) than that which has traveled from slavery to freedom, but still faces discrimination, even when individual members succeed politically and economically. I conclude that reparations are necessary to address the pervasive problems that are continually visited upon the African-American community. Over the past 385 years, African-Americans have contributed mightily to this country, yet still face barriers and burdens unlike those of any other group. Immigrants have received protections from our government, and rightly so, while the same fundamental rights were denied to blacks. Poor whites were allowed to vote and to live wherever they could afford to live, while blacks at every socioeconomic level were denied the same rights during the period of Jim Crow in America. Even today, wealthy African-Americans are victims of racial profiling, when they drive their cars, shop in upscale neighborhoods, or live in places where neighbors believe they don't belong. By the same token, a substantial segment of the black community did not receive the benefits of integration or affirmative action. They are still in those segregated neighborhoods, sending their children to second-rate schools and lingering in poverty. The reparations movement has momentum today because African-Americans have inadequate health care and are more susceptible to disease as a result. All too many are victims of redlining and predatory lending, even though both practices are illegal. Others are denied access to quality education and, as a result, cannot take advantage of opportunities for social mobility. In short, these circumstances have created a frustrated, exasperated, and increasingly angry community that, in ever-increasing numbers, is demanding reparations.

Notwithstanding this support for reparations, my personal view of what to do with this money may differ from that of others in the black community. I propose that the billions, or perhaps trillions, of dollars that come from a successful reparations lawsuit not be distributed in the form of a check to every African-American, even though such equitable distribution may be justified. Indeed, I firmly believe that people like myself who have benefited from *Brown* and affirmative action, and who have overcome the barriers of racism, should not receive reparations. My proposal is that all of the money be placed in a trust fund, administered perhaps through the churches or other reputable organizations in the community, and made available to the "bottom stuck," those African-American families that have not been able to realize the American Dream fully. Furthermore, the funds should be available in a manner similar to the way veterans' benefits are distributed, and their use restricted to such plans to remedy the community's major problems, like health care, housing, employment, and education. This is a way to finally move beyond the idle promises of full integration and to invest in our communities in ways that will generate solutions that are transformative. This will be highly controversial in the black community, I'm sure, because we are telling our people how the money, to which they are entitled, ought to be used. It is a paternalistic approach, of course, but one that is entirely necessary to overcoming the problems we face. In my view, there are few additional ways to address them.

Tragedy sometimes has to remain in our national memory in order to provide meaning. Oklahoma City is an important and defining memory. The Oklahoma City bombing was a tragedy, one that appropriately generated national mourning for the loss of innocent life and destruction of property. In the wake of the bombing, the weight of law enforcement was brought into play, with the accused feeling the full brunt of the criminal justice system. Families have received and will receive some comfort with these convictions and some compensation for their losses. The victims of the bombing have rightfully been exalted as heroes, and their lives are commemorated with an elaborate memorial that is the crown jewel of downtown Oklahoma City.

But there was another tragedy in Oklahoma—the Tulsa race riot of 1921—that many do not even know took place. In terms of human suffering they are clearly comparable; however, the Tulsa race riot has been nearly erased from our memory. Both of these memories are essential to understanding who we are as Americans, and to understanding the need for truth and justice; it is time to bring Tulsa into our national memory.

Not far from the bombing memorial, on May 31, 2005, the eighty-fourth anniversary of the Tulsa race riot of 1921, another terrible instance of domestic terrorism, was observed. Until recently, little was known about the riot. Though they occurred within miles of each other, juxtaposing the events of the 1995 bombing and the Tulsa race riot only underscores the tremendous injustice that has been done to the victims of the Tulsa riot. There is no national monument commemorating the victims of the Tulsa race riot of 1921. In fact, the Riot Commission found that many victims were tossed into unmarked mass graves and never even afforded the dignity of a funeral. Not a single perpetrator has ever been brought to justice, and the survivors have never received compensation.

In the wake of the Oklahoma City bombing, the city, the state of Oklahoma, and the federal government brought every ounce of government machinery to bear to insure that those responsible for the tragedy were brought to justice. As the Riot Commission reported, on May 31 and June 1, 1921, the state of Oklahoma and the city of Tulsa detained only blacks while arming and deputizing members of the white mob, thereby insuring Greenwood's destruction and the death of its citizens. Even today, the state and city continue to pour resources into litigation to see that the survivors of the Tulsa riot never receive a dime of compensation.

It is unfathomable that the victims of domestic terrorism in modern America would ever be prosecuted. Can we even conceive of a system of justice that would not only exonerate Timothy McVeigh but would seek to imprison the victims and their families for the events of April 19, 1995? Yet that is precisely what happened to the victims of the Tulsa riot. They suffered the loss of their loved ones and their homes only to be told by a grand jury and the state of Oklahoma that they brought the destruction upon themselves because they dared to seek the basic human dignity afforded to people with white skin.

The Tulsa race riot and the Oklahoma City bombing are two of the greatest tragedies in our nation's history. Nevertheless, the difference in treatment of the victims of the two atrocities makes painstakingly clear our nation's failure to confront incidents of domestic terrorism perpetrated by the state against African-Americans. Our nation has had little difficulty repudiating Timothy McVeigh's act as evil, and our justice system dealt him its most severe penalty. While we have exalted the victims of one terrorist act and swiftly guaranteed retribution, our country has refused to confront one of the single greatest instances of domestic terrorism in the twentieth century because it was perpetrated by the state against African-Americans.

As we reflect on domestic terrorism and the Oklahoma City bombing, the survivors' litigation and their plea to the Supreme Court ought to shake our nation to its very core. When he established the Supreme Court's power of judicial review in 1803, Chief Justice John Marshall announced that a court's duty is "to say what the law is." Can it be, as the lower courts have said, that our laws deny justice to the victims of the Tulsa race riot?

What can we say about courts that admit that the state of Oklahoma and the city of Tulsa helped to destroy an entire community and kill its citizenry but announce that the survivors cannot seek legal redress? What can we say about laws that would enable the perpetrators of atrocities to escape liability by destroying evidence and denying legal remedies? Is it possible that we still have two standards of justice in America: one for victims of domestic terror perpetrated by individuals and one for victims of domestic terror perpetrated by the state? Is it possible that we still have different standards of justice depending on the race of the victims? If there can be no justice for the victims of the Tulsa race riot, there may be little hope for justice in America.

CHAPTER 18

THE INTEGRATION IDEAL: SOBERING REFLECTIONS

Now that fifty years have passed since the *Brown* decision, we must examine some thorny questions about race matters in America. The years since 1954 have been difficult ones, particularly in addressing matters of race. The false promise of integration—and particularly of the "all deliberate speed" kind embodied in *Bakke*'s diversity rationale—is to perceive integration as an end in itself, rather than a means to an end. Viewing integration as simply an end, some commentators in the wake of *Brown* asserted that it had little impact on desegregation or on the civil rights movement. Gerald Rosenberg, in his book *The Hollow Hope*, was one of the first to do so. He points out, "For ten years, 1954–64, virtually nothing happened."[1] Looking at *Brown*'s effect on public opinion, other branches of government, and the press, Rosenberg doubts that *Brown* had even an indirect impact on any of the three: Instead, he argues that far more than giving the issue prominence, it actually preached to an already committed choir.[2]

Other commentators, such as Michael Klarman, take Rosenberg's argument even further by documenting *Brown*'s "crystallizing effect on southern white resistance to racial change."[3] Yet Klarman's conclusion that *Brown* was to blame for much of the violence against civil rights demonstrators, which in turn was the catalyst for change, seems actually to illustrate *Brown*'s significance. The literature responding to Rosenberg and Klarman is voluminous, and the whole debate is now somewhat dated. The respondents insist that the "cultural significance" of the decision is understated in Rosenberg's analysis, which ignores *Brown*'s importance as a "moral resource" for the civil rights movement.[4] Perhaps the most effective response to Rosenberg details how, merely by becoming law, *Brown* not only "raised new obstacles to segregation" in legal and social contexts but also "challenged the assumption that there was no option but loyalty to the status quo."[5] This view challenges the thesis of the "hollow hope" argument by emphasizing that "[j]udicial decisions can change assumptions not only by opening new options for opposition, but also through their power to grant legitimacy to certain claims and to redefine norms of institutional action."[6]

Moreover, the "hollow hope" view fails to see integration and diversity as instrumental goods—a means of achieving a goal, not the goal itself. The challenge of *Brown* was not only to achieve integration but also to recognize that once integrated, all of us are diverse: we have all given up something to gain something more. Integration does not simply place people side by side in various institutional settings; rather, it remakes America, creating a new community founded on a new form of respect and tolerance. Implicit in that challenge was the recognition that white society had to change to acknowledge in substantive ways the achievements of African-American society. It was not enough simply to admit African-Americans to the table, or even to let them dine, but to partake of the food they brought with them.

The enslaved and segregated African-American community did no less than create the American voice and produce the New World culture that could speak distinctively in contrast to the Old. When Ken Burns creates his documents of American culture, he turns to jazz, to the Civil War, and to modern baseball's flowering out of two leagues, one white, one black. When Mark Twain captured the American voice, it was Huck Finn and Jim, each sounding like the other, black voice mingling with white. By the time F. Scott Fitzgerald captured the spirit of America's emergence as a world power, he called it the Jazz Age; George Gershwin's distinctively American sound was its classical musical expression. In the midst of the worst squalor and deprivation, a people were, if not thriving, then surviving, growing, creating, even celebrating, and what they achieved spoke to and defined much that was America. Some southern segregationists, from *Plessy* forward, even used this evidence of cultural strength to argue that "separate but equal" was good for African-Americans.

By the 1920s, African-American culture was certainly thriving, as around the country middle-class African-Americans engaged in the type of self-reliant enterprise endorsed by Booker T. Washington in his Atlanta Exposition speech of 1895. Many of those communities, however, were formed not from a compromise with southern whites but by an escape north or west to the emerging industrial towns. In New York in the 1920s, Harlem styled itself the black capital of the world. The Harlem Renaissance produced a concentration of talent rarely seen in American letters. But outside the Northeast, other African-American communities were thriving. Of particular note was the Greenwood District of Tulsa, Oklahoma, one of the most successful African-American communities in America.[7] As a result of Jim Crow segregation, Greenwood formed a self-sustaining economy having little contact with the white parts of town.[8]

Often forgotten in the rush toward integration are the community leaders and middle-class entrepreneurs who made these communities flourish. Generations of teachers, newspapermen, shop owners, makers of beauty products, and providers of myriad services for the black community grew in the shadow of segregation. The real challenge of integration was not how to bring black children to white schools, or how to make space at formerly all-white firms for the new black professional class that emerged from the integrated educational spaces. The real challenge was to see how Americans would use the space created by the talents that already existed, by the already skilled—for those spaces existed in the African-American community.

Too often, integration is presented as an unalloyed benefit for African-Americans, as if we all had been clamoring to leave our communities. For many in the African-American community, however, integration was viewed with suspicion or something worse. Many communities at the center of the battle for integration, represented by the crusading lawyers of the NAACP, would have welcomed something less than the full integration demanded by the civil rights lawyers. Instead, these teachers, school principals, and janitors would rather have kept their schools, their jobs, and their positions of power and influence than see their charges bused to white schools run by white principals where white educators often made the children all too grimly aware of their distaste for the new state of affairs.

In fact, integration had a similar effect on large sections of the community. Now not only whites but middle-class blacks as well could live in the suburbs. Although the phenomenon of white flight made clear how ephemeral such an existence could be, many African-Americans chose to leave the inner cities, not so much to integrate with whites—although that was the goal of many—as to create new communities in better areas.

Leaving the black community, however, undermined one of the major goals Du Bois had created for his Talented Tenth: to maintain a connection with the poor and underrepresented in the black community to provide a means of self-betterment for the downtrodden. Disengaging the Talented Tenth from the community created a vacuum that was never properly filled; it led to a spiral of poverty in urban America that has yet to be adequately addressed. For many middle-class African-Americans, moreover, it has created a sense of loss of connection to the community. The current civil rights generation has spent so much time fighting those who would deny equal rights to African-Americans that the question what should be done with integration once it was achieved was put aside.

Does this mean that integration has failed and that African-Americans can thrive only culturally on the margins of American society in the newly resegregated towns and cities? Yes and no. Integration as a one-way street, imagining diversity as all that is not white, has failed. The challenge is for America to see *all* Americans in their diversity—to be not only plural but equal in our plurality. In the meantime, African-Americans, as those closest to their communities, as those most likely to look out for other African-Americans, may be in the best position—if not under the greatest obligation—to make integration work.

Most recently, the failure of the Great Society marked the last time America promised to address the social inequality that predominantly harms African-Americans. For too many Americans, the concept of freedom for African-Americans admits of no degree but is simply based upon the absence of slavery or segregation.

Is there any solution to the problem of discrimination and inequality? There have certainly been moments, for example, after the Civil War and during the civil rights revolution, when America as a whole appears to have manifested a desire to change, to reform, to make whole. My mentor Professor Derrick Bell has provided an account of these moments in terms of "interest convergence,"[9] the claim that only when the interests of the majority converge with those of the minority will the minority achieve its goals. "When whites perceive that it will be profitable or at least cost-free to serve, hire, admit, or otherwise deal with blacks on a nondiscriminatory basis, they do so. When they fear—accurately or not—that there may be a loss, inconvenience, or upset to themselves or other whites, discriminatory conduct usually follows."[10] Bell finds that interest convergence accounts for the successful *Brown* litigation; it also provides a convincing account of the failure of integration in the wake of *Brown*.

There is indeed a cost to be paid for failing to heed the plea of the lawyers in the *Brown* case, half a century ago. In the meantime, we have lost the voice of passion with Dr. King's death and the voice of reason with Justice Marshall's. Many black people have run out of patience waiting for America to address the legacy of slavery. This country's failure to achieve even the modest goals of *Brown*, by providing all children with equal educational opportunities, has resulted in the creation of a movement that we all hoped to avoid: the demand for reparations by blacks. Whereas Justice Brennan's greatest quality was his ability to translate liberal readings of the Constitution into legal doctrine, Marshall's greatest quality was perhaps the empathy he brought to the cases, along with the passion of one seasoned by years of campaigning on behalf of the dispossessed.

The failure of pedagogical diversity at so many of our educational establishments may be an argument for preserving predominantly African-American or female colleges as an educational alternative. That was certainly the position Justice Thomas endorsed in *United States v. Fordice*,[11] an opinion upholding the right of HBCUs to equal funding from the state.

Thomas's answer to the problem of resegregation and unequal funding is deeply radical, pessimistic, and perhaps anticipated by Orlando Patterson, a colleague of mine at Harvard University—that it is the "black person's burden" (to paraphrase Kipling) to reform American society through striving separately for equality. On the one hand, Patterson endorses a view espoused by Justice Ginsburg, that "the purpose of affirmative action is to redress past wrongs." He suggests, however, that an undue reliance on the diversity rationale has transformed this purpose, and that "many of its supporters see affirmative action as an entitlement, requiring little or no effort on the part of minorities." The consequence is that African-Americans must do more of what Patterson terms "the cultural work necessary to create what Martin Luther King, Jr., called the 'beloved community' of an integrated nation."[12] Now, I am as much a fan as anyone of the beloved community. But Patterson seems to have misread the last fifty years of American history as well as the current state of the affirmative action debate if he believes that any but the most extreme supporters of the program view it as an entitlement. It is more accurate to say that we view it as one of the last holdouts in the rollback of the civil rights agenda of the 1960s. Affirmative action is not a substitute for social change and cultural reconstruction. But it is generally regarded as easily the most important means of ensuring the integration Patterson unhesitatingly embraces as the goal of the American community.

The real problem, as I have argued elsewhere[13] and in this book, is not that African-Americans have failed to embrace the beloved community but that the history of integration since *Brown*, and the history of race relations preceding that decision, has been marked by a "go slow" attitude embodied in the phrase "all deliberate speed." For Patterson to suggest that integration has failed so far because of African-American unwillingness or complacency is a myopic indictment of the efforts of the civil rights movement and the actions of those people during the various, often violent, efforts to desegregate school systems throughout the 1970s. Boston, I have made clear, offers one example of the often violent resistance to integration, but there are many others. The failure of American society to live up to Dr. King's ideals is not so much due to the collective failure of African-Americans or some amorphous sense of black entitlement. Rather, it is due to the concrete and often brutally painful failure of many whites to live up to the promises of Reconstruction or the Great Society.

The Boston busing case, along with *Brown* itself, raises an interesting question: Why did the courts (and later the executive branches of the various state and federal governments) ignore the "massive resistance" to these programs and go along with something as socially disruptive as integration? Derrick Bell's discussion of interest convergence provides one answer. Interest convergence explains how African-Americans are able to achieve political gains despite the essentially racist nature of American society. The white majority retains political and social power—in fact, a white minority that has power and wishes to conserve it retains true power, and the rest of white society is empowered only relative to African-Americans. Thus, while not only African-Americans but many whites are without effective political, social, or economic power, the relative position of African-Americans to the rest of society serves to mask the reality of disenfranchisement for the majority of whites.[14] Interest convergence suggests that, against this consolidation of power in an elite, redistributive gains are possible only when the interests of the elite and the rest coincide.

Bell suggests that racism is not some accidental by-product of American society or culture that can be undone by a sustained effort to eradicate it. Rather, racism is endemic in America, a definitive, structural feature of liberal democracy in America.[15] Far from being some problematic, but essentially transient, social or psychological condition, racism is a permanent feature of American society, necessary for its stability and for the well-being of the majority of its citizens.[16] Thus, according to Bell, "black people will never gain full equality in this country. Even those Herculean efforts we hail as successful will produce no more than temporary 'peaks of progress,' short-lived victories that slide into irrelevance as racial patterns adapt in ways that maintain white dominance."[17]

Accordingly, interest convergence works as a safety valve, to permit short-term gains for African-Americans when doing so furthers the short- or long-term goals of the white elite. As a side effect, it has the important consequence of convincing the minority population (or others that lack power) that social change is possible rather than ephemeral and that participation in the social and political system will provide redistributive benefits. This is an important check on widespread disaffection that may end in rioting or even revolution.

In particular, with regard to *Brown*, Bell suggests that the Cold War provided the impetus for a change in the courts' and federal government's attitude to segregation. The American propaganda of equality and democracy was effectively countered in the resource-rich countries of Africa by the communist propaganda surrounding the continued existence of segregation. This foreign policy interest appears in the government brief in *Brown* and is often cited as one of the major influences on the Court's thinking.

In the University of Michigan cases, interest convergence is plainly evident. Ginsburg's and Thomas's opinions in *Gratz* and *Grutter* make clear the symbiosis between elite school status and impoverished and resegregating public education. Affirmative action, whatever its merits, permits the system to exist while abandoning the majority of African-American and Latino students to a second-rate education. Tinkering with affirmative action by introducing income-based qualifications risks further obscuring the real problem: the discriminatory and race-based underfunding of our primary and secondary education systems. On the other hand, failing to address the underlying problem perpetuates it. Unwilling to risk the malign consequences of system failure and unwilling to change the system, majority and minority interests converge around affirmative action.

There is certainly a majority interest in continued participation by minorities in the workplace. The most widely hailed aspect of O'Connor's opinion in *Grutter* has been its acceptance of the business and military community's endorsement of affirmative action.[18] The support of these two vital groups is heartening, suggesting that even if some parts of the population don't "get" the importance of affirmative action, others in power do—and for similar reasons as in *Brown*. Affirmative action is important because the "aesthetic" values derided by Thomas are precisely those that appeal to business and the military: the consumers of their services (a global public; the disproportionately minority noncommissioned ranks) demand it. They want evidence that they can get on in their society regardless of race or that they can do business on equal terms (and thus wish to see such equality manifested in their business partners or superior officers).

As Justice O'Connor put it,

> The benefits [of affirmative action] are not theoretical but real, as major American businesses have made clear that the skills needed in today's increasingly global marketplace can only be developed through exposure to widely diverse people, cultures, ideas, and viewpoints. What is more, high-ranking retired officers and civilian leaders of the United States military assert that, "based on [their] decades of experience," a "highly qual-

ified, racially diverse officer corps . . . is essential to the military's ability to fulfill its princip[al] mission to provide national security."[19]

The causes of educational failure are multiple, but one important factor is the attitude of teachers at public schools toward the minority youngsters in their charge. Many schools are becoming more and more internally segregated, as minority children are assigned to remedial learning classes at a rate that is disproportionately higher than that of white children, and without any justification for the high rate of assignment. Minority children are also more likely to be disciplined, and for longer, than white children for comparable offenses. Finally, because busing was essentially a one-way experience, with whites refusing to travel to African-American schools, the burden of integrated schooling is disproportionately borne by poor African-American children.[20]

So, finally, the wheel has turned full circle. Kenneth Clark's social science evidence, cited by Chief Justice Warren in the now infamous footnote 11 of *Brown v. Board of Education*, to demonstrate that "[s]egregation of white and colored children in public schools has a detrimental effect upon the colored children,"[21] has been trumped, in dissent at least, by Justice Thomas. Roy Brooks, of the University of California at San Diego, also contends that integration has been a failure that may be overcome by a strategy of limited separation. Both theories are pessimistic to the extent that they maintain that integration has failed many African-Americans and that there is lacking in the white community a generalized will to overcome race-based social and economic disparities.[22]

Certainly, there must be some form of social change on the education front. Whether this occurs through separation or in an integrated environment is a matter of great consequence for American society. Our experiment with integration started with a pronouncement, half a century ago in *Brown*, that integration was an important value with positive social consequences that should be embraced by all Americans. Twenty years later, real action to integrate our schools had only just started. We are but one generation into an integrated society, and the signs are that the majority of the population is tired with the process. Those at the top want to stay there, and those in the middle would rather hold on to what they have than give a little to get a lot. We have to decide whether this is a country that is comfortable with discrimination. Are we satisfied with the fact that many whites find minorities so repellent that they will move and change their children's schooling to avoid us? For, make no mistake, that is what underpins the supposedly "rational" decisions based on racial stereotyping: an inability on the part of the majority of Americans to acknowledge that minority citizens are "just like us."

There is little surprise in acknowledging that there was substantial resistance by the white community to integration and later to affirmative action. But the theory of interest convergence suggests that most Americans cannot be bothered to engage that problem unless it directly affects them. They would rather turn away, uninterested, and perpetuate racial disadvantage than acknowledge it, let alone confront it. We have witnessed the *Brown* decision, followed by *Bakke* and, more recently, *Grutter v. Bollinger.* We have witnessed Dr. King's historic "I Have a Dream" speech and his subsequent assassination. We have heard the powerful words of President Johnson in his commitment to affirmative action, and President Bush's criticism of the Michigan plan as a program promoting racial preferences.[23] We have seen diversity plans approved by the Supreme Court and, in the same year, some HBCUs lose their accreditation and close. We continue to make progress, and suffer setbacks, in grappling with the persistent problem of race in America. But we must remain vigilant in our commitment to confront racial inequalities, even when we face persistent, even increasing resistance.

CONCLUSION

As I look back on the fifty years of my life that coincided with the *Brown* decision, the picture is not encouraging. Indeed, I see great disappointment in the effort to achieve a society of equality under the law, blindness to the harm that racial prejudice inflicts on African-Americans, and refusal to address the problem with candor or conviction. If *Brown I* signaled the end of equalization as a permissible educational strategy, *Brown II* indicated that, so far as the legislature was concerned, integration was to be pursued with hesitation. President Eisenhower accepted the *Brown* decision, but emphasized that integration should happen slowly, and it did.

When I turned three years old and the ink on the *Brown* decision was barely dry, there were telling signs that *Brown* was already on unsteady ground, when it was tested in *Briggs v. Elliott* (1955). By the time I uttered my first coherent words as a child and prepared to enter kindergarten, the phrase "massive resistance" had already been coined and the "Southern Manifesto" been signed. Around the time I entered school, and rode on my first yellow school bus to get there, southern cities learned that in preventing desegregation they had a powerful weapon in actually closing schools.

As I moved from one underresourced and largely segregated elementary school in Merced to another, a number of southern states passed pupil placement laws designed to block transfers between white and black schools. The resistance to integration was not limited to the South. The pattern across America—from California to Massachusetts to Michigan—was being replicated along these lines.

In fact, school integration was not achieved until the advent of busing, and then only at great social cost. When I graduated from Stanford in 1975, I recognized that the education I received, largely as a result of the *Brown* mandate, allowed me passage through formerly closed doors in society. I was on my way to the mecca of higher education, Harvard Law School. What could have been better? Well, in the shadow of Harvard, across the river from Cambridge, black, brown, and white children were facing a different reality. As late as 1975, and despite coming under the ambit of the U.S. Constitution and the Massachusetts Racial Imbalance Act, both of which mandated an end to racially discriminatory schooling, Boston resisted the mandate to integrate the local school system fully.

The Boston experience, which was repeated in other parts of the nation, indicates that the country resisted integrating the public school system for decades after the *Brown* decision, and large sections of the nation never entirely embraced integration. During the last thirty years, many Americans, perhaps even a majority, have acted to subvert the ideal of integration announced in *Brown I*. Within thirty years of achieving integration, it has failed de facto and may no longer be required de jure. A major cause of the end of the *Brown* ideal has been a Supreme Court that, once Warren retired, wasted little time in undoing the few gains that were so painstakingly and "deliberately" achieved.

With fifty years of hindsight, I believe that the tragic lesson of the two decisions in *Brown v. Board of Education* is that one described an aspirational view of American democratic liberalism *(Brown I)* and the other *(Brown II)* actually defined the reality of grudging educational reform, and the power of racism as a barrier to true racial progress in twentieth-century and, for that matter, twenty-first-century America. Whereas *Brown I* made possible the institutional equality first promised in 1776 with the Declaration of Independence ("All men are created equal") and again in 1865 with the ratification of the Thirteenth and Fourteenth Amendments, *Brown II* created the method and manner in which America would resist the mandate of the equality ideal. If *Brown I* made integration a legal imperative, *Brown II*, with its decision to proceed "with all deliberate speed," ensured that the imperative was not implemented as a social imperative. Almost immediately, "massive resistance" materialized at virtually every level of society, and it began from the day the decision was issued, through the efforts of national leaders, such as Governor Faubus's appearance on the steps of Little Rock's Central High School in 1957, to the Boston busing crisis of 1975, to the reverse-discrimination arguments that gained popular appeal in the years following *Brown*, and, most telling, to the resegregation of our schools and our communities in the twenty-first century.

As an expression of moral rectitude, *Brown I* was the least the Court could have done, but the timidity expressed in *Brown* II nullified its import. To obtain the requisite unanimity, the Court in *Brown I* went too far to accommodate southern whites' opposition to the morality of segregation. To avoid offending the white segregationists, the Court famously eschewed identifying segregation as immoral or evil— although it was, and everyone knew it to be. Instead, Warren demanded that the opinion be "non-rhetorical, unemotional and, above all, non-accusatory."[1] To identify segregation with evil, Warren and the rest of the Court feared, would provoke a massive rift between South and North and risk the legitimacy of the Court. Given the Court's own reluctance to mandate the forthright enforcement of integration, the legislative and executive branches had all of the reason they needed to ignore or resist urgent and comprehensive remedies.

Forgotten—or, at least, discounted—in all of this were the families and children who petitioned the *Brown* court to end the racial caste system. *Brown I* barely addressed the almost 100 years of Jim Crow suffering and the preceding 250 years of slavery that African-Americans, uniquely as a group in America, had already endured. As a gesture recognizing the pervasive impact of the racial disparity that plagued America then, and the effect of that suffering in the African-American community, *Brown I* included a footnote on the psychological damage inflicted by segregation.[2] If the Court's attitude is one of solicitude toward whites in *Brown I*, in *Brown II*, one can justifiably say, "there is no hint of solicitude for the feelings of Afro-Americans. The Court made no attempt to assuage the inevitable anger and anxiety that the decision would generate within the black community. The rhetoric of the opinion displays . . . complacency [toward the feelings of African-Americans]."[3]

In its solicitude toward the feelings of southern (and many northern) whites in refusing to describe segregation as an evil, the *Brown* decision ignores the restorative function of our legal system. Individuals come to the courts not only to obtain monetary or injunctive remedies but also to seek justice and relief from the suffering they have endured. As Warren surely recognized, *Brown I* offered the opportunity for America to start anew without dividing the nation on the question of race. But forgiveness need not include forgetfulness, and in accounting for *Brown I*'s importance, we should not ignore that it enacted a collective amnesia that haunts the nation to this day.

It is instructive to compare the racial reconciliation enacted through *Brown I* and *II* with that enacted by President Lincoln, faced with similar stakes, during his second inaugural address. Unlike Warren, Lincoln saw slavery as a *national* sin for which the whole country was to be held responsible (and had been held responsible by God). The responsibility for atonement was therefore to be borne by the whole nation, even though the cost would be to account for "all the wealth piled by the bondsman's two hundred and fifty years of unrequited toil."[4]

The restraint shown by Warren in *Brown I* in identifying the magnitude of the evil of segregation led to the predictably modest remedy proposed by *Brown II*. African-Americans would, in theory, have the burden of segregation in public education removed from their shoulders, but the relief would come slowly, deliberately, and at the pace determined by those who resisted the change. *Brown*'s failure to achieve its admirable goals was compounded by the subsequent elimination of the formerly viable, though segregated, black communities and numerous black jobs in education that was a by-product of integration. When schools were integrated, whites did not attend black schools staffed by black teachers and black principals. Instead, blacks went to the better-funded white schools. In this way, integration ended one vital aspect of the "equalization" strategy pursued by the NAACP in the cases leading up to *Brown I*, while at the same time perpetuating the segregation of public education.

The practical effect of judicial, legislative, and personal resistance to *Brown* is manifest today. For example, before *Brown*, the city of Topeka maintained segregated elementary schools. In 1951, there were eighteen elementary schools for whites and four for minorities.[5] After *Brown*, the Topeka board adopted a neighborhood school policy as a result of which three of the elementary schools remained all-black and two others became over 20 percent black. In 1954, less than 10 percent of the elementary students in the district were black.[6]

The Kansas district court reopened the original *Brown* case in 1979, when the lead plaintiff, Linda Brown, along with other parents of school-age children, challenged the continued segregation in Topeka schools. In 1992, the Tenth Circuit concluded—having been asked by the Supreme Court to reconsider its earlier opinion in light of recent desegregation cases—that the Topeka school system had not yet achieved adequate integration of its public schools, and it continued to require court supervision.[7]

While public schools in many parts of the nation are experiencing resegregation in the twenty-first century, some opponents of affirmative action assert that racial diversity can be accomplished through 10 percent and 20 percent plans, as now practiced in California, Texas, and Florida, for example. They present them as diversity-sensitive, but not race-conscious, alternatives to affirmative action, while ignoring the obvious fact that these plans, in order to guarantee admission to state colleges to the top 10 percent of students at every high school, actually depend upon segregated school systems to ensure minority participation at the tertiary level. The predominantly black schools in these states will provide admission to their students, as will the predominantly white schools. Race is the proxy that determines admission to the state university.

Even legally acceptable affirmative action efforts, as sanctioned in the Supreme Court's decision in *Grutter*, will not guarantee a "critical mass" of minorities in elite institutions. The Court, with a 5-to-4 majority vote, approved the admissions policy of the University of Michigan's law school, while at the same time rejecting a policy that ensures minority students access to its undergraduate division, the obvious pipeline to the law school, and ultimately failed to address the type of quality secondary education that is necessary if the affirmative action program is eventually to end. The irony could hardly be more graphic.

There has been no clearer example of the failure to ensure equal educational facilities than the treatment of historically black colleges and universities (HBCUs). Of the 103 currently existing HBCUs, it was reported in 2003, "fifteen percent are on warning or probation status with accreditation agencies. Many can barely meet their payrolls. Two—Morris Brown College in Atlanta and Mary Holmes College in

West Point, Mississippi—have lost their accreditation. Grambling State University in New Orleans is on probation after auditors couldn't make sense of its accounting records."⁸ The focus on integrated schooling has so undermined the status of the HBCUs that only Howard, Morehouse, and Spelman are thriving. Ironically, at a time when affirmative action was under attack by the Bush administration, in the *Grutter* and *Gratz* cases, those colleges that exist to support a predominantly African-American student body were under siege. Many HBCUs have faced discrimination from the states in which they are located, which fund HBCUs at a lower level than other state colleges. In *United States v. Fordice*, the Court found that Mississippi continued to discriminate against its HBCUs in such areas as admission standards and that such discrimination was traceable to the de jure segregation of the Jim Crow era.⁹ The state's proposed solution, to close the HBCUs, was held unconstitutional.

The centrality of the HBCUs to black education can scarcely be overstated. They "helped educate much of the nation's black middle class. Thirty percent of blacks who hold doctorates earned them from black colleges, as did 35% of African-American lawyers, 50% of black engineers and 65% of black physicians."¹⁰ As the Bush administration supports the demise of affirmative action at the college and graduate school levels, such institutions stand to become especially important at a time when many face budgetary crises unlikely to be undone by a proposed 5 percent increase in funding by the federal government.

The decision in *Brown I*, ending segregation in our public schools—and by implication de jure segregation everywhere—is justly celebrated as one of the great events in our legal and political history. Precedent did not compel the result, nor was the composition of the Court indicative of a favorable outcome. There is no doubt that the circumstances of many African-Americans are better now than they were before the *Brown* decision. But the speed with which we have embraced the society made possible by *Brown I* has indeed been all too deliberate. It has been deliberate meaning "slow," "cautious," "wary," as if Americans remained to be convinced of the integration ideal. It has been deliberate in the sense of "ponderous" or "awkward," as if each step had been taken painfully and at great cost. Yet the speed with which we have embraced integration has not been deliberate in the sense of "thoughtful" or "reflective"—on the contrary, our response has been emotional and instinctive, perhaps on both sides of the debate. These reactions, anticipated and epitomized in *Brown II*, I suggest, are the real legacy of *Brown I*.

It would be foolhardy to deny that progress has been made, or to dismiss the reality that *Brown I* is a momentous decision both for what it says and for what it has achieved. But there is more yet to do. *Brown I* should be celebrated for ending de jure segregation in this country—a blight that lasted almost four hundred years and harmed millions of Americans of all races. Far too many African-Americans, however, have been left behind, while only a relative few have truly prospered. For some, the promise of integration has proved ephemeral. For others, short-term gains have been replaced by setbacks engendered by new forms of racism. School districts, briefly integrated, have become resegregated. Some distinctively African-American institutions have been permanently destroyed and others crippled. As we stand near the end or the transformation of affirmative action, things look set to get worse, not better.

For all their clear vision of the need to end segregation, *Brown I* and *II* stand as decisions that see integration as a solution that is embraced only grudgingly. Subsequent courts do not even seem to recognize integration as an imperative. And that, perhaps, is the worst indictment of the *Brown* decisions: their faith in progress and their failure to see how quickly people of a different mind could not only resist but, once the tide had turned, even reverse the progress toward a fully integrated society. This failure compels me to look to the past, and the future, and to suggest both modest and radical solutions to address *Brown*'s failure.

We must not let ourselves be deterred from achieving what so many of our forefathers achieved, in the face of even more formidable challenges. If Africans could survive the innumerable horrors of slavery, and if freed slaves could survive the cruelty and repugnance of the Jim Crow system, we as a nation can, must, and will survive the current manifestations of *Brown*'s failures. It is a challenge that we must face with unrelenting dedication and commitment, and when we do so, we will not fail.

AFTERWORD

THE POST-O'CONNOR SUPREME COURT: THE EMERGENCE OF THE SCALIA COURT?

On July 1, 2005, Justice Sandra Day O'Connor shocked the legal community by announcing her retirement from the U.S. Supreme Court. While many had expected an announcement from Chief Justice William H. Rehnquist, who was diagnosed with thyroid cancer in early 2005, O'Connor's announcement created quite a stir throughout the country, and around the world. Her retirement, as the first woman ever appointed to serve on the Supreme Court, will not only change the ideological tilt but will also profoundly impact the issue of racial justice. Justice O'Connor, more than any other member of the Court, has played a pivotal and defining role in the consideration of race in Supreme Court decisions. She has consistently expressed skepticism about the way race can and should be considered, and used harsh language to criticize some uses of race that she deemed inappropriate.[1]

On July 19, 2005, President Bush resolved all doubt concerning whether he would appoint a conservative jurist to fill Justice O'Connor's seat by nominating a fifty-year-old Harvard Law School graduate and judge of the D.C. Circuit, John G. Roberts. Moreover, in choosing Judge John Roberts, President Bush has rejected the advice of both his wife and Hispanic leaders to appoint either a woman or a Hispanic. He is also choosing a young justice who will be able to serve for decades. When Roberts worked in the Republican administrations in the 1980s, he consistently expressed skepticism about issues of race, and his views as a lawyer were much more aligned with the conservative members of the Supreme Court.

While it is customary to identify the current Court as the Rehnquist Court, it is likely that these developements will enhance the role of one of O'Connor's frequent critics, Justice Antonin Scalia, and lead many to appropriately label the Court that will begin hearing cases on October 3, 2005, as the Scalia Court. It seems certain that the *Grutter v. Bollinger*[2] decision, and indeed the principles underlying *Brown v. Board of Education*,[3] may be in jeopardy.

Justice Scalia's General Jurisprudence

Like Justice Thomas, Justice Scalia adheres to a staunchly conservative ideology. Scalia views the Constitution as a dead document with one discernible meaning for all generations and derides the concept of a living Constitution.[4] Like Thomas, as well, Scalia is an orginalist in the sense that he believes that solely "text and tradition" can resolve constitutional disputes. Unlike Thomas, however, Scalia prefers to rely on the text or wording of a constitutional provision and therefore places less emphasis on history or tradition.

Furthermore, while Thomas supposedly places the original understanding of the Constitution over all else, Scalia is willing to accept the weight of modern precedents. Scalia has noted that this may be the primary difference between their two philosophies: "[Thomas] does not believe in *stare decisis*, period. If a constitutional line of authority is wrong, he would say let's get it right. I wouldn't do that."[5] Still, Justice Scalia is sometimes more dismissive of precedent than he may admit. For example, in *Planned Parenthood of Southeastern Pennsylvania v. Casey*, Scalia declined to join the plurality of justices who, despite having serious reservations about the correctness of *Roe v. Wade*, nonetheless voted to uphold it on the grounds of stare decisis.[6] Similarly, in *Lawrence*, he wrote, "I do not myself believe in rigid adherence to *stare decisis* in constitutional cases" and derided "extraordinary deference to precedent" as nothing more than a "result-oriented expedient."[7]

Since Scalia insists that the Court should look primarily to the text of statutes, he often attacks his fellow justices when they examine reports of congressional committees. He has derided legislative history as "that last hope of lost interpretive causes, that St. Jude of the hagiology of statutory construction."[8] There is even some indication that Scalia's frequent criticisms have caused other members of the Court to cite less frequently to legislative history. As Gregory Maggs reports:

> Over the past few years, in a series of strongly worded concurrences and dissents, Justice Scalia has challenged a number of decisions that rely on legislative history. His writings appear to have had a substantial effect. Even if the entire Court does not accept his arguments at this point, the force of his assaults has made other Justices hesitant to cite extrastatutory sources in their opinions.[9]

When Scalia steadfastly adheres to his textualist methodology, he occasionally reaches more liberal results. For example, in one of his early opinions (in which Justices Brennan and Marshall joined), Scalia held unconstitutional a state statute intended to protect child victims of sexual abuse by placing a screen between the accused and the victims during their testimony. The Court held that this procedure violated the defendant's Sixth Amendment right "to be confronted with the witnesses against him." Writing for the Court, Scalia interpreted "confront" to mean a face-to-face meeting:

> [A]s Justice Harlan put it, "[s]imply as a matter of English" [the Sixth Amendment] confers at least "a right to meet face to face all those who appear and give evidence at trial." Simply as a matter of Latin as well, since the word "confront" ultimately derives from the prefix "con-" (from "contra" meaning "against" or "opposed") and the noun "frons" (forehead). . . . We have never doubted, therefore, that the Confrontation Clause guarantees the defendant a face-to-face meeting with witnesses appearing before the trier of fact.[10]

More recently, in both *Crawford v. Washington* and *Blakely v. Washington*, Justice Scalia relied on constitutional text and myriad historical sources to extend additional procedural protections to criminal defendants facing trial. In *Crawford*, Justice Scalia, writing for the majority, held that out-of-court witness statements that are testimonial in nature (for example, statements made in the course of police interrogation) are barred by the Confrontation Clause unless the witness is unavailable and the statements were made subject to cross-examination by the defendant.[11] In *Blakely v. Washington*, Scalia, again writing for the Court, held that the Sixth Amendment right to a jury trial requires that any fact that increases the sentence for a crime beyond the "statutory maximum"—that is, the maximum penalty a judge may impose without any additional factual findings—must be found by a jury beyond a reasonable doubt.[12] In both cases, then, Scalia's textual and historical methodology led him to reverse a criminal conviction on the grounds that procedural infirmities in state court denied a criminal defendant his constitutionally protected rights.

Even in the realm of federalism and separation of powers, moreover, Scalia's methodology sometimes leads him to results that conflict with his conservative ideology. For example, in *Gonzalez v. Raich*,[13] Scalia voted to uphold Congress's power to regulate marijuana grown and sold purely intrastate, even though his conservative politics would tend to lean toward protecting federalism and states' rights. Similarly, in *Hamdi v. Rumsfeld*, Scalia wrote a forceful dissenting opinion rejecting the government's claims of national security and arguing instead that a citizen held by the government as an enemy combatant is entitled to release "unless (1) criminal proceedings are promptly brought, or (2) Congress has suspended the writ of habeas corpus."[14]

However, as several scholars have noted, the instances in which Scalia's decisions have conflicted with his conservative ideology are few and far between, and many of them occurred during his early years on the Court.[15] Most of the time, Scalia is able to manipulate his textualist inquiry to achieve results in line with his conservative philosophy.[16] This should not be surprising: the textualist inquiry seldom allows for clear answers; if a text truly were unambiguous, there would be no grounds for litigation. In particular, the character of Scalia's approach tends to hinge on what types of rights are at issue. For example, as William Eskridge writes, "In Scalia's approach to issues of constitutional federalism or separation of power, there is usually little or no analysis of specific constitutional provisions but much emphasis on general principles drawn from the overall structure of the document and its history."[17] However, when interpreting the Bill of Rights, Justice Scalia (like Justice

Thomas) employs a narrow, often ahistorical, view of tradition.[18] For example, Scalia has written that "when a practice not expressly prohibited by the text of the Bill of Rights bears the endorsement of a long tradition of open, widespread, and unchallenged use that dates back to the beginning of the Republic, we have no proper basis for striking it down."[19] This narrow view of tradition makes it difficult, if not impossible, to root out traditions discriminatory in nature such as racism, sexism, and homophobia because it subverts the values of the Constitution to these antithetical traditions.[20]

Scalia's view of tradition often leads to no constitutional protection for many modern practices because they were condemned either based on religious or moral precepts of the time or because the practices were unknown to the framers. In light of this view of tradition, many scholars have argued that Scalia would have dissented in *Brown* (although in several interviews, he has expressed support for the principles in *Brown*).[21] After all, the Fourteenth Amendment does not expressly forbid segregation. Racial segregation has a long history in this country, and segregation was relatively "open, widespread, and unchallenged" at the time of *Brown*.

When deciding constitutional cases, at least to some extent, all judges weigh the appropriate aims of the state and what rights and liberties are fundamental. Scalia's supposedly "neutral rules" of text and tradition are all the more insidious because they camouflage the tenets of his otherwise conservative ideology. By taking a more fluid and all-encompassing view of tradition in the context of federalism and executive power while adopting a narrow view of tradition in the context of individual and minority rights, Scalia is able to have it both ways. He is able to reach conservative conclusions in both areas, even though a careful reading of the Constitution's text would require otherwise.

Among the overarching conservative values that inform Scalia's constitutional jurisprudence are a commitment to individualism and an American identity. In the area of educational desegregation, Scalia's individualism is even more radical than Thomas's. The measure of his extremism is exemplified by his partial concurrence in *United States v. Fordice*. In *Fordice*, on the basis of his concern for individual choice, Scalia rejected the Court's decision to require greater integration in Mississippi universities. Scalia argued that once discriminatory admissions standards were eliminated it would be a denial of the equal protection of the law to limit student "choices among public university offerings."[22] Justice Scalia further rejected the existence of group rights and group identity in *Adarand Constructors, Inc. v. Pena*,[23] again because of the "Constitution's focus upon the individual" and Scalia's commitment to a national identity.[24] Although "[i]ndividuals who have been wronged by unlawful racial discrimination should be made whole," Scalia maintained that "under our Constitution there can be no such thing as either a creditor or a debtor race . . . we are just one race here. It is American."[25]

This focus on national identity carries over into the widely publicized debate between Justices Scalia and Breyer with regard to international jurisprudence. Scalia has criticized both the general methodology of citing foreign law in judicial opinions as well as what he perceives as a biased application of foreign law by Breyer and other justices. For example, in *Roper v. Simmons*, Scalia chastised the majority for citing foreign sources of law to support their holding that the juvenile death penalty constituted "cruel and unusual punishment" prohibited by the Eighth Amendment. According to Scalia, "[t]o invoke alien law when it agrees with one's own thinking, and ignore it otherwise, is not reasoned decisionmaking, but sophistry."[26] Similarly, in *Lawrence v. Texas*, Scalia quoted Justice Thomas in referring to the Court's discussion of foreign views as dangerous dicta and as an "impos[ition] of foreign moods, fads, or fashions on Americans."[27]

Scalia is perhaps most conservative in his assessment of the role of the Court. In particular, Scalia manifests his belief in limited judicial intervention with strong preferences for majoritarian political processes and bright-line judicial rules. Scalia has stated that "the most significant development in the law over the past thousand years . . . is the principle that laws should be made not by a ruler, or his ministers, or his appointed judges, but by representatives of the people."[28] Scalia has shown himself especially willing to defer to the political process in defending majority decisions that limit equal protection, and has vehemently criticized judicial decisions that protect political minorities such as women or homosexuals at the expense of popular lawmaking.[29] In doing so, Scalia has emphasized the "countermajoritarian" nature of the Supreme Court, which—according to Scalia—has no business imposing its elitist views. Inconsistently, however, Scalia appears quite willing to second-guess the political process "when it produces an outcome he disfavors," consistently striking down, for instance, affirmative action plans.[30]

To further limit judicial discretion, Scalia demands clear rules from the Court, as necessary to further what he has termed the "Rule of Law." As Scalia held in criticizing the Court in the context of affirmative action in higher education, "[u]nlike a clear constitutional holding that racial preferences in state educational institutions are impermissible, or even a clear anticonstitutional holding that racial preferences in state educational institutions are OK, [the Court's decisions on affirmative action] . . . [seem] perversely designed to prolong the controversy and the litigation."[31] In so holding, however, Scalia made clear that he is not above suggesting avenues of litigation that are left open due to these vague standards. Justice Scalia strongly suggested, for instance, that he would support challenges to affirmative action that question the diversity motives of universities. Somewhat in tension with his generally formalist framework, Scalia also seems to suggest that practical concerns with excessive litigation also motivate his preference for bright-line rules.[32]

Surprisingly, in light of his unique brand of textualist and originalist methodology, Scalia might be best known for his *style* of attack in dissent when he believes that the Court has failed to follow important aspects of this jurisprudence. Scalia's rhetoric gives the impression that he is personally devastated and morally outraged by the decisions of his fellow justices. Scalia has lamented, for example, that "[t]he Court must be living in another world," in which "[d]ay by day, case by case, it is busy designing a Constitution for a country I do not recognize."[33] And he has frequently questioned the integrity of the Court, especially when it extends equal protection: "Today the Court shuts down an institution that has served the people of the Commonwealth of Virginia with pride and distinction for over a century and a half. To achieve that desired result, it rejects (contrary to our established practice) the factual findings of two courts below, sweeps aside the precedents of this Court, and ignores the history of our people."[34]

Scalia is also quick to refer to the "slippery slope" implications of the Court's decisions if followed to their logical conclusions. In particular, he often describes results that would be likely to shock broad segments of the American public. In *Lawrence v. Texas*, for instance, Scalia argues that what he sees as the majority's reasoning in striking down a state's antisodomy laws would render laws against drugs and prostitution similarly illegal. With scathing rhetorical flourish, he adds that gay marriage will not soon follow "only if one entertains the belief that principle and logic have nothing to do with the decisions of this Court. Many will hope that, as the Court comfortingly assures us, this is so."[35]

Justice Scalia and Race

The central distinguishing feature of Justice Scalia's jurisprudence on race is his adherence to the principle that "[o]ur Constitution is color-blind, and neither knows nor tolerates classes among citizens."[36] Race-conscious policies, according to Scalia, have no place in society because they are inherently divisive.[37] Scalia's hostility toward race-conscious policies thus unsurprisingly extends to all government discrimination on the basis of race, including so-called benign measures aimed at remedying past injustices.[38]

In *City of Richmond v. J.A. Croson Co.*, Scalia sided with the majority in striking down an affirmative action program favoring minority-owned business enterprises for city government subcontracts. He wrote a separate concurrence, however, expounding a significantly narrower view of when states may use remedial race-conscious policies. According to Scalia, "there is only one circumstance in which the States may act by race to 'undo the effects of past discrimination': where that is necessary to eliminate their own *maintenance* of a system of unlawful racial classification."[39] Under Scalia's approach, the critical question is whether the continuing segregative effects of prior discriminatory policies can be equated with the ongoing perpetuation of a discriminatory state regime.

The desegregation of primary and secondary schools is one context —and perhaps the only context—where Scalia accepts the validity of race-conscious remedial policies. Scalia recognizes that the Court has adjudged race-neutral policies in this context to be "so ineffective that they might 'indicate a lack of good faith.' "[40] He acknowledges that as a result of this ineffectiveness, the Court has not only permitted, but sometimes required states to adopt race-conscious remedial policies as part of their "affirmative duty to disestablish the dual school system."[41] Scalia thus accepts the use of broad, remedial race-conscious policies—such as attendance zones and out-of-zone assignments by race—where they are necessary for primary and secondary schools to comply with *Brown*'s mandate to desegregate.[42]

Outside the narrow context of elementary and high school education, however, Scalia consistently rejects the use of remedial race-conscious policies. In both *Croson* and *Adarand*, Scalia joined the majority in striking down affirmative action programs designed to remedy prior societal discrimination against minorities in the awarding of government contracts. Yet Scalia went even further by explicitly rejecting the majority's suggestion in *Croson* that states "may in some circumstances discriminate on the basis of race in order . . . 'to ameliorate the effects of past discrimination.' "[43] Scalia's opinion in *Adarand* similarly rules out remedial race-conscious policies on the ground that "under our Constitution there can be no such thing as either a creditor or a debtor race."[44]

In addition to rejecting race-conscious remedial measures, Scalia also imposes a much lower threshold for state compliance with *Brown I* in areas outside of *Brown*'s core concern. For example, in his partial concurrence in *United States v. Fordice*, Scalia emphasized that unlike elementary schools or high schools, "attending college is voluntary, not a legal obligation, and which institution particular students attend is determined by their own choice. . . ."[45] As a result, unlike the *Fordice* majority, which put the burden on the state to eliminate all "policies and practices traceable to its prior de jure dual system that continue to foster segregation,"[46] Scalia would place only one condition on historically segregated state universities: the elimination of discriminatory admissions standards.[47]

Scalia's opinion in *Fordice* drew heavily from *Bazemore v. Friday*,[48] a case involving state financing of single-race university-operated youth clubs decided shortly before Scalia joined the Court in 1986. In *Bazemore*, the Court distinguished voluntary 4-H and Homemaker Clubs from primary and secondary public schools where "schoolchildren must go to school" and "school boards customarily have the power to . . . designate the school that particular students may attend."[49] The *Baze-*

more Court noted that state funding of these voluntary youth clubs "presents no current violation of the Fourteenth Amendment since the [state] has *discontinued its prior discriminatory practices and has adopted a wholly neutral admissions policy.* The mere continued existence of single-race clubs does not make out a constitutional violation."[50] In *Fordice*, Scalia seized upon this language to argue that historically segregated universities that continue to exhibit "vestigial" effects[51]—for example, racially identifiable student populations—nonetheless may achieve full compliance with the Constitution simply through the adoption of race-neutral admissions policies.

For Scalia, then, the import of *Brown I* seems largely cabined to the elementary and high school context. Although he grudgingly accepts the principle that mere presence of "freedom of choice" in primary and secondary schools cannot satisfy a state's affirmative duty to integrate,[52] Scalia turns around and elevates the concept of "freedom of choice" to constitutional significance in virtually all other contexts. In Scalia's view, the stigmatic harms of *Brown* simply are not present in contexts outside of primary and secondary schools so long as individuals are granted equal access through race-neutral criteria. Thus *Brown* and its progeny, according to Scalia, require nothing more in these other contexts than nondiscriminatory admissions policies.

The problem, however, is that Scalia's approach to *Brown*-related cases (at least outside primary and secondary education) effectively elevates form above substance—that is, Scalia's brand of equal protection requires merely formal equality of access (i.e., race-neutral admissions criteria) and thus ignores the very real impediments to substantive equality that stem from the continuing effects of historically segregated institutions. According to Scalia's opinion in *Fordice*, "There is nothing unconstitutional about a 'black' school in the sense, not of a school that blacks *must* attend and that whites *cannot*, but of a school that, as a consequence of *private choice* in residence or in school selection, contains, and has long contained, a large black majority."[53] Although such an argument might be persuasive if blacks and whites started from a baseline of substantive equality, the reality is that the discriminatory effects of segregation continue to plague blacks and constrain the range of "private choices" available to them. Scalia's requirement that states eliminate discriminatory policies is necessary but not sufficient to achieve substantive equality, because blacks and whites simply do not share the same opportunities for "private choice." Indeed, Scalia's approach to *Brown*-related cases not only frees states from their obligation to address racial disparities in wealth, education, and other resources traceable to prior discriminatory practices but actually *prohibits* states from adopting any race-conscious policies (outside of primary and secondary education) designed to remedy those disparities.

Recent cases cast further light on Scalia's hostility toward affirmative action programs of all varieties. Presently, such benign race-conscious policies can overcome the Court's strict scrutiny test only if they are narrowly tailored to achieve one of *two* compelling government interests: remedying past, identified discrimination, or in the education context, promoting classroom diversity. However, Scalia contemptuously casts aside both of these interests. As discussed above, Scalia believes that government may never act on the basis of race to remedy the effects of past injustices because to do so would be to "reinforce, a manner of thinking by race that was the source of the injustice and that will, if it endures within our society, be the source of more injustice still."[54] Scalia similarly rejects those benign classifications that the government justifies based on the compelling interest of fostering diversity.

The Michigan cases, *Grutter v. Bollinger* and *Gratz v. Bollinger*, provided Justice Scalia with his first opportunity to address the diversity rationale, and he took that opportunity to soundly ridicule it. Unsurprisingly, he joined the *Gratz* majority, which held unconstitutional the University of Michigan's practice of adding points to the applications of its minority undergraduate applicants.[55] But Scalia vehemently dissented from the majority's decision in *Grutter*, which upheld the consideration of an applicant's race as one factor in admissions.[56] Scalia began his opinion by agreeing with Justice Thomas's view that the university's interest in diversity was a sham; if the university were truly interested in diversity, it could simply lower its admissions standards to capture more minorities.[57] Instead, Michigan's true interest, according to Scalia, was "in maintaining a 'prestige' law school whose normal admissions standards disproportionately exclude blacks and other minorities."[58] After endorsing that notion, Scalia proceeded to quip that

The "educational benefit" that the University of Michigan seeks to achieve . . . [is] "cross-racial understanding" and "better prepara[tion of] students for an increasingly diverse workforce and society." . . . This is not, of course, an "educational benefit" on which students will be graded . . . (Works and Plays Well with Others: B+) or tested by the bar examiners (Q: Describe in 500 words or less your cross-racial understanding). For it is a lesson of life rather than law. . . . [Diversity] is surely not [a benefit] that is either uniquely relevant to law school or uniquely "teachable" in a formal educational setting.[59]

Two points should be noted: First, and less important, is the slippery slope that Scalia fears—he argues that it would not make sense to cabin the diversity rationale to the university setting; rather, it would have to provide an employable justification in the context of both government and private workplaces. And that, he claims, would usher in "a patriotic, all-American system of racial discrimination in hiring."[60] The second and more important element to Scalia's *Grutter* opinion is the overt disdain with which he treats the diversity rationale. His "report card" and test question examples evince a clear impatience with government claims of "diversity"; moreover, his view of cultural sensitivity as inherently a "lesson of life"—rather than something to be learned in schools—suggests that Scalia would not even find diversity a legitimate state interest under a *rational basis* test.

Taken as a whole, the combination of Scalia's evaluations of both government interests—past discrimination in *Croson* and diversity in *Grutter*—demonstrate that, for him, no avenues of permissible affirmative action are open. Beyond desegregation litigation and affirmative action, moreover, de jure classifications based on race will be permissible only in the most *extreme* of circumstances.[61] This commitment seemingly comes from two distinct principles: first, Scalia's textualist approach, which insists that the Equal Protection Clause applies equally and consistently to *all* distinctions based on race; and second, Scalia's commitment to *individualism*. As noted above, he has gone so far as to insist that race does not exist[62] and that therefore all distinctions based on that nonexistent identity are illegitimate.

Yet Scalia's commitment to searching scrutiny of racial classifications has been the Court's uncontested norm since *Adarand*, and few justices today question it.[63] What distinguishes Scalia from both his fellow justices, and from his own jurisprudence in other areas of the law, is his repudiation of nearly all government interests regarding race-based action, and in particular the diversity interest. Six justices approve of the use of diversity as a factor in admissions.[64] Public universities for some time have used it as such, and private universities and institutions of all sorts do the same. Former U.S. military leaders also filed an amicus brief in the Michigan cases, extolling the importance of diversity.[65] More than a half-century after *Brown*, diversity—at least as a concept —is a ubiquitous piece of American fabric, both public and private.

This is what makes remarkable Scalia's refusal to see *any* merit in the diversity interest. The Court's various tests exist to ferret out legitimate exceptions to an otherwise absolute constitutional text, and it is Scalia who most frequently defers to government action by urging judicial restraint. This is, of course, due to the heightened respect he accords the democratic decision-making process and the concomitant sentiment that the unelected judiciary is incompetent to question most government action. The Court, as a countermajoritarian institution, should step in to correct the political process only in cases of clear mistake. It follows, then, that when the government legislates and acts by classification, it will typically be sufficiently rational such that the Court should abstain from invalidating that action.[66]

Scalia's extreme deference is perhaps best demonstrated by the recent case of *Lawrence v. Texas*, where the Supreme Court ruled on substantive due process grounds in favor of a homosexual man arrested for engaging in sodomy.[67] Addressing in dicta the issue whether the discriminatory arrest of persons engaged in homosexual and not heterosexual sodomy violates the Equal Protection Clause, Scalia's dissent noted that "[e]ven if the Texas law *does* deny equal protection to 'homosexuals as a class,' that denial *still* does not need to be justified by anything more than a rational basis,"[68] which is met by society's long-standing and general distaste for homosexual behavior.[69]

No such deference was paid to the professed interest in diversity in *Grutter*. Admittedly, the sexual orientation classification at issue in *Lawrence* was subjected to a mere rational basis test, as compared to the strict scrutiny employed for the race-based classifications at issue in *Grutter*. But as I suggested above, Scalia's repudiation of diversity as a government interest is so strong as to likely render it suspect under even the rational basis test; scrutiny levels aside, therefore, it is clear that Scalia is susceptible of interrupting government programs based on personal ideology in the same manner as that by which he criticizes his fellow justices. To track the same example: his jurisprudence would defer to a political process that acts to *criminally punish* a person based on his sexuality but not hesitate to undo a politics that acts to ensure that our institutions of higher education represent a diverse cross-section of America. Diversity cannot be encouraged by government, but heterosexuality can be: it is hard to avoid noticing that the justice's legal conclusion conveniently tracks his conservative political ideology.

Scalia is similarly committed to another conservative tenet: the utopian or libertarian commitment to colorblindness. For him, problems of race are best solved by simply ignoring race.[70] Indeed, it is *only* race that spurs Scalia to insist that all Americans are the same, and to disparage the practice of grouping citizens into categories of distinct identities. His understanding of a common American identity typically makes room for the recognition of our differences—for example, among and between persons of different faiths, between women and men,[71] and between gay and straight. But race alone prompts the claim that "there is only one race here. It is American."[72] Scalia believes that the important lesson from America's shameful history on race is that government should always stay out of the racial arena: it is simply too dangerous and too divisive for government to engage in race-conscious action.[73] While the lesson of *Brown* is that this very history mandates reparative government *action*, not inaction, Scalia's position is decidedly the reverse.

For those committed to reviving the flagging success of *Brown*, this position should inspire fear. In fact, signs abound that Scalia's adamancy against race-based action threatens to infiltrate one of the only remaining bastions of his willingness to entertain racial motivation—*Brown*-mandated elementary school desegregation. In *Freeman v. Pitts*, a 1992 case involving federal court supervision of a school desegregation plan,[74] Scalia's concurring opinion acknowledged that primary and secondary schools have an "affirmative duty to desegregate," but he also emphasized that "federal supervision of local school systems was intended as a *temporary* measure to remedy past discrimination."[75] Scalia's opinion noted that in the context of primary and secondary schools, the Court has recognized an "effectively irrebuttable" presumption that current racial imbalances that have existed continuously since *Brown* are a product of the state's prior unlawful segregation.[76] Scalia argues, however, that such a presumption is unwarranted today as "the *de jure* system and the school boards who produced it recede further into the past."[77] According to Scalia:

> Since a multitude of private factors has shaped school systems in the years after abandonment of *de jure* segregation—normal migration, population growth . . . "white flight" from the inner cities, increases in the costs of new facilities—the percentage of the current makeup of school systems attributable to the prior, government-enforced discrimination has diminished with each passing year, *to the point where it cannot realistically be assumed to be a significant factor.*[78]

Scalia's remedy is to effectively reverse the presumption and require plaintiffs to prove causation as they would in "ordinary" equal protection cases—that is, plaintiffs alleging a violation of *Brown* would have to prove "that the racial imbalance they wish corrected is at least in part the vestige of an old *de jure* system." The result of such a reversal, as Scalia himself admits, would be that "the plaintiffs will almost always lose."[79]

While de jure segregation ended fifty years ago, in many places America's schools today remain more segregated than ever. Racial disparities abound as nearly 50 percent of black students are not finishing high school[80] and over 1 million blacks are in state and federal prison—an immensely disproportionate number of the 2 million people who are incarcerated.[81] The Court itself has taken notice of the achievement gap between blacks and whites, with the *Grutter* majority expressing the hope that the gap—and the remedial measures designed to erase that gap—will be eradicated within twenty-five years.[82] That sentiment will remain wishful thinking if those in Scalia's position continue to deny the link between our nation's troubled racial past and the disparities that exist today and refuse to mandate—or even to permit—reparative government action. Steadfastness to *Brown I* and vigilance to the evils it was intended to undo are essential commitments for our judges to undertake—commitments that Justice Scalia sadly deems prudent to discard.

A New Chief Justice: John G. Roberts?

With the resignation of Justice Sandra Day O'Connor, many raised concerns about what impact her resignation would have on issues of race and justice. To fill the first vacancy on the Supreme Court since 1994, President Bush nominated fifty-year-old John G. Roberts, a Harvard Law School graduate who was confirmed by the Senate just two years earlier to a seat on the D.C. Circuit Court of Appeals. After the death of Chief Justice William H. Rehnquist on September 3, 2005, President Bush re-nominated Judge Roberts to serve as Chief Justice of the Supreme Court.

When President Ronald Reagan made the historic judgment to appoint the first woman to the Supreme Court, it was clear that he wanted someone who would express conservative views similar to his own. That brand of conservatism, however, pales by comparison to that which has been advocated by President George W. Bush. Indeed, in public comments while he was running for president in 1999–2000, and repeated again during the 2004 campaign, President Bush has consistently stated that he wants conservative judges in the mold of Justice Antonin Scalia and Justice Clarence Thomas.

Although Judge Roberts's views on race, affirmative action, and civil rights are not plainly evidenced by an extensive paper trail, President Bush's vision of the Court is undoubtedly reflected in his choice. It is clear that if confirmed, Judge Roberts will have the opportunity to exert a profound impact on the future of the Supreme Court. Justice O'Connor, always a skeptic on issues of race, held a position of tremendous influence during her final years on the Supreme Court. Indeed, she was the author of perhaps the most significant race case yet, *Grutter v. Bollinger*, which upheld affirmative action at the University of Michigan Law School. In so doing, Justice O'Connor noted the significant strides that have been made in the armed forces, corporate America, and at many of American's top universities, in considering race as an important factor in hiring and admissions.

During the twenty-four years that Justice O'Connor served on the

Supreme Court, she was consistently conservative, but also a pragmatist. She looked suspiciously upon any claims regarding race that might benefit or burden a group, and she was the swing vote in virtually every significant case involving race. Her skepticism found expression on such issues as whether or not there should be minority set-asides for employment, whether majority-minority districts were constitutional, and to what extent race could be considered in any respect when we are striving for a race-neutral society.

As we reflect upon the legacies of Justices O'Connor and Rehnquist, the question remains —what can we expect if Judge Roberts is confirmed for a seat on the Supreme Court? From all that Judge Roberts has said and written, the picture that emerges is one of great skepticism toward issues of race and civil rights. In 1981, for example, while working as a lawyer in the Justice Department, Roberts authored a memorandum criticizing a report outlining the need for affirmative action. Roberts wrote: "The logic of the report is perfectly circular: the evidence of structural discrimination consists of disparate results, so it is only cured when 'correct' results are achieved through affirmative action quotas."[83] Roberts further noted that a minority recruitment effort failed because "'the affirmative action program required the recruiting of inadequately prepared candidates."[84] Roberts's work as a lawyer for both the Reagan and Bush administrations in the 1980s and early 1990s reveal a shared ideology with the conservative members of the Supreme Court—most prevalently, Chief Justice Rehnquist (with whom he clerked), Justice Scalia, and Justice Thomas.

To be sure, while Judge Roberts is a brilliant man with considerable intellectual talent, his conservatism will weigh heavily on issues of race. The loss of Justice O'Connor's pragmatism, and the expected elevation of Judge Roberts to fill the Chief's position, is likely to strengthen the hold of the conservative arm of the Court. In particular, Justice Scalia will likely assume a position of considerable influence in driving the Court's conservative direction in the coming decades. As a result, it is all too likely that the recent progress made in the Michigan affirmative action case, and indeed, the very principles underlying *Brown v. Board of Education* may soon be in serious jeopardy.

September 2005

NOTES

CHAPTER 1: THE SIGNIFICANCE OF *BROWN*

1. *Brown v. Board of Education*, 347 U.S. 483, 495 (1954).
2. "All God's Chillun," *New York Times*, May 18, 1954.
3. James T. Patterson, Brown v. Board of Education: *Civil Rights Milestone and Its Troubled Legacy* (2001), 88 (internal quotation marks omitted).
4. Jack Bass, *Unlikely Heroes: The Dramatic Story of the Southern Judges of the Fifth Circuit Who Translated the Supreme Court's* Brown *Decision into a Revolution for Equality* (New York: Simon and Schuster, 1981), 117.
5. The others were: *Briggs et al. v. Elliott et al.; Davis et al. v. County School Board of Prince Edward County, Virginia, et al.; Gebhart et al. v. Belton et al.;* and *Bolling v. Sharpe*, 347 U.S. 497 (1954).
6. Richard Kluger, *Simple Justice: The History of* Brown v. Board of Education *and Black America's Struggle for Equality* (New York: Vintage, 1975), 302, 349.
7. "Combined *Brown* Cases, 1951–1954: *Briggs v. Elliot*," Brown v. Board of Education *Orientation Handbook* (Brown Foundation for Educational Equity, Excellence and Research, 1996–2003), available at http://brownv board.org/research/handbook/combined/briggs.htm.
8. Jack Greenberg, *Crusaders in the Courts: How a Dedicated Band of Lawyers Fought for the Civil Rights Revolution* (New York: Basic Books, 1994), 119.
9. Clark's conclusion in the Clarendon County tests, which were consistent with the results of the same test he had previously given to over three hundred children, was that the "Negro child accepts as early as six, seven or eight the negative stereotypes about his own group and that a fundamental effect of segregation is basic confusion in the individuals and their concepts about themselves conflicting in their self-images. [The child has] basic feelings of inferiority, conflict, confusion in his self image, resentment, hostility towards himself, hostility towards whites, intensification of sometimes a desire to resolve his basic conflict by . . . escaping or withdrawing." Ibid., 124.
10. *Brown*, 347 U.S. 483, 486 n. 1 (1954).
11. Kluger, *Simple Justice*, 408.
12. Ibid., 409.
13. "Combined *Brown* Cases."
14. *Davis*, 103 F. Supp. 337, 338 (1952)
15. Kluger, *Simple Justice*, 434.
16. Ibid., 521.

17. *Bolling*, 347 U.S. 497.
18. *Brown*, 347 U.S. 483, 493.
19. Greenberg, *Crusaders in the Courts*, 175.
20. Ibid., 171.
21. *Plessy*, 163 U.S. 537 (1896).
22. Greenberg, *Crusaders in the Courts*, 175.
23. Juan Williams, *Thurgood Marshall: American Revolutionary* (New York: Random House, 1998), 219.
24. Greenberg, *Crusaders in the Courts*, 178–82.
25. Morton J. Horwitz, *The Warren Court and the Pursuit of Justice* (New York: Hill and Wang, 1999).
26. *Korematsu*, 323 U.S. 214, 215 (1944).
27. Greenberg, *Crusanders in the Courts*, 188–89.
28. *Brown v. Board of Education*, 349 U.S. 294, 301 (1955).
29. Patterson, Brown v. Board of Education.
30. The word "deliberate" derives from the Latin *deliberatus,* or the past participle of *deliberare,* which means "to consider carefully." Scholars believe *deliberare* is an alteration of the Latin *delibrare,* from *de-* + *libra,* which implies justice or fairness. The Latin *libra* loosely translates to "scale." See *Merriam-Webster's Collegiate Dictionary,* 11th ed., s.v. "deliberate." Deliberate speed in literary terms can be described as an oxymoron, a phrase built on the seemingly absurd juxtaposition of opposites. See William Safire, *Safire's New Political Dictionary* (New York: Random House, 1993), 881.
31. *Virginia*, 222 U.S. 17, 20 (1912).
32. *Sutton v. Leib*, 342 U.S. 402, 414 (1952) (Frankfurter concurring) ("I would remand the case to the Court of Appeals to be held by it until the plaintiff seeks *with all deliberate speed* a decision on the crucial question of the case"); *First Iowa Hydro-Electric Co-op. v. Federal Power Commission*, 328 U.S. 152, 188 (1946) (Frankfurter dissenting) ("In any event, mere speed is not a test of justice. *Deliberate speed* is. *Deliberate speed* takes time. But it is time well spent."); *Radio Station WOW v. Johnson*, 326 U.S. 120, 132 (1945) ("We think that State power is amply respected if it is qualified merely to the extent of requiring it to withhold execution of that portion of its decree requiring retransfer of the physical properties until steps are ordered to be taken, *with all deliberate speed*, to enable the Commission to deal with new applications in connection with the station"); *Addison v. Holly Hill Fruit Products*, 322 U.S. 607, 619 (1944) ("the case should be remanded to the district court with instructions to hold it until the Administrator, by making a valid determination of the area *with all deliberate speed*, acts within the authority given him by Congress"); *Chrysler Corp. v. United States*, 316 U.S. 556, 568 (1942) (Frankfurter dissenting) ("In order to justify a modification having such drastic

business consequences, it was surely incumbent upon the Government to show that it had proceeded *with all deliberate speed* against General Motors") (all emphasis in note added.)

33. Also translated as "hurry slowly."

34. Abraham Lincoln, *Great Speeches* (New York: Dover, 1991).

35. Lincoln's response is consistent with the *Black's Law Dictionary* definition of "with all deliberate speed": as quickly as the maintenance of law and order and the welfare of the people will allow. *Black's Law Dictionary*, ed. Matthew Garner (West Group: St. Paul, Minncsota, 7th ed. 1994), 438.

36. *Safire's New Political Dictionary*, 882.

37. Former President Clinton recently used "all deliberate speed" to describe his promise to remove the military ban on homosexuality. Clinton is quoted shortly after his first election as saying, "[I] will proceed with all deliberate speed to lift the restriction." Ibid.

38. *Cooper*, 358 U.S. 1 (1958).

39. Constance Baker Motley, *Equal Justice under Law: An Autobiography* (New York: Farrar, Straus, and Giroux, 1998), 187.

40. *Mayor of Baltimore v. Dawson*, 350 U.S. 877 (1955).

41. *Holmes v. City of Atlanta*, 350 U.S. 879 (1955).

42. *Gayle v. Browder*, 352 U.S. 903 (1956).

43. *New Orleans City Park Improvement Association v. Detiege*, 358 U.S. 54 (1958).

44. *Johnson v. Virginia*, 373 U.S. 61 (1963).

45. *Lee v. Washington*, 390 U.S. 333 (1968).

46. *Palmer v. Thompson*, 403 U.S. 217 (1971).

47. Ibid., 218–19.

48. Ibid., 220–27.

49. See *Brown v. Bd. of Educ.*, 347 U.S. 483 (1954); *Bolling v. Sharpe*, 347 U.S. 497 (1954); *Brown v. Bd. of Educ.*, 349 U.S. 294 (1955); *Fla. ex rel. Hawkins v. Bd. of Control*, 350 U.S. 413 (1956); *Cooper v. Aaron*, 358 U.S. 1 (1958); *Goss v. Bd. of Educ.*, 373 U.S. 683 (1963); *Griffin v. County Sch. Bd.*, 377 U.S. 218 (1964); *Bradley v. Sch. Bd.*, 382 U.S. 103 (1965); *Green v. County Sch. Bd.*, 391 U.S. 430 (1968); *Raney v. Bd. of Educ.*, 391 U.S. 443 (1968); *Monroe v. Bd. of Comm'rs*, 391 U.S. 450 (1968); *United States v. Montgomery County Bd. of Educ.*, 395 U.S. 225 (1969); *Alexander v. Holmes County Bd. of Educ.*, 396 U.S. 19 (1969); *Dowell v. Bd. of Educ.*, 396 U.S. 269 (1969); *Swann v. Charlotte-Mecklenburg Bd. of Educ.*, 402 U.S. 1 (1971); *Davis v. Bd. of Sch. Comm'rs*, 402 U.S. 33 (1971); *McDaniel v. Barresi*, 402 U.S. 39 (1971); *N.C. State Bd. of Educ. v. Swann*, 402 U.S. 43 (1971).

50. *Dred Scott v. Sandford*, 60 U.S. 393, 407 (1857).

51. *Plessy v. Ferguson*, 163 U.S. 537, 544 (1896).

CHAPTER 2: THE LEGACY OF SEGREGATION: WHAT *BROWN* MEANT IN MERCED

1. "Mr. Charlie" is a term made popular by African-American art, music, and folklore. In 1964, James Baldwin produced and published a three-act tragedy titled *Blues for Mister Charlie*. A denunciation of racial bigotry and hatred, the play was based on a murder trial in Mississippi in 1955. Richard Henry, a black man who returns to the southern town of his birth to begin a new life and recover from drug addiction, is killed for "not knowing his place" by Lyle Britten—a white bigot. Britten is later acquitted by an all-white jury. See also *Random House Historical Dictionary of American Slang*, ed. J. E. Lighter (New York: Random House, 1994).

CHAPTER 3: *BROWN*'S PROMISE: BLACK STUDENTS AT STANFORD

1. *Stanford Daily*, April 17, 1967.
2. For a discussion of the event, see "Shockley Seeks Study of Racial Ancestry IQ," *Stanford Daily*, Jan. 24, 1973.
3. Office of Policy Planning and Research, U.S. Dept. of Labor, *The Negro Family: The Case for National Action* (Washington, D.C.: GPO, 1965) (hereafter Moynihan Report), available at http://www.dol.gov/asp/programs/history/webid-meynihan.htm.
4. Nathan Glazer and Daniel Patrick Moynihan, *Beyond the Melting Pot: The Negroes, Puerto Ricans, Jews, Italians, and Irish of New York City* (Cambridge: MIT Press, 1963): 26.
5. Ibid., 49.
6. Ibid., 50.
7. Frazier's works include *Black Bourgeoisie* (New York: Collier Books, 1962), *The Negro Family in the United States* (Chicago: Univ. of Chicago Press, 1939), and "Problems and Needs of Negro Children and Youth Resulting from Family Disorganization," *Journal of Negro Education* 19 (1950): 269–77.
8. Glazer and Moynihan, *Melting Pot*, 52.

CHAPTER 4: *BROWN*'S FAILURE: RESISTANCE IN BOSTON

1. See Ronald P. Formisano, *Boston Against Busing: Race, Class, and Ethnicity in the 1960s and 1970s* (Chapel Hill: Univ. of North Carolina Press, 1991), 64.
2. *Green*, 391 U.S. 430, 437–38 (1968).
3. Ibid., 435.
4. Other mandates included requiring certain faculty and staff racial rations,

and pairing geographically and racially dispersed neighborhoods within the district. *Swann*, 402 U.S. 1, 22–31 (1971).

5. Erica Frankenberg et al., "A Multiracial Society with Segregated Schools: Are We Losing the Dream?" (Cambridge: Civil Rights Project, Harvard Univ., Jan. 2003), 37, tbl. 9. For a graphical representation of gains and reversals of desegregation for black students in the South from 1954 to 2000, see ibid., 38, fig. 10.

6. See Erica Frankenberg and Chungmei Lee, "Race in American Schools: Rapidly Resegregating School Districts" (Cambridge: Civil Rights Project, Harvard Univ., 2002), tbl. 9. Districts with countywide metropolitan desegregation plans in the 1980s experienced less resegregation than school districts that implemented partial desegregation plans or that included only central-city regions. Furthermore, these metropolitan districts were more likely to have higher levels of interracial exposure by 2000, even in districts in which the court order was no longer in place. Ibid., 12.

7. Ibid., 23.

8. Ibid.

9. Ibid., 25.

10. Ibid., 27.

11. Ibid., 28–29.

12. Ibid., 41.

13. Ibid., 40.

14. Ibid.

15. *Morgan v. Hennigan*, 379 F. Supp. 410, 417 (D. Mass. 1975).

16. Steven J. L. Taylor, *Desegregation in Boston and Buffalo: The Influence of Local Leaders* (Albany: State Univ. of New York Press, 1998), 5. The law exempted suburban school districts and was targeted only on the three largest urban districts with the largest number of African-Americans. See also George R. Metcalf, *From Little Rock to Boston: The History of School Desegregation* (Westport, Conn.: Greenwood Press, 1983), 197–98.

17. Formisano, *Boston Against Busing*, 44–46. From 1965, the year the Racial Imbalance Act was passed, to 1972, the number of imbalanced schools increased from forty-six to seventy-five, with the proportion of nonwhite students in imbalanced schools hovering around 80 percent. Ibid., 46, tbl. 3.1.

18. Ibid., 36.

19. Ibid., 22.

20. *Morgan*, 379 F. Supp. 415.

21. Ibid., 424, 435.

22. Ibid., 482.

23. Peter Irons, *Jim Crow's Children: The Broken Promise of the* Brown *Decision* (New York: Viking Press, 2002), 250; Taylor, *Desegregation*, 77; Formisano, *Boston Against Busing*, 66; Metcalf, *From Little Rock*, 199.

24. Formisano, *Boston Against Busing*, 66; J. Anthony Lukas, *Common Ground: A Turbulent Decade in the Lives of Three American Families* (New York: Alfred A. Knopf, 1985), 266.
25. Lukas, *Common Ground*, 227–28; Metcalf, *From Little Rock*, 199–200.
26. Formisano, *Boston Against Busing*, 67.
27. Metcalf, *From Little Rock*, 200.
28. For the history of the NAACP's plan and fight for desegregation in Boston public schools from 1963 to 1972, see Formisano, *Boston Against Busing*, 22–54.
29. Morgan v. Hennigan, 379 F. Supp. 410, 482 (D. Mass. 1974).
30. Lukas, *Common Ground*, 239, 241.
31. Irons, *Jim Crow's Children*, 254.
32. Ibid.
33. Taylor, *Desegregation*, 77.
34. Lukas, *Common Ground*, 244.
35. Ibid., 244–46.
36. Formisano, *Boston against Busing*, 178.
37. *New York Times*, Dec. 16, 1974, at 19.
38. Ibid., Dec. 17, 1974, at 10.
39. Irons, *Jim Crow's Children*, 252–53; Lukas, *Common Ground*, 245.
40. Irons, *Jim Crow's Children*, 255.
41. Lukas, *Common Ground*, 245.
42. Formisano, *Boston Against Busing*, 82.
43. *New York Times*, Dec. 16, 1974, at 19.
44. Ibid., Oct. 5, 1974, at 1.
45. Metcalf, *From Little Rock*, 206–7. On his visit to South Boston, ironically in support of the white Irish Catholics, David Duke echoed the concerns of the demonstrators, proclaiming, "The Federal government is taking little white children out of their homes and sending them into black jungles."
46. Taylor, *Desegregation*, 74, 79, 81, 85–86.
47. Brian J. Sheehan, *The Boston School Integration Dispute: Social Change and Legal Maneuvers* (New York: Columbia Univ. Press, 1984), 253.
48. Formisano, *Boston Against Busing*, 209–11.
49. Taylor, *Desegregation*, 73–74.
50. *Boston Globe*, Dec. 12, 1975, p. 28.
51. Sheehan, *Integration Dispute*, 248.
52. Metcalf, *From Little Rock*, 207.
53. Sheehan, *Integration Dispute*, 193.
54. Formisano, *Boston Against Busing*, 80.
55. In 1971, just 45% of blacks said they favored busing. George H. Gallup, *The Gallup Public Opinion 1935-1971* (Random House, 1972), 2323. By 1980, however, 59% of blacks (including 73% of Southern blacks) supported busing as a way to better achieve racial balance in schools. Gallup

Report, Feb. 1981, p. 29. In 1977, 92% of young white Southerners were opposed. Gerald D. Jaynes and Robin M. Williams, Jr., eds., *A Common Destiny: Blacks and American Society* (Washington D.C.: National Academy Press, 1989) 128–29.

56. For a discussion of this evidence, see Frankenberg et al., "A Multiracial Society," 9–14.

57. This was most notably so in Charlotte-Mecklensburg in 2001. Since then, massive resegregation has occurred. See Roslyn Mickelson "The Academic Consequences of Desegregation and Resegregation: Evidence from Charlotte," in Jack Boger and Gary Orfield, *Black, White, and Brown: A Segregated Future for Southern Schools?*, forthcoming.

CHAPTER 5: *BROWN'S* CHALLENGE: CARRYING THE TORCH

1. For a complete listing of presidential appointments of African-American federal judges, see http://www.jtbf.org/pres_appt.htm (compiled by Elaine Jones and Edward B. Toles) (last visited December 24, 2003).

2. A person who mobilized considerable public support for the King holiday was the popular recording artist Stevie Wonder. He wrote and performed a song entitled "Happy Birthday," which spread the message of a King holiday far and wide.

3. For a description of the work, see Public Defender Service website, http://www.pdsdc.org/AboutUs/index.asp.

4. Prepared testimony of Cynthia E. Jones before the House Committee on Government Reform Subcommittee on the District of Columbia (May, 11, 2001), available at LEXIS, Federal News Service Folder.

5. See Claudia Johnson, "Without Tradition and Within Reason: Judge Horton and Atticus Finch in Court," *Alabama Law Review* 45 (1994): 483, 489–91.

CHAPTER 6: LIFE BEFORE *BROWN*

1. Richard Wormser, *The Rise and Fall of Jim Crow* (New York: St. Martin's Press, 2003), xi.

2. National Public Radio (NPR), "Remembering Jim Crow: A Documentary by American RadioWorks" (radio broadcast, Oct. 2001), (available at http://www.americanradioworks.org/features/remembering/transcript.html) (last visited December 24, 2003).

3. See Leon Litwack, *Been in the Storm So Long* (New York: Alfred A. Knopf, 1979), 336–38.

4. 83 U.S. 36, 71 (1873); see *Slaughter-House Cases*.

5. 109 U.S. 3 (1883); see *Civil Rights Cases*.

6. Ibid, 22.

7. John Hope Franklin and Alfred A. Moss, Jr., *From Slavery to Freedom: A History of African Americans*, 8th ed. (New York: Alfred A. Knopf, 2000), 288.
8. Todd Lewan and Dolores Barclay, "Black Families Lose Land Through Legal Maneuvering," Associated Press, Dec. 4, 2001, available at LEXIS, U.S. Newspapers and Wires Folder.
9. Franklin and Moss, *From Slavery to Freedom*, 275.
10. W. Fitzhugh Brundage, *Lynching in the New South: Georgia and Virginia, 1880–1930* (Urbana: Univ. of Illinois Press, 1993), 8.
11. Alfred L. Brophy, *Reconstructing the Dreamland: The Tulsa Riot of 1921: Race, Reparations, and Reconciliation* (New York: Oxford Univ. Press, 2002), 8–9.
12. "Norman Mob after Singie Smith Jazz," *Oklahoma City Black Dispatch*, Feb. 9, 1922 (cited in ibid., 9).
13. For an account of the Helene riot in particular, see "A Painful Present as Historians Confront a Nation's Bloody Past," *Los Angeles Times*, Feb. 22, 2000, at A5.
14. Franklin and Moss, *From Slavery to Freedom*, 385–86.
15. See, e.g., 74 Okl. St. § 8000.1(1) (2003).
16. NPR, "Remembering Jim Crow."
17. Wormser, *Rise and Fall*, 58.
18. Franklin and Moss, *From Slavery to Freedom*, 317.
19. PBS, "The Rise and Fall of Jim Crow: Jim Crow Stories" (available at http://www.pbs.org/wnet/jimcrow/stories_org_nacw.html).
20. Wormser, *Rise and Fall*, 58.
21. Cornel West, *Race Matters* (Boston: Beacon Press, 1993), 15.
22. W. E. B. Du Bois, "Does the Negro Need Separate Schools?" *Journal of Negro Education* 4 (1935): 329, 334.
23. *Cumming*, 175 U.S. 528, 544–45 (1899).
24. Franklin and Moss, *From Slavery to Freedom*, 445.
25. Ibid., 445.
26. Ibid., 446–50.
27. Roy L. Brooks, *Integration or Separation?* (Cambridge: Harvard Univ. Press, 1996), 126–27.
28. Ibid., 128.
29. Joanna Schneider Zangrando and Robert L. Zangrando, "Black Protest: A Rejection of the American Dream," *Journal of Black Studies* 1 (1970): 145.
30. W. E. B. Du Bois, *Dusk of Dawn: An Essay Toward an Autobiography of a Race Concept*, 2d ed. (New York: Schocken Books, 1968), 197–98.
31. P. L. Prattis, "Race Relations and the Negro Press," *Phylon* 14 (1953): 373.
32. Franklin and Moss, *From Slavery to Freedom*, 415.
33. David Levering Lewis, *W. E. B. Du Bois: Biography of a Race* (New York: Henry Holt, 1993), 409–10.
34. Ibid., 410–11.
35. Ibid., 416.

36. Robert C. Kenzer, *Enterprising Southerners: Black Economic Success in North Carolina, 1865–1915* (Charlottesville: Univ. Press of Virginia, 1997), 1.

37. Wilmoth A. Carter, "Negro Main Street as a Symbol of Discrimination," *Phylon* 21 (1960): 236–37.

38. Franklin and Moss, *From Slavery to Freedom*, 311.

39. Ibid., 312–13.

40. Ibid., 312.

41. Ibid., 313.

42. Wormser, *Rise and Fall*, 94.

43. Ibid., 95.

44. George M. Fredrickson, *The Black Image in the White Mind: The Debate on Afro-American Character and Destiny, 1817–1914* (New York: Harper and Row, 1971).

45. Lewis, *Du Bois*, 278.

46. C. Vann Woodward, *The Strange Career of Jim Crow* (New York: Oxford Univ. Press, 2002), 125.

47. Ronald L.F. Davis, "The History of Jim Crow: Resisting Jim Crow," available at http://www.jimcrowhistory.org/history/resisting.htm (last visted December 24, 2003).

48. Robert A. Bone, *The Negro Novel in America*, rev. ed. (New Haven: Yale Univ. Press, 1965), 55–56, 62.

49. Ibid., 62.

50. Franklin and Moss, *From Slavery to Freedom*, 404.

51. Ibid., 409.

52. Ibid., 417.

53. *Plessy*, 163 U.S. 537, 559 (1896) (Harlan, J., dissenting).

54. Scott Ellsworth, *Death in a Promised Land: The Tulsa Race Riot of 1921* (Baton Rouge: Louisiana State Univ. Press, 1982), 15.

55. Scott Ellsworth, "The Tulsa Race Riot," in *Tulsa Race Riot: A Report by the Oklahoma Commission to Study the Tulsa Race Riot of 1921* ([Oklahoma City]: The Commission, 2001), 42.

56. Alfred Brophy, "Assessing State and City Culpability: The Riot and the Law," published with *Tulsa Race Riot*, 153, 156.

57. Ellsworth, "The Tulsa Race Riot," 64.

58. Brophy, *Reconstructing the Dreamland*, 69–87.

59. "Negro Tells How Others Mobilized," *Tulsa Tribune*, June 4, 1921 (quoted in ibid., 13).

CHAPTER 7: DEFEATING JIM CROW

1. Genna Rae McNeil, *Groundwork: Charles Hamilton Houston and the Struggle for Civil Rights* (Philadelphia: Univ. of Pennsylvania Press, 1983), 26–27, 31–33.

2. Ibid., 35–34.
3. Ibid., 42.
4. Ibid., 52–53.
5. Ibid., 112–15.
6. Mark Tushnet, *The NAACP's Legal Strategy Against Segregated Education, 1925–1950* (Chapel Hill: Univ. of North Carolina Press, 1987), 15, 26–28.
7. Ibid.; McNeil, *Groundwork*, 115–16.
8. McNeil, *Groundwork*, 64–68.
9. Ibid., 70.
10. Roscoe Pound, *Introduction to the Philosophy of Law,* rev. ed. (New Haven: Yale Univ. Press, 1954), 47.
11. McNeil, *Groundwork*, 82.
12. Ibid., 134–35.
13. Charles Hamilton Houston, "The Need for Negro Lawyers," *Journal of Negro Education* 4 (1935): 40.
14. Ibid., 49–52.
15. McNeil, *Groundwork*, 71.
16. Ibid., 134–35.
17. Tushnet, *Legal Strategy*, 34.
18. Ibid., 36.
19. Ibid., 44.
20. Ibid., 69.
21. Ibid. 103.
22. *Pearson*, 182 A. 590 (Md. 1936).
23. Missouri, 305 U.S. 337 (1938).
24. Ibid., 349–52.
25. Tushnet, *Legal Strategy*, 74.
26. *Sipuel*, 332 U.S. 631 (1948).
27. Tushnet, *Legal Strategy*, 121–23.
28. Ibid., 125–30.
29. *Sweatt*, 340 U.S. 846 (1950); *McLaurin*, 339 U.S. 637 (1950).
30. *Sweatt*, 340 U.S. at 850.
31. *McLaurin*, 339 U.S. at 640.
32. Tushnet, *Legal Strategy*, 135.

CHAPTER 8: RESISTANCE TO *BROWN*

1. James Hunt, "*Brown v. Board of Education* after Fifty Years: Context and Synopsis," *Mercer Law Review* 52 (2001): 549, 565.
2. *Goss v. Board of Education of Knoxville*, 373 U.S. 683, 684 (1963).
3. U.S. Commission on Civil Rights, *Survey of School Desegregation in Southern and Border States, 1965–66* (Washington, D.C.: GPO, 1966), 51–52.

4. *Briggs v. Elliott*, 132 F. Supp. 776, 777 (E.D.S.C. 1955).
5. See, e.g., *Missouri v. Jenkins*, 515 U.S. 70, 119 (1995) (Thomas, J., concurring) (arguing that a district court's conclusion that "racial imbalances constituted an ongoing constitutional violation" was based on "a misreading of our earliest desegregation case").
6. Patterson, Brown v. Board of Education, 80.
7. Ibid.
8. Ibid., 82 (citing quotations found in Stephen Ambrose, *Eisenhower: Soldier and President* [New York: Simon and Schuster, 1990], 367–68, and Emmet John Hughes, *The Ordeal of Power: A Political Memoir of the Eisenhower Years* [New York: Atheneum, 1963], 201).
9. J. W. Peltason, *Fifty-eight Lonely Men: Southern Federal Judges and School Desegregation* (New York: Harcourt, Brace and World, 1961), 47.
10. Patterson, Brown v. Board of Education, 98.
11. Peltason, *Fifty-eight Lonely Men*, 49.
12. Carl T. Rowan, *Dream Makers, Dream Breakers: The World of Justice Thurgood Marshall* (Boston: Little, Brown, 1993), 251.
13. *Brown v. Board of Education*, 349 U.S. 294, 301 (1955).
14. Ibid., 300.
15. On this lack of direction, see Peltason, *Fifty-eight Lonely Men*, 4.
16. Derrick Bell, "Heretical Thoughts on a Serious Occasion," in Brown *Plus Thirty: Perspectives on Desegregation*, ed. LaMar P. Miller (New York: Metropolitan Center for Educational Research, 1986), 70.
17. Peltason, *Fifty-eight Lonely Men*, 55.
18. Gary Orfield and Susan E. Eaton, *Dismantling Desegregation: The Quiet Reversal of* Brown v. Board of Education (New York: New Press, 1996), 7–8.
19. Carl Tobias, "Public School Desegregation in Virginia during the Post-*Brown* Decade," *William and Mary Law Review* 37 (1996): 1261.
20. Peltason, *Fifty-eight Lonely Men*, 96.
21. Tobias, "Public School Desegregation," 1266–67.
22. Patterson, Brown v. Board of Education, 94.
23. *Cooper*, 358 U.S. 1, 12–13 (1958).
24. Ibid., 15.
25. Ibid., 17 (quoting *Marbury v. Madison*, 5 U.S. [1 Cranch] 137, 177 [1803]).
26. Patterson, Brown v. Board of Education, 112.
27. *Briggs v. Elliott*, 132 F. Supp. 776, 777 (E.D.S.C. 1955). See also Patterson, Brown v. Board, 85.
28. *Briggs*, 132 F. Supp. at 777–78.
29. Greenberg, *Crusaders in the Courts*, 216.
30. Peltason, *Fifty-eight Lonely Men*, 93.
31. Patterson, Brown v. Board of Education, 99.
32. Ibid., 91.

33. Ibid., 90.
34. Ibid., 123–24.
35. Orfield and Eaton, *Dismantling Desegregation*, 8.
36. Ibid., 9 (citing H. R. Haldeman, *The Haldeman Diaries: Inside the Nixon White House* [New York: Putnam, 1994], 120).
37. *Swann*, 404 U.S. 811 (1971).
38. Orfield and Eaton, *Dismantling Desegregation*, 9.
39. Ibid. Kluger, *Simple Justice*, 770–71.
40. *Milliken*, 418 U.S. 717 (1974).
41. Ibid., 741–42, 744–45.
42. Orfield and Eaton, *Dismantling Desegregation*, 12.

CHAPTER 9: MARSHALL AND KING: TWO PATHS TO JUSTICE

1. 169 Md. 478 (1936). For a discussion of the *Murray* case, see Kluger, *Simple Justice*, 186–94.
2. *Allwright*, 321 U.S. 649, 666 (1944).
3. *Morgan*, 328 U.S. 373, 376 (1946).
4. *Shelley*, 334 U.S. 1, 20–21 (1948).
5. Martin Luther King, Jr., "I Have a Dream," in *A Testament of Hope: The Essential Writings and Speeches of Martin Luther King, Jr.*, ed. James Melvin Washington (San Francisco: Harper, 1986), 217.
6. Martin Luther King, Jr., "Remaining Awake through a Great Revolution," in *Testament of Hope*, 271.
7. Lyndon B. Johnson, Howard University commencement speech (1965), available at http://usinfo.state.gove/usa/civilrights/s060466.htm (last visited Sept. 24, 2003).
8. Rowan, *Dream Makers*, 297.
9. King, Jr., "Letter from Birmingham City Jail," in *Testament of Hope*, 292.
10. *Walker*, 388, U.S. 307, 327.
11. Ibid., 320–21.
12. Taylor Branch, *Parting the Waters: America in the King Years, 1954–1963* (New York: Simon and Schuster, 1988), 190.

CHAPTER 10: REVERSING THE *BROWN* MANDATE: THE *BAKKE* CHALLENGE

1. *Green v. County School Board*, 391 U.S. 430, 437–38 (1968).
2. Morton Keller and Phyllis Keller, *Making Harvard Modern: The Rise of America's University* (New York: Oxford Univ. Press, 2001), 34.
3. Ibid.
4. Ibid., 294.
5. *Civil Rights Cases*, 109 U.S. 3, 25 (1883).

6. Bernard Schwartz, *Behind* Bakke: *Affirmative Action and the Supreme Court* (New York: New York Univ. Press, 1988), 13.

7. Joel Dreyfuss and Charles Lawrence, *The* Bakke *Case: The Politics of Inequality* (New York: Harcourt Brace Jovanovich, 1979), 15.

8. Ibid. During his time in the marines, Bakke commanded an antiaircraft unit in Vietnam. Ibid., 8.

9. Ibid., 3, 15.

10. Schwartz, *Behind* Bakke, 2.

11. Dreyfuss and Lawrence, Bakke *Case*, 4. Bakke's work with NASA brought him into contact with physicians who were studying the effects of outer space on humans. This prompted his interest in medicine. See Timothy J. O'Neil, Bakke *and the Politics of Equality* (Middletown, Conn.: Wesleyan Univ. Press, 1985), 21. Bakke also attributed his decision to pursue a career in medicine to his time in Vietnam, where he became fascinated with the work of physicians. See Schwartz, *Behind* Bakke, 2. He stated that his change in career paths was prompted not by financial considerations but by his belief that he could contribute more to society as a physician than as an engineer See Ball, Bakke *Case*, 47. In preparation for medical school, Bakke began taking premedical courses and volunteering at a local hospital while working at NASA. Ibid., 21.

12. Schwartz, *Behind* Bakke, 3; Dreyfuss and Lawrence, Bakke *Case*, 16.

13. Schwartz, *Behind* Bakke, 5.

14. Ibid., 6. While developing his strategy, Bakke considered reapplying to both UC San Francisco and Stanford. Because both schools also used a quota system, he considered suing them as well if he was not admitted. See Dreyfuss and Lawrence, Bakke *Case*, 26.

15. Schwartz, *Behind* Bakke, 6–7.

16. Dreyfuss and Lawrence, Bakke *Case*, 29.

17. *Bakke v. Regents of University of California*, 18 Cal. 3d 34, 387 (1976).

18. Ibid., 39.

19. Ibid.

20. Ibid., 52–56, 64.

21. Ibid., 64.

22. Keller and Keller, *Making Harvard Modern*, 350

23. Ibid., 344.

24. Dreyfuss and Lawrence, Bakke *Case*, 165, 190.

25. Brian C. Kalt, "Wade H. McCree, Jr., and the Office of Solicitor General," *Detroit College of Law at Michigan State University Law Review* (1998): 704.

26. Ibid.

27. Dreyfuss and Lawrence, Bakke *Case*, 191.

28. Schwartz, *Behind* Bakke, 52–53.

29. Ibid., 128.

30. Ibid.
31. Ibid., 41–42.
32. Memorandum of Justice Marshall, Apr. 13, 1978, at 203 (unpublished memorandum, from Thurgood Marshall Papers, Library of Congress, box 204, folder 3) (quoted in Michael Selmi, "The Life of Bakke: An Affirmative Action Retrospective," *Georgetown Law Journal* 87 [1999]: 981, 994). Marshall added, "This case is here now because of that sordid history. So despite the lousy record, the poorly reasoned lower court opinion, and the absence as parties of those who will be most affected by the decision (the Negro applicants), we are stuck with this case. We are not yet all equals, in large part because of the refusal of the *Plessy* Court to adopt the principle of color-blindness. It would be the cruelest irony for this Court to adopt the dissent in *Plessy* now and hold that the University must use color-blind admissions." Ibid.
33. *Bakke*, 438 U.S. at 310–15.
34. Justice White wrote a separate opinion, arguing that there was no private right of action under Title VI. Ibid., 379–87. Justice Blackmun also wrote a separate opinion. Ibid. 402.
35. *Bakke*, 438 U.S. at 362 (opinion of Brennan, White, Marshall, and Blackmun)(quoting Gerald Gunther, "The Supreme Court, 1971 Term—Foreword: In Search of Evolving Doctrine on a Changing Court: A Model for a Newer Equal Protection," *Harvard Law Review* 86 [1972]: 1, 8).
36. *Bakke*, 438 U.S. at 387 (Marshall, J., concurring in part and dissenting in part).
37. Ibid., 387–94.
38. Ibid., 395–36.
39. Ibid., 396.
40. Ibid., 396–98.
41. Ibid., 400. Marshall went on to recite the troubled history of race in America, noting:

> It is unnecessary in 20th-century America to have individual Negroes demonstrate that they have been victims of racial discrimination; the racism of our society has been so pervasive that none, regardless of wealth or position, has managed to escape its impact. The experience of Negroes in America has been different in kind, not just in degree, from that of other ethnic groups. It is not merely the history of slavery alone but also that a whole people were marked as inferior by the law. And that mark has endured. The dream of America as the great melting pot has not been realized for the Negro; because of his skin color he never even made it into the pot.
>
> These differences in the experience of the Negro make it difficult for me to accept that Negroes cannot be afforded greater protection under

the Fourteenth Amendment where it is necessary to remedy the effects of past discrimination. In the *Civil Rights Cases* . . . the Court wrote that the Negro emerging from slavery must cease "to be the special favorite of the laws." We cannot in light of the history of the last century yield to that view. Had the Court in that decision and others been willing to "do for human liberty and the fundamental rights of American citizenship, what it did . . . for the protection of slavery and the rights of the masters of fugitive slaves," (Harlan dissenting) we would not need now to permit the recognition of any "special wards."

Most importantly, had the Court been willing in 1896, in *Plessy v. Ferguson*, to hold that the Equal Protection Clause forbids differences in treatment based on race, we would not be faced with this dilemma in 1978. We must remember, however, that the principle that the "Constitution is color-blind" appeared only in the opinion of the lone dissenter. The majority of the Court rejected the principle of color-blindness, and for the next 58 years, from *Plessy* to *Brown v. Board of Education*, ours was a Nation where, *by law*, an individual could be given "special" treatment based on the color of his skin.

It is because of a legacy of unequal treatment that we now must permit the institutions of this society to give consideration to race in making decisions about who will hold the positions of influence, affluence, and prestige in America. For far too long, the doors to those positions have been shut to Negroes. If we are ever to become a fully integrated society, one in which the color of a person's skin will not determine the opportunities available to him or her, we must be willing to take steps to open those doors. I do not believe that anyone can truly look into America's past and still find that a remedy for the effects of that past is impermissible.

It has been said that this case involves only the individual, Bakke, and this University. I doubt, however, that there is a computer capable of determining the number of persons and institutions that may be affected by the decision in this case. For example, we are told by the Attorney General of the United States that at least 27 federal agencies have adopted regulations requiring recipients of federal funds to take "'*affirmative action* to overcome the effects of conditions which resulted in limiting participation . . . by persons of a particular race, color, or national origin.'". . . I cannot even guess the number of state and local governments that have set up affirmative-action programs, which may be affected by today's decision.

I fear that we have come full circle. After the Civil War our Government started several "affirmative action" programs. This Court in the *Civil Rights Cases* and *Plessy v. Ferguson* destroyed the movement toward complete equality. For almost a century no action was taken,

> and this nonaction was with the tacit approval of the courts. Then we had *Brown v. Board of Education* and the Civil Rights Acts of Congress, followed by numerous affirmative-action programs. *Now*, we have this Court again stepping in, this time to stop affirmative-action programs of the type used by the University of California.

Ibid., 400–402 (citations omitted).

42. Derrick Bell, "*Bakke*, Minority Admissions, and the Usual Price of Racial Remedies," *California Law Review* 67 (1979): 3, 6.

43. *Bakke*, 438 U.S. at 403 (Blackmun, J., concurring in the judgment and dissenting in part).

44. Akhil Reed Amar and Neal Kumar Katyal, "Symposium on Affirmative Action: *Bakke's* Fate," *UCLA Law Review* 43 (1996): 1745, 1775.

45. Ibid. Amar and Katyal note that *Brown technically* held only that "in the field of public education the doctrine of 'separate but equal' has no place." Ibid. (quoting *Brown v. Board of Education*, 347 U.S. 483, 495 [1954]).

46. Samuel Issacharoff, "Law and Misdirection in the Debate over Affirmative Action," *University of Chicago Legal Forum* 11 (2002): 23.

47. Charles Lawrence, "Two Views of the River: A Critique of the Liberal Defense of Affirmative Action," *Columbia Law Review* 101 (2001): 928, 930.

48. Ibid., 942.

49. Ibid., 966.

50. Ibid., 967.

51. Susan Sturm and Lani Guinier, "The Future of Affirmative Action: Reclaiming the Innovative Ideal," *California Law Review* 84 (1996): 953, 956.

CHAPTER 11: THE LEGACY OF THURGOOD MARSHALL

1. *Buckley v. Valeo*, 424 U.S. 39–59 (1976).

2. *Austin v. Michigan State Chamber of Commerce*, 494 U.S. 652, 668–69 (1989).

3. *Linmark*, 431 U.S. 85 (1977).

4. *Rodriguez*, 411 U.S. 1 (1973)

5. Ibid., 43–55.

6. Ibid., 63 70 (White, J., dissenting).

7. Ibid., 70–71. (Marshall, J., dissenting).

8. Ibid., 71–72.

9. Ibid., 112–15.

10. Ibid., 122–23.

11. *Kadrmas v. Dickinson Public Schools*, 487 U.S. 450, 469–71 (1988).

12. Ibid., 469. The closest the Court came to adopting Marshall's view was in *Plyler v. Doe*, 457 U.S. 202 (1982), where it invalidated Texas's complete

exclusion of undocumented children from Texas public schools. Again Marshall stood up for the powerless, undocumented workers, when a near majority of the Court was prepared to rule in a way that denied them the basics rights of all people. *Plyler*'s scope is limited, however, by *Martinez v. Bynum*, 461 U.S. 321 (1983), and *Kadrmas v. Dickinson Public Schools*.

13. *Green*, 391 U.S. 430 (1968).

14. *Swann*, 402 U.S. 1 (1971).

15. *Keyes*, 413 U.S. 189, at 201 (1973). Justice Rehnquist dissented, arguing that deliberate segregation in one part of a unitary school system should create no presumption of intentional segregation in other parts of the system. Ibid., 254–65 (Rehnquist, J., dissenting). It is worth remembering that Rehnquist, while a law clerk for Justice Jackson in the 1950s, expressed in a memo his view that the "separate but equal" rule of *Plessy* should be upheld. In "A Random Thought on the Segregation Cases" (memorandum to Justice Jackson), he wrote, "I realize that it is an unpopular and unhumanitarian position, for which I have been excoriated by 'liberal' colleagues, but I think *Plessy v. Ferguson* was right and should be re-affirmed." See 117 *Cong. Rec.* S44, 880 (1971) (quoting memorandum).

   This was not the only occasion on which the then judicial clerk Rehnquist expressed such views. In a memo to Justice Jackson on *Terry v. Adams*, 345 U.S. 461 (1953), the case holding that political parties could not deny blacks the right to vote in party "pre-primaries," Rehnquist said, "The Constitution does not prevent the majority from banding together, nor does it attain success in the effort. It is about time the Court faced the fact that the white people in the South don't like the colored people; the Constitution restrains them from affecting this dislike through state action, but it most assuredly did not appoint the Court as a sociological watchdog to rear up every time private discrimination raises its admittedly ugly head." Memorandum to Justice Jackson (quoted in John A. Jenkins, "The Partisan: A Talk with Justice Rehnquist," *New York Times Magazine*, March 3, 1985, at 28, 32).

16. William J. Brennan, Jr., "A Tribute to Justice Thurgood Marshall," *Harvard Law Review* 105 (1991): 23, 25–26.

17. *Milliken*, 418 U.S. at 752–53 (1974).

18. Ibid., 782–83 (Marshall, J., dissenting).

19. Ibid., 785 (quoting *Keyes*, 413 U.S. at 201) (internal quotation marks omitted).

20. Ibid., 786.

21. Ibid., 799, n. 19, 801–2. Marshall went on,

   The State must also bear part of the blame for the white flight to the suburbs which would be forthcoming from a Detroit-only decree and would render such a remedy ineffective. Having created a system where

> whites and Negroes were intentionally kept apart so that they could not become accustomed to learning together, the State is responsible for the fact that many whites will react to the dismantling of that segregated system by attempting to flee to the suburbs. Indeed, by limiting the District Court to a Detroit-only remedy and allowing that flight to the suburbs to succeed, the Court today allows the State to profit from its own wrong and to perpetuate for years to come the separation of the races it achieved in the past by purposeful state action.

Ibid., 806.
22. Ibid., 802–3.
23. *Milliken v. Bradley*, 433 U.S. 267 (1977).
24. Brennan, "Tribute," 26.
25. One such example was his dissent in *Pasadena City Board of Education v. Spangler*, 427 U.S. 424 (1976). The majority held that since yearly shifts in schools' racial composition resulted from private choices, not state action, the district court could not continue requiring yearly shifts in attendance zones to ensure "no majority of any minority" in any school. Ibid., 435–40. Marshall supported the district court's conclusion that the achievement of "no majority of any minority" did not necessarily mean a unitary school district had been achieved, and he urged that district courts be permitted to exercise caution in relinquishing supervision over recently segregated school systems. Ibid., 441–44 (Marshall, J., dissenting).
26. *Crawford*, 458 U.S. 527 (1982). The California state constitution forbade de facto as well as de jure segregation. The Court held that California had no obligation to do more than the federal constitution required and that the provision was not facially discriminatory, and there was no evidence that California voters adopted it with discriminatory intent. By contrast, in *Washington v. Seattle School District No. 1*, 458 U.S. 457 (1982), Marshall was part of a five-justice majority that struck down a statute that forbade school boards from requiring students to attend a school other than the geographically nearest one, but made exceptions for virtually all purposes except racial desegregation.
27. *Crawford*, 458 U.S. at 554 (Marshall, J., dissenting).
28. *Board of Education v. Dowell*, 498 U.S. 237, 252 (1991) (Marshall, J., dissenting).
29. *Fullilove*, 448 U.S. 448 (1980).
30. Ibid., 477–78.
31. Ibid., 522 (Marshall, J., concurring in the judgment).
32. *Croson*, 488 U.S. 469 (1989).
33. Ibid., 507.
34. Ibid., 529 (Marshall, J., dissenting). Marshall asserted that the city had proven its role in past discrimination and that the program was substan-

tially related to the interest of eradicating such discrimination. He noted how similar the program (including the 30 percent quota) was to that in *Fullilove* and urged that Richmond need not try race-neutral alternatives first, given that it had already found mere prohibition against discrimination in public contracts and by public contractors to be ineffectual and that Congress had made similar findings. Finally, he argued,

> In concluding that remedial classifications warrant no different standard of review under the Constitution than the most brutal and repugnant forms of state-sponsored racism, a majority of this Court signals that it regards racial discrimination as largely a phenomenon of the past. . . . I, however, do not believe this Nation is anywhere close to eradicating racial discrimination or its vestiges. In constitutionalizing its wishful thinking, the majority today does a grave disservice not only to those victims of past and present racial discrimination in this Nation whom government has sought to assist, but also to this Court's long tradition of approaching issues of race with the utmost sensitivity.

Ibid., 552–53.
35. Ibid., 555.
36. *Batson*, 476 U.S. 79, 96–98 (1986).
37. Ibid., 102–3. In *Holland v. Illinois*, 493 U.S. 474 (1990), Marshall articulated his understanding of the Sixth Amendment's purpose: "(1) guard[ing] against the exercise of arbitrary power and ensuring that the commonsense judgment of the community will act as a hedge against the overzealous or mistaken prosecutor, (2) preserving public confidence in the fairness of the criminal justice system, and (3) implementing our belief that sharing in the administration of justice is a phase of civil responsibility." Ibid., 495. He argued that race-based peremptory challenges undermined all those values.
38. *Robinson*, 414 U.S. 218 (1973).
39. Ibid., 255–59 (Marshall, J., dissenting).
40. *Furman*, 408 U.S. 238 (1972).
41. Ibid., 360–63 (Marshall, J., concurring).
42. *Gregg*, 428 U.S. 153 (1976).
43. Ibid., 241–51 (Marshall, J., dissenting).
44. *Ford*, 477 U.S. 399, 409–10 (1986).
45. *Payne*, 501 U.S. 808 (1991).
46. Ibid., 844–45, 856 (Marshall, J., dissenting).
47. Williams, *Thurgood Marshall*, 391.
48. William H. Rehnquist, "Tribute to Justice Thurgood Marshall," *Stanford Law Review* 44 (1991): 1213.
49. Brennan, "Tribute," 23.
50. Sandra Day O'Connor, "Thurgood Marshall: The Influence of a Raconteur," *Stanford Law Review* 44 (1991): 1217.

51. Anthony M. Kennedy, "Tribute to Justice Thurgood Marshall: The Voice of Thurgood Marshall," *Stanford Law Review* 44 (1992): 1221.
52. A. Leon Higginbotham, Jr., "A Tribute to Justice Thurgood Marshall," *Harvard Law Review* 105 (1991): 55.
53. Brennan, "Tribute," 25.
54. O'Connor, "Thurgood Marshall," 1217.
55. Ibid.
56. Brennan, "Tribute," 23.
57. Neil A. Lewis, "Marshall Urges Bush to Pick 'the Best,' " *New York Times*, June 29, 1991, at A8.

CHAPTER 12: THE RISE OF CLARENCE THOMAS

1. Robert Dallek, *Flawed Giant: Lyndon Johnson and His Times, 1961–1973* (New York: Oxford Univ. Press, 1998), 471.
2. Senate Committee on the Judiciary, *The Nomination of Clarence Thomas to the Supreme Court: Hearings of the Senate Judiciary Committee* (Sept. 10, 1991), available at LEXIS Federal News Service Folder.
3. Ronald Taylor, "Black Lawyers Split on Thomas," *Washington Times*, Aug. 6, 1991, at A1.
4. "Most Blacks Back Thomas, Core Leader Says," *Seattle Times*, Aug. 29, 1991, at B4.
5. *Farrakhan v. United States*, No. 90-3150, 1990 WL 104925 (July 5, 1990).
6. *Boyd*, 906 F.2d 783 (1990).
7. In "Civil Rights as a Principle versus Civil Rights as an Interest," in *Assessing the Reagan Years*, ed. David Boaz (Washington, D.C.: Cato Institute, 1998), 399, Thomas wrote,

> The always arduous task of preserving freedom was a simpler task when limited government was respected. The question now becomes, how do we achieve this object? That its defense is still possible was seen in the testimony of Oliver North before the congressional Iran-Contra committee. Partly disarmed by his attorney's insistence on avoiding closed sessions, the committee beat an ignominious retreat before North's direct attack on it and, by extension, on all of Congress. This shows that people, when not presented with distorted reporting by the media, do act on their common sense and good judgment.

8. National Association for the Advancement of Colored People, "A Report on the Nomination of Judge Clarence Thomas as Associate Justice of the United States Supreme Court," 49–60 (hereinafter NAACP Report). Thomas's thinking was reminiscent of nineteenth-century laissez-faire capitalists' call for limited government intervention in the affairs of people, and of their devotion to market principles as guides to policy and as guarantors of national prosperity. Ibid.

9. Ibid., 50. While Thomas occasionally and begrudgingly acknowledged the importance of civil rights leaders in opening up opportunities formerly denied to blacks because of their race, he was not reluctant to express his opposition to some of the civil rights movement's successes. As I noted in my analysis for the NAACP Report, "Thomas' speech to the Heritage Foundation on 'Why Black Americans Should Look to Conservative Policies' (June 18, 1987), is an interesting case in point. The speech has an extensive autobiographical introduction in which Thomas speaks about the environment in which he was raised. Though it may be natural for Thomas to attribute his success to his fine upbringing, his complete silence on the social struggles of African-Americans is striking. From reading Clarence Thomas one would never gather that a civil rights struggle ever took place in this country." Ibid., 50, n. 80.
10. "Black Conservatives, Center State," *Washington Post*, Dec. 16, 1980, at A21.
11. NAACP Report, 51–52.
12. Fred Barnes, "Weirdo Alert," *New Republic*, Aug. 5, 1991, at 7.
13. Thomas, "Civil Rights as a Principle," 394. Later, in "Affirmative Action Goals and Timetables: Too Tough? Not Tough Enough!" *Yale Law and Policy Review* 5 (1987): 403, n. 3, Thomas wrote, "I continue to believe that distributing opportunities on the basis of race or gender, whoever the beneficiaries, turns the law against employment discrimination on its head. Class preferences are an affront to the rights and dignity of individuals— both those individuals who are directly disadvantaged by them, and those who are their supposed beneficiaries."
14. National Research Council, *A Common Destiny: Blacks and American Society* (Washington, D.C.: National Academy Press, 1989), 7.
15. Carol Kleiman, "More Black Women Tied to Low-Wage Jobs," *Chicago Tribune*, business sect., at 5.
16. Equal Employment Opportunity Commission, EEOC Decision no. 85-9, June 11, 1985, available at LEXIS, EEOC Private Sector Decisions Folder.
17. Thomas, "Civil Rights as a Principle," 399.
18. "Climb the Jagged Mountain," *New York Times*, July 17, 1991, at A21.
19. See NAACP Report, 56.
20. "Climb the Jagged Mountain," at A21.
21. See NAACP Report, 57–58.
22. See Clarence Thomas, "Why Black Americans Should Look to Conservative Policies" (speech at the American Heritage Foundation, June 18, 1987). Thomas's defenders have dismissed his characterization of the Lehrman essay as a "splendid example of applying natural law" as nothing more than a rhetorical compliment (this, even though Thomas was speaking in the Lehrman auditorium). However, even for those not concerned about a woman's right to choose an abortion, the prospect of his applying this method of jurisprudence should still be profoundly troubling.

23. *Griswold*, 381 U.S. 479 (1965).
24. *Roe*, 410 U.S. 113 (1973).
25. Perhaps the best example of Thomas's thinking on the subject was his article "The Higher Law Background of the Privileges or Immunities Clause of the Fourteenth Amendment," *Harvard Journal of Law and Public Policy* 12 (1989): 63–67. He wrote that "[N]atural rights and higher law arguments are the best defense of liberty and limited government." Ibid.
26. Clarence Thomas, "Toward a 'Plain Reading' of the Constitution—The Declaration of Independence in Constitutional Interpretation," 1987 *Howard Law Journal* 691, 698–99.
27. Douglass's position that the Constitution could be interpreted for abolition was not intended as a detached analysis of the Constitution's historical meaning. Rather, it was an abolitionist strategy at a time when there was little hope that the Constitution would ever be changed and no anticipation that there would be a Civil War. Thomas used Douglass's statement, taken out of historical context, to lambaste Marshall for saying that the framers of the Constitution put provisions in it to uphold slavery. Marshall's position was plainly correct: the Constitution provided that the slave trade would end in 1820, clearly indicating that slavery would continue until at least that time, and presumably for the lifetime of the slaves purchased in the last year of the trade. It also made special provision for counting slaves in the census. Given that Thomas believes that the Constitution's meaning never changes, he can scarcely argue that slavery was constitutional in the 1790s but not in the 1850s.
28. Frederick Douglass, "The Meaning of July Fourth for the Negro," in Philip S. Foner, *The Life and Writings of Fredrick Douglass*, vol. 2 (New York: International Publishers, 1950), 192. Moreover, Douglass's views on racism and its impact on blacks were unrepentant, unequivocal, and dramatically different from what Thomas claimed they were. His statements about the Declaration of Independence make that abundantly clear:

> What have I, or those I represent, to do with your national independence? Are the great principles of political freedom and of natural justice, embodied in that Declaration of Independence, extended to us. . . . Would to God for your sakes and ours that an affirmative answer could be truthfully returned to those questions. . . . But such is not the case. I say it with a sad sense of the disparity between us. I am not included within the pale of this glorious anniversary! The rich inheritance of justice, liberty, prosperity and independence, bequeath by your fathers, shared by you not by me. . . . This Fourth of July is *yours*, not *mine*.

> Ibid., 188–89.

29. Thomas, "Toward a 'Plain Reading,' " 703.

CHAPTER 13: WHO'S GETTING LYNCHED?: HILL V. THOMAS

1. Senate Committee on the Judiciary, *The Nomination of Clarence Thomas to the Supreme Court: Hearings of the Senate Judiciary Committee* (Sept. 11, 1991), available at LEXIS, Federal News Service Folder.

CHAPTER 14: JUSTICE THOMAS:
A NEW ERA IN RACE MATTERS

1. A. Leon Higginbotham, Jr., "An Open Letter to Justice Clarence Thomas from a Federal Judicial Colleague," *University of Pennsylvania Law Review* 140 (1992): 1007, 1010, 1015–18.
2. See Herman Schwartz, ed., *The Rehnquist Court: Judicial Activism on the Right* (New York: Hill and Wang, 2002), and Martin H. Belsky, ed., *The Rehnquist Court: A Retrospective* (Oxford University Press, 2002).
3. Charles Ogletree, "The Rehnquist Revolution in Criminal Procedure," in *The Rehnquist Court: Judicial Activism on the Right*, ed. by Herman Schwartz (New York: Hill and Wang, 2002). See also Charles Ogletree, "*Arizona v. Fulminante*: The Harm of Applying Harmless Error to Coerced Confessions," *Harvard Law Review* 105 (1991), 152–75.
4. For example, after the Court's decision in *Romer v. Evans*, 517 U.S. 620 (1996), a case involving gay rights legislation, Justice Scalia quipped that his colleagues had been subjected to a case of "terminal silliness." In *Texas v. Lawrence*, 123 S.Ct. 2472 (2003), Scalia lamented the Court's "sign[ing] onto the so-called homosexual agenda, by which I mean the agenda promoted by some homosexual activists directed at eliminating the moral opprobrium that has traditionally attached to homosexual conduct." Ibid., 2496 (Scalia, J., dissenting). Scalia, in *United States v. Virginia*, 518 U.S. 515 (1996), angrily criticized his colleagues by observing: "to counterbalance the Court's criticism of our ancestors, let me say a word in their praise: They left us free to change. The same cannot be said of this most illiberal Court. . . ." Ibid., 567 (Scalia, J., dissenting).
5. *Grutter*, 123 S.Ct. 2325 (2003).
6. For an example, see *United States v. Lopez*, 514 U.S. 549 (1995). While Scalia joined the majority opinion invalidating the Gun Free School Zones Act under the Court's existing commerce clause test, Thomas concurred to suggest that the Court roll back its "substantial effects" approach and return to an originalist understanding of the commerce clause. Ibid., 584–602 (Thomas, J., concurring).
7. Booker T. Washington, "Atlanta Exposition Address," in *African American Political Thought, 1890–1930*, ed. Cary D. Wintz (Armonk, N.Y.: Sharpe, 1996), 26.
8. Act of April 9, 1866, ch. 31, 14 Stat. 27 (reenacted as amended pursuant

to ratification of Fourteenth Amendment at Act of May 31, 1870, ch. 114, 16 Stat. 140, codified as amended at 42 U.S.C. § 1981 [2000]). It provides, in part, "All persons within the jurisdiction of the United States shall have the same right in every State and Territory to make and enforce contracts, to sue, be parties, give evidence, and to the full and equal benefit of all laws and proceedings for the security of persons and property as is enjoyed by white citizens. . . ." Ibid.

9. *Slaughter-House Cases*, 83 U.S. 36 (1873).

10. See, e.g., Laurence H. Tribe, *American Constitutional Law*, 3d ed. (New York: Foundation Press, 2000), 1297–1303.

11. *Slaughter-House*, 83 U.S. at 71.

12. Ibid., 74, 79. Included among the federal privileges were the rights to vote in a national election, to gain access to a federal courthouse, and to petition the national government; but in all those other laws established by the various states—such as the right to vote in state elections, the means of obtaining, owning, using, and disposing of property, criminal laws, etc.—the states reigned supreme. Ibid., 79–81.

13. *Civil Rights Cases*, 109 U.S. 3, 25 (1883).

14. Ibid., 22–23. The denial of public accommodations to people of color was not found firmly illegal until eighty years later, when the Court in *Katzenbach v. McClung*, 379 U.S. 294 (1964), found Congress's use of the commerce power to ban such denials to be constitutional. Ibid., 305.

15. Furthermore, in *United States v. Reese*, 92 U.S. 214(1876), the Court held that the Fifteenth Amendment did not confer a positive right to vote: that lay in the grant of states. Ibid., 218. Instead, the amendment prohibited states only from *denying* right to vote on basis of race. When taken in conjunction with *United States v. Cruikshank*, 92 U.S. 542 (1876), which found that "the right of suffrage is not a necessary attribute of national citizenship" (ibid., at 545), *Reese* clearly denied the ballot to a majority of Americans, and particularly to African-Americans, for the foreseeable future.

16. *Hudson*, 503 U.S. 1 (1992).

17. See, generally, David M. Oshinsky, *"Worse Than Slavery": Parchman Farm and the Ordeal of Jim Crow Justice* (New York: Free Press, 1997).

18. See, generally, Malcolm M. Feeley and Edward L. Rubin, *Judicial Policy Making and the Modern State: How the Courts Reformed America's Prisons* (New York: Cambridge Univ. Press, 1998).

19. A. Leon Higginbotham, Jr., "Disinvitation: Talking Back to Thomas," *National Law Journal*, Aug. 3, 1998, col. 1.

20. Washington, "Atlanta Exposition Address," 24.

21. *Adarand*, 515 U.S. 200, 204–5 (1995).

22. In *Richmond v. J. A. Croson Co.*, 488 U.S. 469 (1989), a majority of the Court held that strict scrutiny should be applied to all racial classifications by state and local governments, ibid., at 490–92, but had no occasion to

address the standard for federal programs. *Metro Broadcasting, Inc. v. FCC*, 497 U.S. 547 (1990), which upheld two FCC "minority preference policies" under intermediate scrutiny, ibid., at 564–66, was overruled by *Adarand*.
23. *Adarand*, 515 U.S. at 240.
24. Ibid., 241.
25. *Reynolds*, 377 U.S. 533 (1964).
26. *Shaw*, 509 U.S. 630 (1993).
27. Ibid., 646–47.
28. Ibid., 646–48. Thomas's opinion in *Easley v. Cromartie*, 532 U.S. 234 (2001), continued this trend. The Court faulted the district court for relying on evidence of voter registration, rather than voter behavior, to strike down a redistricting plan: at least in North Carolina, African-American registered Democrats vote Democratic much more reliably in national elections than do white registered Democrats, and the evidence "clearly" demonstrated that the legislature was just using this fact about African-Americans to create safe seats for Democrats. Ibid., 244–45.
29. *Holder*, 512 U.S. 874 (1993).
30. Ibid., 892 (Thomas, J., concurring).
31. Ibid., 907 ("The clear premise of the system is that geographic districts are merely a device to be manipulated to establish 'black representatives' whose real constituencies are defined, not in terms of the voters who populate their districts, but in terms of race").
32. *Jenkins*, 515 U.S. 70 (1995).
33. Ibid., 101.
34. Ibid., 114, 118–19 (Thomas, J., concurring). Thomas went on to note, "'Racial isolation' itself is not a harm; only state-enforced segregation is. After all, if separation itself is a harm, and if integration therefore is the only way that blacks can receive a proper education, then there must be something inferior about blacks. Under this theory, segregation injures blacks because blacks, when left on their own, cannot achieve." Ibid., 122.
35. Ibid., 120. It is true that the methodology of the *Brown* studies, particularly Clark's doll study, has been undermined, but many studies since have confirmed both the psychological harm from segregation and the educational benefits from integration. In fact, Thomas cites two such studies. Ibid.
36. Ibid., 121–22.
37. See, e.g., ibid., 126, 131.
38. 536 U.S. 639 (2002).
39. *Zelman v. Simmons-Harris*, 122 S.Ct. 2460, at 2480 (2002) (Thomas, J., concurring)
40. Ibid., 2483.
41. Ibid., 2484.

CHAPTER 15: THE MICHIGAN CASES: MIXED SIGNALS

1. See *Hopwood v. Texas*, 78 F.3d 932, 944 (1996).
2. *Neumyer v. Lynn School Committee*, 263 F.Supp.2d 209 (D.Mass.)
3. *Gratz*, 123 S.Ct. 2411 (2003); *Grutter*, 123 S. Ct. 2325 (2003).
4. "[I]t is not too much to say that the nation's future depends upon leaders trained through wide exposure to the ideas and mores of students as diverse as this Nation of many peoples." *University of California Regents v. Bakke*, 438 U.S. 265, 313 (1978). (internal quotation marks and citation omitted).
5. *Grutter* 123 S.Ct. at 2326. (emphasis added and citation omitted.)
6. *Ibid.*, 123 S.Ct. at 2343.
7. The facts are not quite this clear, as Justice Ginsburg noted in dissent. Gratz, 123 S.Ct. at 2442–46 (Ginsburg, J., dissenting).
8. *Gratz*, 123 S.Ct. at 2432. The Court continued, "This policy stands in sharp contrast to the law school's admissions plan, which enables admissions officers to make nuanced judgments with respect to the contributions each applicant is likely to make to the diversity of the incoming class." Ibid.
9. *Grutter*, 123 S.Ct. at 2341.
10. Ibid., 2337.
11. Ibid., 2339.
12. *Gratz*, 123 S.Ct. at 2414.
13. Lee Bollinger and Nancy Cantor, "The Educational Importance of Race," *Washington Post*, April 28, 1998, at A17, available at http://www.umich .edu/~urel/admissions/statements/washpost.html.
14. Gerhard Casper, Speech to Stanford Faculty Senate: Statement on Diversity, Oct. 4, 1995, available at http://www.stanfordalumni.org/news/magazine/ 1996/sepoct/articles/casper.html. In my view, the recurring accusation that African-American candidates are underqualified is deeply troubling and speaks volumes about the continued persistence and expression of prejudice in this country. Accusing a qualified African-American of not deserving his or her place at an educational establishment is an expression of prejudice and one of the quite common examples of racial discrimination tolerated openly today. See, generally, Patricia J. Williams, *The Rooster's Egg* (Cambridge: Harvard Univ. Press, 1995).
15. *Gratz*, 123 S.Ct. at 2442–43 (Ginsburg, J., dissenting). In his brief and somewhat elusive opinion in *Gratz*, Justice Breyer said that he "agree[d] with Justice Ginsburg that, in implementing the Constitution's equality instruction, government decisionmakers may properly distinguish between policies of inclusion and exclusion." Ibid., 2434 (Breyer concurring in the judgment). Nonetheless, while expressly declining to endorse the majority's reasoning, he agreed with its conclusion.
16. Brief for the NAACP Legal Defense and Education Fund, Inc. and the American Civil Liberties Union as amici curiae in support of respondents at 29, *Grutter v. Bollinger* (No. 02–241).

17. *Grutter*, 123 S.Ct. at 2349–50 (Scalia, J., dissenting).
18. Ibid., 1247.
19. Lani Guinier, "Admissions Rituals as Political Acts: Guardians of the Gates of Our Democratic Ideals," *Harvard Law Review* 117 (2003): 197–98.
20. *Grutter*, 123 S.Ct. at 1147–48 (Ginsburg, J., concurring).
21. This is certainly how Justice Thomas regards it.
22. In *Bakke*, no one concurred in Justice Powell's opinion. It has been, however, regarded by some lower courts as the narrowest of the opinions concurring in the judgment and, on that basis, adopted as the precedent. See *Grutter*, 123 S.Ct. at 2343–44.
23. *Gratz*, 123 S.Ct. at 2443–44 (Ginsburg, J., dissenting). Ginsburg notes, "Actions designed to burden groups long denied full citizenship stature are not sensibly ranked with measures taken to hasten the day when entrenched discrimination and its after effects have been extirpated." Ibid., 2444. To support her proposition, she cites Stephen Carter's article "When Victims Happen to Be Black," *Yale Law Review* 97 (1988): 4320, which states, "To say that two centuries of struggle for the most basic of civil rights have been mostly about freedom from racial categorization rather than freedom from racial oppression is to trivialize the lives and deaths of those who have suffered under racism. To pretend . . . that the issue presented in [*Bakke*] was the same as the issue in [*Brown*] is to pretend that history never happened and that the present doesn't exist." Ibid., 433–34.
24. *Grutter*, 123 S.Ct. at 2348 (Ginsburg, J., concurring).
25. Ibid., 2351 (Thomas, J., dissenting).
26. Ibid., 2352–53 n. 3, 2354–56. Note Thomas's sophistry here. It is impossible for all fifty states to have top-fifteen law schools. A look at *U.S. News and World Report*'s top fifty, however, reveals that most states are actually represented in that list.
27. Thomas fails to consider that other students, including legacy students and former military personnel, are given preferential status comparable to African-Americans even at the graduate level. He does not suggest that the university forgo the financial advantages (the alumni and federal funding) that come with admitting these students.
28. 505 U.S. 717 (1992). Thomas did not participate in the consideration or decision in *Freeman v. Pitts*, 503 U.S. 467 (1992), which held that a district court could relinquish supervision over a school district in stages as it came into compliance with particular aspects of a desegregation decree.
29. *Fordice*, 505 U.S. at 731–32.
30. Ibid., 745 (Thomas, J., concurring) (quoting Du Bois, "Schools," *Crisis* 13 [1917]: 112).
31. Ibid. Thomas characterizes the standard applied to grade schools under *Green v. School Bd. of New Kent County*, 391 U.S. 430 (1968), and its progeny this way because "[a]lthough racial imbalance does not itself

establish a violation of the Constitution, our decisions following *Green* indulged the presumption, often irrebuttable in practice, that a presently observed imbalance has been proximately caused by intentional state action during the prior *de jure* era." Fordice, 505 U.S. at 745 (Thomas, J., concurring).

32. Ibid., 748.

33. Ibid.

34. See David Levering Lewis, *W. E. B. Du Bois: The Fight for Equality and the American Century, 1919–1963* (New York: Henry Holt, 2000), 330–32.

35. *Grutter*, 123 at 2350.

36. Derrick Z. Jackson, "Mugging Frederick Douglass," *Boston Globe*, July 4, 2003, at 15.

37. Ibid.

CHAPTER 16: MEETING THE EDUCATIONAL CHALLENGES OF THE TWENTY-FIRST CENTURY

1. Jack M. Balkin, ed., *What* Brown v. Board of Education *Should Have Said* (New York: New York Univ. Press, 2001), 6–8.

2. *Miliken*, 418 U.S. 717 (1974).

3. Ibid., 752.

4. *Loving v. Virginia*, 388 U.S. 1 (1967).

5. *McLaughlin v. Florida*, 379 U.S. 184 (1964).

6. See ibid., 192.

7. *Washington v. Davis*, 426 U.S. 229 (1976).

8. *Jenkins*, 515 U.S. 70 (1995).

9. Ibid., 525 (Thomas, J., concurring)

10. *McDowell*, 498 U.S. 237 (1991).

11. Ibid., 249–51.

12. *Jenkins*, 515 U.S. at 86–103.

13. Balkin, *What* Brown *Should Have Said*, 8.

14. Orfield et al., "Deepening Segregation," 2, 16–19; Gary A. Orfield and John T. Yum, "Resegregation in American Schools" (Cambridge: Civil Rights Project, Harvard University, June 1999).

15. Frankenberg et al., "A Multiracial Society," 28, fig. 4.

16. Ibid.

17. Gary Orfield and Susan E. Eaton, "Back to Segregation," *Nation*, Mar. 3, 2003, at 5.

18. Weekly Dig, "Segregation in Boston, Part 1: A City Divided," by Seth McM. Dolin, http://weeklydig.com (accessed July 16, 2003).

19. Nancy McArdle, "Race, Place, and Opportunity: Racial Change and Segregation in the Boston Metropolitan Area, 1990–2000" (Cambridge: Civil Rights Project, Harvard Univ., rev. 2003).

20. See Barry Bluestone, "Greater Boston in Transition" (Urban Policy Seminar, Center for Urban and Regional Policy: Northeastern Univ.), available at http://www.curp.neu.edu/visualdata/pdfs/Urban%20Policy%20Seminar. Triple%20Revolution.ppt.
21. See Weekly Dig, "Segregation in Boston."
22. J. R. Logan et. al. "Segregation in Neighborhoods and Schools: Impacts on Minority Children in the Boston Region" (paper presented at the Color Lines Conference, Harvard University Civil Rights Project, Cambridge, September 1, 2003), at 7.
23. Figures analyzed by the Mumford Center for Comparative Urban and Regional Research at the Univ. at Albany.
24. See Cindy Rodriguez and Megan Tench, "White Student Ratios Falling Pattern in Boston's Elementary Schools," *Boston Globe*, Jan. 25, 2002, at A1.
25. Ibid.
26. Nancy McArdle and Guy Stuart "Race, Place, and Segregation: Redrawing the Color Lines in Our Nation's Metros: Boston" (Cambridge: Civil Rights Project, Harvard Univ., May 2002).
27. Douglas S. Massey and Nancy A. Denton, *American Apartheid: Segregation and the Making of the Underclass* (Cambridge: Harvard Univ. Press, 1993).
28. Student data report of 1993–94, Cambridge public schools.
29. Letter from Benjamin Banneker to Thomas Jefferson, Aug. 19, 1791, available at http://extext.lib.virginia.edu/readex/24073.html.
30. Letter from Thomas Jefferson to Benjamin Banneker, Aug. 30, 1791, available at http://etext.lib.virginia.edu/readex/24073.html.
31. http://www.metcoinc.org.

CHAPTER 17: ADDRESSING THE RACIAL DIVIDE: REPARATIONS

1. Martin Luther King, Jr., "I Have a Dream," in *A Testament of Hope: The Essential Writings and Speeches of Martin Luther King, Jr.*, ed. James Melvin Washington (San Francisco: Harper, 1986), 217.
2. Lyndon B. Johnson, "To Fulfill These Rights" (commencement address at Howard Univ., June 4, 1965). Johnson continued,

> We seek not just freedom but opportunity. We seek not just legal equity but human ability, not just equality as a right and a theory but equality as a fact and equality as a result. For the task is to give 20 million Negroes the same chance as every other American to learn and grow, to work and share in society, to develop their abilities—physical, mental and spiritual, and to pursue their individual happiness. To this end equal opportunity is essential, but not enough, not enough. Men and women of all races are born with the same range of abilities. But ability is not

just the product of birth. Ability is stretched or stunted by the family that you live with, and the neighborhood you live in—by the school you go to and the poverty or the richness of your surroundings. It is the product of a hundred unseen forces playing upon the little infant, the child, and finally the man.

3. Ibid.
4. Ibid.
5. There are also various lawsuits seeking reparations for theft of Jews' belongings during World War II. See *Rosner v. United States*, 01-CV-1859 (S.D. Fla.), order on motion to dismiss dated Aug. 28, 2002; *Deutsch v. Turner Corp.*, 2003 WL 139746 (9th Cir. 2003) (Japanese and holocaust litigation case).
6. See *Porter v. Lloyds of London*, Docket No. 02-CV-6180 (N.D. Ill. filed Aug. 29, 2002); *In re: African-American Litig.*, 02-CV-7764 (N.D. Ill.).
7. See Darryl Fears, "Slaves' Descendants Sue Firms: Filing Seeks Reparations from Profits on Free Labor," *Washington Post*, Sept. 4, 2002, sec. A, at 22.
8. See *Carrington v. Fleet Boston Fin. Corp.*, Docket No. 2002cv01863 (E.D.N.Y. filed March 26, 2002); *Farmer-Paellmann v. Fleet Boston Fin. Corp.*, Docket No. 2002cv01862 (E.D.N.Y. filed March 26, 2002); *Ntzebesa v. Citigroup, Inc.*, Docket No. 2002cv04712 (S.D.N.Y. filed June 19, 2002).
9. See *Barber v. New York Life Ins.*, Docket No. 02-CV-2084 (D.N.J. filed May 2, 2002).
10. See *Johnson v. Aetna Life Ins. Co. et al.*, 02-CV-9180 (E.D. La).
11. See *Hurdle v. Fleet Boston*, Docket No. CGC-020412388 (Cal. Sup. Ct. filed Sept. 10, 2002); *Hurdle v. Fleet Boston*, 02-CV-4653 (N.D. Ill., transferred from N.D. Cal.).
12. See *Alexander v. Governor of the State of Oklahoma*, Docket No. 03cv00133 (N.D. Okl. filed Feb. 24, 2003).
13. *In re: African-American Litig.* 02-CV-7764 (N.D.Ill.) Minute Order dated Jan. 17, 2003 (noting that the following cases had been transferred to the Northern District of Illinois pursuant to 28 U.S.C. 1407: "02c6180 [*Porter*], 02c7765 [*Barber*], 02c7766 [*Farmer-Paellman*], 02c7767 [*Carrington*], 02c9180 [*Johnson*], 02c9181 [*Bankhead*], and recently transferred *Timothy Hurdle v. Fleet Boston Financial Corp.* [02-CV-4653]").
14. Fla. Legis. 94-359 (2002 Fl. ALS 387 § 210 [codified at Fla. Stat. 1004.60 (2002)]).
15. Cal. Ins. Code §§ 13810–13 (2003).
16. Oklahoma House Joint Resolution 1035 (1997) (codified as amended at 74 Okl. Stat. § 8201.1 [2003]).
17. Sabrina L. Miller and Gary Washburn, "New Chicago Law Requires Firms to Tell Slavery Links," *Chicago Tribune*, Oct. 3, 2002, west. ed., at 1.
18. Commission to Study Reparations for African Americans Act, H.R. 40, 108th Cong. (2003).

19. For a useful synopsis of the modern attempts to obtain reparations from corporations that profited from the Holocaust, see Michael J. Bazyler, "Nuremberg in America: Litigating the Holocaust in United States Courts," *University of Richmond Law Review* 34 (2000): 1.

20. On the Japanese American reparations movement, see, generally, Lilian Baker, *The Japanning of America*: *Redress and Reparations Demands by Japanese-Americans* (Oregon: Webb Research Group, 1991); Peter Irons, *Justice at War: The Story of the Japanese American Internment Cases* (Oxford: Oxford Univ. Press, 1983); Mitchell T. Maki, *Achieving the Impossible Dream: How Japanese Americans Obtained Redress* (Chicago: Univ. of Illinois Press, 1999); Charles McClain, ed., *The Mass Internment of Japanese Americans and the Quest for Legal Redress* (New York: Garland, 1994); Eric K. Yamamoto, "Beyond Redress: Japanese Americans' Unfinished Business," *Asian Law Journal* 7 (2000): 131. The Civil Liberties Act of 1988, Pub. L. No. 100-383, 102 Stat. 903 (1988) (codified at 50 U.S.C. app § 1989 [2003]) awarded reparations to Japanese Americans and Aleut Indians. For a discussion of the events leading to the passage of the Civil Liberties Act, see Leslie T. Hatamiya, *Righting a Wrong: Japanese Americans and the Passage of the Civil Liberties Act of 1988* (Stanford: Stanford Univ. Press, 1993). The two major Japanese American reparations cases that eventually forced passage of the act are *Hirabayashi v. United States*, 828 F. 2d 591 (9th Cir. 1987), and *Hohri v. United States*, 586 F. Supp. 769 (D.D.C. 1984) (dismissing reparations claim on statute of limitations grounds) *aff'd* 847 F. 2d 779 (Fed. Cir. 1988).

21. In 1829, David Walker "passionately protested the lack of compensation for the labor of slaves." See Ewart Guinier, "Book Review," *Yale Law Journal* 82 (1973): 1719, 1721.

22. Vincene Verdun, "If The Shoe Fits, Wear It: An Analysis of Reparations to African-Americans," *Tulane Law Review* 67 (1993): 597, 600–601.

23. Ibid., 602–3.

24. Ibid., 603–4.

25. King, "I Have a Dream," 217.

26. The Muslim program is reprinted in every issue of the *Final Call*—e.g., in that of Sept. 7, 1990, at 39, cited in Verdun, "If the Shoe Fits," 604.

27. See Verdun, "If the Shoe Fits," 604; Boris I. Bittker, *The Case for Black Reparations* (New York: Random House, 1973), 2–6.

28. See Verdun, "If the Shoe Fits"; see also Rhonda V. Magee, "The Master's Tools, from the Bottom Up: Responses to African-American Reparations Theory in Mainstream and Outsider Remedies Discourse," *Virginia Law Review* 79 (1993): 863; Mari Matusda, "Looking to the Bottom: Critical Legal Studies and Reparations," *Harvard Civil Rights–Civil Liberties Law Review* 22 (1987): 323; Charles Ogletree, "Repairing the Past: New Efforts in the Reparations Debate in America," ibid., 38 (2003). For an earlier

example, see Graham Hughes, "Reparations for Blacks?" *New York University Law Review* 43 (1968): 1063.

29. Randall Robinson, *The Debt: What America Owes to Blacks* (New York: Dutton, 2000), 8.

30. Ibid., 62–63.

31. Pub. L. No. 100-383, §1, 102 Stat. 903 (codified at 50 U.S.C. app. 1989 [2003]).

32. Lori Horvitz, "Race Adviser Says Payback Impractical," *Orlando Sentinel,* April 28, 1998, at C1 (noting that the African-American historian John Hope Franklin, head of the advisory board to President Clinton's Initiative on Race, objected to the payment of reparations). For further discussion of the attacks on the feasibility of reparations, see Ogletree, "Repairing the Past," 290–94.

33. Some members of the caucus still have not endorsed H.R. 40.

34. *Johnson,* 45 U.S. App. D.C. 440 (1915).

35. *Cato,* 70 F.3d 1103 (9th Cir. 1995).

36. Ibid., 1106. *Cato* sought damages for "forced, ancestral indoctrination into a foreign society; kidnapping of ancestors from Africa; breakup of families; removal of traditional values, deprivations of freedom; and imposition of oppression, intimidation, miseducation, and lack of information about various aspects of their indigenous character."

37. Ibid., 1111.

38. See Scott Ellsworth, *Death in a Promised Land: The Tulsa Race Riot of 1921* (Baton Rouge: Louisiana State Univ. Press, 1982), 46–50.

39. Alfred L. Brophy, "Assessing State and City Culpability: The Riot and the Law," in *Tulsa Race Riot: A Report by the Oklahoma Commission to Study the Tulsa Race Riot of 1921* ([Oklahoma City]: The Commission, 2001), 153, 155. One estimate places the number of whites' deputies at over five hundred. See Alfred L. Brophy, "Reconstructing the Dreamland: Contemplating Civil Rights Actions and Reparations for the Tulsa Race Riot of 1921" (preliminary draft of report to Tulsa Race Riot Commission), 32, available at http://www.law.ua.edu/staff/bio/abrophy/reparationsdft.pdf (last visited Jan. 1, 2004).

40. Ellsworth, *Tulsa Race Riot,* 156.

41. Brophy, "Reconstructing the Dreamland," 42.

42. Ibid., 107 and n. 85.

43. Ibid.

44. Ellsworth, *Tulsa Race Riot,* 20.

45. See *Alexander v. Governor of the State of Oklahoma,* Docket No. 03cv00133 (N.D. Okl.), First Amended Complaint filed Feb. 28, 2003, at 417–20.

46. *Alexander v. Governor of the State of Oklahoma,* Docket No. 03-C-133-E (N.D. Okl.), Order filed March 19, 2004, at 11.

47. Ibid., 13–14.
48. Ibid., 21–22.
49. Ibid., 25–26.
50. *Alexander v. Oklahoma*, 391 F.3d 1155, 2–4 (10th Cir. 2004) (Lucero, dissenting).
51. *Alexander v. Governor of the State of Oklahoma*, 487–90.
52. "Norman Mob after Singie Smith Jazz," *Oklahoma City Black Dispatch*, Feb. 9, 1922, cited in Brophy, *Reconstructing the Dreamland*, 8–9.
53. For a further discussion of the statute of limitations in the context of reparations lawsuits, see Ogletree, "Repairing the Past," 299–305.
54. "The Decision: Tulsa Race Riots Lawsuit Dismissed," *Tulsa World*, March 24, 2004.
55. "JPMorgan Apologizes for Connections to Slavery," *USA Today*, available at http://www.usatoday.com/money/industries/banking/2005-01-20-jpm slavery_x.htm?csp=34.
56. Ibid.
57. Katie Benner, "Wachovia Apologizes for Slavery Ties," *CNN Money*, available at http://money.cnn.com/2005/06/02/news/fortune500/wachovia_slavery/.

CHAPTER 18: THE INTEGRATION IDEAL:
SOBERING REFLECTIONS

1. Gerald Rosenberg, *The Hollow Hope: Can Courts Bring About Social Change?* (Chicago: Univ. of Chicago Press, 1991), 52.
2. Ibid., 156.
3. Michael J. Klarman, "*Brown*, Racial Change, and the Civil Rights Movement," *Virginia Law Review* 80 (1994): 7, 10, 13.
4. Mark Tushnet, "The Significance of *Brown v. Board of Education*," *Virginia Law Review* 80 (1994): 173, 176–77.
5. David Schultz and Steven E. Gottlieb, "Legal Functionalism and Social Change: A Reassessment of Rosenberg's *The Hollow Hope: Can Courts Bring About Social Change?*" *Journal of Law and Politics* 12 (1996): 63.
6. Ibid.
7. Ellsworth, *Tulsa Race Riot*, 22.
8. See, generally, Alfred L. Brophy, *Reconstructing the Dreamland*.
9. See Derrick A. Bell, Jr., "*Brown v. Board of Education* and the Interest Convergence Dilemma," in *Critical Race Theory: The Key Writings That Formed the Movement*, ed. Kimberlé Crenshaw et al. (New York: Basic Books, 1992), 22.
10. Derrick A. Bell, Jr., *Faces at the Bottom of the Well: The Permanence of Racism* (New York: Basic Books, 1992), 7.

11. *Fordice*, 505 U.S. 717, 748–49 (1992) (Thomas, J., concurring).
12. Orlando Patterson, "Affirmative Action: The Sequel," *New York Times*, June 22, 2003, sec. 4, at 11.
13. See Ogletree, "Repairing the Past," 282–84.
14. See Bell, *Faces at the Bottom of the Well*, 7.
15. Bell considers the relationship between racism and liberal democracy to be "symbio[tic]" such that "liberal democracy and racism in the United States are historically, even inherently, reinforcing; American society as we know it exists only because of its foundation in racially based slavery, and it thrives only because racial discrimination continues." Ibid., 10.
16. As evidence of the permanence of racism, Bell points to the "unstated understanding by the mass of whites that they will accept large disparities in economic opportunity in respect to other whites as long as they have a priority over blacks and other people of color for access to the few opportunities available." Ibid., 9.
17. Ibid., 12.
18. See *Grutter*, 123 S.Ct. 2325, 2334–43 (2003).
19. Ibid., 2340.
20. Ibid., 2330–31.
21. *Brown*, 347 U.S. 483, 494 n. 11 (1954).
22. See Roy L. Brooks, *Integration or Separation?: A Strategy for Racial Equality* (Cambridge: Harvard Univ. Press, 1996), 185–213. Brooks's analysis is similar to Derek Bell's work on interest convergence.
23. As an alternative to Michigan's diversity plan, President Bush recommended the race-neutral percentage plans. In my view, the arguments for these plans to achieve diversity are unsophisticated and unpersuasive; when closely examined, the plans, advanced by opponents of diversity, perpetuate a more sinister brand of racism. Moreover, percentage plans are inapplicable to the Michigan Law School. Most Michigan Law School students leave the state, any attempt to provide education benefits or access to leadership paths is addressed as a national problem, and under *Adarand* states cannot adopt race-conscious solutions to address generalized national race problems. Finally, recent empirical evidence suggests that these plans are not as effective as race-conscious plans in achieving diversity. See Catherine L. Horn and Stella M. Flores, *Percentage Plans in College Admissions: A Comparative Analysis of Three States' Experiences* (Cambridge: The Civil Rights Project at Harvard University, 2003).

CONCLUSION

1. Randall L. Kennedy, *"McCleskey v. Kemp:* Race, Capital Punishment, and the Supreme Court," *Harvard Law Review* 101 (1988): 1388, 1418.
2. *Brown I,* 347 U.S. at 494, n. 11.
3. Kennedy, *"McClesky v. Kemp,"* 1418.
4. Abraham Lincoln, *Great Speeches,* 107.
5. *Brown v. Board of Education,* 98 F. Supp. 797, 797 (D. Kan. 1952).
6. *Brown,* 892 F.2d 851, 856 (10th Cir. 1989).
7. *Brown v. Board of Education,* 978 F. 2d 585, 587 (10th Cir. 1992).
8. Ruby Bailey, "Colleges in Budget Squeeze; Crisis Hits Historically Black Schools as Lawsuits Threaten Affirmative Action," *Milwaukee Journal Sentinel,* March 9, 2003, news sec., at 7A.
9. *Fordice,* 505 U.S. 717, 733–35 (1992).
10. Bailey, "Colleges in Budget Squeeze."

AFTERWORD: THE POST-O'CONNOR SUPREME COURT: THE EMERGENCE OF THE SCALIA COURT?

1. See *Shaw v. Reno,* 509 U.S. 630 (1993). See also *Adarand Constructors, Inc. v. Pena,* 515 U.S. 200 (1995).
2. See *Grutter v. Bollinger,* 539 U.S. 306 (2003).
3. *Brown,* 347 U.S. 483 (1954).
4. Antonin Scalia, *A Matter of Interpretation: Federal Courts and the Law* (Princeton: Princeton University Press, 1997), 7.
5. Ken Foskett, *Judging Thomas: The Life and Times of Clarence Thomas* (New York: HarperCollins, 2004), 281.
6. *Planned Parenthood,* 505 U.S. 833, 979–84 (1992) (Scalia, J., concurring in the judgment in part and dissenting in part).
7. *Lawrence v. Texas,* 539 U.S. 558, 587, 592 (2003) (Scalia, J., dissenting).
8. *United States v. Thompson/Center Arms Co.,* 504 U.S. 505, 521, 112 S.Ct. 2102, 2111 (1992) (Scalia, J., concurring in the judgment).
9. Gregory E. Maggs, "The Secret Decline of Legislative History: Has Someone Heard a Voice Crying in the Wilderness?," *Public Interest Law Review* (1994): 57, 58. Justice Scalia's criticisms of legislative history, however, seem to have had much less impact on the congressional drafting of statutes. In a recent case study of staffers on the Senate Judiciary Committee, most staffers said that Scalia's critique "has had little resonance." Victoria F. Nourse and Jane S. Schacter, "The Politics of Legislative Drafting: A Congressional Case Study," *NYU Law Review* 77 (2002): 575, 606.
10. *Coy v. Iowa,* 487 U.S. 1012, 1016, 108 S.Ct. 2798, 2800–2801 (1988) (citations omitted).
11. *Crawford,* 541 U.S. 36, 50–53, 59 (2004).

12. *Blakely*, 124 S.Ct. 2531, 2536–37 (2004).
13. *Gonzalez*, 125 S. Ct. 2195 (2005) (Scalia, J., concurring in the judgment).
14. *Hamdi*, 124 S.Ct. 2633, 2671 (2004) (Scalia, J., dissenting).
15. See, e.g., Erwin Chemerinsky, "The Jurisprudence of Antonin Scalia: A Critical Appraisal," *Univeristy of Hawaii Law Review* 22 (2000): 385, 394–95.
16. See, e.g., *Alexander v. Sandoval*, 121 S.Ct. 1511 (2001) (finding no right of action under Title VI of the civil rights laws).
17. William N. Eskridge, Jr., "Textualism, the Unknown Ideal," *Michigan Law Review* 96 (1998): 1509, 1517 (reviewing Antonin Scalia, *A Matter of Interpretation: Federal Courts and the Law* [1997]).
18. *Michael H. v. Gerald D.*, 491 U.S. 110, 127, n. 6, 109 S.Ct. 2333, 2344 n. 6 (1989) ("We refer to the most specific level at which a relevant tradition protecting, or denying protection to, the asserted right can be identified").
19. *Rutan v. Republican Party of Illinois*, 497 U.S. 62, 95, 110 S.Ct. 2729, 2748 (1990) (Scalia, J., dissenting).
20. See David Schultz, "Scalia on Democratic Decision Making and Long-standing Traditions: How Rights Always Lose," *Suffolk University Law Review* 31 (1997): 319.
21. David M. Zlotnick, "Justice Scalia and His Critics: An Exploration of Scalia's Fidelity to His Constitutional Methodology," *Emory Law Journal* 48 (1999): 1377, 1404.
22. *Fordice*, 505 U.S. 717, 758 (1992) (Scalia, J., concurring in the original in part and dissenting in part).
23. *Adarand*, 515 U.S. 200 (1995).
24. Ibid., 239 (Scalia, J., concurring in part and concurring in the judgment).
25. Ibid.
26. *Roper*, 125 S. Ct. 1183, 1228 (2005) (Scalia, J., dissenting).
27. *Lawrence*, 539 U.S. 558, 598 (2003) (Scalia, J., dissenting) (citing *Foster v. Florida*, 537 U.S. 990, 990n.* [2002] [Thomas, J., concurring in denial of certiori]).
28. Antonin Scalia, "How Democracy Swept the World," editorial, *Wall Street Journal*, Sept. 7, 1999, at A24.
29. See, e.g., *United States v. Virginia*, 518 U.S. 515 (1996); *Lawrence v. Texas*, 539 U.S. 558 (2003).
30. Schultz, "Scalia on Democratic Decision Making," 319, 336.
31. *Grutter v. Bollinger*, 539 U.S. 306, 348 (2003) (Scalia, J., concurring in part and dissenting in part).
32. See *United States v. Virginia*, 518 U.S. 515 (1996); *Wabaunsee County v. Umbehr*, 518 U.S. 668 (1996).
33. *Wabaunsee County v. Umbehr*, 518 U.S. 668, 711 (1996) (Scalia, J., dissenting).
34. *United States v. Virginia*, 518 U.S. 515, 566 (1996) (Scalia, J., dissenting).

35. *Lawrence*, 539 U.S. 558, 587 (2003) (Scalia, J., dissenting).

36. *City of Richmond v. J.A. Croson Co.*, 488 U.S. 469, 521 (1989) (Scalia, J., concurring in the judgment) (quoting *Plessy v. Ferguson*, 163 U.S. 537, 559 [1896] [Harlan, J., dissenting]) (alteration in original).

37. See ibid., 528 ("Racial preferences appear to 'even the score' [in some small degree] only if one embraces the proposition that our society is appropriately viewed as divided into races, making it right that an injustice rendered in the past to a black man should be compensated for by discriminating against a white. Nothing is worth that embrace").

38. See *Adarand Constructors, Inc. v. Pena*, 515 U.S. 200, 239 (1995) (Scalia, J., concurring in part and concurring in the judgment) ("To pursue the concept of racial entitlement—even for the most admirable and benign of purposes—is to reinforce and preserve for future mischief the way of thinking that produced race slavery, race privilege and race hatred").

39. *Croson*, 488 U.S. at 524 (Scalia, J., concurring in the judgment) (emphasis added). In the nonremedial context, Scalia maintains that the only other valid race-based action is that which deals with "a social emergency rising to the level of imminent danger to life and limb—for example, a prison race riot, requiring temporary segregation of inmates." Ibid., 521 (citing *Lee v. Washington*, 390 U.S. 333 [1968] [per curiam]).

40. Ibid., 524–25 (citing *Green v. New Kent County School Board*, 391 U.S. 430, 439, [1968]).

41. *McDaniel v. Barresi*, 402 U.S. 39, 41 (1971).

42. See *Croson*, 488 U.S. at 525 (Scalia, J., concurring in the judgment) (citing *McDaniel*, 402 U.S. at 40–41).

43. Ibid., 520 (Scalia, J., concurring in the judgment). The majority in *Croson* held that remedial race-conscious policies were permissible if such policies targeted specific or "identified" past discrimination but not general "societal" discrimination. Ibid., 507.

44. *Adarand*, 515 U.S. 200, 239 (1995) (Scalia, J., concurring in part and concurring in the judgment).

45. *Fordice*, 505 U.S. 717, 757 (1992) (Scalia, J., concurring in the judgment in part and dissenting in part).

46. Ibid., 728.

47. Ibid., 758 (Scalia, J., concurring in the judgment in part and dissenting in part) ("Only one aspect of a historically segregated university system need be eliminated: discriminatory admissions standards").

48. *Bazemore*, 478 U.S. 385 (1986).

49. Ibid., at 408.

50. Ibid. (emphasis added).

51. *Fordice*, 507 U.S. at 757 (Scalia, J., concurring in the judgment in part and dissenting in part).

52. See *Freeman v. Pitts*, 503 U.S. 467, 504 (1992) (Scalia, J., concurring) ("We

concluded in *Green* that a 'freedom of choice' plan was not necessarily sufficient and later applied this conclusion to all jurisdictions with a history of intentional segregation. . . ." [citing *Green v. County School Board of New Kent County, Virginia*, 391 U.S. 430, 439–40 (1968)]).

53. *Fordice*, 507 U.S. at 760–61 (Scalia, J., concurring in the judgment in part and dissenting in part). See also ibid., 754–55 ("Legacies of the dual system that permit [or even incidentally facilitate] free choice of racially identifiable schools—while still assuring each individual student the right to attend *whatever* school he wishes—do not [implicate *Brown*]").

54. Ibid., 527-28 (Scalia, J., concurring in the judgment).

55. *Gratz*, 539 U.S. 244, 274–75 (2003).

56. *Grutter*, 539 U.S. 306 (2003).

57. Ibid, 349–78 (Thomas, J., concurring in part and dissenting in part).

58. Ibid., 347 (Scalia, J., concurring in part and dissenting in part).

59. Ibid., (Scalia, J., concurring in part and dissenting in part).

60. Ibid., 348 (Scalia, J., concurring in part and dissenting in part).

61. See, e.g., *City of Richmond v. J.A. Croson Co.*, 488 U.S. 469, 521 (1989) (Scalia, J. concurring in the judgment) ("[O]nly a social emergency rising to the level of imminent danger to life and limb—for example, a prison race riot, requiring temporary segregation of inmates can justify an exception to the principle embodied in the Fourteenth Amendment that '[o]ur Constitution is color-blind, and neither knows nor tolerates classes among citizens' " [citing *Lee v. Washington*, 390 U.S. 333 (1968) (per curiam); *Plessy v. Ferguson*, 163 U.S. 537, 559 (1896) (Harlan, J., dissenting)]); *Johnson v. California*, 125 S. Ct. 1141, 1157 (2005) (Thomas, J., dissenting, joined by Scalia, J., dissenting) (arguing that temporary racial segregation of prisoners in state prison does not violate Equal Protection).

62. *Adarand Constructors, Inc. v. Pena*, 515 U.S. 200, 239 (1995) (Scalia, J., concurring in part and concurring in the judgment).

63. An important exception would be Justice Ginsburg, whose dissent in *Gratz* noted the perversion of failing to distinguish between discrimination and affirmative action. See *Gratz v. Bollinger*, 539 U.S. 244, 301–2 (Ginsburg, J. dissenting).

64. Justice Kennedy agreed that educational diversity was a compelling state interest but did not join the majority opinion in *Grutter* because he felt it applied an insufficiently rigorous form of strict scrutiny. See *Grutter v. Bollinger*, 539 U.S. at 387–90 (Kennedy, J., dissenting).

65. Ibid., 330.

66. For example, in *Employment Division v. Smith*, 494 U.S. 872 (1990), Scalia ushered in the famous "neutral and generally applicable laws" principle of Free Exercise jurisprudence, denying Native Americans the ability to be exempt from criminal punishment for violating a general law against

the ingestion of peyote. But he noted that the religious group could have recourse to the legislature to give them a specific exemption from the law. Ibid., 890. This discriminatory exemption, according to Scalia would not be problematic; while acknowledging "that leaving accommodation to the political process will place at a relative disadvantage those religious practices that are not widely engaged in," he found that effect to be an "unavoidable consequence of democratic government." Ibid.

67. *Lawrence*, 539 U.S. 578 (2003).
68. Ibid., 602 (Scalia, J., dissenting).
69. Ibid.
70. Indeed, Scalia has suggested that government remedial programs should be race-neutral. See *Croson*, 488 U.S. at 528 (Scalia, J., dissenting) ("Since blacks have been disproportionately disadvantaged by racial discrimination, any race-neutral remedial program aimed at the disadvantaged *as such* will have a disproportionately beneficial impact on blacks").
71. See *United States v. Virginia*, 518 U.S. 515, 566 (1996) (Scalia, J., dissenting) (finding "gender-based developmental differences" a compelling reason for Virginia's maintenance of an all-male military school).
72. *Adarand Constructors, Inc. v. Pena*, 515 U.S. 200, 239 (1995) (Scalia, J., concurring in part and concurring in the judgment).
73. See *Croson*, 488 U.S. 521 (Scalia, J., dissenting) ("I share the view expressed by Alexander Bickel that '[t]he lesson of the great decisions of the Supreme Court and the lesson of contemporary history have been the same for at least a generation: discrimination on the basis of race is illegal, immoral, unconstitutional, inherently wrong, and destructive of democratic society' " [quoting Alexander Bickel, *The Morality of Consent* (New Haven: Yale University Press, 1975), 133]).
74. In *Freeman*, Scalia joined the majority in holding that a federal court may end its supervision of certain aspects of a desegregation order that the school district had successfully implemented, even though other parts of the order remained unfulfilled. *Freeman*, 503 U.S. 467, 500 (1992) (Scalia, J., concurring).
75. Ibid., 505 (Scalia, J., concurring) (quoting *Board of Education of Oklahoma City Public Schools v. Dowell*, 498 U.S. 237, 247 [1991]) (emphasis added).
76. Ibid.
77. Ibid., 506.
78. Ibid. (emphasis added).
79. Ibid., 503.
80. See Gary Orfield, ed., *Dropouts in America: Confronting the Graduation Rate Crisis* (Cambridge, MA: Harvard Education Press, 2004).
81. See Margo Schlanger, "Inmate Litigation," *Harvard Law Review* 116 (2003): 1555, 1557; Paul Butler, "Affirmative Action: Diversity of Opin-

ions: Affirmative Action and the Criminal Law," *University of Colorado Law Review* 68 (1997): 841, 868 n. 97 (noting there are more black than white men in prisons nationwide).

82. *Grutter v. Bollinger*, 539 U.S. 306, 343 ("We expect that 25 years from now, the use of racial preferences will no longer be necessary to further the interest approved today").

83. See *Dropouts in America: Confronting the Graduation Rate Crisis* (Gary Orfield ed. 2004).

84. See Margo Schlanger, *Inmate Litigation*, 116 *Harvard Law Review* 1555, 1557 (2003); Paul Butler, *Affirmative Action: Diversity of Opinions: Affirmative Action and the Criminal Law*, 68 U. Col. L. Rev. 841, 868 n.97 (1997) (noting there are more black than white men in prisons nationwide).

FREQUENTLY CITED CASES

Sipuel v. Oklahoma, 332 U.S. 631 (1948)

Slaughter-House Cases, 83 U.S. 36, 71 (1873)

Smith v. Allwright, 321 U.S. 649, 666 (1944)

Swann v. Charlotte-Mecklenburg Board of Education, 402 U.S. 1, 22–31 (1971)

Sweatt v. Painter, 340 U.S. 846 (1950)

United States v. Fordice, 505 U.S. 717 (1992)

United States v. Robinson, 414 U.S. 212 (1973)

University of California Regents v. Bakke, 18 Cal. 3d. 34. 387 (1976)

Virginia v. West Virginia, 222 U.S. 17, 20 (1912)

Zelman v. Simmons-Harris, 122 S. Ct. 2460, 2480 (2002)

INDEX

ABOUT THE AUTHOR

Charles J. Ogletree, Jr., the Harvard Law School Jesse Climenko Professor of Law and founding and executive director of the Charles Hamilton Houston Institute for Race and Justice, is a prominent legal theorist who has made an international reputation by taking a hard look at complex issues of law and by working to secure the rights guaranteed by the Constitution for everyone equally under the law. He is the coauthor of the award-winning book *Beyond the Rodney King Story: An Investigation of Police Conduct in Minority Communities* (1995) and frequently contributes to many publications. In 2002, Professor Ogletree contributed a chapter entitled "The Rehnquist Revolution in Criminal Procedure," which appears in *The Rehnquist Court: Judicial Activism on the Right* (Herman Schwartz, ed., 2002). He has also published a number of law review articles concerning the 1921 Tulsa race riot reparations case on which he is currently working. In 2005, Professor Ogletree was honored with the Martin Luther King, Jr., Legacy Award for National Service and presented with the Morehouse College Candle in the Dark Award in Education and Law. In 2004, the Clio Exchange presented Professor Ogletree with the Carter G. Woodson History Maker Living Legend Award. He lives in Cambridge, Massachusetts, with his wife, Pamela, and attends St. Paul AME Church.